THE IRISH WAR

Tony Geraghty

THE IRISH WAR

The Hidden Conflict between the IRA
and British Intelligence

The Johns Hopkins University Press
Baltimore and London

Originally published by HarperCollins*Publishers*, London, 1998
Johns Hopkins edition, 2000
2 4 6 8 9 7 5 3

The Johns Hopkins University Press
2715 North Charles Street
Baltimore, Maryland 21218-4363
www.press.jhu.edu

Library of Congress Cataloging-in-Publication Data

Geraghty, Tony.
The Irish War : the hidden conflict between the IRA and British Intelligence /
Tony Geraghty.
p.   cm.
Originally published: London : HarperCollins Publishers, 1998.
Includes bibliographical references and index.
ISBN 0-8018-6456-9 (alk. paper)
1. Ireland—History, Military.   2. Political violence—Northern Ireland—
History.   3. Counterinsurgency—Northern Ireland—History.
4. Political violence—Ireland—History.   5. Terrorism—Northern Ireland—History.
6. Counterinsurgency—Ireland—History.   7. Northern Ireland—History, Military.
8. Terrorism—Ireland—History.   9. Irish unification question.   10. Great Britain. Army.
11. Irish Republican Army.   12. Irish question.   I. Title.

DA914.G47 2000
941.60824—dc21
99-087238

A catalog record for this book is available from the British Library.

DEDICATION

This history is dedicated to all the victims, tens of thousands of them, of an unnecessary war. No one knows the exact number. For every direct victim of the violence there were many more bereaved, ruined people who gave up the will to live. In both parts of Ireland, Britain and the Continent, about 4,000 have been killed by military action. The overwhelming majority were civilians. More than fifty were children aged fourteen or younger. These juvenile victims included Patrick Rooney, aged nine, hit in his bedroom by a police machine-gun bullet; Angela Gallagher, aged seventeen months, cut down in the street by IRA gunfire, her death shrugged off by a leading Republican as 'one of the hazards of urban guerrilla warfare'; Majella O'Hare, shot by a British soldier whose spokesmen initially blamed the IRA; Jonathan Ball, aged three and Tim Parry, aged twelve, blown up by the IRA while shopping in Warrington.

Most of the victims lived and died in Northern Ireland. The total of 3,251 fatalities there between 1969 and 1998 translated as a percentage of the British population would create a bodycount of 100,000. More than 30,000 people have been injured or maimed: in percentage terms, this is the equivalent of a million British people.

Milestones on this Calvary include bomb attacks on pubs in Belfast, Birmingham and the streets of Dublin and Monaghan. At McGurk's Bar, fifteen people were murdered by Loyalist UVF terrorists. In the first, British edition of this history, the author wrongly ascribed this atrocity to an IRA own-goal. This is the proper place to apologise to the McGurk family, who lost a mother (Mrs Philomena McGurk) and a daughter (Marie, aged fourteen). In May 1974, more than thirty people died and the gutters ran with blood after more Loyalist bombing in Dublin and Monaghan. Six months later, bombs in two Birmingham pubs killed nineteen people and injured another 180. The IRA denied responsibility.

Not all these victims died quickly. Jim Seymour, an RUC constable shot in the head by the IRA, took twenty-two years to expire, lying in his hospital bed, unable to speak or to move. A child of twelve, watching her father dying over a period of eleven days, later wrote: 'The smell of burning flesh never really goes away.' Some victims, the disappeared, abductees of terror groups that now have pretensions to become community police forces, have no known grave. They include Jean McConville, a mother of ten, aged thirty-seven when she was taken away by an IRA gang of eight men and four women in 1972. Her crime had been to place a cushion beneath the head of a fatally wounded soldier, who was shot outside her house, and to say a prayer for his departing soul.

May they rest in peace.

CONTENTS

ACKNOWLEDGEMENTS

Many minds and much conflicting experience of the Irish tragedy have contributed to this history, though the author alone is responsible for the end result, with all its imperfections, real and – since the Irish quarrel vigorously these days over historical revisionism – apparent. The contributors, all indispensable, included veterans of the British armed services, among them the SAS Regiment, the Parachute Regiment (with which I served in the 1950s, though not in Ireland), Royal Military Police, Royal Army Ordnance Corps, Intelligence Corps and the less public faces of the Security Service MI5, the Metropolitan Police Special Branch, the covert reconnaissance organization known as 14 Company ('The Detachments', or 'Dets') and the agent-handling team known as FRU.

On the other side of the conflict I have drawn from interviews with and memoirs of men and women of the Official IRA, Provisional IRA, INLA and Loyalist terror groups. Over the years that I reported on the emerging conflict in Northern Ireland I have made personal contacts with such people as Seamus Twomey (Officer Commanding the Provisionals' Belfast Battalion), the hospitable Maire Drumm, later murdered by Loyalists, and more recently, Sean O'Callaghan, a former head of the Provos' Southern Command and later the movement's most informed and articulate enemy, whose health is imperilled by his chain-smoking as much as a Provisional's bullet.

Journalists deserve recognition from a former member of their tribe, and thanks for their help. My former editor at the *Sunday Times*, Harold Evans, described the best journalism as 'the first rough draft of history'. Such minds as David McKittrick of the *Independent* and Peter Taylor, a television journalist, have stayed the course of this long conflict more consistently than any soldier or politician and have provided the clearest contemporary analyses of a murky war we can hope to get.

Certain individuals have made a particularly valuable contribution to the thinking that has shaped this book. They include Field Marshal Lord Carver, the Army Chief of the General Staff at a critical period; Lieutenant-Colonel Michael Mates MP, who saw active service as a soldier in the Province and was later, as Minister of State for Northern Ireland, political supremo there; and Mr John Alderton, a liberal-minded and sane former Chief Constable.

My wife, Gillian Linscott (a successful fiction writer these days), drew on her experience as a reporter in the Province, where she interviewed IRA leaders at the Derry Gasworks and elsewhere during the first phase of the renewed conflict. She also applied her sharp mind and phenomenal reading speed to the task of researching the eighteenth- and nineteenth-century coverage of this book, with the aid of that superb research tool known as The London Library

A 'library' of another sort was opened to me by my friend Peter Thompson, whose collection of preciously preserved left-wing journals from the 1960s and 1970s offered a unique insight into the motives of those whose street politics detonated the latest troubles.

To these and many others I am grateful. All of us have been changed, in some measure, by our exposure to the Irish experience. Ireland being the special place it is, the change wrought in us was not always bad.

LIST OF ILLUSTRATIONS

PREFACE

In a famous – even hackneyed – comment about the purpose under-pinning the apparent insanity of armed conflict, General Karl von Clausewitz wrote: 'War is nothing but the continuation of politics by other means.' The Irish have reversed that doctrine. In a land of gunmen (and women) it is the soldier who calls the shots, not the politician.

The problem is not new. It took the massive energy and fascist organization of Ancient Rome to subdue the loosely structured Celtic empire that once stretched from Ireland to the Adriatic. But if the politics of peace-making have remained unconvincing since 1969, the style of warfare in John Bull's Other Island has mutated to embrace forms of surveillance and counter-surveillance, blackmail, interrogation, chemical analysis and electronic eavesdropping, bur-glary and assassination beyond the dreams, or nightmares, of Clausewitz or Orwell, or for that matter, the practices of the East German Stasi. A machine has been created – necessary for the purpose – out of sight of the British public that is capable of con-trolling entire populations if it is allowed its full potential. Both sides have succeeded in manipulating media and law alike. If the Irish War ever ends, the war machine cannot be disinvented. Like expatriate Roman legions turning against Rome, it would be available for domestic service. Were that 'boomerang effect' to happen, the Celts' final victory over their ancient Anglo-Saxon enemy (as the English begin the search for the next enemy within) could fulfil the Latin saying: 'Those whom the gods would destroy, they first make mad.'

On 3 December 1998, almost two months after the first hardback edition of this book appeared, the Irish War boomerang came through the author's front door in a remote Herefordshire hamlet. Six detectives from the UK's Ministry of Defence Police Agency arrived before dawn to arrest the author on suspicion of breaching the Official Secrets Act, 1989. In particular, the Defence Ministry police were excited about references in the book to electronic surveillance systems linked to computers. More than a year later, Geraghty still awaits the UK government's decision about whether to put him on trial and if so, when.

The other message of this history is that the current Troubles have their roots not in the division of Ireland by the Treaty of 1921 but in 1691, before the word 'Republican' had become a synonym for 'Irish Patriot'. In 1691 the last professional soldier to fight the English on Irish soil led his men into permanent exile. Resistance henceforth was in the hands of amateur warriors, who refined terrorism into an art form. The peculiar Irish knack of running a viable war machine as a cottage industry is the other deadly obstacle to any 'peace process', however well-meant, however ingenious. In 1998, the war looks set to continue indefinitely even though there may be occasional remissions, which politicians describe as 'complete ceasefires', in the progress of the Irish disease.

The pursuit of Irish history is a sometimes foggy affair, a meandering track that leads into a dark political wilderness and an ambiguous landscape that reflects a Gaelic language in which there is no simple word for 'Yes' or 'No'. This narrative, perhaps arbitrarily, attempts to follow stepping stones across the Irish bog, stones that trace the history of the conflict waged against the English in Ireland and beyond. As the Contents page indicates, those stones are as follows.

Parts I to III: the current Troubles, since those represent present griefs which politicians still aspire to end. Since 1968 the renewed conflict has evolved into a sophisticated type of revolutionary and counter-revolutionary warfare of interest beyond these islands: hence the partition (if that is not too dangerous a word in the Irish context) of the contemporary war into three separate arenas. For completeness and to illustrate the immutable basis of the conflict, as well as its recent evolution, Part IV rehearses the story from the end of professional, disciplined military resistance to Britain in Ireland in 1691, to the end of the Anglo-Irish War of 1919–21, the war the English lost, the war that still inspires the IRA.

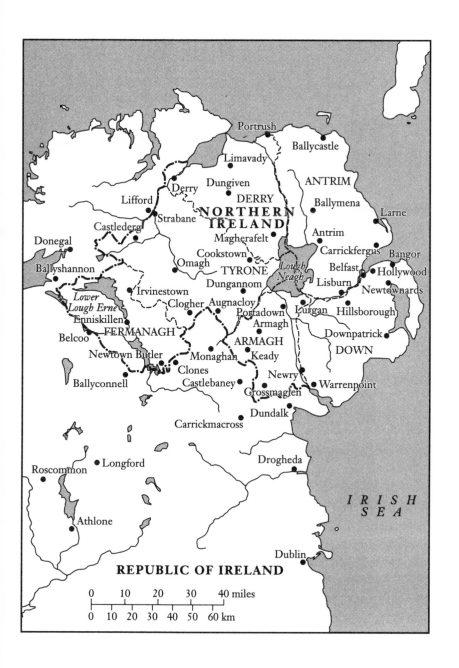

Portrush

Ballycastle

Limavady

ANTRIM

Derry   Dungiven

Lifford   DERRY   Ballymena

Larne

NORTHERN
Strabane   IRELAND

Castlederg

Magherafelt   Antrim

Donegal   Cookstown   Carrickfergus   Bangor

Omagh   TYRONE   *Lough*   Belfast   Hollywood
Ballyshannon   *Neagh*

Irvinestown   Dungannon   Lisburn   Newtownards

Lower   Clogher   Augnacloy
Lough Erne   Portadown   Lurgan   Hillsborough
Enniskillen   FERMANAGH   Armagh

Belcoo   ARMAGH   Downpatrick

Newtown Butler   Monaghan   Keady   DOWN

Clones   Newry
Ballyconnell   Castlebaney   Warrenpoint
Crossmaglen

Carrickmacross   Dundalk

Roscommon   Longford   Drogheda

IRISH
SEA

Athlone

Dublin

REPUBLIC OF IRELAND

0   10   20   30   40 miles

0   10   20   30   40   50   60 km

INTRODUCTION

Every war generates its 'old soldier' stories, first-hand and usually credible memories of the minutiae of the conflict, as well as eye-witness accounts of the major turning points. The Irish War has killed 650 British soldiers, 302 RUC police officers and 2,270 others since 1969, yet most of the books are written by the Irish, for the Irish. This absence of British testimony after thirty years of conflict 'across the water' (as soldiers describe Ireland) is surprising. The 1982 Falklands conflict, in which 237 British soldiers lost their lives in three months, generated shelves of memoirs, as did the one-month 1991 Gulf War (British bodycount: twenty-eight.) Another paradox is that British writing about the Irish War *is* prolific when it comes to fiction, often disguised as fact. That genre is so rich that Patrick Magee, the Brighton bomber, spent some of his time in prison working on a thesis analysing 'Troubles Fiction'.

In those circumstances – as one who was a close eye-witness of the key street battles of the renewed Troubles from 1969 until 1971 – I conclude it is legitimate, for once, to drop the mask of the uninvolved historian, for part of this book at least. To quote a well-tried cliché: I was there.

One warm Wednesday afternoon I took a walk up the Falls Road, Belfast. It was early September 1969 and people were still in a state of shock after what they had done to their neighbours and what their neighbours, decent enough people normally, had done to them. You could still catch the odour of burnt Catholic homes in Conway Street – it was the odour of the blitz, one that the people of London and Dresden had come to know a generation earlier. There were other intimations of terror. Three officers of the Royal Ulster Constabulary, left to defend their building at Springfield Road, had discovered the unique fear of the lynch-mob as they had fired volleys of automatic fire into the night sky. A mile away the parents of Patrick Rooney, aged nine, were mourning his loss. He had been cowering in his bedroom at the ugly Divis Street apartment block when he was killed by bullets fired by a heavy machine-gun, a .3 Browning. The gun was brought to the forecourt of the apartments by a police armoured car and the finger on the trigger, a mere 100 metres away, was that of a police officer who was himself terrified by petrol bombs raining on the turret above him from the darkened street. The gun had a lethal range of 3,000 metres. The police machine-gunner was unacquainted with the weapon or the vehicle and he fired blindly into the night on the orders of a senior officer, himself already half-mad with anxiety.

By this Wednesday, a week or so later, there was something that could be relied upon. The British Tommy, dependable as ever, had been sent by a reluctant Labour government to restore order. Tommy believed he'd be home by Christmas, unaware that the first soldier had already died in this renewed conflict. He was Trooper McCabe, Royal Irish Rangers, home on leave and probably shooting at the Royal Ulster Constabulary when a police marksman killed him with one 7.62mm high velocity round fired from the roof of Hastings Street police station. The bullet entered McCabe's body under a cheekbone and exited through his ribs on the other side of his body, indicating that he was in the prone position when he died.

My purpose that day, as Chief Reporter of the *Sunday Times*, was to have a word with Mrs Agnes McKenna, who ran a newsagent's shop on the corner of Dover Street. Mrs McKenna was a great source, better informed (like most people at street level) than government spokesmen at Stormont, a remote Victorian building on a green hill 15 miles outside the city. No paramilitary group had yet organized its thugs to intimidate people such as Mrs McKenna. I was within sight of her shop when a British army staff car drew up and a major-general stepped out, uttered a word to his driver and then strode on alone, walking tall like the sheriff of Dodge City, before swinging left into a back alley. Unlike the sheriff, he was unarmed.

I dropped in beside him and introduced myself.

'I'm not supposed to be here,' he told me. 'I'm on my way to see Father Murphy.'

I guessed, correctly, that he was not about to make confession to the good father, who was one of those larger-than-life priests celebrated in song like Father O'Flynn, lifting the lazy ones on with the stick. Major-General Tony Dyball, it turned out, was also on his way to see 'these Citizens' Defence Committee chaps' to discuss with them the removal of barricades across key routes in West Belfast. The barricades, creating the first no-go area in Belfast, were a public reproach to the Unionist government. At his destination – St Patrick's Pro-Cathedral – the general went upstairs to meet the committee. Some time later, as the meeting ended, he ducked away from my questions but one friendly face did appear. This was Jim Sullivan, chairman of the CCDC and a prominent member of the Irish Republican Army, a movement deeply fissured by attempts to modernize it and already split into opposed Official and Provisional factions.

'We's got this back-of-envelope treaty with the British military,' said Sullivan. He read from the notes he had made. The barricades would be removed on Saturday and joint security guards would be mounted by British soldiers and local vigilantes. The Royal Ulster Constabulary would be excluded.

I watched the Sullivan–Dyball 'treaty' take effect. There was some resistance from local people, arms linked across Albert Street, but both Father Murphy and Jim Sullivan reassured them that all was well. General Sir Ian Freeland, the military supremo in the Province, pronounced the operation 'an outstanding triumph for the forces of good reason, moderation and common sense, the basis on which the whole community can work together towards an early return to normal life'.

The reality was that, in order to remove the barricades and the image of no-goism, a British general had been obliged to negotiate with, among others, the IRA. Such secret negotiations were not the first, nor the last, but in order to reassure Unionists who feared that their world was on the brink of collapse, the reality had to be denied. My account of events in the *Sunday Times* sent a shudder through Whitehall and Stormont and precipitated a Protestant riot in Belfast. The official Whitehall line, purveyed by *The Times* on the day after my report, was that my story 'relies for its impact on the rather shaky assumption that the IRA is now much more than a slogan out of the past. Diligent investigations by journalists have failed to reveal that it is anything more.'

I now entered Ireland's political hall of mirrors. Facts which were mundane political furniture in Belfast were declared in London, ninety minutes away by air, not to exist. A second brigadier appeared on my horizon. This one was in charge of army public affairs in London. He called on the editor of the *Sunday Times* and I was summoned back to London to answer for my 'slogans'. This was Kafka territory. So matters stood until the end of the same week when, by a useful coincidence, the Scottish judge Lord Cameron reported on the civil rights disturbances of preceding months. He confirmed that the civil rights movement was well penetrated by the IRA, which had provided marchers and, more critically, stewards for protest marches.

During the first four years of the renewed war between Irish Republicans and England, I had no time to reflect on the useful lesson of the Sullivan–Dyball 'treaty'. Close encounters with guerrilla fighters of all sides, sometimes when they were shooting at one another, were not conducive to detached, long-term analysis. My arrest at gunpoint during the Falls Road 'curfew' of 3–4 July 1970 (which Parliament was told later was not a curfew at all but a 'restriction on movement'); a criminal charge of breaching the peace by impeding the army, carrying a mandatory prison sentence on conviction (a piquant prospect, since I seemed to be the only unarmed man on the street where they lifted me); a routine beating by RUC batons on the steps of Stormont; the curiously soft interrogation by well-spoken Englishmen in the privacy of an interrogation centre; my sometimes dangerous quarrels with IRA leaders in Belfast and Derry, one of whom placed his pistol on the kitchen table as we talked; my more amicable encounters with one of the godfathers over poteen in Roscommon – all these gave an adrenaline boost but they did not help me to comprehend the rich, historical symbolism of the Belfast Central Citizens' Defence Committee.

Nor indeed did my own education as an expatriate Irish Catholic, born in Liverpool, educated at the London Oratory (where I was told, aged about twelve, that I was leaving it somewhat late to discover my 'vocation'), help me to comprehend what the CCDC symbolized. The Troubles, my Dublin-born mother had implied, were something buried in the past and they involved two groups of people – the Irish and the English – who were in some curious fashion not us or our neighbours in working-class, wartime Pimlico, though she limped from a bullet wound in the ankle collected during an earlier phase of Irish resistance. The process of denial was aided by such distractions as Luftwaffe bombs and landmines, flying bombs and v2 missiles during which boys like me – blitz kids – collected such interesting 'souvenirs' as shrapnel, shell caps and the human hand that appeared in the back yard of our basement apartment.

It took me a long time to comprehend that the importance of the CCDC was that it was a sort of historical signpost creaking uneasily in a storm, a flimsy coalition held together only in its opposition to an external threat and a shared hatred. The theme recurs throughout this history of the war of three centuries between the Irish and England. As Brendan Fitzpatrick, a historian at Trinity College, Dublin, put it: 'The "unity" of Ireland may well be its greatest myth.'

The force that has bound the Irish nation through 300 years has been opposition to the English presence in Ireland; the obverse of which, some might argue, has been the presence of the Irish in England. But there was an important distinction. The 'aboriginal' Irish were underdogs in both countries. In the nineteenth century and beyond, together with a huge growth in popular literacy and democratic, liberal government, England became a superpower, governing a worldwide empire thanks to the Industrial Revolution and the Royal Navy. Ireland, a land of peat, had no such revolution. (As the West enters a post-industrial age, it is the Irish economy that is thriving thanks to the non-industrial, electronic revolution.) The urbanization of Britain had no parallel in Catholic Ireland.

One effect of urbanization was to create a viable sense of national identity which could be readily manipulated into jingoism, as any student of music-hall songs in nineteenth-century England ('Soldiers of the Queen, My Lad'; 'The Boers Have Took My Daddy') will have noticed. No similar force could be at work in Ireland.

Instead, there was a powerful oral culture, fuelled by a Gaelic idiom. This passed from one generation to another the woes and resentments of the Irish from Cromwell onwards. The hatred was undiluted by the passage of time for it was encapsulated in a cultural time-machine. Such a culture needed a focus for resentment. The expat English, whose behaviour overseas was usually a parody of England-at-Home, obligingly refreshed Ireland's well of bitterness with new atrocities, more blood, at regular intervals.

With the defeat and exile of General Patrick Sarsfield, first Earl of Lucan, in 1691 the last nationally organized resistance to English rule in Ireland ended and with it the control of Irish resistance by professional soldiers. If resistance was to continue thereafter, it had to be through a conflict waged without rules, by irregulars and amateurs, unrestrained by a trained officer class.

The new war against England, post-Sarsfield, would be one of dirty tricks and dirty hands on all sides; a war which England-at-Home did not usually notice even as it wailed and raged against its back door like the unquiet banshee. When Bernadette Devlin pronounced, in 1969, 'Beware of the wrath of the risen people!' such a sentiment and such a spectre prompted incredulity in the London of the Swinging '6os. It was as if Henry VIII himself had reappeared, alive and well, to claim the English throne. It could not really be like that, the English told themselves. In any case, the soldiers knew they would be home by Christmas. No one believed the war would last another thirty years or so and claim another 3,000 dead, most of them innocent non-combatants. And even then, most of England did not seem to notice the significance of a virtual British surrender in 1993, in which a London government publicly professed 'no selfish, strategic interest' in Ireland (denying centuries of history) as well as acknowledging 'the right of the Irish people to self-determination'.

Were these malevolent ghosts laid to rest at last in 1998? The great majority of the Irish, north and south, voted for exorcism, as they had done so once before in the twenty-six counties, in 1922. Loyalist terrorists were marginalised. This was a new experience for them, for this was no longer a Protestant state for a Protestant people. The Orange Order, like a headless chicken that continues to strut about briefly after decapitation, believed that its version of law and order was to be imposed on the moderate majority, as if nothing had changed. Throughout the years of Stormont government, it had threatened a Doomsday (also known as the Protestant Backlash) and with good reason. The threat the Orangemen identified was Dublin's claim to 'the whole island of Ireland' – De Valera's 1937 rewrite of the 1921 treaty – enforced by an IRA war of attrition aimed at making the Province ungovernable. Loyalists were ensnared in a reactive military strategy, the strategy of status-quo symbolised by an attachment to ritual parades and funny walks. The real possibility that a million angry, armed and righteous Protestants backed the strategy was unfunny and recognised as such by intelligent, reconstructed Republicans like Sean O'Callaghan.

The momentous decision of ninety-four per cent of the southern Irish to abandon a flawed claim to jurisdiction over the North undermined Loyalist extremists, whose armed forces had in any case been thoroughly and effectively penetrated by the RUC Special Branch. Trapped between the pincers of penetration and adverse public opinion, the Loyalist backlash, hitherto credible, was one of the major sources of conflict removed by the Assembly election result of 25 June 1998. Even if 'No'-Unionists, including the Reverand Ian Paisley's people, were somehow to manipulate a political crisis within the new structure, there was no hope that they could press on from there to impose their will by force of arms. The Tories of 1998 were not the same animals as those of 1912. British officers engaged in the Irish War in its latest phase simply look puzzled when you ask if they could respond to a Loyalist appeal to 'kith-and-kin'. The British Army's Curragh Mutiny, like the Tory party of Balfour, is part of a long-buried and now irrelevant past.

But what of the IRA? Republican purists, rejoicing in their isolationist zeal, could never foreswear the armed struggle. It was written into their constitution that the British must be expelled and Ireland reunited as a precondition of all and any political progress. As the Proclamation of 1916 has it: 'Until our arms have brought the opportune moment for the establishing of a permanent National Government, representative of the whole people of Ireland, and elected by the suffrages of all her men and women, the Provisional Government, hereby constituted, will administer the civil and military affairs of the Republic in trust for the people.'

Sinn Fein's acceptance of partition under the leadership of Adams and McGuinness until such time as a democratic majority in the North decreed otherwise, marked the parting of the ways, the final recognition, after sixty years of subterfuge and self-delusion, of the essential difference between Sinn Fein's constitutional patriots – represented by the 1918 Dail – and the fanatics of the Irish Republican Brotherhood and the IRA. Adams, after his election to the Northern Ireland Assembly, shrugged off questions about the armed struggle. Was the war over, he was asked. 'You tell me,' he responded. Was he selling-out to the Establishment? He would, he promised, 'always be a subversive' but 'this Assembly doesn't stand alone. It is inextricably linked to the cross-border bodies, to the Council of Ministers, and through the Cabinet is the *only* route into that all-Ireland dimension' [my italics].

Such assertions of sanity over bloodlust were not well received in New York where – as before – Irish-Americans exiled more by time and history than distance, saw peace as a sell-out. What then? Could the 'dissident' Republican groups, loyal to the old agenda, run a viable war on the same terms as before? Probably not for some years, though in the months after the 1998 Good Friday Agreement, military intelligence chiefs confessed, in private, that they could no longer 'read' the Balkanised politics and control of the Provisionals. The tigers of South Armagh and East Tyrone, like everyone else, faced a totally new situation, one in which the old verities had been dismantled overnight. No Irish government now dare repeat the mistakes of 1969. There could be no reliable safe havens; no blind eyes turned to training camps; no political hard-of-hearing as bombs were tested; no arms slush funds back-channelled through the Red Cross. If there was a historical precedent it was 1962, when the old IRA acknowledged defeat for the very good reason that it had been rejected as irrelevant by the people it claimed to lead.

On that occasion the IRA set about reinventing itself. Aided by a reactionary Belfast government and the naivety of student street politics, the Republicans turned their situation around in a mere six years. The big question for the people of Ireland and Britain in 1998 was whether the momentum towards peace could be sustained. The IRA's command structure and its other sinews of war were intact. The Semtex and the guns were still available, though in much-diminished quantities from the heyday of Libyan supplies. The 'decommissioning' promised in writing to the Unionists by Prime Minister Blair would not happen, but after his electoral victories on both sides of the Irish Sea he could afford to shrug off that promise. Like all shrewd observers of the history, he knew that the IRA's strategic weapons were not the Armalites or the Semtex high explosive used in the bloody campaign in Ulster. The weapons that made the difference politically were the big bombs that penetrated to the heart of the City of London (London's Wall Street): lorry-loads of home-made explosive created from materials no more exotic than icing sugar and fertiliser.

The trial of James McArdle, a twenty-nine-year-old Crossmaglen farm labourer optimistically described as 'the last IRA terrorist', revealed how the odds had moved against the chances of success in such bombings. McArdle helped deliver to South Quay, London, the bomb that ended the IRA ceasefire in February 1996. By that time, the Metropolitan Police anti-terrorist squad had investigated 1,300 bombings over a period of twenty-seven years and charged nearly 700 suspects.

After South Quay, an inquisitive lorry driver reported seeing an unfamiliar trailer and truck parked nine miles from Docklands on the day of the explosion. He was the 199th out of 850 people who rang the anti-terrorist hot line. A forensic team took a look at the place where the mystery lorry had been parked hours before an attack planned and prepared during the IRA's ceasefire. Commander John Grieve, head of the anti-terrorist branch, said that the parking spot at River Road, Barking, 'was like a quarter-mile rubbish tip, and officers crawled on their hands and knees picking up every bit of paper'. In an old tyre they found tachograph records revealing the movement of a lorry from an Irish ferry port. A trucking magazine bore a thumbprint. Other clues were pieces of false number plates, traces of explosive on a trailer used in the operation, paint scrapings that identified the exact source of the lorry and finally, closed-circuit television recordings of the truck as it passed beneath motorway bridges on its way across England. At a truckers' halt in Carlisle, a matching thumbprint (the second) was found on an ashtray. A ferry ticket stub bought at Stranraer for a dummy run was uncovered, revealing a third matching thumbprint. Police nicknamed their quarry 'the triple thumbprint man'.

Evidence of this sort of density put McArdle in the dock in 1998, to be sentenced the day the people of Northern Ireland voted in their new Assembly, and he was convicted of conspiracy to cause explosions. The police continued their investigations into bombings at Manchester, Warrington, Deal and the Baltic Exchange. The lesson was clear, even to a farm labourer of average intelligence. It was that making a bomb to attack London is comparatively simple. All necessary technical information is available on the Internet. But delivering a device to the target without a premature explosion, penetrating the screen of surveillance and intelligence now around British key points undetected, is another matter.

The IRA old guard made it clear where they stood in 1998. A generation of its veterans, some surprised to be alive, had now lived long enough to grow up to reject the option of violence. They were led by – of all people – Joe Cahill, a seventy-eight-year-old veteran of IRA action since the 1940s, sentenced to death for the murder of Constable Patrick Murphy in Belfast in 1942. It is said among Republicans that the IRA oath is only the first stage in the making of a Volunteer, that when prison and beatings, self-starvation and isolation do not break an IRA man, the end result is called Joe Cahill. Cahill, in 1998, stood for election at Antrim North, unsuccessfully, with a twinkle in his eye. He also had a message for the next generation of Irish patriots. It was this: 'I've always believed that somewhere along the line, armed struggle would have to stop, negotiations would take place and the political way would be the way forward.' He also regretted 'all the deaths including those of British soldiers. They've been victims of this conflict too. I do believe that there is a real opportunity now for peace and that people sense that.'

This was a long way from the rhetoric of Pearse. It would be no surprise if 'the last terrorist', and others of the last year of the conflict felt that they had been misled. Only time will demonstrate whether the war is truly at an end. By the year 2008 or perhaps a little beyond that, a new generation of young Irishmen will reach adolescence. By then also, the demographic changes on which the Blair government secretly placed its hopes of a gradualist, Fabian-like process will have ripened a little, shifting the Irish centre of gravity towards peaceful evolution.

Meanwhile, incorrigible English optimism, wishing away the Irish problem, remained a constant theme after the Good Friday peace deal of 1998. On Saturday, 15 August that year, the irreconcilable 'Real IRA' replaced the defeated Provisional IRA and murdered twenty-nine civilians in Omagh, ten of them minors, including unborn twins. A theoretical political peace thus became the occasion for the worst atrocity of the renewed Troubles. But this obscures the fact that all bombs are indiscriminate weapons. The means to make more was still in the wrong hands. It was not a good time to drop one's guard.

Addendum to the 2000 Edition

The Belfast Good Friday Peace Agreement of 1998 and its massive endorsement by all the people of Ireland was the high water mark of political optimism that the Irish War could be ended without further loss of life; that the gun would cease, at last, to be the determining factor in Irish public life. Just before Good Friday 1998 Blair envisioned 'an end to bombings, killings and beatings, claimed or unclaimed' as a result of paramilitary ceasefires. By the end of 1999, events had not matched up to that prediction. Faced with the hard reality of the IRA's unique interpretation of the word 'ceasefire' – one that placed British security forces off-limits but permitted the continued murder of informers and others who offended Republican susceptibilities – Britain's idealistic Minister for Northern Ireland, Dr Mo Mowlam, concluded, on balance, that the ceasefire was intact. She did not regard the IRA's control of the Catholic ghettoes by violence as acceptable, but she did perceive it as a fact of life about which she could do nothing much. Her most telling point was that 'the peace we have now is imperfect, but better than none.'

Her critics were not convinced. Vincent McKenna, a disillusioned IRA intelligence officer who now runs the Northern Ireland Human Rights Bureau, calculated that in the first sixteen months of this imperfect peace, the IRA had carried out 5 murders, 61 shootings, 152 beatings and had forcibly exiled 432 people. His statistics did not include the victims of Omagh. During the same period, 147 Republican terrorists had been released from prison ostensibly because the IRA was now committed to non-violent politics. Loyalist terrorists were not inactive during this time, either. They murdered the three Quinn brothers, aged ten, nine and eight, by arson and killed the civil rights lawyer Rosemary Nelson with a car bomb. But Loyalist opponents of the peace process were not strong enough to destabilise it, running the risk of provoking the IRA to all-out war once more.

Mowlam's idealism was blended with a poker player's sense of realpolitik. The cards in this game were less stable than say, the Ace of Spades. This was poker played with tarot cards. The unstable, ambiguous nature of the game made it impossible to stick to clear-cut rules. It was entirely apt that one British cartoon should depict Mowlam as a character in a Lewis Carroll fairy story, declaring: 'When I choose a word it means just what I choose it to mean.'

What was consistent was the determination of the British government not to provoke the IRA to return to war and the IRA's care not to destablise entirely an arrangement that secured freedom for its prisoners. By May 2000 they would all be out. Was there an agenda beyond that? The British clearly hoped that the habit of peace would stick, but both sides could in any case read the future demography of Northern Ireland. By 1999 the Protestant population was an ageing one, as more of its young people emigrated to Scotland and England, and the Catholic population was growing, encouraged by the success of the Dublin economy. One calculation was that Republican aspirations of reunification would become reality over time. That, however, would be to misunderstand the nature of hardline Republicanism and its tradition of physical force.

According to the hardliner's mythology, reunification had to come about as a result of force, not natural evolution. As one leading hardliner, Brian Keenan, put it during the long debate about the 'decommissioning' of IRA weapons: 'The only thing to be decommissioned in Ireland is the British state.'

Meanwhile, Mowlam's acceptance of a mutilated peace agreement subtly undermined her security forces' most important weapon against terrorism: the use of informers, whom the IRA proceeded to murder or exile.

The fruits of the peace process, 1998–99, might therefore be summarized as follows:

- Release of virtually all terrorist prisoners.
- Continued 'complete cessation' of military operations by the IRA (but no cessation of extreme violence against Catholic informers, dissidents, drug dealers and social misfits including children). As Sinn Fein's Gerry Adams saw the situation: 'The very fact that the IRA has taken its weapons out of commission, is on cessation and is maintaining that cessation despite killings by the Loyalists, despite the activities of British forces on the ground, despite the refusal of the Unionists to keep their commitment [to shared government] I think is proof of the goodwill of the IRA to make this peace process work.'
- Continued IRA punishments as part of the movement's own law-enforcement program. (Could Sinn Fein have prevented those? Vincent McKenna believed so. He said: 'There were no punishment beatings or shootings in the four weeks leading up to President Clinton's visit to Belfast in 1995. Nor were there any in the six weeks leading up to the Belfast Agreement in April last year.')
- Loyalist terrorists' parallel campaign of punishment attacks combined with sectarian bomb outrages against vulnerable Catholics.
- UK government's confirmation that the IRA ceasefire was 'intact' laid it open to a charge of abandoning its own network of informers to their fate, surrendering the most important weapon available to either side in this war: accurate intelligence.

- Clear IRA preparations for a return to the armed struggle, including an 'unsanctioned' Republican gun-running operation from Florida and the discovery of a monumental two-tonne cache of Semtex held by 'dissident' Republicans in the Irish Republic.
- Catholic families of some of the IRA's 'disappeared' – people abducted more than twenty-seven years before – finally received the remains of the victims for burial, but only after guarantees that the remains would not be used by the authorities for forensic investigation.
- British proposals for reconstruction of the Royal Ulster Constabulary included cutting the RUC strength from 13,000 to 8,000, a move that prompted Chief Constable Sir Ronnie Flanagan to threaten resignation if the terrorist threat remained undiminished.
- INLA (Irish National Liberation Army) – a left-wing Republican splinter group responsible for at least 140 murders – announced that its armed struggle was over.

At the core of the continued failure of a democratic peace process was the profound enigma of IRA/Sinn Fein relations, Ireland's own heart of darkness. Who, if anyone, was in charge of the Republican army? It was a question that had remained unresolved within the movement since the first independent Irish Dail (parliament) in 1918.

In public Sinn Fein insisted that it did not control the IRA. Indeed, Martin McGuinness, a former IRA leader himself, asserted that it was an insult to misidentify his party by calling it 'IRA/Sinn Fein.' At the first formal Assembly meeting with Ulster Unionists in February 1999 Sinn Fein again insisted that it had no link with the IRA and there was no requirement for IRA arms to be surrendered before the party took its two seats on the Northern Ireland executive.

Gerry Adams created a chic analogy in 1997, plucked from the world of international business. He suggested: 'Think of the IRA as a corporate organisation. People leave all the time, people come in all the time, people have rows all the time, people die, take career breaks and so on . . . but the organisation goes on.'

If Sinn Fein and the IRA were quite separate entities then it would be unconstitutional – and a betrayal of Good Friday '98 – to exclude Sinn Fein from the government of a reformed Northern Ireland. If Sinn Fein and the IRA *were* two sides of one coin, then continued IRA violence, backed by the threat of an untamed arsenal, properly disqualified the party from political power in a democracy that relied on persuasion rather than torture.

The truth of this symbiotic relationship will not emerge for a generation or so, if ever. But there are some useful signs pointing to it. The most significant of these is the relationship between Sinn Fein and IRA prisoners. For Republicans, prisoner-release has been the undiluted success of the peace process. During the first ten months, 242 terrorists, of which 120 were Republican, walked free, including the Shankill bomber. As the first IRA men were set free on 11 September 1998, the reception party was led by Gerry Kelly and Brendan McFarlane of Sinn Fein, both of whom were old IRA hands themselves.

The hectic soap opera that is Northern Ireland makes for a complicated plot. To comprehend it, there is merit in returning to view an earlier episode: the negotiations between Sinn Fein and the prisoners that preceded Good Friday '98. Before the Agreement, the prisoners were a potent – even a dominant – political force within Republicanism, all the more coherent for being contained within the same walls, in their 'University of Terror,' for years before the peace agreement. And beyond the walls, as perceived by a Catholic nun, Sister Sarah Clarke, there was 'a whole community around each prisoner.' Three years before Good Friday '98, a conservative Northern Ireland Secretary, Minister Sir Patrick Mayhew, had pressed the quick-release button by changing the rules on the remission of sentences. This was done, as government spokesmen hinted, 'in an effort to kick-start the stalled peace process' after twelve months of the IRA ceasefire.

In the spring of 1998, at a pivotal point of the negotiations, prisoner power was exercised over two governments as well as Sinn Fein. In April, Sinn Fein's annual conference was addressed by IRA men given special leave by Dublin for the event from Portlaoise Prison, in the Republic. The IRA delegates included Michael O'Brien, the Provisionals' 'Officer Commanding' in the gaol. As one commentator noted: 'The prisoners are a vital constituent that Sinn Fein must keep on board.'

On 10 May Sinn Fein took the momentous step of recognising and participating in the political process of Northern Ireland, ending seventy-five years of abstentionism. A special conference voted for the Good Friday Agreement only after it had received the public blessing of a Who's Who of IRA prisoners from both sides of the Irish border. Those released for this political jamboree, before a brief return to prison, included the Balcombe Street gang; Padraic Wilson, the IRA's OC in the Maze Prison; Ella O'Dwyer and Martina Anderson, serving life at Maghaberry Prison for a bomb plot; and Anderson's husband Paul Kavanagh, serving life for murder.

Mo Mowlam's office explained that the prisoners had been freed 'to promote a full discussion on the agreement and to encourage the peace process.' When 311 out of 350 Republicans voted in favour, the minister herself recognised 'how significant this decision is for Republicans.' She applauded the leadership of Gerry Adams.

Everyone was happy, including Sinn Fein's two most public faces, Adams and McGuinness. The solidarity between active IRA men and Sinn Fein politicians was total. Adams soothed the soldiers' feelings with two promises of his own: Taking part in a Northern Ireland Assembly would be 'another staging post' on the road to a united Ireland, and calls for the IRA to disarm were 'nonsense' and would be resisted. Activists such as John Kelly from South Londonderry said that the agreement was 'an extension of the armed struggle.'

Whatever else these jesuitical words meant, they illustrated the hard truth that even if Sinn Fein had no ostensible influence over the IRA, the IRA assuredly ruled Sinn Fein when it mattered. The nature of this relationship continues to fulfill the bleak lesson that in the Irish War it is physical force, not normal political dialogue, which shapes events regardless of what the Irish majority, outside the hermetically sealed world of fundamentalism, might wish. In pursuit of their aims the terrorists will not stop at any atrocity. After each new outrage they will make a tactical withdrawal, to wait until the bloodstains have dried and popular indignation has cooled. Then, as the representatives of the Real IRA and Continuity IRA have confirmed, the war against the English – and many others – will resume.

Throughout the Irish War – most particularly when Republican fortunes were low – the fianna could always fall back upon one consistent source of hope: nourishment and weapons. That source (as much of this history demonstrates) is the United States. During the most recent phase of the conflict, however, another sort of American influence has made its impact. It has forced the British and the Ulster Protestants to open up the airless politics of Northern Ireland to international opinion and (with the end of the Cold War in 1990) to what is called the New World Order, effectively a *Pax Americana*.

Sinn Fein can rightly claim that its political power now rests upon legitimate electoral support won fair and square, at open election. This resulted from the political backlash provoked by the Republican hunger-strike deaths of 1981. Those were a slow, calculated, theatrical self-sacrifice unmatched in any western country this century. But there was another force at work to anoint Sinn Fein with the sweet oil of political legitimacy. In 1994, in the teeth of official British protests, President Clinton granted Gerry Adams an audience at the White House that transformed Adams's status and that of Sinn Fein internationally. The gesture did not please all Americans. Former Secretary of State James Baker told a US Republican Party convention at San Diego on 15 August 1996: 'We have seen a representative of the IRA hosted in the White House just prior to its resumption of terrorist bombings in London. The result has been the worst relationship with our closest ally, Britain, since the Boston Tea Party in 1773.' Clinton's numerous critics recalled an IRA briefing paper in 1994 that described him as the first president in decades to be influenced by the Irish-American lobby. David Wilshire, vice-chairman of the ruling Conservative

Party's Northern Ireland Committee hurrahed: 'Hallelujah! At long last a note of realism in America. At last someone is putting people's lives above grubbing for votes. I applaud Baker for it. He is absolutely right.'

What no one noticed at the time was that the born-again Gerry Adams was now a political counterweight to the IRA within the Republican movement. The IRA's decision to resume the war with a new blitzkreig against London in February 1996 without prior warning was, in part at least, the terrorists' response to Adams's growing – and as they saw it – dangerous influence. This dislocation of the two parts of the Republican war machine went unrecognised by British politicians and journalists who could only perceive 'Sinn Fein/IRA' as a single entity.

The other significant and benign transatlantic influence was Senator George Mitchell. He deserved the Presidential Medal of Freedom awarded to him on St Patrick's Day, 1999. As the citation put it: 'As judge, lawmaker and statesman, George Mitchell has devoted his life to the determined pursuit of the common good. No one contributed more than he to bringing about the Good Friday peace accord in Northern Ireland in 1998. In displaying exceptional qualities as a patient listener, determined chairman and above all, a fair man, he built the trust essential to reaching an agreement among eight parties and two governments. He has helped bring the people of Northern Ireland closer to lasting peace than they have been in thirty years of sectarian conflict.'

Not even Mitchell's wisdom and cunning could wish away the structural flaw at the heart of the Belfast Agreement: the possession of an arsenal by a secret army dedicated to force of arms rather than force of opinion. In the autumn of 1999, after his latest attempt to breathe life back into the peace process, Mitchell conceded: 'The whole process is under stress. There is a very real threat of its not proceeding. The result of that happening would be entirely unpredictable. There is no credible alternative to the Good Friday Agreement. If it is not implemented, I think the people in Northern Ireland face a highly uncertain future. The outcome is not assured. I hope that there will be full implementation of the Agreement but the pro-Agreement parties remain in disagreement over some of the principal areas needed for implementation. The review I am engaged upon will be concluded in the near future. I have not set a specific time, but I do not intend this to be an open-ended process.'

PART I

The Great Deception

1

Back from the Dead, 1962–1969

In 1962 the IRA was a spent force, a ragged-trousered army scratching at wounds still festering from the venom of a civil war in Ireland, a disastrous bombing campaign in England and a tragi-comic dalliance with Nazi intelligence in Ireland during the Second World War. As an embittered German spymaster, Captain Hermann Goertz, noted in 1940:

> The IRA's intelligence system was as primitive as that of children playing cops and robbers. They hid their messages in the girls' socks . . . They refused to learn even the simplest code by heart. They preferred to sacrifice their men and women. I once told them: 'You know how to die for Ireland but how to fight for it you have not the slightest idea.'

The IRA also knew how to kill people, usually the wrong people. Eight months before Britain declared war on Nazi Germany, the IRA yet again declared war on England. A Republican bomb in the front pannier of a delivery bicycle was bounced recklessly on cobblestones and then abandoned in panic against a Post Office wall in Coventry, where it blew up five innocent people. The Luftwaffe returned to Coventry a few months later to wreak more efficient havoc.

In 1956 the Republicans tried and failed again, with raids on military armouries in Britain and Northern Ireland. The campaign was stopped in its tracks by internment of known IRA men in the Irish Republic as well as the Six Counties. The same prescription – a double-dose of internment – might succeed again, in the view of some former IRA men, but the movement, learning from past mistakes, has usually taken care not to alienate Dublin, even if it does not regard the regime there as politically legitimate.

So it was that on 26 February 1962, the IRA issued a communiqué admitting that its latest campaign in the Six Counties and in England was not supported by the people it was intended to 'liberate'. It said: 'Foremost among the factors motivating this course [ending the campaign] has been the attitude of the general public whose minds have deliberately been distracted from the supreme issue facing the Irish people – the unity and freedom of Ireland.' In practice it did not give up. If an MI5 report made public in 1997 was correct, the movement secretly recruited and trained a new generation of volunteers. Within four years a shadowy army of 3,000 men had passed through one or other of thirty-four camps across the Republic. British Intelligence monitored the process with growing concern as the fiftieth anniversary of the 1916 Easter Rising loomed. It warned the Prime Minister, Harold Wilson, that 3,000 armed Republicans 'could be called out in an emergency'.

The British government considered sending troops into the Province for the anniversary but it did not wish to provoke trouble. As Wilson's Home Secretary, James Callaghan, told the Ulster Labour MP Gerry Fitt: 'I can get the Army in all right, but it will be the devil of a job to get it out again.'

Easter 1966 passed without trouble for one very good reason: the fertile minds running the IRA were busy constructing a new war strategy which would command popular support, one which, furthermore, could be camouflaged as something much more innocent than renewed terrorism. The IRA Chief of Staff in 1962 was a house-painter named Cathal Goulding. In 1970, he gave a remarkably frank interview about the means by which a broken guerrilla army had resurrected itself during the preceding eight years. What he described was a masterpiece of political deception, an armed Marxist revolution dressed up as an acceptable demand for basic civil rights in Northern Ireland. After the 1962 communiqué an IRA conference, meeting almost nightly for nearly two years, studied past failures, starting with 1798 and Wolfe Tone. 'Why was the movement unable to succeed in spite of the fact that people engaged in revolutionary activities were willing to make any sacrifice for it?' The reason was: 'We were separated from the people of Ireland, in the sense that we were a secret organisation. The people had no real knowledge of our objective . . . They didn't understand our tactics or our motives . . . Without the support of the majority of the people, we just couldn't succeed.'

Goulding was right. In practice, the Fenian Irish Republican Brotherhood and its offspring the IRA had never felt themselves answerable to a public, political process for which many of the founding fathers had only contempt. As Liam Lynch, a Cork IRA veteran and the hardest of anti-treaty hardliners, once wrote: 'The Army has to hew the way for politics to follow.'

> How could we get the people to support us? [Goulding asked] The evidence was that the Republican movement had no real policies. Without objectives, we couldn't develop a proper strategy. Tactics were all that we had employed. The actual fight for freedom had become an end in itself to us. Instead of a means, it became an end. We hadn't planned to achieve the freedom of Ireland. We simply planned to *fight* for the freedom of Ireland. We could never hope to succeed because we never planned to succeed.

The way out of this cul de sac, said Goulding, was populist, street politics,

> to involve ourselves in the everyday problems of people . . . better houses . . . working conditions . . . jobs . . . pay . . . education. By doing this we felt that we could involve the people, not so much in supporting the Republican movement for our *political* ends but in supporting agitation so that they themselves would be part of a revolutionary force demanding what the present system just couldn't produce.

The IRA's self-examination continued until 1965, at which point 'we produced a nine-point document dealing with social agitation'. Point no. 9 was to break with the tradition of electing MPs who then refused to take their seats, by electing compliant individuals to 'extend our guerrilla activities and tactics into the very Parliament

5

itself'. Such people were not to be 'elected as Sinn Fein candidates, merely as such'. The agenda was to stir agitation and then put up candidates to represent the trouble. This was entryism, a well-tried strategy adopted by extremists elsewhere to penetrate more reputable political organisms like a virus. As Goulding put it: 'If our people were elected from an area *where agitation had developed to such an extent that the majority (or a large number) of people in the area were disgusted and disillusioned with the establishment* [his emphasis] we could put up a candidate, representing that agitation. That is a revolutionary use of political agitation.'

By 1967, according to Goulding, the IRA as such had become dormant, though (see above) that was not MI5's assessment. The view from Dublin was that 'units of the IRA and the Cumainn of Sinn Fein had become almost non-existent'. In practice, in hardline areas such as Kerry, the Thompson sub-machine-guns were still concealed in barns, oiled and ready for use, as the IRA apostate Sean O'Callaghan discovered when he joined the movement at the age of fifteen. Goulding's view, however, was that 'something dynamic was needed or the Movement was going to break up'.

A meeting of local IRA leaders was convened at the end of August 1967 in which they were told that 'they had no Movement at all: they only thought they had a Movement'. The new policy, explicitly based on the doctrines of the Marxist James Connolly, was for a socialist republic directed towards worker-control. A programme for socialism in a Catholic/nationalist and instinctively right-wing culture at the same time as abandoning another cherished tradition – non-participation in democratically elected parliaments – was another recipe for failure, but in the 1960s, when much of the free world was blazing with youthful street violence disguised as political protest, the new IRA approach had one huge advantage: it could catalyse popular discontent so as to destabilize the existing order.

As Goulding put it:

> When we decided on the agitation campaign, we first of all decided that we would become engaged in the things I've referred to: housing, land, fisheries, Trade Union agitations

and so on. We realized that in the Six Counties, however, before launching these activities, we would have first to work for the establishment of basic Civil Rights in order to establish democracy and abolish discrimination. This would also give us the political manoeuvrability to establish the Republican Movement openly ... We decided to support a Civil Rights campaign in the North, we took part in marches and demonstrations. We acted as stewards on these occasions.

While the new IRA preferred to be non-sectarian, unifying the Protestant and Catholic working class in conformity with Marxist dedication to a dictatorship of the proletariat,

> we felt that as a result of the Unionist 'super-race' complex and its attendant bigotries, the Catholics had a kind of sub-race spirit – that they hadn't got the spirit or the will to revolt effectively. They would at different times attempt a revolt, but their rebellion was never cohesive, never really organized. This, we felt, was due to something within their own minds: they were a beaten people before they started.

The campaign for agitation would inevitably lead, in the febrile atmosphere of Northern Ireland, to an armed struggle. Here, the IRA faced two problems. One was lack of popular support within the Catholic community. Asked if the IRA's new preoccupation with politics had rendered it psychologically incapable of supporting the Catholics with physical force when the time came in 1969, Goulding replied:

> There is no foundation for this. As a famous revolutionary once said: 'A guerrilla must move through his people like a fish moves through water.' We ... moved through our people like a fish through a desert: we were sticking out a mile. When the guerrilla campaign [of the 1950s] finished, because of the efficiency of the Security Forces there and because of the lack of support for us among the ordinary people, the actual fight was dying down. We weren't able to sustain it.

This in turn led to a decision by American Republicans – who were still dedicated to physical force – to withdraw financial support.

> In 1964, when the [IRA review] conference was going on, I spent three or four weeks in America with the Clann na Gael. I was constantly pointing out to them why we needed support and emphasizing the changes in our policy and the reasons for them. The reaction I got there was that they couldn't support us financially unless there was some form of revolutionary activity, particularly military activity, actually going on in Ireland. Exiles will support activity, but they won't help prepare for it. Irishmen . . . in the Bronx or Boston would say: 'What is the IRA doing anyway? Their military campaign is over. All they'll do with the money is live a soft life.'
>
> We decided to go ahead with the agitationary campaign anyway. Maybe they would see that as real revolutionary 'activity'. If not, we were committed to going ahead with it, to develop the revolutionary potential in Ireland . . . But we didn't get the support we needed from America. Most of our organizations in America were oriented towards supporting physical force. In the Constitution of the Clann na Gael it stated that they would support the people in Ireland who were working for the freedom of Ireland, but they would only support those that were using force alone. Those two words, 'force alone', meant that they wouldn't support political or agitationary activities in Ireland.

Nevertheless, Goulding persuaded the Americans to change Clann na Gael's Constitution to admit 'any means to attain the freedom of Ireland'. This had an unexpected side effect:

> After this time, whatever support did come [from America] was diverted into the Civil Rights Movement, instead of coming to us. So, we were broke. We hadn't got the where-withal to buy arms. We were in no position . . . to get arms by military means . . . Any arms raids or military activities

would obstruct the development of those political and agitationary tactics.

We were in a cleft stick. We couldn't be militarily active because we hadn't got the resources and we hadn't conditioned the people for military activities. We knew from all our discussions . . . that military activity *alone* couldn't make the revolution. We would first have to get the support of the people for military activity. We *had* to start at the beginning, we had to start with our economic resistance campaign and our political activities from scratch.

The elements were now assembled for a lethal experiment in political agitation of a kind that was certain to lead to insurrectionary violence, but the IRA, although it held stocks of weapons in the Republic, would choose not to deploy those when the agitation provoked a violent reaction by Ulster's security forces, notably the Ulster Special Constabulary. The policy of old-fashioned Fenian provocation dressed in new clothes was combined with incredible optimism: 'We didn't think that the police would come in and deliberately shoot up people in the Falls Road area [of Belfast]'

As it happened, the sacrifice of Catholics as a result of deliberately induced street violence worked to the advantage of the 'physical force' element within the IRA rather than political theorists working to a Stalinist programme of step-by-step revolution known as Stages. Once the violence had started in earnest, as Goulding admitted,

we were able to organize a system whereby we could filter arms into the areas where they would be needed for defence . . . We got better support from America and other areas for the Movement itself. This gave us the necessary facilities to obtain the materials that we hadn't been able to get previously. The fighting that had taken place in August of '69 emphasized to our people in America that a section of our people in the North were behind barricades, that they were practically undefended and that it was the duty of the Republican movement, whether in America or anywhere else, to supply the finance and other means to procure defensive weapons.

Two years after that interview, in March 1972, Goulding shed fresh light on the realities of 1969 when he told the left-wing journal *7 Days* that the IRA *could* have provided guns to defend Catholic ghettos from attack by the RUC. The IRA leadership apparently persuaded itself that the police assaults its agitation had provoked were a trap set by the authorities. As Goulding put it:

> The aim of the day was to bring the IRA out with its guns. We were 'cute' and we got a lot of criticism for being so. We didn't give what guns we had out. We hadn't thought there would be organised pogroms because of the worldwide publicity attracted by Derry [a year earlier]. We miscalculated there . . . this miscalculation had two effects. It wasn't Protestant sectarianism that developed after August 1968 so much as Catholic sectarianism. The demand was raised to throw away our pamphlets and get bullets and this brought the Provisionals, who were always in the IRA, into action again and we were swamped by this right-wing reactionary group.

This was an impressive miscalculation, yet its effect was successful in destabilizing the existing state of Northern Ireland. The Catholics were made to suffer for it. What is still unproven is the extent to which elements within the IRA intended it to happen that way.

The Provisional Sinn Fein President Ruairi O'Bradaigh (Gerry Adams's predecessor) also talked frankly to the press in 1972. He confirmed that the traditionalists identified civil rights agitation as an exploitable revolutionary situation. He said: 'There is a tide in the affairs of men, that taken at the flood leads on to success . . . We recognised that this was the tide, the first real tide in fifty years.' O'Bradaigh's interviewer, Richard Trench, also learned that as part of the takeover strategy,

> Sean Mac Stiofain, then IRA Director of Intelligence, had already made contingency plans for the split with his leading ally in Belfast, Leo Martin. When it came out into the open, eighty per cent of Belfast's post-August 1969 recruits sided with the Provisionals. They were eagerly joined by the 'old

men' who had dropped out of republican politics after the shift to Marxism in 1962. An extraordinary situation occurred where impatient leftists, political illiterates and bitter nationalists walked hand in hand. It seemed that the only force that could unite them was their belief in the gun.

The combination of agitation and street violence, described in the next chapter, gave new life and credibility to the old IRA tradition, dedicated to the gun rather than the ballot box and bank-rolled by sinister forces in the Dublin government of the day (see Chapter 10). As a sharp-minded left-wing revolutionary of the period, Eamonn McCann, admitted in 1972: 'We had been working . . . on a conscious, if unspoken strategy to provoke the authorities into overreaction and thus spark off a mass response. We certainly succeeded. But when the mass response came we were not capable of handling it.'

In the same article, he said wryly:

The Provisionals filled the vacuum created by the effective absence of the left and the irrelevance of the right. Had there been a consistent attempt between October 1968 and August 1969 to build a vigorous socialist movement . . . then we *might* have had, when the explosion came, an organisation sufficiently clear in its perspectives, sufficiently confident of its politics to intervene decisively and seize the initiative. Instead, taking leadership from the left had proved as easy as taking candy from a baby.

The political front that disguised the truth of the civil rights disturbances had many aliases in the pioneering days of the Ulster civil rights campaign. One was the Young Socialist Alliance, described by McCann as 'the semi-clandestine core of People's Democracy'. The student-led PD, in its turn, was to be a major destabilizing influence, in open alliance with the Provisionals after the IRA split, through a joint enterprise known as the Northern Resistance Movement. Another group was the Wolfe Tone Society, a republican–socialist 'study group' formed in 1963.

The gathering that spawned the Northern Ireland Civil Rights

Association (an umbrella organization known as NICRA) at Maghera, Derry, on 13 August 1966, was held under the auspices of the Wolfe Tone Society. It was attended by Goulding and the IRA's leading theoretician, Dr Roy Johnston, a nuclear scientist, as well as moderate, constitutional reformists from the Six Counties. The fuse was now discreetly laid for a renewed IRA campaign. It would be ignited in due course by People's Democracy enthusiastically, if unwittingly, assisted by the Royal Ulster Constabulary.

Nine years after the conflict was renewed, the traitorous Customs clerk Eamon Collins, engineering the deaths of colleagues in Newry, still believed that he was being influenced by 'a very ultraleft kind of Marxism. I believed that the IRA could be turned into an organisation which could take on the capitalist state and the agents of that state, as the Red Brigades had done in Italy.'

Collins renounced the IRA and became one of its foremost critics. He was murdered as a result on 27 January 1999 in a killing similar to that of another critic, Andrew Kearny, a few months earlier. Kearney was shot dead in Belfast in July 1998 after he emerged as the victor in a brawl with a local IRA leader. As the victims' support group, Families Against Intimidation and Terror, argued, such attacks were 'designed to maintain power and control over communities.'

This was not what the idealistic majority of civil rights campaigners thought they were in business for. Their peaceful revolution was hijacked even before it got started. The true objective, concealed from journalists and others, was the discredited IRA aim of reunification at the point of a gun, rather than equal rights for Catholics in a democratized Northern Ireland. But in 1968, no one was saying that out loud.

2

Confrontation, 1968–1970

After almost fifty years, Northern Ireland was a political slum, a huge ghetto isolated from the values of a world changing around it. It was a place where a homeless Catholic family could be thrown out of a squat to make room for a single nineteen-year-old Protestant woman. It was tailor-made for street protest, 1960s style. At that time, the violence had to be seen to be done *to* the Republicans, not *by* them. The first protest march at Dungannon on 24 August 1968, to the surprise of the organizers, attracted 4,000 marchers, including a local girl, then a student at Queen's University Belfast, named Bernadette Devlin. In spite of Unionist threats the march went off peacefully. The lesson for the future was not lost on chairman of the Civil Rights Association Betty Sinclair, a veteran communist and trade unionist, who concluded: 'We had been looking for a spark for years. At Dungannon we realized that we had found it.' To underscore the international, human rights dimension of their protest, the marchers sang 'We Shall Overcome'. The local RUC estimated that seventy of the stewards were Republicans and at least ten were fully fledged IRA men. They were right.

Lord Cameron, a Scottish judge who reported on the disturbances of 1968, declared that the IRA men were

> efficient and exercised a high degree of discipline. There is no evidence . . . that such members either incited to riot or took part in acts of violence . . . While there is evidence that members of the IRA are active in the organisation there is no sign that they are in any sense dominant or in a position to control or direct policy of the Civil Rights Association.

Further research by the IRA historian Tim Pat Coogan confirmed that the association 'worked brilliantly: Unionist spokesmen thundered that CRA was only another way of saying IRA, but never a shot was fired, never an IRA man showed himself as such and the IRA deserves some of the credit.'

On 5 October 1968, a peaceful protest march at Londonderry was baton-charged by the RUC. Television film of the attack appeared around a world already sensitized by scenes of police brutality in Paris and at Kent State. The crucial difference between those places and Londonderry was the Irish sectarian fault-line combined with a tradition of armed revolution. As Northern Ireland slid towards the precipice, its reformist leader, Captain Terence O'Neill, conferred with British premier Harold Wilson and the Labour Home Secretary, James Callaghan. By 22 November, O'Neill – to the disgust of his own ultras – had announced a reform package that went a long way towards meeting Catholic demands. It was the only hope for peace, as Wilson acknowledged in the House of Commons. If O'Neill or his ideals were sabotaged, then the British government would consider 'a very fundamental reappraisal' of relations with the Province. It was a thinly veiled threat of direct rule and it was a dangerous bluff.

Following the police attack upon marchers at Derry in November and the O'Neill peace package, there were more marches and a violent response by Protestant ultras trying to stop peaceful protests that had been recognized by the police as legal events. O'Neill, in an emotional televised appeal to all sections of the community just before Christmas 1968, asked: 'What kind of Ulster do you want? A happy and respected province . . . or a place continually torn apart by riots . . . regarded by the rest of Britain as a political outcast?' The appeal struck a chord with the moderate majority, including the civil rights movement which called a 'truce' – a pause in street politics – over Christmas.

Bernadette Devlin and others in the People's Democracy had another agenda. She described O'Neill's appeal as 'hilarious', adding: 'The students called no truce.' Mid–December was an eventful time for the main participants in the disastrous cycle of events that was to follow. O'Neill's appeal on the 10th coincided with the death of George Forrest, the Unionist MP for Mid-Ulster, a constituency dominated by Catholics. By Christmas, it was being hinted to Bernadette Devlin that she might stand as a candidate to unite the various strands of anti-Unionist sentiment and win the seat. The political group most able to manipulate the situation, in a state where Sinn Fein was outlawed, was the Republican Party. It was an enticing prospect for a talented, twenty-one-year-old activist.

On 1 January 1969, defying the Civil Rights Association, the Derry Citizens' Action Committee and the Catholic hierarchy, the People's Democracy started a 73-mile march from Belfast to Derry. As Bernadette Devlin put it later:

> Our function in marching from Belfast to Derry was to break the truce, to relaunch the civil rights movement as a mass movement, and to show people that O'Neill was, in fact, offering them nothing. We knew we wouldn't finish the march without getting molested and we were accused of going out looking for trouble. What we really wanted to do was pull the carpet off the floor to show the dirt that was under it, so that we could sweep it up.

The self-appointed avengers dedicating themselves to the task of cleaning up Ulster's Augean stables were an assorted bunch: twenty-five people, including Republicans, anarchists, Young Socialists, Marxists of various kinds and Trotskyists. The new Left ecumenicalism of the march was symbolized by the presence of four banners. The marchers predictably came under threat, particularly when they crossed Protestant territory. For centuries in Ireland, marches have been a signal of triumphalism or defiance, inviting a response. Forty miles along the way, at the Republican village of Brackaghreilly on Slieve Gallion mountain, the marchers slept in a hall guarded by IRA men. In the immediate vicinity, fifty armed men – one of a series of shifts available that night – had set up roadblocks at approaches to the village. It was an impressive show of strength, confirmation that the IRA still had guns and that they were in the hands of disciplined men. This would make even more astonishing the failure of the IRA to use its guns a few months later, when it mattered.

Earlier that day, confronted by a mob of Protestant extremists at Randalstown, Bernadette Devlin and another marcher, Fred Taggart, had paused to telephone the Prime Minister's office. Mr Wilson, they proposed, should order the RUC to clear a way for the march or others would do the job.

'Who do you mean?' asked a bewildered Whitehall functionary.

'Have you ever heard of the Irish Republican Army?' his caller demanded.

The third night, the marchers rested in a hall at Claudy. They were due to arrive at Derry, eight miles away, next day. While the marchers slept, Protestants supporting Ian Paisley held a rally in the city's Guildhall. The audience included families with their children. On the streets outside, a different kind of gathering was assembling: drunken Catholic youths attacked the hall and burned the car of one of Paisley's lieutenants, Major Ronald Bunting. As stones came through the windows, Bunting called on the men present to turn chairs and banisters into clubs so as to defend their loved ones. Nothing could have been more perfectly calculated to exacerbate an already dangerous situation than this attack, attributed by Lord Cameron to random hooliganism. As it happened, there was to be a considerable amount of random hooliganism later, often at a point when one more push would send a delicately balanced situation over the brink.

Shaken and angry Protestants, before they left the Guildhall, were told to be at Brackfield Church next morning, near Burntollet bridge. The bridge was a vulnerable bottleneck overlooked by hills on the route that the PD march would take on the last phase of its journey to Derry. It was the ideal spot for an ambush. At 11 a.m., the marchers were punished for what had happened at the Guildhall: bricks, boulders and bottles rained down upon them. It was, in Cameron's phrase, 'a calculated martyrdom' on the part of the student activists.

The RUC failed to stop the violence, in which eighty-seven people were injured so severely as to need hospital treatment. Bernadette Devlin, a lucky survivor, had been near the head of the march alongside Gerard (Gerry) Lawless, a former member of a breakaway, left-wing Republican group known as Saor Eire (Free

Ireland). His combination of fiery Republicanism and grass-roots socialism chimed well with much that People's Democracy now expressed.

The violence now had its own momentum. Immediately after the Burntollet ambush, RUC officers made an unauthorized, punitive raid on the Catholic Bogside district of Londonderry. As Cameron put it: 'Our investigations have led us to the unhesitating conclusion that on the night of 4–5 January a number of policemen were guilty of misconduct which involved assault and battery, malicious damage to property, to streets . . . and the use of provocative sectarian and political slogans.' After that rampage, 163 people needed hospital treatment.

In Newry, as a recently arrived *Sunday Times* correspondent, I witnessed the PD's interpretation of non-violent protest at first hand when a leading member of the movement tried to set fire to a police bus before releasing the brakes, to roll it downhill on to a static police line. Meanwhile another PD leader cried: 'People of Newry, occupy your Post Office!' No one did so, but the shout owed nothing to the Gandhi tradition of passive resistance.

Meanwhile, the subversion of the civil rights movement continued. Large numbers of People's Democracy activists joined the CRA not as PD members but as sympathetic individuals. The association chairman, Betty Sinclair, criticized for her cautious warnings against premature action, was voted out of office. People prominent in PD moved on to the CRA executive.

In February, during a crisis election for the Stormont Parliament called by O'Neill, the People's Democracy contested eight seats. Bernadette Devlin in South Derry picked up a creditable 6,000 votes against the 9,000 for the new Unionist Prime Minister Major James Chichester-Clark. She was now identified by the IRA as a strong contender for the forthcoming Westminster parliamentary by-election at Mid-Ulster. Two anti-Unionist candidates – the veteran Republican Kevin Agnew and the nationalist Austin Currie – were on hand to split the Catholic vote and ensure another Unionist victory. The new, political IRA was determined to keep the momentum of its non-violent policy moving as effectively as the street protests it had helped to orchestrate. The dilemma it faced in Mid-Ulster was that an overtly Republican candidate, to be loyal to the tradition of winning the vote but declining to take the oath of loyalty at Westminster, thereby withdrew (the Republicans use the word 'abstain') from useful political activity in or out of London. Bernadette Devlin, the naive socialist daughter of a Republican who probably served as an IRA volunteer, was – as she later admitted – totally ignorant of formal politics. She was ideally suited to keep the momentum going without compromising IRA tradition. A stalemate developed between Agnew and Currie.

Devlin later recalled:

> In the middle of this situation, some of the Republicans came informally to me, observing in a casual way, 'You could hold this seat.' They came to me because I was becoming known as a speech-maker at civil rights meetings and as the Republicans told me, 'You never *say* anything but we know what you mean.' It was a dishonest little game they were playing: they weren't prepared to allow a Republican to take the oath of allegiance, but they were prepared to go outside the party, find someone who believed what they professed to believe, and stuff that person up to Westminster to take the oath.

A joint convention was arranged for 2 April, at which a single anti-Unionist candidate would be chosen. The night before, as an intensive *Sunday Times* Insight inquiry confirmed,

> the IRA took a hand ... At 11.30 that evening, in a house in the upland village of Pomeroy, the Republican executive of Mid-Ulster met. Present as 'advisers' were Tom Mitchell [a former abstentionist MP] and Tomas Mac Giolla, the president of Sinn Fein. Both had driven that day from Dublin. Their advice was clear: the Republicans should not field a candidate against Bernadette Devlin.

Next day, as arranged, both Agnew and Currie withdrew in favour of the only other serious candidate. Miss Devlin was selected. Two weeks later, she was elected with a comfortable majority on a turn-out of 91.5 per cent.

As the dawn of promise broke over the eastern horizon in 1969, so did the polluted cloud of Ireland's most deadly Orange Order marching season for a century or more. This hellish, drumming brew of Protestant triumphalism and Catholic defiance had pro- voked riots in 1857, 1864 and 1886 in Belfast and in 1869 and 1883 in Derry. All were examined by official inquiries. As the his- torian A. T. Q. Stewart points out: 'With depressing frequency the nineteenth-century commission laid the blame squarely on two main factors: the partiality and inefficiency of the police and the provocative nature of Orange celebrations.' In 1997, an inquiry conducted by Dr Peter North, an Oxford academic, sought solu- tions to similar problems, thanks to the Drumcree march of 1996.

In May 1969, IRA leaders in Belfast, reading the runes correctly, went in person to Dublin to ask their Army Council for substantial supplies of weapons. The plea was rejected. As Tim Pat Coogan rightly concluded: 'In the event of weapons being discovered in the North, the work for the Civil Rights movement would have been discredited and a stick given to Stormont to beat the IRA out into the open from behind its façade of Republican clubs.' There was another reason, which was the new doctrine defined in Cameron's luminous phrase, 'calculated martyrdom'. The calculation was being made in Dublin. The martyrs-in-waiting were to be found in the Catholic ghettos of Belfast and Derry. Hardline Northern Republi- can leaders, such as Sean Keenan of Derry and Jimmy Drumm of Andersonstown in Belfast, were less than happy. There was talk of a separate Northern command; in effect, a breakaway movement whose spirit might be labelled the Traditional IRA. With Irish irony it was soon to become a body called the Provisional Irish Republican Army.

As the British government sat on its hands, the summer violence of 1969 swept across the Province. On 12 July, the anniversary of the Boyne victory over the Catholic King James, the Orangemen marched in twenty places throughout Ulster. There was routine violence in Belfast. At Dungiven, that day and the next, Catholics repeatedly tried to burn down a new Orange hall. At Derry, at least sixteen RUC men and twenty-two 'civilians' were injured in a street battle during which the Catholics hurled at least forty petrol bombs. The Protestant militia, the B Special Police Reserve, was turned loose on Dungiven, firing wildly, causing no casualties, in response to a volley of stones and bottles.

On 11 August, the Unionist government at Stormont gave in to demands to permit the most provocative march of all next day by 15,000 Apprentice Boys of Derry, on a route overlooking the Bogside. 'Whitehall', as Insight noted, 'was unruffled.' In a replay of the force reductions of 1919 in Cork and Dublin, 'in the first days of August, with General Freeland [military supremo in the Province] pleading for reinforcements, the Ministry of Defence actually reduced the number of troops in Northern Ireland,' so that a light infantry battalion could be sent to Kenya for routine training.

An RUC line cordoned the Catholic Bogside. Half of the march had passed without trouble at about 4 p.m. when youths emerged from within the ghetto to hurl stones, bottles and marbles or to fire catapults against the Apprentices. It was a bleak mirror-image of the ambush at Burntollet bridge. At Burntollet, RUC police officers had been ineffectual in preventing the violence against non-violent, if provocative, marchers. At Derry, Catholic stewards – IRA and otherwise – were invisible as the Apprentice Boys swaggered past in their sashes. Fifty hours of continuous fighting which became known as the Battle of the Bogside now began. Police, responding to the youths' opening salvo, charged into the ghetto. In a well-organized defensive manoeuvre planned by the Derry Citizens Defence Association headed by Sean Keenan, barricades went up before the RUC and petrol-bombs descended upon them. The RUC replied with tear-gas.

The conflict was now deliberately spread to ten other urban areas by elements within the Civil Rights Association 'to take police pressure off Derry'. Scenting a wholesale revolution, the Stormont government panicked and mobilized B Specials throughout the Province. Still the British government did not intervene.

At Dungiven, the Court House and Orange hall were burned down. In Armagh, thirteen members of a B Special platoon of seventeen men fired twenty-four shots, killing John Gallagher, a Catholic, and wounding two others. Worse, much worse, was to come in Belfast. Again, the catalyst was a wolfpack of youths apparently beyond the control of the IRA or other stewards at a time when their intervention might have cooled the situation. Using rocks and petrol bombs, they attacked the police station (or barracks) at Hastings Street in the Catholic Lower Falls Road area. The RUC over-reaction was more than any *agent provocateur* had a right to anticipate. The RUC drove Shorland armoured cars at the crowd threatening the police building.

The rioters now shifted their attacks to another police station, half a mile away at Springfield Road, and shots were exchanged. More than one person in the crowd was armed. Meanwhile in Republican Leeson Street, Lower Falls, a grenade was thrown at RUC men using batons to repel an attack. The authorities were now certain that a full-scale, pre-planned IRA uprising was in progress. That night, heavy .30 Browning machine-guns, with a killing range of two miles, were mounted on the Shorlands.

Not until the following afternoon, 14 August – by which time the police had committed all their resources including the B Special reserve – did Prime Minister Harold Wilson and his Home Secretary James Callaghan finally give their consent for troops to intervene. Though they were to restore order at the request of the RUC, they were to use common-law powers which require any citizen, military or civilian, to assist a constable if called upon. This is a vague, unwritten arrangement that includes the doctrine of 'citizen's arrest'. In the early evening a company of soldiers of the Prince of Wales' Own moved by truck from a stand-by base into Derry. A Whitehall spokesman was reassuring. The soldiers, he promised, would be back in their barracks by the weekend. It was now Thursday.

As the first British troops entered Derry in a convoy of trucks, B Specials 70 miles away in Belfast were preparing to take on, as they saw it, a Republican insurrection. Catholic civilians, fearing a pogrom, threw up barricades and prepared petrol bombs. Hastings Street was attacked again. This time, the armoured cars were ready to hit back with automatic gunfire. Each community believed the other had a massacre in mind. Paranoia took over. A mob of 100 Catholic youths marched to the edge of the Catholic area, displaying the tricolour of the twenty-six counties and singing Eire's national anthem, 'The Soldier's Song'. The Protestants counter-attacked. Fire-bombs went into Catholic homes on the fringes of the two districts. From the Catholic St Comgall's School a burst of automatic fire from the IRA's favourite automatic weapon, a Thompson sub-machine-gun, killed Herbert Roy, a Protestant. At close range the Shorlands poured heavy bursts into nearby Divis Streets high-rise flats, where Patrick Rooney, aged nine, cowered in his bedroom. A .3 shell from one of the Shorlands blew his head off as it passed through the building.

On the night of 14–15 August, ten civilians were killed and four RUC men and 145 civilians were wounded by gunfire. The partition fault-line inherent in the 1921 Anglo-Irish Treaty – the best that could be achieved, and endorsed, by a majority of people in Eire – was torn apart and a community traumatized. The strategy of provocation and calculated martyrdom, thanks to the brittle quality of the Stormont regime and the pusillanimous response of the British government, had broken the uneasy, but viable, mixture of peace and gradual reform. In its place, the Irish War had started again with a vengeance. The civil liberties campaign, in so far as this meant equal rights for all civilians before the law in Northern Ireland, would soon be acknowledged by many campaigners to be an irrelevance. The strategy of provocation was working. For Republicans the penalty was that the beleagured Catholics of Derry and Belfast had greeted the British Tommies as saviours, welcoming them with cups of tea. I recall the unease with which Republican leaders at Unity Walk Flats, a Belfast flashpoint, deflected the efforts of a Hampshire regiment major (who did not know that a journalist was present) to persuade them that they needed no fire-arms. The thrust of the exchange, from memory, was along the following lines:

'Come on, Mr Brady, we're here to protect you now . . . You don't need any hardware around the place.'

'Ah, well, that's as may be, Major . . . But we don't know what the future holds, do we?'

Soon, a British army post, with light machine-gun, would perch on top of the building like a stork's nest. Republicans concluded that the bird was actually a cuckoo.

Even harder to swallow for the local IRA was the issue of relations with the Dublin leadership and those supporting it in Belfast. Throughout the history of the Northern state, Belfast Catholics had known that they were effective hostages in any sectarian doomsday scenario. For them, survival had been of greater moment than reunification. The Belfast IRA now had to come to terms with the ugly fact that when they had needed support, none was forthcoming. There was no sign of the 3,000 armed Republicans identified by MI5 three years earlier, or of the teams of fifty who had guarded the PD marchers at Brackaghreilly.

Surprisingly, in August 1969 and even into early September, none of the correspondents swarming over the Province seemed to notice the IRA's role in events. Two who did – one from London, the other from Dublin – kept silent. One reason for this failure to recognize the truth was that Lord Cameron's report into the earlier disturbances, identifying the IRA presence, had not yet been published. When it appeared, it noted that in those initial riots, 'when the so-called Free Derry was set up following the rioting … members of the IRA were active in the organisation of defence committees set up on a street by street basis.'

In the week following my unwelcome *Sunday Times* report, a delegation of Catholic leaders spent seven hours talking with Home Secretary Callaghan. The deal offered was the presence of soldiers to guard the ends of every Catholic street to keep hostile Protestants out, in exchange for bringing down the barricades now declared an act of unlawful defiance by the Unionist Prime Minister Chichester-Clark. The next weekend, as Insight established, was spent trying to sell the deal to the rest of the Central Citizens' Defence Committee. This turned out to comprise 120 men from all over Belfast, a 'tough crew' whose dissenters were 'led by Francis Card, Billy McKee and Leo Martin, three men who were later to emerge as leaders of the Provisional IRA. This was the first meeting at which this identifiable hard-line group emerged inside the Catholic community.'

The deal went through only in response to pressure from the Roman Catholic Bishop of Down and Connor, Dr Philbin, who had 'to work over the CCDC leadership'. The fact remained that the barricades came down only with the assent – given reluctantly – of the IRA.

For many months before the fatal breakdown of law and order in the Province – a legal precondition of the provision of soldiers under their common law obligations, rather than an operation of military aid to the civil community – some soldiers had taken an intelligent interest in what was going on 'across the water', and what that might imply for the familiar strategy of defending the North German plain against the Warsaw Pact. One of them was Major Michael Mates, a cavalry officer who had started his career with the Royal Ulster Rifles. In time, Mates became Northern Ireland Minister but in 1967, serving in Berlin, he agreed with most professional soldiers that Northern Ireland was 'Sleepy Hollow'.

After the PD march was ambushed at Burntollet, Mates's perception changed. It occurred to him that the small peacetime garrison in Northern Ireland might need reinforcement. If the soldiers were to be provided from the British Army of the Rhine, then that had implications for the military planners in Germany. He discussed the issue with his Chief of Staff who promptly sent him to Northern Ireland to find out what the commitment might be.

In about March of 1969, some two months after Burntollet, Mates arrived at the army's headquarters at Lisburn, County Down. He joked later: 'It was my tiny niche in history. I can say I was the first reinforcement!' He carried out a serious assessment of the threat.

> Our evaluation was that the problem at the time was one of civil disobedience [which implied passive resistance, Gandhi-style] rather than a resumption of the IRA campaign. As we went on through that summer it was quite clear that the Protestants, the B Specials, were over-reacting. It is often forgotten now that it was Cardinal Conway and other leaders of the Nationalist or Catholic communities who begged the British government to send the military in.

Mates proposed that selected fighting units, including infantry and gunners, should train reinforcement 'bricks' of around 100 men to be earmarked for attachment to Northern Ireland as required.

The teams were trained to contain street disturbances and to run cordon-and-search operations, using the doctrines taught for generations and last used in Aden and Cyprus and before that in the Suez Canal Zone and Palestine. The difference this time was that no one could be sure who was the enemy. It was the beginning of what one SAS veteran describes as 'a war without a strategy, run with sometimes brilliant tactics'.

The training was not a waste of time, however. As Mates recalled: 'I came back [to Berlin] and did the planning. Lo and behold, in August/September 1969 we went out trained.' And in the first use of British troops to quell civil disturbances in the United Kingdom for generations, even limited preparation, in good time, ensured that the army did not compound the over-reaction of the indigenous police forces.

The Mates initiative seems to have gone unremarked in Downing Street. Harold Wilson had first discussed with O'Neill the possible need for troops three years earlier, in 1966, the year he received the MI5 report warning of 3,000 armed IRA volunteers. As the civil rights campaign stirred up violent reaction, the Labour government became increasingly concerned not to become directly involved. As the July Orange marching season began in 1969, the British military supremo in the Province, Lieutenant-General Ian Freeland, had 2,500 soldiers on strength, but half of these were guarding water pipelines and electricity pylons after a UVF (Loyalist) bombing campaign in April. (The attacks were attributed to the IRA at the time and helped to depose O'Neill.) In the Defence Ministry meanwhile, senior staff officers produced nine scenarios to anticipate the possible course of events. None had a happy ending. All estimated that as many as 20,000 to 30,000 soldiers might be required to hold the ring in a civil war across the water, even if Dublin did not intervene.

Dennis Healey, Labour's Defence Minister, was not alone in expressing dismay at such calculations. In the Far East, where Britain still had bases in Singapore and Malaysia, a senior Royal Navy admiral snorted when I discussed such estimates with him. He growled: 'I don't care a fish's tit what Freeland wants. We have commitments here.'

Towards the end of July, as the situation worsened, the Cabinet sought a device to avoid the commitment of direct rule of the Province from London. It was the Attorney-General, Sir Elwyn Jones, who identified the soldier's duty to act as a 'common-law constable'. This ignored the fact that a soldier, armed with a lethal weapon, could be victimized by military law if he disobeyed an order to shoot an unarmed civilian. Equally, excessive force would expose him to a murder charge. The fudge conjured up to cover such a risk was the doctrine of 'equivalent force' through which the soldier would be justified in opening fire if he had good reason to think that the risk he faced required it. Worse, the common-law response required that the RUC should have exhausted all its resources – including the B Specials – before it could legitimately seek army help. It was a recipe for a disaster that would spread far beyond Ulster.

As the situation spiralled out of control in Belfast, on Sunday 3 August Belfast Police Commissioner Harold Wolseley asked for help. The appeal went to Freeland, who sent a company of soldiers of about 100 men – one of Mates's 'bricks' – to stand by at the RUC headquarters in East Belfast. Freeland then tried to get his decision endorsed by London. This was not forthcoming. The troops were withdrawn, pending the use of B Specials. As the log of 39 Brigade, Northern Ireland, noted: 'No question of committing troops until all methods exhausted by the police.'

By 13 August, it was obvious even to Downing Street that troops must, after all, be provided if lives were not to be at risk. As Freeland moved his first contingent into Derry the next day, it was clear that the scenarios were right: more troops would be required, quickly, if the situation was to be held in Belfast, Dungannon and elsewhere. But as the Insight inquiry confirmed: 'no reinforcements were sent to Freeland until more than forty-eight hours afterwards. According to an excellent source, this stemmed from a decision on Friday 14 August by Wilson and Callaghan that the troops should only go into Derry. They were still trying to minimise the British military involvement.'

It was late on Friday night when a battalion of the 3rd Light Infantry touched down at Aldergrove airport, outside Belfast; later still when they drove down the Crumlin Road. By that time, Catholic homes were ablaze. The soldiers, greeted as saviours, would be treated as the enemy within twelve months as they acted in support of the RUC, as the Attorney-General's legal fudge required. In the short run, however, it was the Protestants who were outraged. Secret negotiations between army chiefs and IRA leaders in September 1969 and the 'back-of-envelope treaty' on the Falls Road, which I exposed at the time, provoked a Protestant riot in Belfast. Reform of the RUC following the April police rampage in Bogside meant that the B Specials were disbanded and the RUC disarmed. The result was an armed uprising by Belfast Loyalists, who shot dead an RUC officer, PC Victor Arbuckle, in an irrational attempt to bring about the restoration of the RUC's right to carry firearms. The British army responded with sixty-six shots, killing two rioters and wounding many others.

These events should have reassured the Catholics that the change was for real and that the British army was serious about defending Catholic rights. This was not what the IRA old guard wanted. The Tommies were an army of occupation. Somehow, relations between them and the Catholics had to be poisoned. Within a few months that would happen, thanks in large measure to the ham-fisted nature of the British military command in Northern Ireland as well as, paradoxically, efforts to convert the RUC into an orthodox police force acceptable to both communities. The RUC had a new Chief Constable, Sir Arthur Young, former boss of the City of London force. He proposed joint army/police riot squads armed only with batons. Freeland did not think that a good idea. In riot conditions, he argued, soldiers carried guns 'to show they mean business'. This was already a long step away from the common-law doctrine of equivalent force, though the first victims were Protestants.

Young's ideal of a community police force was doomed by the hostages to fortune left from the preceding months. Who were the officers who had beaten up the Devenny family in their own home in Derry without provocation in April? Who were the crews who blazed away at Divis Street flats with machine-guns from Shorland armoured cars, killing Patrick Rooney, in August? These questions were unanswered then and remain so almost thirty years later.

Inside the newly-created no-go areas, though riven by internal feuds between the Official (left-wing) IRA and the re-emerging traditionalists of the Provisional movement, the Republicans were able to prey on the fears of Catholics without interference from outside Intelligence agencies. No stranger could enter, say, Leeson Street, or take a beer in the Long Bar there, without being noted by the old men, or small boys, lounging on the corner. The challenge 'Who are you? What are you doing here?' would be delivered to the visitor soon afterwards by someone more able-bodied.

After a series of convoluted meetings in Belfast, Donegal and Dublin, the split between the two wings of the IRA was formalized in December. The new Official IRA policy was to acknowledge the reality of two Irish Parliaments and another at Westminster: a remarkable change of direction, and perhaps of heart, that came too late to arrest both the destabilization of the North and the calculated martyrdom for which the organization had worked so successfully through its surrogates in PD and elsewhere. By now, the violence had acquired its own momentum in a society where the most exciting events of any day were the horse-racing or Gaelic football results. The Officials got the worst of both worlds. The new line was more than the traditionalists could stomach after the use of RUC machine-guns in Belfast and the betrayal by the Dublin high command, a process compared by one Provisional to the Russians' cynical sacrifice of the Warsaw ghetto resistance to the retreating Wehrmacht in 1944. A minority of hardliners walked out and on 10 January 1970, they formed their own separate organization.

Within a few days, three Official IRA units based in the Republic threw their weight behind the Provisionals. As a token of good faith they donated thirty Thompson sub-machine-guns, twenty-seven bolt-action rifles and a varied collection of pistols. It was further evidence that the Officials, having stirred up the Troubles anew, could have defended the beleaguered Belfast Catholics had they so chosen.

The Provisionals now had two targets in their sights: British soldiers, still regarded as friendly by most Catholics, and their erstwhile comrades of the Official IRA. The stern, teetotal fanatics of Pira set about both tasks with fundamental zeal.

3

Amritsar, UK,
1970–1972

The period between the renewed Troubles of 1969 and June 1970 marked a transition from peace-keeping to confrontation. The confrontation led to the British army's adoption of a style of counter-insurgency that ignored the valuable lessons of the successful Malayan campaign, which had stressed the need to win hearts and minds if terrorism was to be beaten by government; it reverted instead to a more primitive security style that alienated the civil population with its use of collective punishment. Riots were to be contained, according to a military staff college training manual still used in the 1960s, as if General Reginald Dyer were still in charge at Amritsar. (In that Indian city on 13 April 1919, Dyer ordered his soldiers to open fire on a non-violent crowd attending a banned meeting. A total of 379 people were killed, the youngest a child aged three. Another 1,000 were wounded.) British ideas about Intelligence-gathering had not advanced beyond the cordon-and-search tactics of the eighteenth century. As Major (later Lieutenant-Colonel and Northern Ireland Minister) Michael Mates put it in an interview with the author: 'The threat evaluation in 1969 was one of civil disobedience rather than a resumption of the IRA campaign.' The doctrine governing internal security 'was a counter-insurgency philosophy from the Cyprus campaign that was not particularly sophisticated'. Intelligence about the IRA was 'pathetic'. When street violence boiled over, Northern Ireland was treated as just another rebellious colony, to be punished accordingly. This policy would prove to be the IRA's most able recruiting sergeant.

On 26 June 1970, a week after Edward Heath defied poll predictions to win a general election in Britain, Bernadette Devlin MP, on her way to address a meeting, was snatched by police at a roadblock in Northern Ireland and taken to prison. This was punishment for her vividly photographed part in the Battle of the Bogside the preceding August. None of the police thugs who had disgraced their uniforms during the preceding eighteen months or more was arrested. Miss Devlin alone, out of thousands of rioters, was imprisoned. At a time when the tension of a hot summer was approaching boiling point, thanks to Loyalist marchers and Catholic stone-throwers, Devlin's imprisonment was an error of epic proportions. It was in keeping with Heath's hardline style of government at the time in such places as Oman as well as Ireland.

In Bogside – 'Free Derry', a no-go area to Security Forces – an angry audience, waiting to touch the hem of their Jeanne d'Arc, expressed their disappointment with stones and petrol-bombs. This time the targets were soldiers, twenty of whom were injured. The troops hit back with CS riot 'gas'.

The violence was warming up again as I drove into Belfast early next morning down the drab Victorian canyon of Crumlin Road towards the pall of smoke and dirt that lay like a permanent shroud over the city centre. It was an extraordinary scene. At one end of the road, Saturday shoppers came and went to their Co-op store, ignoring what was happening 200 yards away, just out of sight though not out of earshot, round a gentle bend. The boundary between peace and war was marked by bricks in the road and an absence of people.

The war, when it came into view, took the form of a three-cornered gunfight, an Irish version of the OK Corral. On the right-hand side of the road, a British military truck faced me. Alongside it, rifles poised, were Royal Marine commandos in green berets. A civilian body lay near the truck in a puddle of blood. From the Catholic Hooker Street on the left swarmed the youths. This time they were armed with revolvers. They knelt down and took careful aim, like the trained marksmen they were, at the Protestant enemy on the other side of the main road, emerging from Palmer Street. From the Protestant side, one rifle – a bolt-action .303 Lee Enfield

– was firing back. The Marines dashed forwards across the road, and into the cover of a derelict building. I joined them.

It was the beginning of a long day, much of which was overlayed in a blur of CS gas and violence by other, worse violence that day and for many days after. But the main events are clear enough: the swirling clouds of CS around the youths of the deprived and angry Ballymurphy estate, within which the rioters danced, handkerchiefs over their faces, hurling stones back at the troops and chanting, rhythmically, 'Eee-zy! Eee-zy!'; the scene across the River Lagan, at evening, when I was halted by a team of RUC men, with their Land Rover. 'Sor,' said a sergeant the size of Divis Mountain. 'It's bad down the Newtonards Road tonight. I wouldn't go down there if I were you . . . In fact, we're just about to evacuate ourselves.'

The redoubt of Short Strand in East Belfast was a mere pocket of 6,000 Catholics surrounded by 60,000 Protestants. That night, the street lights had been extinguished by an unseen hand. The Protestants were about to exact vengeance. Earlier, an Orange band had swaggered past. Its favourite lyrics included the line: 'You've never seen a better Taig [Catholic] than with a bullet in his back.' The stones flew. A pub on the Protestant side of the road was broken into, looted and then set ablaze. Protestant gunmen, armed with Lee Enfields and emboldened by drink, screamed obscenities at their opponents a mere 50 yards away across the road. Their target was the church of St Matthew. They were not to know it, but the Provisionals were present, armed with sub-machine-guns, winning their spurs, thirsting for blood. The gunfire eased long enough to allow an occasional British army personnel carrier (a 'Pig') to whine past, illuminated by the flames in a token gesture of law-and-order. The army had also cordoned off the area. The effect of that was to deny the Provisionals any hope of reinforcement. The Provos prepared for a last stand, as their enemy swarmed across the road armed with petrol-bombs. An IRA Volunteer named Henry McIlhone emerged from cover to stand in the church door. His sub-machine-gun jammed. His opponent, also armed with a carbine, fired first, pouring bullets into his chest and neck. That, at least, was the approved Republican version of events soon afterwards. Local Catholics, close eye-witnesses of events that night, have since told me that McIlhone was actually killed in a battle accident by one of his own side, a diminutive man incapable of controlling the swing of his Thompson sub-machine-gun once he pulled the trigger. The accident apparently occurred as the IRA men were ordered to withdraw tactically. The man with the Thompson was several feet behind McIlhone.

The battle paused for a time, as each side cleared the wounded and foraged for more ammunition and, perhaps, more alcohol. By now, my newspaper deadline had long passed. Unable to leave, I listened to a strange sound in the sudden silence. It was long and sibilant, a swishing noise which stopped briefly and then resumed. In the insanity of that night, it seemed bizarre. Then, silhouetted as black against near-black, I could see the figure of a man, bent over, walking backwards in a laboured fashion. He was pulling something along, something heavy, pausing every now and again to rest. It was a body.

The battle resumed. It turned when the Protestants came under fire from somewhere behind them. This time the gunfire seemed to be high-velocity, modern, 7.62mm rifle fire. Either the British army was shooting at them, or an IRA sniper had infiltrated the cordon. Either way, the effect was electrifying. Everyone scattered.

The sun rose early, for this was June and the weather was fine. The gunmen were nowhere in sight. The smouldering pub, the blood, the broken glass that fine summer morning were a confirmation that what had just occurred was uncontrolled urban warfare. I had filed some early accounts from a minicab office, which I approached horizontally, but my editors did not believe a word of it – this was, after all, the United Kingdom of Great Britain and Northern Ireland, where such things could not happen – and spiked the copy. I walked back to the Europa Hotel feeling a primitive, animal euphoria. From other battlegrounds I also knew that the gunmen would soon provide more excitement, in a higher dosage.

Later accounts, researched by Insight and others, concluded that the Catholic side of the action was run by Billy McKee, the Pira Belfast Brigade commander and Billy Kelly, commanding the movement's 3rd Battalion. McKee was wounded. Meanwhile, appeals to the army and the RUC to intervene fell on deaf ears. One army officer allegedly told Kelly: 'You can stew . . .' If true, it was a big mistake. The Provos were gaining in credibility in the only arena that mattered. A total of 276 people were injured in the riots on Day 1. Three Protestants were killed during the first shooting engagement, on the upper Crumlin Road, on Day 2. At East Belfast, two Protestants were killed outright, two more fatally wounded, while IRA casualties included McIlhone and others not confirmed.

Ironically, military studies back in Britain foresaw under-employment for professional soldiers. Early in 1969 an SAS officer concluded that since 1830 there had been only one or two years in which the army was not fighting a war somewhere. The preceding year of 1968 had been remarkable in that it was not one in which a British soldier was killed in action somewhere. In SAS eyes, Ireland was a peace-keeping job, not a real war. SAS eyes turned towards Oman, where the Heath government was about to mastermind a *coup d'état* against an unpopular client-ruler, Sa'id bin Taimur. After a flurry of gunshots, Taimur was put aboard an RAF flight to Britain, to die in exile. His son, Qaboos, was appointed in his stead with an SAS bodyguard to ensure he did as he was told.

Three weeks before Taimur was overturned by force of arms, Heath's team in Belfast imposed a curfew on the troublesome Falls Road, as if this were the rebellious Crater District of Aden Colony. It was 3 July, one week after the Battle of Short Strand. Two days earlier, the Joint Security Committee for Northern Ireland had decided upon a hard military crackdown, upon any signs of further street violence. A single incident was all that was required to turn a bad situation into a hopeless one. That duly occurred when a search team from the Royal Scots swept into a terraced house at Balkan Street and found a small cache of arms: twelve pistols, some explosives, ammunition and a quick-firing Schmeisser carbine of Second World War vintage. It was teatime on Friday. A crowd gathered. Stones were thrown. An army driver crushed a civilian against railings. More stones brought an army truck to a halt. The searchers were surrounded and trapped. A second infantry company was deployed to extract the first. More troops were deployed. They used CS gas. The locals, supporters of the Official IRA, threw nail-bombs, petrol-bombs and hand-grenades. Five soldiers were hurt. The army retreated to the edge of the area, put a cordon round it and awaited reinforcements. Soon, 3,000 soldiers were massed, ready to invade the Falls Road where the locals were erecting barricades. A helicopter flying over the streets carried a public address system through which an English voice announced that a curfew had been imposed. Everyone was to clear the streets.

In a surprising show of solidarity, as the troops prepared to smash their way into the Lower Falls, the Provisional chieftain Billy McKee telephoned his opposite number commanding the Official IRA team and offered support. The Officials rejected the offer, adding: 'We're going to take on the British army ourselves.' The Officials, Goulding's people, were no longer being 'cute' about their weapons; instead they were now preparing to use them. Goulding said soon afterwards:

> We used the lull – from the time the August [1969] fighting had finished – and we were able to organize a system whereby we could filter arms into the areas where they would be needed for defence . . . The accusation that we were simply interested in politics, that we weren't interested in armed revolution, was a big help to us. Not only did [our accusers] succeed in getting a lot of other people . . . to believe that we had gone soft by going 'political', they also got the Establishment to believe it! This was into our barrow. This was one of the factors that enabled us to supply material to the areas to establish a proper defensive fight when that fight came off.

In practice, yet again, the Provisionals would be the long-term beneficiaries of the British army's latest fatal mistake in Ireland. At 8.20 that Friday evening, the British army was ordered to attack. I had returned to my hotel to complete filing my report to the *Sunday Times*. An executive liked the analysis I had written but wanted 'a bit more colour'. I explained that a curfew was in force. I could try my luck, but I would probably be arrested. Having been already locked up in Lagos during the Biafran War and in Paris during the student troubles, I knew that misplaced bravado on a

Friday night, near the final edition, was not a good way to win applause from desk editors in London. This time I was told to go back on to the street.

It was now around 8 p.m. and a lot of gunfire echoed around the Lower Falls where it crossed Dover Street. Some of the soldiers, freshly disembarked that day in Belfast harbour, had no knowledge of local geography and for some it was their first time under fire. Urban warfare is a dodgy business. It can be peculiarly difficult to identify the direction from which shots come, as the Paras and journalists were to discover in Londonderry two years later. It was inevitable that some rounds were fired at the wrong targets.

A tower crane overlooked the area, from which an IRA sniper was firing carefully aimed shots. Some of these hit the road near me as I moved towards the army cordon. I dived for cover behind a street telephone and landed on a soldier who was already in the prone position, lining up his self-loading rifle. He was not pleased. We exchanged increasingly friendly words. He was Light Infantry, as I had once been. I wished him luck.

I wanted to penetrate the cordon, to see what was happening to the people bottled up inside it. At first, it seemed, my luck was in. In a doorway I encountered a big man wearing a white suit. He said, in Catholic-Belfast, 'Yer man on the crane's a friend of mine. He can see me in this suit all right. Stick with me and yuz'll be OK. Now, we's going to zig-zag. We'll hit that door over there. Ready? Go!' It worked like a charm. Each time White Suit crossed the street, the sniper stopped. What we did not know was that about 200 yards away, in the direction in which we were moving, an army truck facing away from us was the firing point for British soldiers. Each time we moved, their rifles were trained on us. They did not fire, but waited for us to close on their position. We turned left, down cramped Ardmoulin Street and then right, into an alley-way near St Patrick's Pro-Cathedral, the scene of the not-so-secret talks between Brigadier Dyball and Jimmy Sullivan. As we came round the corner a powerful searchlight snapped on. The effect was blinding.

'Halt!' I came to a halt, military style, hands raised high. White Suit shambled on a few steps, shielding his eyes.

'You! The man in white. Come forward.'

The first voice was an NCO's. The second belonged to Sandhurst.

White Suit moved as instructed. I could see his silhouette as they put him hands-against-wall while another figure hit his head with a rifle butt.

'Now you, Second Man. Come forward.'

'My name is Geraghty,' I said before moving. 'I represent the *Sunday Times* of London.'

'Oh, yes. We know who you are.'

I marched forward, expecting the rifle butt treatment; it would not be the first beating I had received on this assignment. Guns were trained on me but it seemed reasonable to expect that the safety-catches were on. I was handcuffed to White Suit who was not steady on his feet and needed support. We were then marched slowly across the wide, exposed killing ground of Albert Street. There seemed to be a lot of gunfire at that moment. We turned right and then left, back on to the Lower Falls and encountered the truck with its soldiers whose guns had been aimed at us and had not fired. It was one of many military lorries being used that night to take curfew-breakers to prison. We were bundled inside it. I noted that the sides were covered by canvas; it was not bullet-proof. My fellow prisoners included some volunteer first-aid crews and a little man who said he was a journalist. Interested as ever in the strength of the professional competition around me, I asked: 'What sort of journalist?'

'I'm a racing journalist,' he said. I believe he added: 'I do the tips for the *Irish News*.'

A light rain was falling. It was now dark. The soldiers half-carried, half-dragged a dead body from the direction we had come and let it drop heavily on the greasy pavement. Then they took turns to kick the corpse and curse it. They thought they had killed a terrorist, but the victim was more enigmatic and interesting than that. He was, almost certainly, Zbigniew Ugilik, a Pole who had been working as a postman in West London until the day before. Then, for no obvious reason, armed with expensive camera equipment, he flew to Belfast to take photographs. In the gloom, a camera with a long lens can seem like a gun as it is pointed over a wall. The chances are that he was working for British Intelligence.

The soldiers were receiving a lesson from their platoon NCO in demythologizing the enemy.

'You ever seen a dead enemy before, lad? Well, you have now. Look at him. Shake his hand. Go on then, shake his hand!'

Even by the surreal standards of Belfast, this was unusual. It struck me that if I reported it, my editors were unlikely to believe me. After more of this, the soldiers discussed what they should do with the body. They finally put it in the truck parked in front of ours. This contained their urn of warm tea. They had a jokey conversation about the effect of the corpse on the quality of the tea.

Later, we were taken to an interrogation centre which I suspect was Castlereagh. I was interviewed with great courtesy and some humour by men dressed in civilian clothes. The humour even extended to the criminal offence with which I was charged and which carried, on conviction, an automatic prison sentence of the sort Bernadette Devlin was now serving. I was one of the few people not armed and ready to kill on the Falls Road that night. I was charged with impeding the army by being on the street against a military order to civilians.

I was given bail and set free next day just in time to join the rest of the press corps at a briefing for journalists. The Defence Ministry was to claim that British gunfire amounted to just fourteen rounds. The claim was challenged. Much later, the real figures were published. In all, the soldiers had fired 1,454 rounds. This included seventeen rounds of .303 from sniper rifles, ten rounds of 9mm from Sterling sub-machine-guns and 1,427 rounds of 7·62mm high velocity ammunition, the NATO standard for battlefield use, from self-loading rifles. In addition, 1,600 cartridges and canisters of CS gas were poured into the narrow streets, penetrating every crevice. As well as Ugilik, three Catholics were killed and sixty-eight injured by gunfire or grenade splinters, as were nineteen soldiers.

As Simon Winchester of the *Guardian* wrote later: 'Ever since those later figures were quietly published, many reporters found it terribly hard to accept contemporary accounts of a serious disturbance by the army public relations' men. Never, since then, have I found myself able to take the army's explanation about any single incident with any less a pinch of salt than I would take any other explanation.'

What had the army achieved? It had flattened the instant barricades erected as the original riot began two nights earlier. It had also uncovered a formidable armoury: 107 guns, 25lb of high explosive, one hand-grenade, 21,000 rounds of ammunition, eight respirators and eight radios. This collection, later displayed for press photographers at Springfield Road police barracks, gave the lie to the claim, a few months earlier, that the Official IRA had no access to weapons.

The army had also shown that if it were prepared to use its muscle it could impose its will, for a short time, upon a large area of a modern city, but at a terrible cost. As Winchester put it:

> No-one could escape the terror. Bullets whined around like furious bluebottles; the gas seeped everywhere. The shouts and screams of panic, especially from the children and the older women, were awful. Nothing seemed able to stop the nightmare, as on it went, screeching and crying and whining and belching its terror out into the fast-growing dusk.

The curfew remained in force throughout the weekend and was lifted only after thirty-four hours. While an angry, sullen civil population remained penned in their homes in sweltering weather, the army ran a triumphal convoy through the deserted streets, ostensibly as part of the process of briefing the media.

Military PR added an additional twist to this macabre event. It presented triumphantly, riding high on top of the leading vehicle, two Unionist ministers from the hardline Stormont government: Captains William Long and John Brooke. Local people had viewed the army's offensive as an invasion. The presence of Long and Brooke confirmed that they were now victims of alien occupation, not friendly protection. At Springfield Road barracks, as press cameras clicked and whirred over captured IRA arms, Captain Brooke squeezed the arm of a young RUC constable. I stood close as Brooke murmured: 'It's a grand day for us.'

My own position was serious. I was remanded several times over a period of months. Lawyers agreed that although 113 people had been charged with defying the curfew, mine would be the 'test case'. This focused attention on me and did not make the job of objective reporting easy. When, in September, we got to court, the magistrate ruled that I had no case to answer. However, other civilians were later convicted. The Belfast magistrate concluded that every soldier had a common-law duty to suppress riot 'by every means in his power', setting the scene for the use of lethal force eighteen months later on Bloody Sunday.

By Monday morning, official doctrine surrounding the weekend's events was already rewritten. In Parliament a ministerial statement insisted that there was no curfew as such, but a 'restriction on movement'. The same absurd claim was made in the courts.

The army's position was much more serious and longer lasting. As well as the deaths, injuries, intimidation and imprisonment of thousands of people in their own homes, the arms search had resulted in widespread damage to homes by soldiers. The worst damage, however, was to the tentative trust that Belfast Catholics had placed in the British army. The IRA knew that and turned its thugs loose on anyone fraternizing with the Tommies. Thanks to Heath's hardline approach, alienation had started. Over the next two years, it would tip the country into an armed conflict that would last for thirty years or more. In Oman, by contrast, a hearts-and-minds campaign spearheaded by the SAS, providing veterinary and medical aid, water wells and even firearms for former enemies, combined with a full-blooded use of military force against active insurgents from 1970 onwards, brought lasting peace to the country in six years.

In Ireland the opposite occurred. Fearing civil war after the Curfew, the Dublin government declared it knew 'very well that partition is basic to the whole problem. There can be no doubt whatsoever about our commitment to the reunification of our country and to the safety and well-being of all the Irish people.' The IRA created new facts to fit the propaganda, aided by British incomprehension of the forces against them. The Curfew was followed in 1970 by the Six-day riots in Belfast in July and August and in Derry between 2 and 5 August. The Orange marches were permitted to proceed. The army shot dead one rioter. By the end of the year, two IRA officers had been killed along with twenty other people.

The year 1971 was far worse, as the British army piled on the pressure in Belfast with more cordon-and-search operations. The Provisionals hit back with automatic fire in New Lodge Road, seriously wounding five soldiers with a single burst. The General Officer Commanding the Army, Major-General Anthony Farrar-Hockley – known as 'Farrar-the-Para' – made a television broadcast in which he declared that a contentious arms search was carried out in a Catholic area 'because we have good evidence that it harbours . . . IRA Provisionals' who had paraded their activities 'with some braggadocio'. They were correctly identified as Francis Card, Billy McKee, Leo Martin, Liam Hannaway and Kevin Hannaway. This was a second fatal error, for the army had been negotiating with the same men in an effort, ostensibly, to control the wilder elements of such places as Ballymurphy estate. The Pira leaders regarded the broadcast as proof of the army's bad faith.

Two nights later, on 6 February, terrorists shot dead Gunner Robert Curtis. He was the first British soldier to die on duty in Northern Ireland for almost half a century. The Ulster Unionist Prime Minister, James Chichester-Clark, announced on television: 'Northern Ireland is at war with the Irish Republican Army Provisionals.' In due course, to their cost, soldiers were to discover that they did not enjoy the usual legal immunity granted to acts committed on the battlefield which would elsewhere have been categorized as criminal. It was not real war but virtual war, soon to be controlled by virtual justice for everyone caught up in it.

Over the following weeks, armed demonstrations at IRA funerals for two Provisional volunteers killed by the army cranked up Unionist demands for an even harder line. Court cases arising from the riots in which outrageously partial judgments were handed down, favouring Protestant offenders, poisoned the atmosphere further.

Much worse followed in the coming month. On 10 March, three young Scottish soldiers of the Royal Highland Fusiliers, one aged seventeen, were 'walking out', off-duty, in civilian clothes and unarmed. In a Belfast pub they were picked up by some Republican women and lured to their deaths. Their bodies were recovered from desolate Squire's Hill, near Divis Mountain. Two of the men, including the seventeen-year-old, were brothers. Each was shot in the back of the head by three separate assassins, one of whom put a bullet into all three victims. It was an atrocity as cold-blooded as the execution of two British soldiers hanged in a eucalyptus grove in Palestine by the Zionist terror group, Irgun Zwei Leumi, in 1947. Squire's Hill was even more effective in polarizing events. The army now saw all Catholics as the enemy and the Catholics were propelled into the arms of the IRA. The murders also added pressure to Unionist demands for the internment of Catholic activists. A joint RUC–army 'internment working party' was set up within a few weeks. Internment itself – another political disaster – followed in August. During the intervening period, from March onwards, two bombs were detonated almost every day. During a twelve-hour period in July, twenty blasts destroyed pubs, shops and banks. Another four soldiers were murdered and almost thirty wounded. Four civilians, including one known Provisional, were shot dead by the army.

The statistics for 1971 still make grim reading. Security Forces recorded 6,948 violent incidents of all types during the year, including more than 1,000 bombs that caused fifty deaths. Security Forces were shot at 1,500 times. Police stations were attacked 261 times. The SF lost fifty-nine men killed in action and another 180 people met violent deaths. Arms searches recovered more than 700 firearms, 1,681 grenades and similar devices.

The year 1972 saw more bombings than ever: around four each day, which killed a total of 136 people. With other violence, the overall death toll was 478, of whom 146 were soldiers or policemen. Three dark events overshadow this sad catalogue. The first was internment, on 9 August 1971. The second was Bloody Sunday on 30 January 1972. The third was Bloody Friday on 21 July 1972.

Internment, bungled in its planning, brutal in its execution, had one lasting effect upon the British army: it was a catalyst for violence on a scale that led the Westminster government to acknowledge that this was now a military campaign for which military decorations should be awarded, even if the rules of war were not to apply in this new war zone. This acknowledgement was made only reluctantly. On 23 May 1971, three months before internment, the Prime Minister was asked if he would recommend the award of a special medal to troops deployed in Northern Ireland. Mr Heath replied: 'No, but individual awards are of course available for gallantry and especially meritorious service in Northern Ireland as elsewhere.'

At that stage, six soldiers had been killed. They were Gunner Curtis; Lance Bombardier John Laurie (shot on 8 February); Corporal Jolliffe, Royal Military Police; and the three Royal Highland Fusiliers – Joseph and John McCaig and Dougald McCaughey. In the four months after internment, thirty soldiers were killed as were eleven members of the RUC and UDR and seventy-three civilians.

On 21 October, three months after internment, Heath told the Commons: 'In recognition of the services of Her Majesty's Armed Forces in Northern Ireland, The Queen has approved proposals for the grant of the General Service Medal and clasp for specified service in the province.' A white paper fleshed out this reply. The first sentence was historically significant. It said: 'The Committee on the Grant of Honours, Decorations and Medals have had under consideration the need for the general recognition of service in Northern Ireland from 14th August 1969, inclusive, to *a future date to be decided in due course*, with special regard to the hardships and dangers which have accompanied duty there' [my italics]. In 1998, that situation remained unchanged. It was a testament to the strategy that evolved during the next twenty-six years or more, a 'low intensity' conflict of attrition, a component of which, according to an official document by one SAS officer, was 'an acceptable level of violence' or, as Home Secretary Reginald Maudling put it more publicly in December 1971, the fact that Britain might have to accept as normal a certain level of violence for the indefinite future.

4

A Very Public War,
1972–1974

In 1971, Unionist hardliners reasoned that internment had worked before in stopping the IRA in its tracks and it could do so again. The precedent they had in mind was 1956–58, when 187 Republicans were locked up without trial. The key difference between that successful outcome and the world as it existed in 1971–72 was that the Dublin government had also interned IRA leaders, denying them sanctuary and an operational base beyond the reach of the British. On 8 July 1957, the Irish Special Branch lifted just sixty key people. It was enough to break the back of the IRA as it then existed.

The 1972 exercise might have worked if the right people had been arrested again on both sides of the Irish border, preferably in a co-ordinated, simultaneous swoop. But in the 1970s there was no hope that Dublin would co-operate. Attacks on Catholic areas, perceived as the latest in a long series of pogroms within the Six Counties, and the failure to bring to book RUC officers probably guilty of murder meant that an attack by the Irish government on the IRA – by now self-appointed defenders of the Catholic ghettos – would have been political suicide. The need for joint action did not go unnoticed at Stormont. The long-standing advocate and architect of internment was Captain Brian Faulkner, who succeeded Chichester-Clark as Ulster Prime Minister on 23 March 1972. A week later, Faulkner took his case to the British Cabinet's Committee on Northern Ireland, known as GEN 42. It was an eerie occasion attended by the newly appointed GOC Northern Ireland, General Harry Tuzo, and Field Marshal Lord Carver for whom this was his first day as Chief of the General Staff. Carver later wrote:

One remark of Faulkner's stuck in my memory. When asked what had made it possible to bring IRA terrorist activity to an end on a previous occasion, he replied that the decisive factor had been that the Dublin Government had then also taken tough measures . . . including the use of internment. *This did not prevent him and some of our own senior ministers from suggesting action that would inevitably have aroused the anger of the Republic.* [my italics]

According to the Irish historian Tim Pat Coogan, Faulkner also wanted the army to send snatch squads into the Republic to kidnap known members of the IRA. This was wishful thinking. Carver would not have sanctioned it. In any case, the inaccuracy of the RUC list of suspects was such that the wrong people would probably have been lifted. Equally hawkish suggestions came from the Cabinet itself, which Carver had to deter. Years later, he confirmed that some senior ministers wanted him to operate an unlawful 'shoot-to-kill' policy. He said:

> It was being suggested that it was perfectly legal for the Army to shoot somebody whether or not they thought they were being shot at, because anybody who obstructed or got in the way of the armed forces of the Queen was, by that very act, the Queen's enemy and this was being put forward by a legal luminary in the Cabinet.

Who was that legal luminary? In a letter to me in 1996, Lord Carver said: 'The legal luminary in the Cabinet was the Lord Chancellor, Lord Hailsham.'

Faulkner, apparently reading from the same brief, told the Stormont Parliament on 25 May: 'Any soldier seeing any person with a weapon or acting suspiciously may, depending on the circumstances, fire to warn or with effect without waiting for orders.'

Carver believed that

> the army has always been trained to shoot to kill and not to fire either over the heads of a crowd or to shoot to wound. Both are likely to kill the wrong people. What one has to determine are the circumstances in which a soldier, acting

in aid of the civil power, is justified in using his firearm. If he does use it, he must aim carefully to kill a specific person. If the situation does not justify using a firearm, but soldiers are being used for riot control, they should be using other methods, such as incapacitating gases or plastic bullets.

On 7 July two Bogside rioters, Desmond Beattie and Seamus Cusack, were shot by soldiers who claimed the two were armed. No one else believed that. Beattie was killed outright and Cusack died of his wounds soon afterwards, in the Republic. The killings would have been in line with the Hailsham–Faulkner doctrine that anyone obstructing a soldier courted instant death. Non-Unionist moderates at Stormont, led by Gerry (later Lord) Fitt, walked out and formed their own 'alternative Parliament'. They were not to know then that powerful elements within the British government were advocating an illegal shoot-to-kill policy.

When the Stormont Cabinet met on 3 August to consider internment yet again, it agreed that, to be effective, it would have to happen in the Republic at the same time. But, said Faulkner, 'London will have to pursue that.' It was not only an unrealistic policy but a doomed one, rooted in the urge to do something, anything, as IRA bombs tore the fabric of Ulster's commercial life to shreds. The Heath government, meanwhile, was discovering that it would have to back Faulkner, however reluctantly, or impose direct rule and thereby commit itself to an Irish war of indeterminate duration.

On 5 August Faulkner again met the British Cabinet, which over-rode the objections of the Security Forces represented by General Tuzo. Between 23 July and 3 August there had been ninety riots and attacks on military posts with petrol-bombs and three or four high-explosive bombs daily. Car-bombs, mainly the work of the Provisionals, consumed around two tons of high explosive within three weeks. The next banana skin lying in the path of the Security Forces was the Apprentice Boys' March in Londonderry, a chronic source of trouble, on 12 August.

Carver wrote: 'While Faulkner represented the situation as deteriorating, I recommended to Ministers on 3 August that internment should only be introduced as a last resort and that we should "ride it out" in the face of threats from both sides ... My view was accepted ... On 5 August, Faulkner decided, in spite of Tuzo's advice, and almost certainly for political reasons, to ask for the "double act".' (The 'double act' was a shorthand phrase for a ban on the Apprentice Boys' March as an emollient to moderate nationalist opinion in parallel with the internment of militant Irish Nationalists.) At the Cabinet that day:

> Ministers finally gave way to Faulkner's demand. As a quid pro quo they tried to extract from him a permanent ban on all marches and the disbandment of rifle clubs. He agreed to a six-month ban, but evaded the rifle club issue ... In retrospect, I believe that my advice to ride out the Apprentice Boys' March without the 'double act' was sound. I have no doubt that internment would have been necessary later on in the year but the haste with which it was decided upon and implemented was undoubtedly largely responsible for the intense emotion it aroused and the criticism it received.

Physical implementation of internment, Operation Demetrius, and the interrogations which followed were now left, disastrously, to military technicians without supervision from senior officers or politicians. Most military interrogation is apolitical and tactical. That is, the job is designed to extract from the prisoner-of-war instant information about his formation: its location, its arms, its leaders and morale. It cannot be a subtle process, since time is of the essence. The Geneva Convention rule that obliges a POW to provide only his name, rank and number is the first obstruction to rapid access to information a battlefield commander needs. The methods used in Ireland in 1971 were fundamentally the same as those intended for use in a tactical military situation, refined by way of the Korean conflict through colonial wars in Malaya, Cyprus, Kenya, Aden and Borneo.

The refinement required for low-intensity conflict was that the prisoner's resistance had to be broken without his suffering any serious, visible physical harm. The answer was to disorient the captive by using a combination of sensory deprivation, exhaustion, humiliation (for example, exposing genitalia to ridicule) and fear (for example, placing a prisoner, handcuffed, in a helicopter and threatening to pitch him through the open door from a great height). Throughout the Cold War years most of these techniques were routinely inflicted on RAF aircrew, special forces soldiers, submariners and others likely to fall into the hands of the Soviet enemy during clandestine operations. The intention was to 'blood' these people and harden them psychologically to what might befall them.

The techniques, though horrific to civilians in a society unaccustomed to warfare, were less brutal than the use of electric shock employed by the French in Algeria (successfully, as it happens, in breaking a terrorist urban bombing campaign); assuredly less barbaric than the methods employed by IRA enforcement squads against their own people then and later. To illustrate the point: the French army arrested 24,000 people in Algiers in the first seven months of 1957, of whom – it was officially admitted – 3,024 died in custody. Though Irish internees in 1971 were traumatized and suffered long-term psychological damage, none died during internment.

No one seems to have explained to the professional British interrogators who went to work in Ireland that they were not running tactical, battlefield interrogation sessions; nor were they engaged, officially, in a colonial war or even an acknowledged counter-insurgency campaign. They were still relying on their powers at common law and, probably illegally, the Civil Authorities (Special Powers) Act (NI) 1933.

The interrogators were drawn from the Interrogation Wing of the Joint Service Intelligence School at Ashford, Kent, comprising men of the Intelligence Corps and RAF Intelligence under the command of the Director General of Intelligence in the Defence Ministry. Lord Carver, the most senior soldier, recalled: 'I was not aware of, and had not enquired into, the details of the methods to be employed.' He concluded that Heath (Prime Minister), Carrington (Defence Minister), Maudling (Home Secretary), Faulkner, General Tuzo and the RUC Chief Constable, Graham Shillington, had been misled, as he had been.

Preparations for the great round-up of IRA suspects – no Loyalists were arrested – went ahead in a feverish atmosphere as the operational deadline of 9 August approached. The RUC supplied its 'hit list' of 520 names, a vast number, many of whom were already on the move from one safe-house to another. I recall asking the Provisional IRA chieftain Leo Martin where he slept. He replied by holding up a key ring from which hung about thirty different door keys. In the event, the army arrested 326 suspects. Since the law required that each arrest be made in the presence of a police officer – an impossibility in these circumstances – many of the arrests were illegal acts in themselves.

At 4 a.m. on 9 August the round-up began. It bagged 342 suspects, ranging from a seventy-eight-year-old Republican sympathizer to young People's Democracy activists. Worse, it included many people who thought they had no personal involvement in the Troubles. They were about to be politicized by their experience. All were men. Civilian furniture vans were pressed into service to take them to three 'assembly centres'. The biggest number, 185, went to Girdwood barracks, Belfast. Others were held at Ballykinler camp, County Down and Magilligan camp at the eastern end of Lough Foyle. The main interrogation centre was at Ballykelly barracks, a former RAF base north-east of Londonderry. By mid-December the total arrested by the army under the Special Powers Act rose to 1,576, of whom 934 were released.

Many of these people were deprived of food, sanitation and sleep. A fair number were kicked and beaten by soldiers. A minority suffered treatment that was denounced by the European Court as 'degrading and inhuman'. In some cases it came perilously close to torture. Pat Shivers, aged thirty-seven, of Toomebridge, a man with no IRA connection, was awarded £15,000 damages against the government by the Belfast High Court when he proved he had been hooded, handcuffed, stripped and deprived of sleep for most of the eight days he was in custody. Paddy Joe McClean, a remedial school teacher from Bergagh, Tyrone, was arrested early on 11 August. He also had no IRA record. In a statement to the Association for Legal Justice, he said:

A hood was pulled over my head and I was handcuffed and subjected to verbal and personal abuse, which included the threat of being dropped from a helicopter which was in the air, being kicked and struck about the body with batons on the way. After what seemed about one hour in the helicopter I was thrown from it and kicked and batoned into what I took to be a lorry. The lorry was driven only a couple of hundred yards to a building. There I was given a thorough examination by a doctor. After this all my clothes were taken from me and I was given a boiler suit to wear which had no buttons and which was several sizes too big for me. During all this time the hood was still over my head and the handcuffs were removed only at the time of the 'medical examination.'

I was then taken into what I can only guess was another room and was made to stand with my feet wide apart and my hands pressed against a wall. During all this time I could hear a low droning noise, which sounded to me like an electric saw or something of that nature. This continued for . . . an indefinite period . . . My arms, legs, back and head began to ache. I perspired freely, the noise and the heat were terrible. My brain seemed ready to burst. What was going to happen to me? Was I alone? Are they coming to kill me? I wished to God they would, to end it. My circulation had stopped. I flexed my arms to start the blood moving. They struck me several times on the hands, ribs, kidneys and my knee-caps were kicked. My hood-covered head was banged against the wall.

McClean estimates that this went on for 'about two days and nights'. He collapsed regularly.

I came to in what I believed to be Crumlin Road gaol, having been pushed into a chair. The hood was removed and I was handed what I was told was a detention form. [He could not focus his eyes but believed his ordeal was over. Then the hood was put back again.] I was roughly jerked to my feet and half pulled, half kicked and beaten for about 400 yards . . . the worst sustained beating to date. Fists, boots and batons crashed into my numbed body . . . Hands in handcuffs behind my back . . . Pain! Someone pulling and jerking my arms. Thrown headlong into a vehicle – soft seats, beating continued, boots, batons, fists. Then the noise, that dreaded helicopter again. Dragged out of the vehicle by the hair, thrown onto the floor of the helicopter. Blacked out.

Conscious again. Hands manacled in front of me. Pushed against a wall, legs wide apart . . . Dug fingernails into wall. Pain all over me . . . My mind began to drift. I tried to sing to myself. I was going mad.

[Someone, probably a military doctor breaching his Hippocratic oath, checked his pulse and chest.]

Dragged along. Pushed into a chair, hood pulled off. Screaming, blinding light, questions fast and hard, couldn't speak. 'Spell your name.' Tried to find the letters . . . couldn't spell my name. I must be insane. More questions – blows, hair pulled. Still can't see well. A table – three men at it – all writing – blinding light.

I was told I would be given half an hour to rest and think. Then I would be asked more questions and if I didn't answer them I would be taken back to the 'music room' . . . Sleep, deep, black sleep. Pulled to my feet. Back to the questions again. Would not give answers. Back to 'music room'. Feet wide apart. Hands handcuffed against the wall. Droning noise fills my head. By this time I could feel no pain. Just numb. Dragged away from the wall, legs buckled under me, fell to the floor. Dragged by the ankles up and down shallow steps. Didn't care. Past feeling pain. Didn't have a body.

For some time thereafter, McClean was propelled through a nightmarish cycle of interrogation, 'music room' punishment and sleep. At last the beatings eased off and he was given water, bread, a blanket and a cold cell in which to sleep. The hood was removed. He was taken by lorry, helicopter and Land-Rover to Crumlin Road Prison, Belfast, and was subsequently released.

The violence outside Ballykelly interrogation centre was more spectacular and virulent than the violence within. Belfast erupted.

During the forty-eight hours after internment, seventeen people were killed in street fighting. On average the IRA killed a British soldier every second day in August. The IRA also took on the army in a series of major gun battles in which tens of thousands of rounds were fired on both sides. The IRA took heavy, often concealed casualties but – like other revolutionary manoeuvres, such as the Vietcong's Tet Offensive in 1968 – won the war of political credibility in so doing. Barricades went up around Bogside and were still there at the beginning of September.

There was another penalty. At that time and for long after, British Intelligence did not have good sources within the IRA from which reliable information could be drawn. Interrogation, properly run, did yield the answers. The political storm raised by internment resulted in official limitations on interrogation which gave the IRA a real military prize. The value of intelligent interrogation was revealed by one of the government inquiries into the internment scandal. A committee headed by Lord Parker asserted:

On the introduction of internment two operations of interrogation in depth took place involving the use of these techniques. In August 1971 twelve detainees and in October 1971 two detainees were interrogated in depth. As a result . . . the following information was obtained.

(1) Identification of a further seven hundred members of both IRA factions and their positions in the organisations;

(2) Over forty sheets giving details of the organisation and structure of IRA units and sub-units;

(3) Details of possible IRA operations; arms caches; safe houses; communications and supply routes, including those across the border; and locations of wanted persons;

(4) Details of morale, operational directives, propaganda techniques, relations with other organisations and future plans;

(5) The discovery of individual responsibility for about eighty-five incidents recorded on police files which had previously remained unexplained.

The rate at which arms, ammunition and explosives were recovered increased markedly after 9th August (largely on account of information obtained as a result of interrogation in depth):

	1 Jan. – 8 Aug.	9 Aug. – 31 Dec.
Machine Guns	1	25
Rifles	66	178
Pistols/Revolvers	86	158
Shotguns	40	52
Rockets	Nil	55
Ammunition rounds (in units of ten thousand)	4.1	11.5
Explosives (lbs)	1,194	2,541

The Provisional IRA's answer to such claims was to run a press conference in Belfast to demonstrate that their command structure was undamaged and that the wrong people had been lifted. They turned the knife further by making anonymous telephone calls to the Security Forces to misidentify people in the Catholic Ardoyne area as IRA activists. A flurry of arrests followed in which innocent people became victims and for which the British were blamed. The victims included a mentally retarded man and an ex-regular British army soldier who, ironically, had spent four years as a prisoner-of-war in Germany.

Such was the unmitigated disaster of internment that the days of the independent Protestant government at Stormont were numbered. The Labour government, just before it lost the election of June 1970 to Heath, had prepared a short legislative bill for just this purpose. Military contingency planning for direct rule from London included five options for taking over the Province. One of these, reflecting the experience of the Curragh Mutiny in 1914, raised the delicate question of how many British soldiers might be required to invade Northern Ireland to secure it from the Loyalists.

One more catastrophe was required to discredit the Faulkner hardline, even in the eyes of a hawkish Conservative government at Westminster. That was the event known as Bloody Sunday, 30 January 1972. During the months between internment and that day, the army was carried along by the momentum of information gathered through interrogation. During the last two months of 1971, the army believed it had killed or wounded seventy-seven terrorists. It recovered 884lb of explosive, 87,696 bullets, 1,100 detonators, 20 machine-guns, 126 rifles, 93 pistols and revolvers.

The impending tragedy was also masked by a Loyalist atrocity wrongly described for years by security experts as an IRA own-goal. At 9 p.m. on Saturday, 4 December 1971, a bomb exploded at McGurk's Bar in Belfast, killing fifteen Catholics, including some of the McGurk family, and injuring sixteen others. Six years later Robert James Campbell, a UVF terrorist, confessed that he had accompanied the bomber. He received sixteen life sentences.

In November 1971, it had been in Carver's mind – as he told the Cabinet Committee on Northern Ireland – that normal politics might be restored during a narrow window of opportunity in February or March the following year.

I said that if things went well, by February the IRA might be seen to be ineffective. There might then be a short period before the Protestants would begin to feel that the threat had been removed and that they need not therefore give anything away. If, however, by that time there had been little progress, the Prime Minister might feel that the only answer would be a major operation 'to finish it off once and for all', as he had suggested to me at Chequers on the eve of the visit of Mr Lynch, Prime Minister of the Republic, in June. I said that I did not believe that this was possible . . . without concurrent political action. Either of the situations that I had postulated could involve direct rule.

In mid-December, Carver visited the Province and was convinced that the 'window' was imminent. He suggested to Lord Carrington, the Defence Secretary, that 'we should aim to take the political initiative in mid-February'. The initiative would grasp the nettle which had been manifest since the army was forced to intervene in the crisis in August 1969; who was in charge of security policy?

Any proposal, Carver argued, would have to be acceptable to the RUC, to Faulkner personally 'though not necessarily to his party', to the Catholic hierarchy, Gerald Fitt, leader of the SDLP moderates, and to the Irish Prime Minister Lynch. Reform of public administration was also included in the Carver package, together with reform of the Stormont constitution. The Orange Order, whose baleful influence had opposed earlier reform attempts, was not likely to endorse that. The most prescient of Carver's ideas, however, concerned Londonderry. There, 'I suggested a lowering of provocative activity by security forces to a level which maintained the morale of the Protestants without provoking the Catholics to an extent which caused us severe casualties, further antagonised them and brought no dividends.'

Carver presented his package to a ministerial meeting early in January 1972. The package was set aside for further consideration. The ban on marches in the Province was renewed for six months. The barricades remained up around Bogside. Carver estimated that to break them down would require seven battalions, with four to hold the area afterwards.

By now, a dialogue of violence between Republicans and soldiers on the ground was developing its own momentum regardless of what politicians or generals might decree. During the days preceding Bloody Sunday, bombs went off inside the Parachute regiment's base at Hollywood barracks, Belfast. The army asserted that the IRA had launched eighty attacks in Londonderry during the preceding fortnight. A demonstration on a beach near Derry, to protest against the opening of yet another internment camp, began with good humour but was savagely broken up by the Paras when some marchers tried to penetrate a barbed-wire barricade stretched across the beach, into the sea. This protest, against Magilligan camp, occurred a week before Bloody Sunday and set the agenda for that terrible event. The agenda was this: peaceful marchers – though in breach of Faulkner's law – would be tolerated and contained by non-Para units but if marchers sought confrontation and riot, then this escalation would be handled by the Paras. Soldiers of the 1st Battalion the Parachute Regiment, arguably the most aggressive unit in the British army, were imported specially from Belfast on both Sundays.

The beach protest followed the agenda described above. Soldiers of the Green Jackets were waiting for the demonstrators that cold day with nothing more intimidating than urns of hot tea and buns. The marchers ignored them and took to the beach. At the wire, most marchers halted and sang protest songs. About fifty, including some women, had other ideas. They ran into the ebbing tide and went round the wire. As they did so, the Paras fired volleys of rubber bullets at them. The mêlée developed into a brawl in which the soldiers used batons, fists and more rubber bullets.

During the following days, as both sides considered how to handle NICRA's proposed march at Derry, a number of people including a local MP, Ivan Cooper, sought assurances from the IRA. Cooper, a civil rights champion, pacifist and Protestant, knew the local Pira commander well enough to believe the promise he was given, that the Provisionals would not be in the vicinity of the march. Similar promises were made by the Official IRA.

On the day, around 5,000 people joined the 'peaceful' march, in a carnival atmosphere, to walk from the Creggan estate overlooking Bogside to Bogside itself. Bogside had by now become Free Derry, flying its Irish tricolour, openly patrolled by armed IRA men who checked the identities of anyone driving into or out of the area, including British journalists. The area was effectively no longer part of the United Kingdom. Security Forces had been excluded for six months, but the route of the march was flanked by army barricades, to contain the trouble. The men manning those were Green Jackets. The Paras were held in reserve, ready to enter Bogside to snatch and arrest rioters if the trouble got out of hand. They had been warned that if they went in they might be ambushed by the IRA; a reasonable belief, for between 1 August 1971 and 9 February 1972 there had been 2,656 shots fired at soldiers in Derry, 456 nail and gelignite bombs thrown at them there and 225 bomb attacks on business premises in the city causing £6 million of damage. Although they were ostensibly a snatch squad aimed at arresting rioters, the Paras carried 7.62mm assault rifles – the standard NATO battlefield weapon – as well as riot-control devices.

The civil rights element of the march moved blandly past the potential flashpoint of William Street, the position from which the rioters had hurled stones at Orange Order marchers in August 1969 to start the Battle of Bogside.

The events that followed were observed with clinical care and noted as they occurred by Simon Winchester of the *Guardian*, among others. He wrote later: 'From behind the lorry [leading the march] about two hundred youths, the young boys and girls who appeared each evening at "Aggro Corner" to pelt some hapless infantry platoon, came slowly forward to the head of the column.'

The march leaders turned away from the barriers, abandoning the original plan to reach the old Guildhall and went right into William Street, leading the main part of the crowd to Free Derry Corner on the southern edge of Bogside, farthest away from the Paras' entry point. But, Winchester noted, 'the youths ahead of the lorry wanted confrontation: and accordingly this small sea of angry Derry youth surged forward, not to the meeting but, breaking away from the main march, towards the three army barricades.' A crowd of people who preferred confrontation to peaceful protest built up around the youths at the William Street barricade. 'A smooth-voiced Green Jacket officer explained that the march was illegal, and that soldiers would stop any further progress.' An elderly man tried to rock the wooden barricade out of position. What happened next was intriguing. 'One elderly man tried to rock the knife rest [the wooden barrier] out of position, but march stewards – *who were still among the hooligans* – [my italics] dragged him away.' It seems possible that the elderly man, though no danger to anyone but himself, was an unwanted interference in the choreographed violence that followed. Some of the mob moved round the corner to other barricades, 'relieving pressure in William Street sufficiently for the stone-throwers to begin to swing their right arms. So the stones and bottles began to fly; and within moments the riot guns came smartly up and with the deafening bangs echoing along the tiny lane, a dozen rubber bullets skittled into the mob.'

The youths who threw the stones were exempt, it seems, from arrest by march stewards, some of whom, almost certainly, were among those IRA members who, according to Lord Cameron, had acted as stewards from the inception of the civil rights movement. The youths had been instrumental many times before in Republican Belfast as well as Derry in making a dangerous situation into a lethal one. When they were injured they claimed civilian status, as if they were non-combatants, but Republicans (and, later, Tim Pat Coogan) knew them as 'Derry Fusiliers'. Their ambiguity was almost covered by a new international Red Cross doctrine for the rules of war, which decreed that a guerrilla was entitled to the same consideration if taken prisoner as any regular soldier, provided he donned a recognizable uniform just before he went into action. The only uniforms worn that day were those of British soldiers.

According to Mr Coogan, the fusiliers 'inevitably' began throwing stones as the demonstration was about to reach a peaceful end. The Green Jackets hit the mob with CS riot gas for twenty minutes. As Winchester put it: 'It was a classic and efficient method of riot control: the Green Jackets had proved themselves excellent and disciplined soldiers: a disturbance was being broken up with brutal efficiency.'

Shortly after, as he sheltered in the doorway of a taxi company a few dozen yards from the barricade on the same side as the demonstrators, 'a single crack of a rifle rang out. "They're shooting at us," a woman cried. "Make sure you put that down, and get it right, you English reporter."'

Winchester noted the shot and the time, 4.05 p.m., 'and I noted the direction of the shot – it came, it seemed, from behind me, from where, had they been on duty that day, the IRA could have expected to have positioned their snipers.'

Others heard this first shot and saw its effects. Well before the Paras stormed into Bogside, a single, high-velocity bullet aimed at an army wire-cutting party on a wall outside the area, apparently fired from Rossville Street flats dominating the centre of the Republican no-go area, struck a drainpipe on the Presbyterian church outside it. A Parachute regiment officer saw the impact of this bullet and was clear about that, twenty-six years later, in an interview with me. Lord Widgery's inquiry report noted:

Whilst some soldiers from the [Paras'] Mortar Platoon were cutting the wire a single high velocity round was fired from somewhere near the Rossville Flats and struck a rainwater pipe on the side of the Presbyterian church just above their heads. A large number of witnesses gave evidence about this incident, which clearly occurred and which proves that at that stage there was at least one sniper, equipped with a high velocity weapon, established somewhere in the vicinity of the Rossville Flats and prepared to open fire on the soldiers.

Winchester, writing a considered account after the tribunal, concluded:

Most of us agreed there had been one shot fired at around 4 p.m. It turned out to have been from an IRA gun, fired at an army wire-cutting party. It injured no-one; but it gave an indication that there were IRA guns in the Bogside that day, despite the assurances given to me earlier, and that they had been used prior to the Paras' coming over the wire.

Within a few minutes of the first shot, Winchester heard voices screaming, 'The soldiers, the soldiers!' A line of armoured personnel carriers, engines revving angrily, roared into the no-go zone accompanied by two 3-ton lorries. Parachute regiment soldiers, easily identified by their round jump helmets and para wings on the right sleeve, jumped out and took up firing positions. Then the firing started: as many as a dozen high-velocity cracks from the assault rifles. People began falling, screaming, cursing, praying and dying. Winchester, his mind still coolly recording what was happening, took shelter in Rossville Flats stairwell.

From here I could discern both the hard rifle fire of the Army self-loading rifles and what I thought might have been the sharper cracks of .22s and the low steady thudding of a sub-machine gun. But there was a helicopter chugging

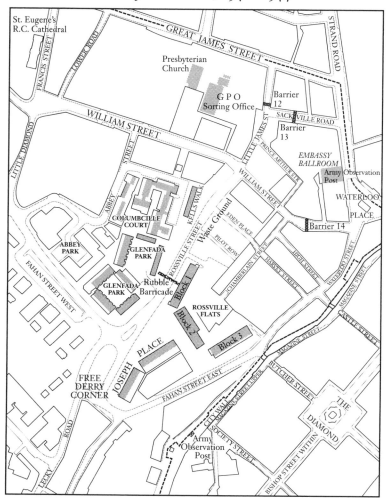

Bogside 1972

overhead as well and gas guns were still discharging in the background, and men and women screamed and glass crashed and voices were raised in hysterical panic, so it was difficult to be very sure. But gunfire was raging

59

out in the open and people, it seemed clear, were being hurt.

It was not only the British soldiers who were shooting. The eye-witness testimony to Widgery of two priests (Fathers Edward Daly and T. O'Gara) and journalists C. J. Donnelly (*Irish Times*), David Capper and P. E. C. Beggin (BBC), David Phillips, Gerry Seymour, P. F. Wilkinson and R. E. Hammond (ITN), W. J. Mailey (freelance), Nigel Wade (*Daily Telegraph*) and Simon Winchester confirms the soldiers' claims that once they entered the Republican area to arrest rioters, they came under fire from revolvers and machine-guns (not used by the army that day) from several positions including the ten-storey Rossville Flats. Other independent witnesses included a Londoner on holiday in the area, a Mr L. Bedell. He told Widgery that he

> saw the [Paras'] armoured vehicles arrive in Rossville Street and heard firing. Some minutes later he saw several cars drive down from the Creggan. About two dozen men armed with rifles and automatic weapons got out, dispersed amongst the flats on the north side of Westland Street and fired about fifty rounds at the soldiers. When the gunmen withdrew, Mr Bedell saw a crowd of about fifty civilians surround and give cover to one of the gunmen who had been separated from the main body, so that he was able to rejoin the others in safety. Mr N. Kunioka, a Japanese student at the London Film School, saw a man armed with a rifle in Westland Street [a position well to the south of the killing zone].

Twenty-five years later, a television documentary team working for Channel 4's *Secret History* series interviewed 150 eye-witnesses of these events. It found that 'both Provisional and Official IRA gave an assurance [of non-participation] but our research has revealed the presence of up to three gunmen in the Bogside when the Paratroopers came in. We believe they were all Official IRA men, mavericks present in the Bogside against orders. Two were present at Rossville flats. The soldiers say there were four more.'

The weapons described by army witnesses to Widgery included sub-machine-guns, a machine-gun, a rifle and pistols.

The *Secret History* programme turned up a still-photograph of a man in civilian clothes, carrying a half-concealed hand-gun, stalking soldiers near Chamberlain Street. Edward Daly, retired Bishop of Derry and a curate in Bogside at the time, told a television interviewer: 'The fellow came out of Chamberlain Street . . . in his twenties. He had a firearm, a short firearm and he came along to the edge of the wall and fired one or two shots. We screamed at him to go away because we were afraid the Paras would have thought we were firing from where we were.'

No responsible observer, including Roman Catholic clergy, dissents from the proposition that the IRA was present, armed, and opened fire on Bloody Sunday. The moral argument focuses upon who fired first. For example, the day after Bloody Sunday, Catholic priests, while accusing the Paras of 'wilful murder', declared in a prepared statement: 'It is untrue that shots were fired at the troops in Rossville Street *before* they attacked' (my emphasis). This statement overlooks the sniper round that hit the Presbyterian church some yards to the north of William Street, a shot aimed at Paras cutting through a wire on a wall, as a preliminary to their move into Bogside. Father (later Mr) Denis Bradley, a local priest, recalled: 'I was called over to a place in Glenfada park where somebody said there was a gunman in there. And three Provos arrived to take him out. He was obviously a "Stickie" [i.e., a member of the Official IRA] and they told him, "You don't shoot in situations like this."'

What is certain is that the Paras shot at least twenty-six people, killing fourteen of them. There is no convincing evidence that any of the victims was armed at the time. Though local priests, in their statement next day, accused the soldiers of firing indiscriminately into a fleeing crowd, there is evidence that most of the lethal shots were, in fact, aimed expertly and deliberately, if very fast. The technique is known as snap-shooting. The reason why the Paras deliberately shot down unarmed people is at the heart of the moral repugnance felt by most civilian observers who regarded the demonstrators as non-combatants. The Paras, however, saw their targets as combatants. Faced by an armed enemy, screened by a crowd of stone-throwers and others, their training encourages instant life-or-death decisions. As one of them told the *Secret History* team:

> The blokes would be hyped up. They expect a gunman to come. Suddenly four blokes dash out. Bang-bang-bang! You are talking about a split second. He could have thought, 'Oh, maybe this one had his hand in his pocket and his arm down somewhere. Maybe he is going to bring a pistol or a rifle up.' Bang-bang! You don't know. The fellow could be that hyped up with his adrenaline and he has fired first. Maybe it is just the way he [his targets] runs.

That day the Paras' targets were men, usually young men on the move, in what they now regarded as a military battle zone. Anyone whose conduct made him conspicuous was a target once the Paras came under fire.

One of those who took part in the Bloody Sunday operation – a cool, expert freefall parachutist when not at war – admitted in an interview with me that he was sufficiently nervous to sense hairs rising on the back of his neck as he raced across the open ground in front of the Rossville Street flats. 'There was a lot of shooting,' he said, 'but I had no idea where the shots were coming from. My only aim was to get to the far side of the open ground and get under cover.'

He revealed that some of the men with his group that day were not even regular soldiers but part-time Territorials who misidentified General Ford as 'a lieutenant in the Physical Training Corps' on account of the general's rank insignia, embodying a crossed sword. The weekend soldiers attached to 1 Para that day, he said, were noticeably more aroused by the prospect of killing an enemy than the regulars around them.

The IRA, whether they opened fire first or not, were guilty of using their own unarmed civilians as a screen from behind which they tried to shoot soldiers. They would not be the first terrorist group to use such a screen; nor would this be the first time that the IRA had opted for the calculated martyrdom of some of their own if it furthered the greater cause of Irish unity.

The public and political evaluation of Bloody Sunday is that it was a massacre of innocents and a disgrace to a professional army. With the wisdom of hindsight it would assuredly have been wiser to hold the Paras as the first shot was fired so as to identify the sniper position more exactly. Then what? In wartime, missiles, machine-guns, even artillery are used to destroy a sniper. On a civilian battleground, the real victory is in the minds of people afterwards. Front-line soldiers, trained for a sacrificial role behind enemy lines, dedicated to taking as many as possible of the enemy with them before they die, are not the best choice for urban warfare against terrorists dressed as civilians, a war fought in a jungle of moral subtleties. Some Paras thought they had had quite a good day. One of their number later told me that he regretted the deaths of thirteen civilians. 'We probably got as many others who were Pira,' he claimed.

What happened to the bodies? I asked.

'They were smuggled away, across the border,' he replied.

This notion was not universally shared by the men of 1 Para, some of whom dismissed it, years later, as regimental mythology, though one non-Para officer, with access to the slender Bloody Sunday file still held at the army's Northern Ireland headquarters, reports a 'mismatch' between the number of hits claimed by the Paras that day and the number of casualties publicly identified. The 'missing corpses' myth was pervasive because it was not entirely implausible; a number of Catholic civilians have disappeared in similar circumstances. A few months before Bloody Sunday, a Bog-side resident named Seamus Cusack was shot in the leg by soldiers during a riot. As the *Sunday Times* Insight recounted:

> The man fell and was immediately borne away by the crowd
> . . . He was put in a car and driven across the border to
> Letterkenny Hospital, where he died from loss of blood . . .
> As the Army see it, Cusack's fatal removal across the border
> is proof that he was an IRA gunman . . . But Bogside people
> injured in riots regularly cross the border for treatment
> because they fear that Ulster hospitals might give their
> names to the security officers. It was, in other words, a kind
> of routine to take Cusack to Letterkenny.

I was soon to discover for myself (on Bloody Friday) the simple routine for concealing identities in a nationalist hospital in Belfast.

On Bloody Sunday, the Paras were right to regard most of the peaceful demonstrators, that day, as the enemy. By that time, the whole Bogside community was in a state of revolt. Only a tiny minority, however, were culpable. Most of the casualties, I believe, were victims of a provocation to which the Paras, with their customary aggression, over-reacted. The political beneficiaries of the moral outrage that resulted were the I RA.

In the years that followed Bloody Sunday, Irish researchers, historians and polemicists sifted the evidence in obsessive detail, piling on political pressure during the delicate negotiations of the 'peace process' so that, in 1998, the British government promised to hold a new inquiry. In particular, the researches of Don Mullan (one of the demonstrators at Bogside that day), the solicitors Madden & Finucane and Jane Winter, Director of British Irish Rights Watch, focused on the role not only of the Paras but of other soldiers manning positions on the medieval wall and adjoining buildings overlooking Bogside that day. Widgery had little to say about those soldiers. Havine examined the Paras' use of ammunition (each bullet had to be accounted for), the Lord Chief Justice added: 'About twenty more rounds were fired by the Army in Londonderry that afternoon, but not by 1 Para and not in the area with which the Tribunal was primarily concerned.' Mullan suggested that the additional twenty rounds, or some of them, were fired by army snipers from an observation post or derelict building nearby, overlooking Bogside from the south; that is, facing towards the Paras as they entered the neighbourhood from the north. A single military OP is identified on the sketch plan accompanying the Widgery report – the only reference to army action in Derry that day outside the immediate killing ground. The OP was on the medieval city wall approximately 220 yards distant, a comfortable range for a good shot equipped with a .303 sniper rifle and telescopic sight. Mullan's research quotes a witness statement by a soldier not quoted in the Widgery report, identified by his last three regimental numbers (156), admitting that he was at yet another position on the wall, 'at the Double Bastions, by Roaring Meg' (a gun). This position does not even figure on the Widgery plan. In practice, it lined up on exactly 360 degrees, south–north, with the Presbyterian church where the Paras recorded the first incoming high-velocity round 400 yards away. The soldier identified as 156 said his position came under fire. 'An army sniper who was situated on my left about 15 yards away in the attic of a derelict house outside the City Walls returned three shots but I did not see where his shots had gone and there was no return fire.'

In these circumstances, with elements of the Security Forces firing from opposite ends of the contested area, the risk of a battle accident, or 'blue-on-blue' shooting, was considerable. The possibility also arose that not all those killed at Bloody Sunday were actually killed by the Paras. However, after almost thirty years, the hope of establishing the truth of this tragedy, once and for all, is drastically reduced. Several of the Para witnesses to Widgery, for example, are now dead: one killed by the IRA; two in battle in the Falklands; three from other causes. Those who survive have retained only a blurred recollection of Bloody Sunday.

Any new inquiry will be obliged to examine many hitherto neglected civilian witness statements and test the value of the army's testimony, in so far as that is still possible. One former Para allegedly claimed that his true statement was replaced by a fictionalized version. Another asserted that at a briefing the night before the operation, an officer exhorted the Paras: 'Let's teach these buggers a lesson. We want some kills.' This witness added: 'To the mentality of the blokes to whom he was speaking, this was tantamount to an order.'

Had Bloody Sunday occurred after 1976, instead of in 1972, then the killing ground might have been treated as a scene-of-crime from which (the IRA permitting) spent bullets would have been recovered from walls as well as bodies, to provide concrete ballistic evidence pointing to the source of shots now alleged to have been fired into some of the victims from the city wall. But the culture of 1972, under the gung-ho premiership of Edward Heath, was different. This difference is laid bare by a minute drafted by Mr G. L. Angel, a senior civil servant, on 1 February 1972 (HO 129/50 in the Public Record Office) and unearthed by Don Mullan.

The minute records a meeting beginning at 7.20 p.m. (Mr Angel was a meticulous man) on 31 January 1972 between Lord Widgery and the Prime Minister, just as Widgery prepared to take up the burden of the Bloody Sunday inquiry. This reveals: 'The Prime Minister ... said ... it had to be remembered that we were in Northern Ireland fighting not only a military war but a propaganda war.' This did no more than confirm the status of the conflict expressed three months earlier through the decision to award the General Service Medal and Northern Ireland clasp to servicemen who survived three months in the Province. The soldiers' legal position, however, was not that of the battlefield, as many would discover to their cost.

The most likely outcome of the new inquiry into Bloody Sunday promised by London in February 1998 was prolonged controversy and the reopening of old griefs. The coroner concerned, Major Hubert O'Neill, had delivered his verdict long since: 'I would say without hesitation that it was sheer, unadulterated murder. It was murder.'

The unanswered question is, 'By whose hand?' The soldiers on the street? Their political masters in London? The IRA? Their patrons in Dublin?

During the fifty-four days remaining before Edward Heath imposed direct rule on the Province, obliging the Stormont Parliament to conduct its own burial rites, Protestant paramilitaries, from being a joke on the British army's landscape, were revealed as an army capable of fighting a civil war. Thousands of Ulster Defence Association men were able to parade in uniform, as they had done in earlier times, and to give friendly journalists a teasing glimpse of the weapons they had stockpiled: modern new rifles, ready for battle. The Official IRA increased the risk of a sectarian war by firing six bullets into John Taylor, Stormont's Minister for Home Affairs. He survived. The Provisionals, led in Belfast by a bullying ex-bookmaker named Seamus Twomey, exploded a car-bomb at Donegall Street in the city centre, randomly killing six civilians and causing horrific injuries to another 150. One, a young woman, lost both legs. Press cameras clicked as a Para held her in his arms.

I had met Twomey shortly before, at a terraced house in Andersonstown. As I entered the front parlour, his armed bodyguards sat watching the Saturday racing on television, their bulk threatening damage to the worn sofa.

'What yah got?' one joked. Racing tips were not normally my affair but it happened that I had been given one as I left the Grand Central Hotel. The source was a porter whose omniscience I had come to respect. So I repeated his advice: 'Black Dog [or some such name]. Three-thirty. Doncaster. Sure-shot outsider at twenty-to-one.'

The encounter with Twomey, in the back kitchen, was less frivolous. I had got wind of an incident in which Twomey had come near to being blown up by one of his own teams due to a small misunderstanding about where and when the bomb would be laid. I wanted to test his reaction. Given the volatility of the man, himself an explosive substance, this was unwise but educational. We discussed the matter for some time. At last Twomey's temper snapped. He stood and closed his hand. The veins stood out on his forehead. His fist smashed the table for emphasis as he hissed at me: 'I don't give a damn what you put into your British newspaper, Geraghty. Our people will believe what we tell them.' The only witness to this conversation, a Dublin writer known for his Republican sympathies, buried his face in his hands. I concluded it was time to leave, closed my notebook and said: 'Thank you, Mr Twomey. I will go now.' He paused, licked his lips and seemed about to say something. It was a fine Saturday, but if I were to be shot down on the street, no one at Benbradagh Gardens would admit to having seen or heard anything. I moved as casually as I could from the kitchen, Twomey's eyes on me, into the front room, nodded to the heavies and let myself out on to the street. As I did so, one of them called, 'Hey, Mister, fucking good horse, that!'

Two days after the horror of Donegall Street, the Ulster premier, Brian Faulkner, and his deputy Sir John Andrews flew to London to be informed with brutal directness by Edward Heath that, from now on, the Province would be governed from London. All security, including control of the Royal Ulster Constabulary, would be controlled from London, with William Whitelaw as the first Secretary of State for Northern Ireland. This was the first tangible political prize won by the IRA's carefully crafted campaign of murder and agitprop. It was a reform far beyond anything contemplated by the Unionists, who were instantly alienated. Yet for the Republicans it was also a poisoned chalice. For how, having run a campaign directed towards equal rights for Catholics in Northern Ireland, could the Irish now change the question? The IRA's assets were still the physical control of the nationalist ghettos; the legitimate fear among Catholics of sectarian murders at the hands of Protestant death squads; and the knowledge that what were no-go areas for the security forces were a sort of sanctuary for Catholics.

Another emollient, useful for the IRA's credibility, was the steady release of internees from the Long Kesh prison camp. By mid-June, more than 500 were back in circulation. Another 370 were still held. Many of those set free instantly joined or rejoined the terrorists.

On 21 May, two months after direct rule had been imposed, the Official IRA blundered again with an assassination. This time the victim died. Politically he was a bad choice and the impact of his death rebounded. The youth who was killed was William Best, a local Derry Catholic, serving with the Royal Irish Rangers, a unit – like the Irish Guards – not deployed in Ireland. He was home on leave from Germany when the Officials shot him. Such was the stink that the Officials agreed to declare a truce, beginning on 21 May. At the time, as nationalists adjusted to the remarkable fact of life without Stormont, the appetite for peace grew. Moral pressure was now on the Provisionals to follow the example of their rivals. Simultaneously, secret contacts were being built between Whitelaw and the Provisional leadership. On 22 June the Dublin headquarters of Pira announced an indefinite, unconditional ceasefire. It was to last a mere thirteen days, but for many seasoned observers as well as locals of both communities, it seemed like the end of the war. With chilling efficiency the Provisionals shot dead another soldier less than two minutes before the ceasefire took effect at midnight on 26 June. This was Staff-Sergeant Banks, Royal Engineers, killed by a sniper at Ballymacarrett, Belfast.

On 7 July Whitelaw, stretching Protestant tolerance almost to breaking point, tried negotiating with Pira leaders who were guaranteed safe passage to and from London. In a subsequent television documentary Whitelaw said he found in the Provisionals 'no sign that they contemplated politics as they really were'. The terms laid down by Pira in the preceding September explicitly moved the agenda away from the civil rights demands. Pira wanted:

1. An end to the British army's campaign of violence against the Irish people.

2. Abolition of Stormont.

3. Free elections for regional Ulster parliament as the first step towards a new government of a united Ireland.

4. Release of all political prisoners, whether tried or not.

5. Compensation for all who had suffered as a result of British violence.

To this was added the demand that the army be withdrawn to barracks before going back to the British mainland. By July 1972, Stormont had gone and unconvicted prisoners were being released. Whitelaw had abolished the death penalty for murder, which was still in effect in the Province until he took over. He gave a personal promise to guarantee the civil rights of Catholics in Northern Ireland. His powers as Secretary of State, almost those of a monarch ruling the Province, were an assurance that the promise could be fulfilled. But there was no way that Whitelaw could have acceded to the total surrender demanded by the IRA, including British withdrawal by 1 January 1975 and the handover of Northern Ireland to a new form of government for the whole of Ireland. Dublin, for its part, did not relish the prospect of having to deal with a million desperate and armed Protestants, though the IRA delegates seemed to think they could handle that problem if they had to. The gulf between the two sides was redefined but not bridged. The IRA delegation – including Gerry Adams, Martin McGuinness, Seamus Twomey and the English-born Chief of Staff Sean McStiofain – then went home to resume the war.

The mechanical means by which this was engineered lacked finesse. Both communities in Ulster were now victims of ethnic cleansing: the use of force to frighten people out of their homes in mixed areas. Lenadoon Avenue, on the western edge of Republican Andersonstown, a breezy area of modern houses, was one of those. During the summer of 1972 Protestant families had been forced out by IRA threats; others remained, nervous about the future. As the London talks were taking place, the Central Citizens' Defence Committee – ostensibly not part of the IRA structure – decided to move sixteen Catholic families into the empty Protestant houses. The Ulster Defence Association threatened retaliation if that happened. The Provisionals decided to enforce the CCDC decision. Two days later, on Sunday 9 July, 1,000 Catholics marched in front of a furniture van to begin the takeover. British troops set up knife-rest barriers across their path. Hand-to-hand fights began between the two.

Twomey appeared to declare that the British had 'violated' the IRA's indefinite and unconditional ceasefire, now downgraded to a mere 'truce'. Whistles were blown and, soon afterwards, the IRA was firing at the soldiers with rifles and automatic weapons. For the Republicans, it was back to business as usual. For everyone else, it was time to look into the abyss and contemplate the real risk of a sectarian civil war. That night, as the price of Pira's policy of calculated martyrdom, 500 families were burned out of their homes. Within a week, 7,000 Catholic refugees had fled to the Republic. By 1975, the total number of such victims, on one estimate, had reached 60,000. It was an awesome testament to the power of fundamentalism in a modern European country.

The IRA's response was a blitzkrieg against civilians in central Belfast regardless of their affinities. The event which anticipated the worst horrors of Beirut became known as Bloody Friday. It has never been commemorated by the Irish with the same dedication they bring to Bloody Sunday. Bloody Friday – 21 July – began for me in a hospital bed. I had been scheduled to travel to India. An inoculation for the trip, pumped into my arm by an over-enthusiastic nurse, had worked too well. I was now trying to function in Belfast while suffering from some sort of tropical fever. I decided to check into the IRA's favourite hospital, the Mater, for a night. This proved entertaining. Some casualties, presumably IRA men, were brought into intensive care. RUC Special Branch men sat stolidly on a bench outside the ward, waiting to question them. In the early hours, a young student nurse brought the SB men coffee. She walked slowly, as if at a funeral, intoning: 'They're only human, after all . . .'

The hospital was next door to Crumlin Road prison. Next morning, slates started to rise from the prison roof. A hand reached up through the new hole, then the owner of the hand. One by one, prisoners clustered on the roof. A crowd gathered in the road below. They called up: 'Is yiz Fenian or Loyalist?'

The prisoners answered: 'Wiz DOCs [Decent Ordinary Criminals] and wiz want the same treatment as the politicals.'

'No! Yiz Fenians, yiz flickin Fenians!' the mob shouted.

The dialogue ended when someone in the crowd aimed a rifle at the prisoners and opened fire. Soon after that, the first bomb exploded, from somewhere to the left, down the hill as I gazed out of the ward window. Then there came another. And another. Soon a stormcloud of debris was drifting up. Ambulances went past, their sirens adding to the noise. Gillian Linscott, a close friend, reporting for another newspaper, walked purposefully towards the bombs, the ground shaking beneath her, as shocked survivors streamed past her away from the danger. It was time for me to check out of hospital and return to work. I felt embarrassed about doing that. The nursing staff had been kind.

'Sure and that's no trouble at all, Mr McGeraghty,' said the staff nurse, instinctively restoring the missing Gaelic prefix to my name, a prefix expunged by an English law a century or so earlier. 'And what name would you want to sign out under?'

In all, the IRA detonated twenty-one bombs that afternoon within one mile of the city centre, killing nine people and wounding 130. Some casualties were the victims of more than one bomb. Bodies were scraped with shovels off roads and walls, to be poured into plastic rubbish sacks. The millions who saw this on television that night were horrified, but not the IRA. A day or two later, in the Catholic Short Strand area, across the river Lagan, I asked one of the terrorists how long they intended to sustain the bombing. He gave me a lopsided grin and said: 'Till we've flattened everything from here to Peter's Hill.' Peter's Hill was a Catholic outpost at the end of the Protestant Shankill Road and a long way off. His was an agenda written in blood, with death as the only item on it. This was the moment when my sympathy for the nationalist cause in the Province – explicit enough to have earned a few beatings, one by the RUC at Stormont, as well as a reputation among Conservative ministers as 'that IRA reporter' – underwent a radical rethink.

In its publicity value to the Security Forces, Bloody Friday overlay Bloody Sunday sufficiently to make it politically possible for the army to gather its strength at last to destroy the IRA's no-go haven of Free Derry in Operation Motorman, and other operations in Belfast. After the imposition of direct rule, while the London government attempted to talk to the IRA, the army had been ordered to 'respect' the no-go areas. An academic analysis of that policy in 1997 concluded: 'Militarily, this "pause" was regarded as a disaster by the British Army. They believed that behind the barricades the Provisionals were recruiting and regrouping. This proved to be the case.'

The game was up with Operation Motorman when the army committed more British combat units (a total of thirty-eight battalions) to a single operation than it had since 1945, more even than during the invasion of Suez in 1956. At the Ministry of Defence in London, military press officers were concerned that the temporary use of armoured bulldozers, sent by sea from England to remove the barricades, might attract adverse publicity. As press officers usually do, they sought a semantic escape from the difficulty. As one of them revealed:

> A great deal of thought at the highest level went into the Q & A brief for journalists. There was a special brief covering the presence of the Armoured Vehicle Royal Engineers [bulldozer] in Ulster if detected. We feared such headlines as, *Tanks Used to Quell Londonderry*. I was instructed to take the brief to 10 Downing Street. My initial draft had referred to AVREs as 'vehicles', a word less emotive than 'tank'. Some hours later the brief was returned to me with the word 'vehicle' amended to 'tank'. The amendment was initialled, 'EH': that was, the Prime Minister Edward Heath.

Motorman virtually ended the urban guerrilla warfare, played out as public theatre since early 1970, though in rural areas such as South Armagh and East Tyrone traditional military 'contacts' between the opposing armies continued much as they had done for the preceding three centuries. By then, centuries of bitterness and conflict had been resurrected; opportunities for peaceful settlement missed; strategic errors made. Thoughtful and perceptive Irish observers, such as Martin Dillon and Tim Pat Coogan, blame the British and their Unionist allies: the Labour government of Harold Wilson, with its cowardice in failing to grasp the nettle of Unionist repression in 1968–69; and the Heath government's aggressive use of muscle even when top soldiers, including Lord Carver, protested against using the army as a blunt instrument. As Tim Pat Coogan told Dillon: 'The one power that neither the Dublin government nor the IRA nor anybody in Ireland had was the power of initiative. That power lay in London. So obviously, that is where the blame lies.'

That is not entirely true. The revolutionaries had the power to destabilize any emerging non-violent solution by recourse to a use of violence sanctified in nationalist mythology by the phrase 'the physical force tradition', and thereby to command the tribal loyalty of most Catholics in the North. The revolutionaries used their initiative with terrible effect. As Bernadette Devlin put it in her autobiography, *The Price of My Soul*: 'For half a century the Unionist Party Government has misgoverned us, but it is on the way out. Now we are witnessing its dying convulsions. And with traditional Irish mercy, when we've got it down we will kick it into the ground.'

5

Mutation,
1975–1998

The British army's massive occupation of Free Derry in Operation Motorman marked the end of the first phase of the renewed Irish War, one in which antique methods of repressive counter-insurgency failed when faced with a sophisticated combination of modern terrorism and effective propaganda. After about 1975 the conflict mutated into a form of warfare that would defy previous analysis. The elements included the familiar toxins of terrorism and guerrilla warfare, fine-tuned to political demands and propaganda, but still finally distorted to fit the traditional Republican agenda of physical force. What changed was counter-insurgency and the IRA's response. Military thinkers in the British Intelligence community studied the most successful of Britain's post-war campaigns – the war against the communist insurgency in Malaya. They noted that the key element of that was population control, the compulsory resettlement of a million people in heavily policed 'new villages'. Meanwhile, in the jungle and out of sight of journalists and the public, soldiers were licensed to kill on sight.

The new Irish strategy, slow and painful in its evolution, finally combined painstaking, forensic police investigation – treating each act of paramilitary violence as a scene-of-crime – with massive surveillance of suspects as a substitute for enforced resettlement. The 'new village' in Ulster was an invisible cage of electronic and human surveillance thrown around selected homes and neighbour-hoods, Orwellian in its implications for a liberal society. But this was Ireland, where ghettos that were still no-go areas to the RUC were subject to IRA policing from within, rather than the rule of

74

law from without. Special Forces led by the SAS would arrest or kill Republican terrorists caught in the act. At that point, policing crossed over into military action, confirming the hybrid nature of the conflict that now existed.

The philosophy underpinning the new strategy was to play it long, so long that attrition would wear down the opposition over decades if necessary. Not every soldier thought gradualism was a good idea. One was an SAS general involved in the early stages of the Gibraltar operation (Operation Flavius), who described the triple killings on the Rock as 'the Gibraltar cull'. Another was a senior officer quoted by *Time* magazine as follows: 'A majority of officers are now strongly backing a shoot-to-kill policy as the principal method of defeating the IRA. Otherwise we shall be marching toward an eternity of duty in Northern Ireland.'

Such views echoed the hawkish Hailsham sixteen years earlier but they did not prevail. The Security Forces, having stolen the marathon hunger-striker Terence MacSwiney's doctrine of victory to those who endure longest, also accepted that a long war had its price. This was 'an acceptable level of violence'. The arrangement – which might be characterized as refined counter-insurgency – suited professional warriors on both sides. For many Pira veterans, there was a good living to be had from a variety of rackets, from video piracy to protection money, as well as godlike power in their communities.

The RUC, now in the front-line and rearmed, enjoyed greater status and pay benefits than ever before as the overtime piled up with each new crisis. The British army, with a live enemy to fight, built up a uniquely valuable asset: it became the world's most expert counter-terrorist force. It created a whole menagerie of undercover squads, none of them part of the permanent British military order of battle, camouflaged under constantly changing initials such as MRF and FRU. As one Intelligence officer put it, 'What else would you do with 15,000 Toms?'

Largely by chance, the army had struck military paydirt. With the unexpected end of the Cold War in 1990, the New World Order strategy, directed from Washington, required exactly the combination of applied Military Intelligence, police work and unobtrusive firepower, all tailored for consumption by an informed democracy, that the British could now supply. The Gulf War reminded Western politicians that armed conflict was expected to yield big political gains for minimal loss of life. Too many deaths, even among the enemy retreating up the road to Basra, lost votes back home in the new climate. The new strategy aimed to score maximum political points for the lowest possible body count; military glory at no cost. As Saddam Hussein had reminded the US Ambassador to Baghdad just before he invaded Kuwait: 'Yours is not a society that can accept 10,000 dead in one battle.'

The new strategy, initially copied from Israel by the FBI, was to target and shadow individual terrorist leaders and bring them to justice. It rested not just upon the Israeli's Old Testament approach to retribution, but also on a very American notion – that the enemy can be personified by a single, identifiable strong man, to be demonized or deified, bought or butchered. Examples included the Ayatollah Khomeini of Iran and the Somali warlord Aideed. When the first Bosnian war criminals had to be arrested by a military abduction team in 1997, it was British Special Forces – surveillance experts of 'The Dets' and an SAS snatch squad – that did the job. As one of them said later: 'This is what we do all the time in Ireland.'

In the Irish conflict after the late 1970s, civilian peace initiatives had little relevance. They came and went without political reality though often, as Conor Cruise O'Brien has pointed out, they seemed to stoke up violence by raising unrealistic hopes of victory by one side or the other. With such illusions came the greater illusion that 'one last push' would do the trick.

IRA strategy also evolved. From a low point after SAS intervention in 1976, the movement dramatically revived following a reorganization into small, self-contained cells in 1979, when the Northern Command – McGuinness, Adams, etc – took control from Ruairi O'Bradaigh and others based in the Republic. The renascence was aided by the hardline rhetoric of Mrs Thatcher, by eleven hunger-strike deaths and huge arms cargoes from Libya between 1973 and 1987. Starting from scratch the movement created a sophisticated armaments industry tailored like a bespoke suit for the Irish War; that in itself was a stunning technical coup, requiring expert use of machine tools and mastery of complex electronics.

Irish revolutionary history sanctifies two equally valid traditions. One is the physical force tradition (described as such by professional historians, museum curators and academics). The other is the moral force tradition. The embodiment of the first in Irish culture invests violence with a respectability that is part of a martial culture. (The very word 'Celt' comes from the Greek for 'fighter'.) From 1981, in parallel with its arms-manufacturing capability, the physical force movement shrewdly adopted a peace-seeking posture – for propaganda purposes only – which linked the Armalite rifle to the ballot box. Most significantly, it honoured an unwritten but clear agreement not to alienate any Dublin government by mounting attacks on the Security Forces of the Irish Republic. When the IRA did so in June 1996, murdering an Irish detective, it provoked a massive public backlash. There was also a sudden, deadly increase in leaks from within the IRA to British security. The eerie run of success that was enjoyed by MI5 after the killing of Garda McCabe was not a coincidence. It was a reminder to the Provisionals that if Dublin and London became a double act, then the latest campaign was as doomed as its predecessors.

A complete, unedited record of the millions of incidents that combine to create this history would require many volumes and would not, by reason of sheer quantity, provide enlightenment. In any case the Military Chronology (see Appendix) identifies the major actions. What follows is a carefully selected series of examples which, it is hoped, shed light on the means by which the war has been fought since internment without trial ended in 1975, and since the joint RUC/army directive *The Way Ahead* became the blueprint for refined counter-insurgency in January 1977. Refined counter-insurgency, sharpened up in 1986 so as to give the police the leading role against terrorism, has been running for twenty years. There is no guarantee it will not continue for another twenty. In the perspective of the Irish War, that is not so long.

PART II

The British
Soft-War Machine

6

The Forensic Battleground

One of the first to be caught through the new, police-led, strategy was Shane Paul O'Doherty. As the *Listener* journalist Peter Taylor discovered, O'Doherty was recruited into the IRA as a schoolboy in Derry soon after the Troubles began anew in 1969 ('I was no longer an insignificant teenager. I was a secret agent of the IRA – a schoolboy by day and a bomber by night'). O'Doherty abandoned his promising school career and sent shoals of letter-bombs to England, where they mutilated secretaries and other security officers who opened them in the outer offices of the great and the good. In December 1974 his colleague Ethel Lynch blew herself up while making a bomb in Derry. More letter-bombs were found intact, ready to post, in the wreckage. At this point forensic science took over. The letters were addressed in a hand that was unmistakably that of the suspect O'Doherty. Chemical analysis of saliva used to seal the envelopes clinched the case against him. Early in 1975, the first Pira truce was in place. Sinn Fein was legalized by Merlyn Rees and talks were under way with terrorist leaders. O'Doherty thought the war was over. For him, a knock on the door at his home signalled that it was only beginning. He was arrested by Security Forces, taken to the Old Bailey and put on trial, where thirty life sentences were passed on him. In prison he underwent a classic 'gaol conversion', a common phenomenon and a sign of growing maturity. Taylor interviewed O'Doherty in prison and asked whether he thought he had helped to free Ireland: 'His answer was an emphatic no. "You only have to look at the state of Northern Ireland now to see that the fruits of twenty years of violence have put off the very ideals we sought to serve – and will do so for a long time to come."'

O'Doherty was released on licence in 1989, having served his purpose (in IRA terms) and half his lifetime in prison, but he was alive and one Volunteer for whom the cycle of violence was broken. His case represented a small victory for the new, 'soft' strategy.

As the Pira arms-manufacturing industry matured over the years, so the opportunities for forensic defence increased. A secret technical Intelligence analysis of thirty-eight mortar attacks on Security Forces in Ulster between June 1972 and November 1974 noted that the tools and skills were 'beyond the scope of the average handyman'. Equipment included arc welders, mechanical saws, guillotines, drills, lathes, grindstones, bench vices, plumber's vices, pipe-threading facilities and paint sprayers. The report continued:

> The same plumber's vice was used to grasp the Mk 3, Mk 1 40mm and Mk 1 Bombard. A different type of vice was used in the Mk 4 bomb. A blunt wire cutter was linked to a safety fuse on Mk 3/4/40mm Mk 1 bombs. A wire cutter adapted in this way was recovered from the fatal explosion outside Newry on 15 October 1974 when a motor cyclist carrying three bombards was killed. A badly damaged instruction leaflet on the Bombard Mk 1 was recovered at the scene . . . and printed instructions similar to those on an instruction leaflet . . . recovered from Springfield Road, Belfast, on 22 October 1974.

Chemical analysis of the explosives used in the whole series of attacks showed that one type was used throughout. Furthermore, 'in all cases the propellant was a J-cloth impregnated with sodium chlorate; between 75 and 80 per cent of the total propellant weight [prepared by] dipping the J-cloth into warm saturated solution of sodium chlorate and water and hanging up to dry.'

The report concluded: 'all improvised mortars and bombs in the current terrorist use are the product of one design series . . . With a common source of material for the manufacture of the weapons . . . Common selection of tools . . . Same workshop has been involved for some time in the manufacture of improvised grenades.'

The IRA, with customary thoroughness, debriefed Volunteers

who had gone through the process of detection and trial and produced a 9,000-word document whose title could have been 'How not to Incriminate Yourself'. The fact that a copy was found in a tree trunk in a cemetery near an IRA bomb indicated that Pira had failed to follow its own advice. The document, found in 1995 and quoted from here for the first time, notes the change in British strategy from hard to soft. Internment having failed, it says,

> the RUC under [Sir Kenneth] Newman [Chief Constable] sought to put in place a more formal 'legal' process to justify the imprisonment of Republicans . . . by providing the 'evidence' which they did by setting up teams of specially trained interrogators who extracted self-incriminating statements through the use of torture . . . As the training of *Oglaigh* [Volunteers] in anti-interrogation techniques began to take effect and the brutality involved in obtaining forced statements proved to be politically embarrassing to the British, the RUC were once again forced to alter their approach.

Informers (supergrasses) also had been tried and had failed.

This part of the IRA document is illuminating not only for what it says, but as a result of its implicit admission that the Security Forces were not, in general, pursuing a shoot-to-kill strategy, but were collecting evidence that would stand up in court. As the IRA document acknowledges: 'In recent times they have switched their emphasis on Forensic Science from a corroborating role to the position of primary evidence . . . utilising massive scientific resources and applying them meticulously to material gathered up from the scene of operation.'

The document begins with an assertion that says everything about the hybrid conflict.

> Just as we find it absolutely necessary to understand the enemy's interrogation techniques or surveillance and to train to overcome such obstacles, so too we must tackle the problem of Forensic Science. We cannot afford to lose *Oglaigh* at any time, much less through sloppy preparation or execution of an operation. Not only can it cause us major

problems in ... our operational capacity but the political mileage we achieve from a successful operation can be lost, or at the very least reduced, due to arrests.

The RUC, it explains, seals off an area where the IRA has carried out an attack.

They will seek out witnesses not solely for identification but to establish the sequence of events: who came from where, who did what, was a vehicle used, what time did it happen, etc ... It allows them with their Forensic Scientists to search for the type of evidence they would expect to find associated with the type of operation. It may be useful to employ a delaying tactic (such as a hoax bomb or a booby trap) which apart from having obvious military advantages, also allows for time to lapse during which forensic evidence may be dispersed or destroyed.

The forensic laboratory team discuss each case with the investigation officer, then allocate every item of physical evidence to the relevant laboratory division.

In general terms, anything which is of living origin, however remote, is within the province of biology; conversely an item of inanimate origin indicates Chemistry as the right discipline for its examination. Specimens of blood and saliva would go to Biology; contact evidence such as explosive traces, glass particles and paint fragments would go to Chemistry. Bloodstained clothing containing paint fragments might be analysed by both departments.

The IRA document then lists fifteen separate areas of forensic evidence which a Volunteer should plan to nullify before an operation begins. Hair traces, including gels, sprays and dyes in the hair, both collect incriminating evidence, including explosive chemicals, and deposit clues on discarded masks and wigs used for disguise. An arrested Volunteer will find that almost the first step taken by the RUC when they have someone in custody is to run a plastic comb through his or her hair, 'with or without consent'.

The comb, its teeth clogged with cotton wool, will collect a variety of samples. Among other precautions, the Volunteer on active service 'must make certain that the original hair sprays, etc are not in their homes to be taken up by the RUC as additional supportive evidence'.

Firearm residue creates a major headache for IRA men and women. Each time he shoots, a cloud of particles covers the gunman: 'hands, face, hair and clothes are splattered with it and some of the particles even enter the nose and can be recovered from the nasal passage.' Revolvers are more 'leaky' than self-loading pistols. But 'irrespective of the type of weapon . . . we must always assume we have been covered in residue and act accordingly'. Under arrest, the Volunteer's clothes are taken for analysis. Though the courts accept that the only time that lead, antimony and barium – the main trace elements from gunshot – are found is in relation to firearms, 'all three elements are found in paint. Lead is a constituent of petrol and solder; antimony is found in many fire-retardant systems; antimony and lead are found together in battery grids . . . solder and pewter as well as in bullets.'

The prophylactic advice offered is to wear protective outer garments and to avoid capture until these are washed. Overalls and a mask are *de rigueur*. 'However, such steps are not the end of our safety precautions. Even with a mask firearm residue can find its way through the eye holes onto the face.'

The document concedes that bomb-making is not only dangerous to the bomb-maker but extremely messy, unless commercial or military explosives are used. It points out:

> Fertiliser-based explosives tend to be manufactured in vast quantities. Their bulk weight can be anything up to several thousand pounds. The sheer volume of the fertiliser that has to be processed and turned into explosives means that the *Oglaigh* are involved in a forensically messy operation. Working speedily with such a bulk cannot realistically be done without creating a mess; the base will be contaminated with raw material and finished product; the Volunteer's clothes would also be covered . . . They would actually be

breathing in the component particles. Therefore the manufacture of explosives . . . particularly in an urban populated area . . . represents a very great danger.

Ways must be found to reduce the contamination from these 'mixes' . . . We must ensure that the *Oglaigh* who actually plant or use the explosive device are contamination free, forensically clean. Fertiliser-based bombs are usually fairly large and are normally placed in a culvert or a van . . . However, Volunteers carrying small explosive charges such as boobytraps, 'up-and-under' impact grenades (using commercial explosives) are at risk from contamination.

When the RUC arrests a Volunteer suspected of bombing, it 'will attempt to preserve all possible forensic evidence on the *Oglach*'s hands by placing plastic bags over them. At the Barracks these will be removed and swab tests carried out on the hands, and perhaps face and hair. Most certainly they will seize any clothes that may be there and test them for explosive.'

In some cases, the air within plastic bags which are used to store incriminating clothes is sucked out with an electric pump to be captured on absorbent material. Near-microscopic, possibly odourless particles, including Semtex, are then analysed in tests which 'can detect explosive traces weighing between one million millionth of a gram and one thousand times less than this'. The advice adds: 'All explosives must be treated with respect – not just because carelessness when handling such sensitive material can cost lives through premature explosions – but . . . also cause explosive particles to spread over the *Oglach*, his or her clothes and over the surrounding area. Our every action can leave a possible trace.'

In both types of attack – with firearms or bombs – the Volunteer should break the forensic link to incriminating chemical residue.

All clothes used during the operation should be washed immediately. It is now standard practice for the RUC when searching a house for trace evidence to take the filters from washing machines, or waste water from pipes, in order to analyse them for fibres, residues, etc . . . Always wash clothes by hand and dispose of the water into an outside drain, back garden or yard.

The IRA's scientific adviser pays particular attention to the problem of leaving garment fibres as a clue to operational activities. 'Fibres,' says the expert, 'are the major forensic danger. They are links in a chain and can cross transfer in a number of ways . . . For example, if a fibre from an *Oglach*'s sleeve could be found on a glove and a fibre from the glove found on a weapon, a link between weapon and Volunteer could be established.' The mere action of sitting on a chair or wearing one item of clothing over another is sufficient to cause cross-contact. Some fibres are so small that they are barely noticeable to the human eye: 'As we go about our daily business we are constantly shedding and picking up fibres of no significance. If we make such contacts as republican activists while engaged on active service we should understand a very basic yet crucial lesson – applicable to the forensic threat in general – "Every contact leaves a trace" and therefore also a potential link.'

Those most at risk from fibre trace evidence are those captured in the vicinity of an IRA operation or shortly after it:

> In many similar situations in the past, prior to the systematic use of forensic evidence, if the arrested Volunteer maintained silence in the Barracks he or she was released despite the enemy's knowing their involvement. In effect they weren't able to prove it. Today in such situations more is required in terms of pre-operational planning if we are to prevent the enemy from imprisoning *Oglaigh*.

No Volunteer on active service should wear any clothing made of wool, natural or synthetic, since this sheds fibres easily and as readily retains fibres from other materials. Nylon and denim are identified as the safest fabrics. 'Colour, too is important for dyes . . . are good forensic links.' Washed blue denim jeans and similar garments are made from a natural fibre that 'is so common that it is microscopically indistinguishable from all other denim. It is of no use to the forensic scientist'.

Masks made of wool or acrylic should never be used. 'We do

suggest, however, that *Oglaigh* use ladies' nylon stockings as masks. If the *Oglach* is not fully happy with this disguise another mask can be worn over the top of the nylon stocking. The stocking would be a forensic barrier . . . Nylons can be easily burnt, destroying any possible trace evidence. This should be done after every operation.'

The IRA advice document includes a learned essay on glass, including such arcane matters as the 'refractive index' of samples.

If the Volunteer or someone else smashes a window, the pane will not only shatter . . . but dust-fine particles will be created. These can be spread up to twenty feet and can lodge themselves undetected into clothes or hair. Volunteers could walk over particles of glass and carry them with him or her in the soles of shoes. Or the car in which the *Oglaigh* are travelling could crash thus leaving glass from the headlamps for the forensic scientist to follow up on.

Similarly, paint is 'good trace evidence'. The IRA notes:

In an operational role we may need to break into the home of a member of the crown forces or of a loyalist paramilitary . . . We may need to break down the door with a sledge hammer . . . Paint, where dry . . . will shatter and hurl fragments into the air around us . . . We may crash a car into another vehicle or object, transferring paint traces from one to another . . . We may also be involved in handling various types of drums and containers whilst making mines or bombs . . . The forensic scientist can establish who manufactured the paint. Indeed some colours and types of paint are so unique that it has been known for forensic scientists to identify the probable make, model and year of a car from a fragment of its paint.

The IRA acknowledges the power of DNA to identify an individual's body fluids including blood, saliva and semen but stresses:

Taking suitable material for DNA testing from a captured *Oglach* is not a simple task. Under their law they only have the power to carry out non-intimate searches on any 'suspect'

... Even doctors cannot carry out blood tests. The only so-called non-intimate search they can do is the 'mouth swab'. There is however dispute among scientists as to the reliability of this test. [But] if an *Oglach* has been wounded they will take his or her clothing or bandages and use them to make the forensic link.

Fortunately for the wounded IRA soldier, such test material is often liable to contamination and therefore unreliable evidence. This section reflects the main lesson of the O'Doherty case: 'Even the unconscious licking of a stamp before placing it on a letter bomb can give possible clues to the RUC via the forensic scientist.'

The document also examines the problem of the compromising footprint. In a house taken over by an IRA ambush team, prints invisible to the naked eye on carpets and other surfaces can be detected by the Electrostatic Dust Mark Lifter. 'The area under scrutiny is covered with an electrical insulator through which a large voltage (up to 15,000 volts) is applied. When the insulator is finally moved for inspection a footprint, made up from dust particles, would be found fixed to it ... It is also possible through the use of lasers to create a hologram of footprints found on carpet.'

A near perfect match with the IRA suspect's footwear is obtained with a thin layer of oil spread on the sole of the shoe, pressed on to paper to create a print which is dusted with fingerprint powder. Even 'the precise degree of natural wear and tear through walking plus damage by stones, glass, etc' will emerge to convict an accused Volunteer.

An extensive survey of the incriminating nature of documents – including chemical composition of paper and ink, and the idiosyncrasies of syntax and handwriting – as well as the Electrostatic Detection Apparatus Test (ESDA) to reveal impressions made from a top document on to others beneath, concludes: 'An *Oglach* must always rest a single sheet of paper on a hard surface such as a table top.'

The stress laid upon the significance of contact evidence as a result of clues derived from clothes – whether the pollution of gunshot residue or the telltale story of characteristic fibres – reflects one of the IRA's great failures, converted to a triumph, in the early days of the forensic war. The year was 1972, the worst for casualties since the Troubles were renewed, when 468 people died violently in Northern Ireland, 323 of whom were uninvolved civilians. There were 10,268 shooting incidents, 1,382 explosions and 471 bombs disarmed. A total of 36,617 houses were searched. Amid the mayhem, an undercover unit known as the Mobile Reconnaissance Force created a mobile valet service known as the Four Square Laundry. Clothes to be cleaned were collected by van. The driver and his partner, a woman serving with the Royal Military Police, were both natives of Northern Ireland. For some months they trawled the streets of Catholic Belfast, collecting clothes to be cleaned, returning them punctiliously. The service ran with military precision, as did the forensic laboratory examining the clothes before they were cleaned.

In October 1972 the IRA turned a double-agent working for the MRF. He exposed the real nature of the Four Square operation. On 2 October, the van was ambushed by the IRA in West Belfast and raked with automatic fire. The driver was killed. The woman fled to a nearby house and survived to be promoted and secretly invested at Buckingham Palace with an MBE. The incident was one of a series of catastrophes which led to disbandment of the MRF soon afterwards.

Later in the war, the IRA twice bombed the Northern Ireland Forensic Laboratory. On the first occasion, the movement manipulated the routine used to investigate civilian car crimes. Cars recovered from accidents where a crime was suspected were taken to the laboratory for inspection. The IRA set up a 'sting': an accident which Forensic would investigate, using a car which concealed a bomb. This Trojan Horse was taken into the laboratory for investigation of the original 'accident'. It then blew up, destroying much forensic evidence held as part of the war against terrorism. On 22 September 1992, a 3,000lb bomb in a van placed alongside the laboratory's perimeter fence did massive damage to the place. It was one of the largest bombs successfully used in the Province and further proof of the severity of the 'forensic threat', in terrorist eyes.

7

Virtual Justice

The heart of the British army's credibility during the post-1969 Troubles was the claim that the soldier operated within the rule of law while his terrorist opponent did not. Without that, there was moral equivalence between both sides. If, as the IRA insisted, its attacks were part of a just war, then the British army could not assert any claim to legality; it was, in Republican eyes, merely an alien force of military occupation suppressing the rights of the civil population, or at least one segment of it. This matrix of law, morality and brute force contained the key to ultimate victory in a counter-insurgency war: popular support for one side or the other. If this principle held good in Malaya and Oman, it was even more relevant in the quick-witted, idea-loving, gossipy environment of Ireland.

For the British, the law was a minefield from the beginning. Increasing dependence on legal process after the change of strategy made things worse. The way out of the difficulty was to arrange matters so that as the war evolved so did the legal system. It was the only way, short of surrender to the IRA, to contain the contradictions presented by assassins who changed their legal status as readily as their camouflage. As Lord Gardiner, the former Lord Chancellor, put it in March 1972: 'There is virtually a war going on between the Government of Northern Ireland and the Irish Republican Army.' The government's dilemma, in London as well as Ulster, was to disguise this fact through a series of legal stratagems. Virtual warfare begat a virtual legal system. By the 1990s, as the IRA veteran Sean O'Callaghan revealed in 1996: 'The IRA has developed its own in-house lawyers. A lad who wants to join the IRA is sponsored to study law. An IRA person [i.e., a guardian] stays with him all the time. They then have an IRA Volunteer who is a lawyer. I am pretty certain the Security Forces have not yet caught up with the sophistication of it.' Candidates for the IRA's equivalent of the Army Legal Service were not selected at random but tended to come from a tiny elite of Republican families. As O'Callaghan put it: 'Ninety-nine per cent of the core leadership are from families who have been involved in this going back hundreds of years.'

When the troops were sent to Northern Ireland they were despatched by a government that did not wish to lend aid and comfort to a repressive Unionist regime using the draconian Special Powers Act to strip people of their civil rights. Several Cabinet ministers, in fact, favoured reunification as a solution to the Irish problem. 'Our policy in 1969', said one minister, 'amounted to doing anything which would avoid direct rule.' So as Ulster disintegrated into a near civil war, the British government itself was torn by two mutually incompatible imperatives: to restore peace without supporting the local Protestant administration at Stormont; and to avoid direct intervention. This was to have fatal consequences.

Towards the end of July 1969, someone in the Cabinet's Northern Ireland Committee ('Gen. 42') asked what would be the legal position if any soldiers were sent to intervene in the Troubles? The Attorney-General, Sir Elwyn Jones, was reassuring. Soldiers would become 'common law constables', exercising the duty of citizen's arrest to aid the police. This did not satisfy those ministers who argued that soldiers, subject to military, not civil law, might have to shoot their fellow subjects to defend the common law. What then? As Insight discovered: 'The doctrine of equivalent force was wheeled out. Roughly it would be in order for a soldier to shoot someone if they had been prepared to do something equally drastic to him.'

Somewhat later, in August 1996, Field Marshal Lord Carver quoted a ruling by the law officers of the crown dating back to 1911 (an inauspicious year for the British rule of law in Ireland):

A soldier differs from the ordinary citizen in being armed

and subject to discipline; but his rights and duties in dealing with crime are precisely the same as those of the ordinary citizen. If the aid of the military has been invoked by the police and the soldiers find that a situation arises in which prompt action is required, although neither Magistrates nor Police are present or available for consultation, they must act on their own responsibility. They are bound to use such force as is reasonably necessary to protect premises over which they are watching, and to prevent serious crime or riot. But they must not use lethal weapons to prevent or suppress minor disorders or offences of a less serious character, and in no case should they do so if less extreme measures would suffice. Should it be necessary for them to use extreme measures, they should, whenever possible, give sufficient warning of their intention.

The beguiling simplicity of all this was flawed in two respects. First, it did not address the nature of the 'civil power' the troops were to assist. To the beleaguered Catholics of the Lower Falls – the unwitting sacrifice of an American Irish Republican destabilization plan – the civil power was the source of their problems and the threat from which they sought military protection. Recognition of that reality was given briefly in the 'back-of-envelope treaty' agreed between Major-General Dyball and Jimmy Sullivan, the IRA officer ostensibly representing the Belfast Central Citizens' Defence Committee early in September 1969 (see Introduction).

The other, equally deadly, fault in British policy was that the civil police (the RUC) had to expend all its resources before the soldiers could move. As the message log of 39 Brigade noted on 3 August 1969: 'No question of committing troops until all methods exhausted by the police.' Troops already sent to the RUC's Belfast headquarters were withdrawn only three days before the most provocative Orange Order march of the season, that of the Apprentice Boys of Derry. The RUC would now have to scrape the bottom of the security barrel to find more men. That meant mobilizing the RUC reserve force, the Ulster Special Constabulary, or B Specials, a sectarian private army that had its roots in the most bigoted Unionist tradition. Law and order predictably broke down on 12 August. At Armagh a group of B Specials fired wildly into Catholic rioters, killing John Gallagher. The ancient sectarian fault-line was now ripped open and the tigers of Irish tribalism let loose. On 14 August, soldiers from the Prince of Wales' Own Yorkshire regiment moved in their trucks across the river Foyle into Bogside.

As street violence increased, so did the legal embarrassments. The common-law figleaf, the Cabinet discovered, did not cover pre-emptive measures including military roadblocks and checkpoints. These could be made lawful only by reference to the infamous Special Powers Act, the device used by Stormont to override normal civil and criminal law.

The curfew imposed by the army on the Falls Road in July 1970 followed by the arrest of 300 people, the detention of 20,000 people in their homes and the deaths of four civilians was almost certainly unlawful, though a Belfast magistrate found that a soldier, acting on his own authority, could suppress riot 'by every means'. The internment process the following year, with its illegal use of military detention and even more illegal use of military interrogation techniques on civilians detained without authority, led to successful claims for damages against the crown in the civil courts. The European Commission on Human Rights, in a fourteen-volume report, found that the interrogations were not torture as such but did constitute inhumane treatment. Later episodes – including Bloody Sunday, in which fourteen unarmed people were shot dead by soldiers, and in Gibraltar, 1988, in which three unarmed IRA terrorists were similarly killed – could not be said to represent a policy of minimum rather than lethal force. (In September 1995, the European Court of Human Rights found that the Gibraltar Three had a legal right to life that was unlawfully breached.)

In August 1973 the Special Powers Act, which the South African prophet of apartheid, John Vorster, had much admired, was replaced by a new Westminster law, the Northern Ireland (Emergency Provisions) Act, 1973. This gave legal effect to a report by the English jurist Lord Diplock, in which he admitted: 'The only hope of restoring the efficiency of criminal courts in Northern

Ireland to deal with terrorist crimes is by using an extra-judicial process.'

The extra-judicial process was the juryless trial, presided over by a single judge. The Act also regularized the powers of soldiers to act as law-enforcers, giving them powers of arrest for a variety of crimes including possession of any document (such as this book, perhaps) which contained information about security of potential use to a terrorist. The new powers and the Diplock Courts that enforced them, marked the start of the British effort to characterize their armed opponents as criminals, not political guerrillas. This change of policy inherited a new handicap. In June 1972, a Conservative minister, William Whitelaw, had granted 'special category status' to convicted terrorist prisoners, a status not unlike that of prisoners-of-war. This amounted to political recognition of terrorists and was the IRA's third major victory, following the destabilization of the RUC in 1969 and the demolition of Stormont in March 1972. Both Diplock and 'special status' were to cause new griefs for London.

The Diplock Courts often depended on confessions by the accused while in custody, in the hands of the RUC, for proof of guilt. An analysis by John Newsinger argues: 'This was to amount in practice to a replacement of internment by trial by confession.' RUC interrogators had been trained by British Military Intelligence men and women in the spring of 1971 in methods later admitted to be illegal. The planning of the main interrogation centre at Castlereagh in Belfast began at about the same time. As Lord Gardiner noted the following year: 'It was not unnatural that the Royal Ulster Constabulary should assume that the army had satisfied themselves that the procedures which they were training the police to employ were legal.' It was not long before prisoners appearing before Diplock Courts were to be heard complaining of brutal treatment while under interrogation. A police surgeon, Dr Robert Irwin, told Independent Television News that he knew of 150 suspects whose injuries in custody – broken bones and punctured ear-drums – could not have been self-inflicted.

In 1978 Judge Bennett QC looked into such complaints. The British government now headed by James Callaghan (Home Secretary when the troops were first committed to the Province), claimed that Diplock had stopped jury-nobbling by terrorist intimidators. Over three years, 4,650 people had been charged with terrorist crimes. Bennett noted that an impressive 94 per cent of these suspects had been convicted. The government also claimed that out of 3,000 people detained in 1977–78, only fifteen had been shown to suffer injuries in custody that were not self-inflicted. Nevertheless, Bennett recommended the use of closed-circuit television to monitor RUC interrogations and the provision of legal advice for suspects after forty-eight hours in custody.

The other new legal instrument employed to halt terrorism was the Prevention of Terrorism (Temporary Provisions) Act, first passed in 1974 after nineteen people were slaughtered in the Birmingham pub bombings. Until 1977, when a reformed RUC started becoming the leading agent against the IRA as part of the criminalization policy, Britain's laws on terrorism were rooted in traditional military notions of counter-insurgency, particularly the use of 'temporary' emergency laws suspending the usual rights of prompt access to lawyers and court protection. The 1974 Act was in practice a means of gathering Intelligence rather than punishing the guilty. Of 5,500 people detained by the end of 1982, fewer than 2 per cent were charged. The *Criminal Law Review* concluded in 1978 that the authorities seemed to accept that the Act's key provision 'may properly be used to obtain information about terrorism (as distinct from actually detecting offenders and holding suspects)'. Powers provided by this Act to hold suspects for up to seven days without charge were regarded by the European Court of Human Rights as excessive, but the British government claimed its right of derogation from the Convention. As a result, this Intelligence-gathering tool remained part of the British judicial process.

Meanwhile, thanks to Whitelaw's reform, convicted terrorists and others held without trial, under emergency internment regulations, were enjoying special privileges and fast converting their prisons into 'staff colleges' for revolution, taking over the prisons from within and consolidating their hold through threats of intimidation against prison officers' families or, in a few cases, sexual favours on the part of detainees' wives and others. In one way or another, the prison officers – even the majority who remained personally uncompromised – retained only limited control of their charges. By 1975, Lord Gardiner concluded in a second report that the authorities had virtually lost control of the prisoner-of-war compounds. He advised ending special status.

It would be fifteen years before the full extent of the internal corrosion of the political prisons would be laid bare in public. In 1990 John Christopher Hanna, a principal prison officer at the Maze, was himself given a life sentence and concurrent sentences of twenty-seven years for helping the IRA to murder one of his colleagues and conspire with the terrorists in other ways. The colleague, Brian Armour, vice-chairman of the Prison Officers' Association, was killed by a bomb under his car in October 1988.

Hanna, a womanizer, was controlled by 'a Provie woman', in his words, who was an actress doubling as an IRA Intelligence officer. He was now in the 'honey trap'. That was not the only pressure the terrorists brought to bear. They learned that his daughter lived with a former IRA prisoner and had a child by the man. Hanna claimed that he was told that if he refused to co-operate: 'Your grandson might be coming home in a wee brown box.'

Correspondents who followed the case noted that Northern Ireland's 3,000 prison officers were responsible for the most dangerous prison population in Europe, including more than 300 men convicted of terrorist murders. As one report put it: 'Many officers were hastily recruited in the 1970s and the authorities admit that their quality can be patchy. Security sources believe prison officers have been actively involved in . . . smuggling guns into the Maze and Crumlin Road jails on the orders of the IRA.'

Acting on Gardiner's advice, a Labour minister, Merlyn Rees, phased out the special category status from 1 March 1976, having ended internment without trial a few months earlier. A return to cells and penal uniform was bitterly opposed by the IRA and its allies. The 'dirty' protest – using excrement as a weapon to make cells uninhabitable – and the 'blanket' campaign (no dress except a prison blanket) were followed by hunger-strikes.

The IRA is good at hunger-strikes. They combine moral force with political impact; suicide expressed as a ritualized drama guaranteed to run for about sixty-five days plus a theatrically staged funeral, an oration and a hero presented as sacrificial victim. The protests were implicitly encouraged by a British muddle. On 12 February 1976 Frank Stagg, an IRA man sentenced to ten years in October 1973 as one of a bomb team in Britain, died on hunger-strike in Wakefield prison. He had demanded special category status and a transfer to a prison in Northern Ireland. The IRA was determined to milk the event as a propaganda coup. Stagg's widow thought otherwise. She lived in England and wanted a private funeral.

According to former Irish Prime Minister Garret Fitzgerald:

> [Mrs Stagg] was threatened by the IRA with being shot through the head if she pressed her view. We were told that the authorities in Britain had refused to accord her a police guard on her home and had entered into a deal under which it was agreed to ignore her right to her husband's remains and to hand them over to the IRA to bring to Ireland in return for agreement by the IRA to confine their demonstrations to our island. They proposed to parade the coffin through Dublin and various other towns before bringing it to Ballina, County Mayo, for interment.

Fitzgerald called the British minister responsible, Roy Jenkins, and told him that unless the IRA deal was repudiated, he would call a press conference 'to expose this macabre plot between authorities in Britain and the IRA'. The response was immediate. The body was handed over to the Irish police at Heathrow airport and the aircraft carrying it diverted from Dublin to Shannon. Mrs Stagg went to Dublin where, in spite of a police guard, her hotel room was invaded during the night 'and for three hours she had been subjected to intimidation designed to "persuade" her to hand over the remains to the IRA, intimidation that with great courage she had resisted'.

Mrs Stagg offered a compromise: to hold a funeral Mass at Ballina, after which she would not resist an IRA funeral locally. The Irish government accepted that 'but when the IRA heard that they wee not to be allowed to bring the body on a tour of the country, they . . . took no part in the funeral'. Although the grave was secured with concrete, an IRA team dug up the remains to be reburied in a Republican plot. As a pro-Republican American writer Kevin Kelley tells the story: 'On the night of 6 November 1976 an IRA unit dug around the cement casing and transferred the corpse to the republican grave-site. A priest was on hand to say a few prayers, while the volunteers fired one round over the grave as a farewell salute before making off into the night.'

The IRA campaign to prompt more hunger-strikes in response to the end of special category status made a slow start. It was accelerated after the election of Margaret Thatcher in 1979, and possibly as a reaction to her appetite for confrontation. A carefully phased, rolling programme of lethal fasts began in 1981. Bobby Sands, aged twenty-six, Pira's leader in the Maze prison, refused food from 1 March until his death sixty-six days later on 5 May. More than 70,000 supporters followed his coffin at the funeral. On 12 May Francis Hughes – wounded and taken prisoner by the SAS after a prolonged manhunt which ended with his comment, 'Your dogs is no fuckin' good' – died after fifty-nine days. So the macabre drama continued, presented to the world as a battle of wills between Republican zealots and the Iron Lady. Raymond McCreesh died on 21 May; Patsy O'Hara of INLA on 21 May; Joe McDonnell on 8 July; Martin Hurson on 13 July; Kevin Lynch on 1 August; Kieran Doherty on 2 August; Thomas McElwee on 8 August and Michael Devine on 20 August.

The fasts ended on 3 October, after relatives of four prisoners authorized feeding of their men under medical supervision. Three days later, the London government backed down from its insistence on prison uniform and allowed politicals the right to wear their own clothes. Winning this concession, of limited practical use but symbolically important, had taken almost ten years. As well as the lives of ten hunger-strikers, a seven-month fever of street riots and 1,200 public demonstrations killed 101 people. Victims of the backlash included twenty-one RUC officers and fifteen soldiers (five of whom died in a landmine explosion near Camlough, home village of hunger-striker Raymond McCreesh).

The special category campaign had a major impact on Anglo-

Irish politics. Most English people backed the triumphalism of Thatcher, who travelled to Belfast on 28 May to assert that the hunger-strikes 'might well be the last card' of the IRA. The Celtic Irish, equally unanimous, believed that the fast should be recognized as an ethical gesture and statement of Irish identity in defiance of English repression. What was not known was that secret negotiations in which Gerry Adams and Danny Morrison of Sinn Fein/IRA were permitted to talk with the prisoners, to find a formula to end the strikes with British approval, were being undermined by both the IRA and London. The IRA pitched a higher price than the prisoners themselves to end the fasts while the Thatcher government took a harder line in public than in private. The crunch came a few hours after the death of Joe McDonnell. As Garret Fitzgerald wrote later:

> We had been quite unprepared for this [British] volte-face, for we, of course, had known nothing whatever of the disastrous British approach to Adams and Morrison. Nor had we known of the IRA's attempts – regardless of the threat this posed to the lives of the prisoners and especially to that of Joe McDonnell – to raise the ante by seeking concessions beyond what the prisoners had said they could accept.

The political effect of hunger-strike deaths was to build support for Sinn Fein among previously uncommitted people in the Republic. As Fitzgerald – no friend of the IRA – conceded:

> The IRA, with which an organ of the British government had chosen to deal behind our backs, launched a demonstration on our streets that threatened public order in our own state . . . I had written on 10 July to Margaret Thatcher telling her that a rising tide of sympathy for the hunger-strikers was threatening the stability of the Republic.

In Ulster and the Republic, hunger-strikers were elected in their absence to the Parliaments of London and Dublin or to local councils in both countries. As W. D. Flackes noted: 'The nine H-Block [Maze prison] candidates took nearly 40,000 first preference votes' in the June 1981 election in the Republic, playing a major part in the defeat of the Dublin Fianna Fail government. The IRA had now taken a long stride towards establishing a legitimate political mandate on both sides of the border. Although British Intelligence officers and others asserted that the hunger-strike was defeated, the overall result was a brilliant political success for the Republicans and an example of the use of its varied arsenal – psychological and political warfare as well as urban terrorism and guerrilla warfare – in a loosely orchestrated, extemporized fashion that always kept its opponents off balance. The strategy also required a reptilian attitude to the welfare of the hunger-strikers and their next-of-kin. Like the victims of the 1969 pogroms, they were treated as pawns in a bigger game than one of mere personal survival.

In 1982–83, the legal authorities tried a new device: the usually uncorroborated evidence of a converted terrorist ('supergrass') to imprison former friends. The process blossomed remarkably for a year or so. By December 1985 one man – Harry Kirkpatrick of the INLA – had been instrumental in convicting twenty-five alleged terrorists. In all, some thirty supergrass witnesses from all terrorist factions had prompted 600 arrests. The supergrass was granted legal immunity. On appeal, convictions obtained this way were increasingly quashed. For example, on 17 July 1986 the convictions of eighteen men named by the IRA supergrass Christopher Black three years earlier were overturned. On 24 December 1986, twenty-four out of Kirkpatrick's twenty-five suspects were released by the Appeal Court. Thereafter supergrasses were discredited and ditched by the virtual justice system.

If the terrorists were vulnerable once they were in custody, then the soldiers were equally exposed to legal sanction on the street. The law in question was the 1967 Criminal Law (Northern Ireland) Act which states that 'such force as is reasonable' may be used to prevent crime or apprehend offenders or suspects. Here the issue was criminalization of soldiers, not terrorists. A series of cases illustrate the Security Forces' dilemma in fighting a conflict that evolved into 'virtual warfare' after 1967. On 10 July 1978, two SAS soldiers waiting for an IRA team to draw weapons from an arms cache hidden beneath a tombstone in a rural churchyard in Antrim shot dead a youth who went to the cache and extracted an automatic rifle. They were charged with murder, largely because an autopsy suggested that the youth, John Boyle, had been shot in the back when he could have been arrested. The soldiers were acquitted after independent pathological evidence demonstrated that the youth was shot while facing the SAS ambush. Acquitting the two men, Sir Robert Lowry, Lord Chief Justice of Northern Ireland, savagely criticized them for 'a badly planned and bungled exercise'. He added: 'I do not intend to give any currency to the view that the Army is above the general law in the use of weapons.'

That message was blurred by Lord Justice Gibson, who acquitted three RUC officers of murder following the so-called 'shoot-to-kill' deaths of three Republicans in a car riddled with 109 bullets on 11 November 1982. The dead men were unarmed at the time yet the judge commended the officers for bringing the three men 'to justice . . . the final court of justice'. Gibson, in his turn, was blown up and killed on the border in April 1987. The IRA bomber responsible, Brendan Burns, was killed by one of his own devices the following year. By then, as well as Gibson, victims of IRA summary justice, in which Burns played the role of executioner, included the five soldiers murdered at Camlough during the hunger-strikes and eighteen Parachute regiment soldiers at Warrenpoint in August 1979.

Gibson's ruling did not apply in the case of Private Ian Thain, of the Light Infantry, who shot and killed Thomas Reilly, a civilian (and road manager of the pop group Bananarama) on 9 August 1983. Thain was convicted of murder and, as he was not yet twenty-one, sent to the young offenders' wing at Walton prison, Liverpool. On 27 February 1987 he was paroled and resumed military duties, though not in Ireland. He left the army in January 1990.

In December 1990 the brothers Fergal and Michael Caraher were stopped by a burst of fire as they drove out of a pub car park at Cullyhanna, South Armagh. Fergal, aged twenty and a well-known member of Sinn Fein, was killed. Two Royal Marines, Lance Corporal Elkington, aged twenty-three, and Private Andrew Callaghan, were prosecuted for murder and attempted murder. The prosecution claimed that Elkington smashed the driver's widow with his rifle, opened fire and ordered Private Callaghan to do the same. The court was told that Elkington told police he had fired nine aimed shots at the driver, believing that a third soldier was being carried away on the bonnet of the car. Lord Chief Justice Hutton did not believe the testimony of any of the witnesses. There was, however, 'objective and undisputed' scientific evidence to support the soldiers' claim, since fibres from military uniforms were found on the car bonnet. The accused men were acquitted. Seven years later, Michael Caraher was charged with possessing a Barrett sniper rifle and other alleged terrorist offences.

The outcome of the first Caraher case was a sharp reminder of the forensic dangers about which the IRA would later advise its front-line guerrillas. In spite of such evidence, the case provoked disbelief among church and legal leaders in the Province. At that point, 350 people, many civilians, had been killed by on-duty members of the Security Forces during the Troubles. Just under two dozen prosecutions had been brought, with the courts usually acquitting the soldiers and policemen charged. When the peace process brought Sinn Fein/IRA to the peace talks in 1997, only four soldiers (and no police officers) had been convicted of murder. As a veteran reporter of the Troubles, David McKittrick, observed: 'Critics cite this record as statistical evidence for the argument that British governments' primary concern has been not to ensure justice but to protect members of the security forces who pull the trigger. The IRA says it demonstrates there is one law for the Army and Royal Ulster Constabulary and another for everyone else.'

In a culture of virtual warfare and virtual legality, that was probably inevitable. The man and woman in uniform, unlike the civilian or the plain-clothes terrorist, was a ready target, for whom some special protection was imperative if a counter-insurgency campaign was to be effective. The problems were most clearly focused by the case of Private Lee Clegg of 3rd Battalion, the Parachute regiment. Just before midnight on 30 September 1990, a team of Paras on the fringes of West Belfast, one of whom was Clegg, was scattered by a dark blue Vauxhall Astra that paused near their road check, then came through their position at speed. It was the second incident of its sort that night. As the Astra sped past, six of the soldiers including Clegg started shooting. Nineteen bullets hit the car, killing the driver Martin Peake and his rear-seat passenger Karen

Reilly. (The Security Forces killed at least a dozen people in similar circumstances during the renewed Troubles.) The front-seat passenger in the car driven by Peake, Markiewicz Gorman, suffered minor injuries.

Unwisely, the soldiers inflicted injuries on one of their own men in an attempt to mislead the police into believing that the stolen car had hit him. Soon afterwards BBC Panorama reporter John Ware, investigating 154 civilian deaths caused by the army over twenty-five years, spotted a cardboard cut-out dummy of the Astra, decorated with bullet holes, fixed to the wall of 3 Para's canteen near Belfast. In the front seat was a papier mâché head with red paint depicting the shot that had killed Peake. The caption, on the wall above the dummy, was highly damaging for the soldiers' claims that they had used reasonable force, as the law required. It said: VAUXHALL ASTRA: BUILT BY ROBOTS. DRIVEN BY JOY-RIDERS. STOPPED BY 'A' COMPANY.

Ten months after the shooting, BBC's *Panorama* team broadcast a special documentary about lethal force in Northern Ireland. Subsequently, six members of the patrol were charged with various offences.

In June 1993, Clegg was convicted by a Diplock Court of murdering Karen Reilly, the rear-seat passenger, and given a life sentence. The law did not permit a reduced charge of manslaughter in such cases. Equally, the life sentence was an automatic consequence of conviction for murder. The case went through the entire legal system, including an appeal hearing before the Law Lords. For three days, three distinguished judges devoted microscopic attention to the law governing the use of force in self-defence, the common law, citizen's arrest, and the differences between ordinary members of the public and Security Forces in Northern Ireland. It was the most thorough examination of such issues since the Troubles were renewed in 1969. Like the lower courts, the Lords found as a fact that Clegg's first three shots were fired in self-defence or in defence of a colleague, and were fired legally, but that the fourth round, fired when the fugitive car had passed and was 50 feet away, was an act of murder. The basis for this belief was the opinion of a single expert, Mr Gary Montgomery, senior scientific officer at the Northern Ireland Forensic Science Laboratory.

The Law Lords examined parts of the army's guidance document, 'Instructions for Opening Fire in Northern Ireland', also known as the 'Yellow Card'. Paragraph 5 specifies:

> You may only open fire against a person: (a) if he is committing or about to commit an act LIKELY TO ENDANGER LIFE, AND THERE IS NO OTHER WAY TO PREVENT THE DANGER. The following are some examples of acts where life could be endangered, dependent always upon the circumstances: (1) firing or being about to fire a weapon; (2) planting, detonating or throwing an explosive device (including a petrol bomb); (3) deliberately driving a vehicle at a person and there is no other way of stopping him; (b) if you know that he has just killed or injured any person by such means and he does not surrender if challenged and THERE IS NO OTHER WAY TO MAKE AN ARREST.

The Court of Appeal had concluded that, as framed, the Yellow Card 'rules', which have no legal force, would justify a soldier in opening fire where a person had been injured by a car, irrespective of the seriousness of the injury. The House of Lords judgment went on: 'The court considered it desirable for the army authorities to redraft the Yellow Card to make it clear that a minor injury caused by a car does not justify a soldier in opening fire.'

The Lords quoted in full the appeal court's next observation, since it identified an important question of law.

> The trial judge found that the fourth shot fired by Private Clegg killed Karen Reilly and that he had no legal justification for firing that shot. Under the existing law, having found that Private Clegg fired that shot with intent to kill or cause grievously bodily harm, the trial judge was obliged to find Clegg guilty of the heinous crime of murder, which carries a mandatory sentence of life imprisonment, and it was not open to the judge to find Clegg guilty of the lesser crime of manslaughter, where the judge can sentence the accused to

the period of imprisonment which he considers appropriate in all the circumstances of the crime.

There is one obvious and striking difference between Private Clegg and other persons found guilty of murder. The great majority of persons found guilty of murder, whether they are terrorist or domestic murders, kill from an evil and wicked motive. But when Pte Clegg set out on patrol on the night of 30 September 1990 he did so to assist in the maintenance of law and order and we have no doubt that as he commenced the patrol he had no intention of unlawfully killing or wounding anyone. However, he was suddenly faced with a car driving through an army checkpoint and, being armed with a high velocity rifle to enable him to combat the threat of terrorism, he decided to fire the fourth shot from his rifle in circumstances which cannot be justified and the firing of his fourth shot was found to be unlawful.

It is right that Pte Clegg should be convicted in respect of the unlawful killing of Karen Reilly and that he should receive a just punishment for committing that offence which ended a young life and caused great sorrow to her parents and relatives and friends. But this court considers, and we believe that many other fair-minded citizens would share this view, that the law would be much fairer if it had been open to the trial judge to have convicted Pte Clegg of the lesser crime of manslaughter on the ground that he did not kill Karen Reilly from an evil motive but because, his duties having placed him on the Glen Road armed with a high-velocity rifle, he reacted wrongly to a situation which suddenly confronted him in the course of his duties. Whilst it is right that he should be convicted for the unlawful killing of Karen Reilly, we consider that a law which would permit a conviction for manslaughter would reflect more clearly the nature of the offence which he had committed.

What of the soldier's duty? The Lords cast back to a speech of Lord Diplock in 1976:

There is little authority in English law concerning the rights and duties of a member of the armed forces of the Crown when acting in aid of the civil power; and what little authority there is relates almost entirely to the duties of soldiers when troops are called on to assist in controlling a riotous assembly. Where used for such temporary purposes it may not be inaccurate to describe the legal rights and duties of a soldier as being no more than those of an ordinary citizen in uniform . . . [But] a soldier who is employed in aid of the civil power in Northern Ireland is under a duty, enforceable under military law, to search for criminals if so ordered by his superior officer and to risk his own life should this be necessary in preventing terrorist acts. For the performance of this duty he is armed with a firearm, a self-loading rifle from which a bullet, if it hits the human body, is almost certain to cause serious injury if not death.

Taking up that point, Lord Lloyd of Berwick, on behalf of the Lords, commented:

In the case of a soldier in Northern Ireland, in the circumstances in which Private Clegg found himself, there is no scope for graduated force. The only choice lay between firing a high-velocity rifle which, if aimed accurately, was almost certain to kill or injure, and doing nothing at all.

The point at issue here is not whether Pte Clegg was entitled to be acquitted altogether, on the ground that he was acting in obedience to superior orders. There is no such general defence known to English law . . . The point is rather whether the offence in such a case should, because of strong mitigating circumstances, be regarded as manslaughter rather than murder. But so to hold would . . . be to make entirely new law . . . Under the existing law, on the facts found by the trial judge, he had no alternative but to convict of murder.

Lord Lloyd concluded this was not a situation for case law.

The reduction of what would otherwise be murder to manslaughter in a particular class of case seems to me essentially a matter for decision by the legislature, and not by this

House in its judicial capacity. For the point in issue is, in truth, part of the wider issue whether the mandatory life sentence for murder should still be maintained. That wider issue can only be decided by Parliament.

Why Parliament had done nothing to cover soldiers' legal situation after almost thirty years is puzzling as well as a betrayal of the man and woman on the front-line. One explanation might be that the Irish situation is still seen, as it has been for 300 years, as a temporary crisis requiring only temporary, emergency laws. Even in 1997, soldiers being trained for duties 'across the water' were given, on average, only a cursory half-hour of instruction about the law and that was focused upon the flawed and legally ineffective Yellow Card. To amend the law concerning murder and manslaughter would be to effect a permanent change and to acknowledge, at last, that the Irish War is a fact of British political life.

Even before Clegg's appeals had been rejected by the House of Lords in January 1995, his regiment, led by the Paras' 'Tribal Elders' – a group of retired senior officers – were orchestrating an effective media campaign. Meanwhile, the Ministry of Defence compensated both Markiewicz Gorman and the mother of Karen Reilly with undisclosed damages, undeterred by a *Daily Mail* revelation that Karen Reilly's father, James McGrillen, an IRA Volunteer, was shot dead by soldiers while travelling in a stolen car in 1976. Clegg was released on licence in July 1995 and a Republican protest riot duly followed in Belfast.

The Clegg case still held legal surprises. Shortly before Clegg's release and his return to the Paras, the automatic SA80 rifle he had used was tested forensically on an army shooting range in Kent. In January 1997, the Northern Ireland Minister Sir Patrick Mayhew agreed to send the case back to the appeal system in the light of new forensic evidence. Clegg's own evidence, quoted by the Lords, adds further doubt to the issue of whose rifle fired the bullet that killed Karen Reilly. This is the relevant passage:

> In the course of his cross-examination Pte Clegg was asked whether he was aware of any circumstances which would

have justified him in firing after the car had passed. He replied that he had no reason to fire at that stage.

Q: And if you had fired any more you know of no justification for that action?

A: That's correct. That's why I applied my safety-catch as the car went past me.

The significance of that might have been overlooked, since it conveyed the belief that Clegg, *as the car went past*, had made his weapon incapable of firing further shots. Yet the three courts through whose minds the evidence was sifted had found as a matter of fact that Clegg did fire the illegal shot into Karen Reilly *after* the car had passed through Clegg's position.

In November 1997, the Northern Ireland Appeal Court re-examined the case. Mr Anthony Scrivener QC, representing Clegg, recalled that the finding that the fatal, illegal bullet was fired into the rear of the car was based upon the opinion of the scientist Gary Montgomery. Mr Scrivener contended that later tests conducted by Mr Graham Renshaw, a former Home Office scientist, showed that at the 50-foot range postulated by Mr Montgomery, a bullet striking the boot of the car was likely to disintegrate after passing through a metal panel behind the back seat. The bullet recovered from Miss Reilly's body, said Scrivener, was intact and bore none of the marks that would be expected to appear. Mr Renshaw concluded that the bullet found in Miss Reilly's body was more likely to have entered the car through a side door. Furthermore, he claimed, the Renshaw tests were supported by a second forensic report commissioned from the Strathclyde Forensic Science Laboratory at the request of Sir Patrick Mayhew, the then Northern Ireland Secretary. What of the original Montgomery opinion? That, said Mr Scrivener, had never been tested scientifically. While Mr Montgomery was highly qualified and respected, the prosecution had been conducted on the basis of his opinion 'without any expert conducting a single test'. What of the Renshaw report? 'To put it quite bluntly, if that evidence had been available at trial it would have destroyed the prosecution case.'

Though Mr Reg Weir QC, for the Crown, disputed this

conclusion, the Lord Chief Justice of Northern Ireland, Sir Robert
Carswell, concluded in February 1998 that Clegg's conviction was
unsafe 'as it was based on suppositions now shown to be unfounded'.
A retrial was ordered before a juryless Diplock Court though Clegg
had already spent 1,430 days behind bars. On 12 March 1999 Clegg
was finally acquitted of murder after a fifth courtroom battle – though
Mr Justice Kerr, sitting alone, accused him of 'a farrago of untruths'
about his contention that the stolen car had hit one of his comrades.

Another murder prosecution against soldiers followed the death
of a Belfast Catholic in 1992. Jim Fisher, a Gulf War veteran, and
Mark Wright were serving with the Scots Guards, on patrol in
Republican North Belfast when they shot Peter McBride, aged
eighteen, in the back. They believed he was 'acting suspiciously'
and might have been carrying a coffee-jar grenade in a plastic bag.
They claimed they fired warning shots. When he ran away, they
killed him. The victim was unarmed. The soldiers were given life
imprisonment. Lieutenant-General Sir David Scott-Barrett, who
led the Scots Guards Release Group, argued: 'The military side of
their situation was not highlighted in the court case. Men trained
to act under military law are judged by civilian law . . . Only a few
days earlier a Scots Guardsman had been killed by a sniper's bullet
in the same area. These soldiers acted without malice. Neither
should have been judged to be criminal or jailed with criminals.'

An Appeal Court judge took a different view in 1995: 'As the
deceased was shot when he was unarmed the appellants had no
lawful justification for firing.'

In March 1998, Sir Ludovic Kennedy joined the campaign on
their behalf, alleging that three local residents whose evidence convicted the soldiers had crucially changed their statements during
the police inquiry. Worse, a key military witness had not been
called at all. In a *Daily Mail* article, Kennedy commented:

> The rioting, shooting and burning of cars that would have
> followed an acquittal of two soldiers of the occupying power
> chasing and then killing by shooting in the back an appar-
> ently unarmed youth did not bear thinking about. As a fellow
> Scot and long-time campaigner against miscarriages of jus-

tice, I have to say that my heart bleeds for Fisher and Wright, as it does for Peter McBride's mother who has been heard to mutter as she lays flowers on her son's grave, 'Oh Peter, Peter, why didn't you stop?'

Such cases were not the most damaging for the name of British justice in Northern Ireland. That distinction must go to the abuse of process that accompanied the fatal shooting of three unarmed Republicans at an RUC roadblock near Lurgan on 11 November 1982. The affair led to an impartial inquiry by an honest and experienced Manchester detective, John Stalker, Deputy Chief Constable of Greater Manchester. Stalker probed too deeply and was suspended in bizarre circumstances. His report was never published. In 1996, twelve years after three unarmed IRA men had been shot by the SAS-trained special RUC team, the Belfast coroner John Leckey concluded he could not complete the inquest because the House of Lords had ruled that the police officers could not be compelled to give evidence. Another court denied the coroner access to the Stalker report in the interests of national security. Mr Leckey announced in September 1996 that the ruling refusing him access to the Stalker report meant that his effort to examine fully the circumstances surrounding the deaths was 'no longer achievable'.

Almost as damaging was the position of the informer working for one arm or other of British Intelligence, obliged to become a terrorist himself in order to work as an effective agent. Brian Nelson, an agent for Army Intelligence, was sentenced to ten years' imprisonment for terrorist offences on behalf of the Protestant extremist Ulster Defence Association. His defence counsel, Desmond Boal QC, argued that Nelson had been 'invited and encouraged into criminality by people in authority'. People in authority were not courageous enough to face up to that. There was, in fact, 'dishonesty and cowardice at a very high level and it was because of this that Nelson was in the dock'. As his military controller, a lieutenant-colonel of the Intelligence Corps also pointed out, 'at the heart of the informer system lies a legal nonsense'.

It is an open question whether the adoption of virtual justice to contain virtual warfare was an absolute failure. It was assuredly a more legitimate process than the kangaroo courts, execution and punishment squads run by the IRA, but virtual justice was assuredly not an absolute success either. As Lord Colville QC, who was responsible for several reviews of emergency legislation for the British government, observed in 1993: 'The policeman or soldier, his family and friends, say that it is monstrous that a minor misjudgement in a man's reaction to a split-second emergency, should lead to a sentence of life imprisonment. But the victim's family and friends will be outraged by an acquittal.'

The legal dilemma implied a larger one for the British, whose own, often successful, counter-insurgency doctrine had recognized since the 1950s that the essential ingredient in halting terrorism was popular support, known to soldiers as 'hearts-and-minds'. The point was reinforced in 1991 by Father Denis Faul, a campaigning County Tyrone priest regarded as one of the Republican movement's most effective opponents precisely because he has attacked the betrayal of human rights in Northern Ireland more effectively than most journalists. He told David McKittrick:

> Justice is the big thing, justice is the solution. Most of the problems in the 1980s were created by the British government. We could have wiped out the Provos long ago if the Government had put proper discipline into the RUC, the British army and the UDR. All we've ever asked for is the security forces to behave within the law. Don't torture. Don't shoot to kill. Don't unjustly harass people. The Provos rely upon atrocities by the security forces to bail them out. The Provos love harshness and cruelty and misery. It suits them down to the ground . . . The only way to beat the IRA is to be kind and just to the Catholic people and take them away from the Provos. Only the Catholic people will tell them to stop, will throw the guns out on the streets . . . My attitude to the Provos is that they're prodigals. We must always hold out lifelines to them. They've come out of the slums. They've sprung from bigotry and sectarianism; from ill-treatment by the British Army and RUC, from internment, from being burnt out of their homes . . . We must

reconcile them, bring them back into a better way of working for Ireland.

British civil liberties as well as those of Ireland were damaged by virtual justice. John Alderson, former Chief Constable of Devon and Cornwall, argues: 'Failure to provide early redress of grievances of the Catholic/Nationalist minority, or to be seen to be taking steps to do so, led to gradual escalation of violence which eventually caused contamination and diminution of the system of criminal justice not only in Northern Ireland, but also in Great Britain.'

In a society whose judges were obliged to carry guns under their robes, as did Judge Ambrose McGonigal among others, no one could elude the vortex of violence. Even within the legal profession, the rule of law was over-ruled by the brutal law of physical force. From the very beginning, advocates who did not allow politics to pollute their profession were exposed to intimidation and worse. Richard Ferguson QC was Unionist MP at Stormont from 1968 to 1970. A liberal supporter of O'Neill and the reforms of 1969, he resigned from the Orange Order in August that fateful year. The intimidation followed. He resigned as an MP for health reasons in February 1970. In April, his home was bombed. He was not alone in finding that his vocation put him in someone's gun-sights. Patrick Finucane, a Belfast solicitor, was shot dead by a Loyalist assassin in 1989. The New York-based Lawyers Committee for Human Rights investigated. Four years later, its report concluded: 'Finucane's success as a lawyer subjected him to various forms of official intimidation prior to his murder. There is additional evidence pointing to collusion between the Ulster Freedom Fighters and the security forces in the murder itself.' Finucane's problem was that the Protestant terrorists suspected that Finucane and two other solicitors were 'the brains behind the IRA'.

The IRA was just as enthusiastic about killing members of the legal profession, particularly judges and most particularly Catholic judges of various sorts. The victims included Judge William Doyle, shot dead on his way to Mass (January 1973); William Staunton, magistrate, shot collecting his daughter from the Catholic St Dominic's College in Belfast (January 1973); Martin McBirney, magistrate, shot dead at home, East Belfast (1974); Judge Rory Conahan, also murdered at home (1974); Irish home of Sir James Comyn, an Irish judge on the English bench, firebombed (1981); Tom Travers, magistrate, and his daughter, shot as they walked home from Mass (Travers survived, his daughter died; 1984); Lord Chief Justice, Sir Maurice Gibson (blown up, 1987); home of Sir Eoin Higgins rocketed (1987); Donald Murray (survived bomb attack, 1987, and moved house). The wife of a surviving member of the judiciary complained: 'We feel isolated here, as though London doesn't care. They regard us as Paddies who can take care of ourselves.' A dispute flared up in 1988 about the degree of protection such people should have. The IRA, with breathtaking cynicism, offered an 'amnesty' to Judge Donaldson, provided he resigned from the Bench and, as an advocate, refrained from acting for the Director of Public Prosecutions. A barrister who was intimidated into the 'comparatively safe anonymity of the English bar' confided that life in Northern Ireland

> becomes a living nightmare, looking around your shoulder each moment, considering, 'Should I do this? Go there? Are the wife and children safe to take that picnic on the beach this afternoon?' You get tense, knowing the moment you relax and don't take simple precautions, like looking underneath your car before getting into it, could be fatal. In the end some, like myself, say life's just not worth living like that.

The force of those remarks was underlined on 13 June 1981 when the IRA attached a bomb to the car used by Lord Gardiner on a visit to Belfast. A liberal judge, Gardiner was also the official voice of dissent from the use of sensory deprivation to interrogate suspects and the Lord Chancellor who publicly confirmed that 'the normal conventions of majority rule would not work in Northern Ireland'. The IRA failed to kill him only because the bomb fell from his car before it could explode. To justify the attack, the Republicans said Gardiner was 'the political architect of the criminalization policy and the H-blocks'. Like Comyn and others, his natural sympathies were with society's underdogs. That, in the eyes of extremists, made him the more dangerous.

For more than twenty years, virtual justice proved to be a convenient political instrument in presenting a revolutionary military conflict as if it were merely a criminal process responsive to the rule of law. The end result of the experiment, from the falsification of forensic evidence at the scene of a death to the abuse of process by way of official gagging orders (Public Interest Immunity Certificates) to suppress such evidence as was uncovered, was cancerous for the British body politic. Though the dead were interred, the fudging of the surrounding circumstances haunted the British down the years. Bloody Sunday, 1972, was such a case. In 1997 the author Don Mullan cited an official Home Office document, newly released by the Public Record Office, which seemed to suggest that even a Lord Chief Justice was not immune. Lord Widgery was finalizing his report when a minister or senior civil servant annotated it, in handwriting: 'LCJ will pile up the case against the deceased ... but will conclude that he cannot find with certainty any one of the 13 was a gunman.' In 1998, under pressure from Dublin, the London government of Tony Blair conceded a new inquiry into Bloody Sunday as part of the 'peace process'.

After the success of the 1998 Good Friday peace agreement, endorsed by popular vote in Ireland, unrepentant terrorists were promised early release from prison in exchange for a peace pledge by their organisations. Terrorist murderers as yet undetected were invited to hand over weapons with a guarantee that they would not be prosecuted for their crimes. The IRA felt this was an offer it could refuse.

So could their Loyalist counterparts. On 15 March 1999, the Red Hand Defenders killed the civil rights lawyer Rosemary Nelson with a bomb attached to her car. Her friends alleged that she had been under threat from elements within the RUC. Her murder, with its odour of threats by security forces, was a seismic political event as the Patten Enquiry moved towards reform of the police as part of the peace process. The RUC's Chief Constable, Sir Ronnie Flanagan, to demonstrate honest policing, called in an FBI officer and an English Chief Constable to join the investigation. By then, only 20 out of 1,400 solicitors in the Province were willing to defend 'politically-sensitive cases.' No officers were prosecuted.

8

The Hit Squad

When Irish hostilities were put on pause by the 1997 ceasefire, 22 SAS regiment had killed approximately thirty-eight Republican terrorists and arrested several times that number. It also killed five innocents, either in circumstances sufficiently ambiguous to justify opening fire, or as a result of 'battle accidents'. Throughout most of those years the SAS presence in Northern Ireland was tiny, as its own losses – two men killed in action – confirm. Usually, the Irish detachment was the strength of a troop, around thirty men, reinforced by air at short notice from the regiment's base at Hereford.

The real impact of the SAS in this as in other campaigns was as a 'force multiplier' as well as (in Lord Justice Gibson's memorable phrase) the final court of justice. Small was effective if not always beautiful. In Ireland its main adversary, the Provisional IRA, never knew which of its operations had been compromised and, if so, which one would end in an SAS ambush. In practice, cases suitable for SAS treatment were a small fraction of the whole. They were usually those in which no form of legal words would suffice. The ratio between SAS killing and arrest varied wildly. The way the statistics shape up might tell a story, or reflect nothing more than the random nature of the conflict. Conspiracy theorists prefer to read a hidden political agenda into the bodycount.

The bare facts are that between 1976, when the regiment was publicly committed to operations, and 1984, when the IRA's Brighton bomb nearly killed Margaret Thatcher, the regiment had killed nine Republican terrorists. Between 1985 and 16 February 1992, twenty-seven more (or twenty-nine, according to another estimate) were 'malleted' (killed), plus one wounded, escaped. These figures were inflated by eight of the IRA's East Tyrone Brigade killed at a single stroke at Loughgall but even so they represent an increase of 300 per cent during the Thatcher years after Brighton. Between 1992 and 1997, the John Major years, only one Republican was killed by the regiment. This, according to one SAS officer, reflected political and legal imperatives to use minimum force after the blood-letting at Loughgall in 1987 in which two civilians, as well as the IRA, lost their lives. He might have added that the controversial nature of the Gibraltar shootings in 1988 intensified the public relations, and therefore the political, pressure on the SAS. An IRA team allegedly linked to the deadly long-range sniper rifle, the Barrett Light, was arrested by the SAS in 1996 in circumstances which might have justified opening fire. As it was, the arrests were wrapped up with a few bruises on each side.

As the number of Republicans killed by the SAS diminished, so the number of Republicans murdered by Loyalist terror groups increased. Orange killings of all kinds doubled from eighteen in 1990 to more than forty in 1991, to thirty-nine in 1992 and almost fifty in 1993. This might be coincidence. However (see Chapter 9), Loyalist terrorists were also able increasingly to target key Republicans, or their next-of-kin as proxy targets, after 1990, thanks to Intelligence leaked to the killers by Security Forces. It is not impossible that a precisely tuned counter-insurgency strategy, fouled up by bad publicity, was replaced by a Loyalist assassination offensive.

The SAS dipped its toes briefly into the troubled waters of Northern Ireland in 1969, when its soldiers wore uniforms and regimental berets, complete with winged dagger, as they searched the glens of Antrim and incoming ships for Loyalist arms; and again in 1974. It was a time when repressive military force was acceptable. But when a Belfast bank was raided by two SAS soldiers, and when a Protestant was ambushed, shot and wounded with a silenced sub-machine-gun, B Squadron was hastily withdrawn. The victim of the silenced Patchet sub-machine-gun was suspected of being a UVF 'quartermaster'. In time, he was awarded £16,500 compensation, met by the taxpayer.

When the SAS was permanently committed to the Irish War in January 1976, it was in the circumstances of Whitehall farce scripted by Prime Minister Harold Wilson. The regiment was still a colonial counter-insurgency force, not known for limiting the firepower at its disposal. In Ireland, a policy of military counter-insurgency was about to be replaced by one of police primacy, criminalizing those who regarded the gun as a legitimate political instrument. There could not have been a less appropriate time to call in the SAS but that is what a Labour Prime Minister chose to do. If Wilson's response in 1969 was underplayed, this looked like a serious over-reaction. That the policy was a military success owed nothing to him. Through most of the preceding year, the IRA had been running a sectarian war against much of the Protestant community as well as the Official IRA in Belfast, where one Pira hit squad, searching for an Official IRA heretic, murdered a girl aged six instead. The sectarian campaign brought Northern Ireland close to civil war. On 4 June 1975 Francis Jordan, a Provisional, was shot dead by soldiers as he laid a bomb outside a crowded Protestant pub at Bessbrook, South Armagh. The Provisionals publicly confirmed that this was an authorized operation. As the radical American journalist Kevin Kelley noted: 'The Provos' acknowledgement . . . was nothing less than an open admission by the IRA that it was attacking Protestant civilian targets.'

A month later a pop group, the Miami Showband, on its way home to Dublin, was stopped by a Loyalist death squad wearing Ulster Defence Regiment uniforms. One of the gang was also a UDR sergeant. Using high explosives the terrorists killed three of the musicians and two of their own. Tit-for-tat massacres continued into the following January, when a bus carrying twelve unarmed workmen was stopped by an IRA team near Whitecross, South Armagh, and the occupants sorted according to their religions. The only Catholic was told to leave. The eleven Protestants were mown down with long bursts of automatic fire. Only one survived.

In the medium term, the sectarian murders on both sides vindicated the policy of treating the gunmen as mere criminals rather than as soldiers and helped along the emerging policy of criminalization. But in the immediate aftermath of the Whitecross massacre,

Protestant anger was at boiling point. To reassure the community that the government was taking the crisis seriously, Wilson told journalists that the SAS was on its way to South Armagh. He had neglected to mention this inspired idea to the Ministry of Defence or the SAS, who learned about the deployment from the television news. An officer serving with the SAS at the time recalled that its Director, Brigadier John Watts, 'was wheeled in to see the GOC [General Officer Commanding] who tore him off an enormous strip. The GOC was convinced that the SAS had done a backstairs deal with Wilson to get the SAS into Northern Ireland and was very much against it.'

In practice, the SAS – heavily committed in the Dhofar war and with a squadron exercising in Norway – had only eleven men available for Ireland, five of whom were on convalescent leave after being wounded in the Gulf. Wilson's briefers assured *The Times* that up to 150 SAS men were on their way and that 'the decision will be warmly welcomed by the Army'. The officer in charge of the vanguard, who had earlier worked on the Intelligence corridor at the army's headquarters at Lisburn, arrived only to be shown the door with the words: 'You are not allowed up here . . . The SAS is under command of 1 Royal Scots based at Bessbrook Mill [South Armagh]. You will answer to that Commanding Officer and get all your intelligence from the Intelligence Officer of 1 Royal Scots.'

Frozen out of the military establishment in the Province, the SAS now turned to the RUC Special Branch. It was the start of a symbiotic relationship that anticipated the strategic reforms already being planned at the Home Office in London. The Branch, through its network of informers, could identify the IRA's key players but did not have the training, the arms or the capability to act on that information. So, as one SAS veteran of the time put it: 'We could do the dirty work they couldn't do. They weren't equipped. They didn't have the expertise. They didn't have the freedom.'

The regiment soon began work. On 12 March, Sean McKenna Jnr, who later gave a detailed and convincing account of his experiences, was kidnapped by an SAS team. At 2.45 a.m. he was asleep in bed in his family's summer cottage 250 yards south of the border at Edentubber, Dundalk. Two men kicked his bedroom door open and put a 9mm Browning pistol to his head. McKenna was told that if he resisted arrest he would be shot. He was marched through the darkness to the Flurry river, where he was ordered to jump across and not get wet, and handed over to the RUC. The SAS claimed that he was drunk in a field on their side of the border when they found him. He was sentenced to twenty-five years in prison for what Judge Babbington described as 'a whole catalogue of terrorist offences'. Though threatened with death if he resisted, on his own account, he was not a target for SAS assassination, but for arrest, trial and imprisonment.

The SAS's second action, on 15 April, had more impact on the sectarian killers of South Armagh. This was the loss of the unit's treasurer, Peter Cleary, aged twenty-five, of Newry. His day job was as a scrap dealer. Pira acknowledged that he was a staff officer. He was seized by the SAS at his fiancée's home on the border and taken to a field nearby to await a military helicopter. In the dark, four men were to hold lanterns to guide the helicopter to land. A fifth man, an officer, guarded Cleary. The SAS account of what followed is that Cleary, desperate to escape, tried to seize his guard's rifle. In the struggle that followed, the young officer, on his first operation, fired two shots into Cleary.

Though mortally wounded, Cleary did not die immediately. A battle-hardened NCO took the officer's rifle, fired a single *coup de grâce* shot into Cleary to end his misery, wiped the gun clean of fingerprints and handed it back to the officer. At the inquest nine months later, Raymond Anthony Fegan, a witness who was in the house where Cleary was detained, claimed that immediately the soldiers left with Cleary, he heard automatic gunfire. A news report of the hearing continued: 'He heard somebody crying over the ditch and then there was a single shot. He claimed that the soldiers had told them not to leave the house for ten minutes.'

At the inquest, three of the SAS team gave evidence while wearing dark glasses, navy anoraks and polo-neck sweaters. They sat in the witness box with their backs to the main body of the courtroom. This was a novelty in Britain then; a cliché later. The officer did not appear, though a statement was read on his behalf under the *nom de guerre* 'Soldier A.'. Cleary, he claimed, was heavier and stronger than him and a notorious killer. His statement continued: 'As he lurched at me my instinct as an SAS soldier took over. I released the safety catch on my weapon and started shooting. There was no chance to warn Cleary. I kept on firing until the danger to me was over.' The inquest returned an open verdict.

The Catholic population now had confirmation, it thought, that the SAS was indeed a Special Assassination Squad. So did the Provisional IRA, which backed away from operations in South Armagh for twelve months or more. Had matters remained there, the SAS might have kept under some rough control an area that was to be virtually uncontrollable, where public road signs showed the outline of the hooded man with the Armalite rifle and the reminder: 'Sniper at Work.' As one of those involved in the campaign said:

> Our presence on the Border had achieved its aim. But it was never reinforced. The decision was made in Whitehall that the SAS were so successful they would be deployed Province-wide. The regiment's contribution then became a series of penny-packet size teams, having a little impact in little areas. If we had concentrated our efforts in South Armagh we could have held and cleaned the area overnight. For us to develop an expertise in urban as well as rural areas was asking an enormous amount of a tiny regiment. Nobody knew how tiny it was: just 190 individuals. It was so secret and we were so desperately small.

The regiment's reputation for lethality after Cleary's death, though a useful weapon psychologically, did nothing for its image further afield. In these years before SAS men were fêted as heroes thanks to the Iranian embassy operation in 1980, and long before an SAS 'Writers' Circle' (de la Billière, Mitchell, Armstrong and others) produced a torrent of revelations, the regiment's critics on the British Left such as Fred Halliday (who perceived SAS deaths in Oman as an 'optimistic outlook' for revolutionaries), and within the army's own establishment knew they could plant any rumour, however wild, about the unit without risk of rebuttal. The Cleary case, as a first, had to be defused convincingly. What followed was one of the most bizarre exercises in press relations ever mounted by the army. It worked surprisingly well.

A major critic of the regiment, not surprisingly, was the *Guardian*. In collaboration with the MI5 boss in the Province, an SAS officer planted the regiment's version on the paper through an apparently accidental encounter with its staff writer covering Northern Ireland. The writer's movements had to be known in advance. How they were known remains an open question. It may be supposed that this correspondent's Belfast telephone, like others, was monitored by more than one security agency.

The correspondent was on his way to London by train. He was joined on his journey by the officer, in civilian clothes. A conversation began in which, bit by bit, the officer revealed more and more about his role in Ireland and the killing of Cleary. The correspondent did not interrupt his flow; did not say, 'Excuse me, do you appreciate you are talking to a journalist who will publish every word you say?' Instead, according to an SAS source, 'He appeared greedy to take it all up.'

What was planted was not untrue, even if it was not the whole truth. The essential point which the regiment wanted to make public was that Cleary was not set up for assassination. He really had been killed while trying to make a break from legal custody and would have murdered his escort to do so. In view of what had just happened to Sean McKenna, that is credible. The *Guardian*'s man left the train at Birmingham to telephone an account that was headlined: '*How the SAS moved in on the terrorists*.' It began: 'Chance encounters with members of the Special Air Service Regiment are supposed . . . to be as unpleasant as they are infrequent. The torch in the eyes at 3 am, the cold press of blue steel in the back of the neck, the muffled bark of a silenced machine pistol . . . But my chance encounter could hardly have been more civilised . . .' The article faithfully relayed the regiment's apparently unguarded revelations about Cleary. Back at SAS headquarters in Chelsea, London, the officer, identified in the *Guardian* as 'F', was rebuked by Watts, the SAS Director, for his apparent indiscretion.

The war in Dhofar, Oman, was won in late 1975 and confirmed

by treaty early in 1976, releasing more SAS soldiers for the war in Ireland. Until then, apart from one disastrous 1974 experiment, the SAS role had been to provide skilled Intelligence officers to run the undercover surveillance team described in Chapter 9. After 1976 – as Intelligence groups of various kinds came of age and evolved separately from the SAS – the regiment's role increasingly was to ambush IRA terrorists known to be on their way to a target and unlikely to surrender without a fight. These were cases where minimum force, reasonable force, legal and illegal lethal force were so close as to be indistinguishable. Many of those killed by the SAS had already been through the criminal courts at least once and had chosen to live as armed outlaws rather than making their political point without violence by leaving the IRA to become Sinn Fein politicians. The SAS campaign, from now on, was a conflict in which orthodox soldiers had little or no part.

At dusk one Sunday in January 1977, as the regiment reclaimed South Armagh, Seamus Harvey, aged twenty, armed with a sawn-off shotgun, walked into an SAS ambush and was hit by bullets from his own side as well as the SAS. Another Sunday evening, a year later, Paul Duffy – aged twenty-three, carpenter, IRA Volunteer – was cut down by Security Forces at a deserted farm used as an IRA explosives store. His wounds suggested summary execution. British army headquarters in the Province promptly credited this one to the SAS. Subsequently the regiment asserted that 'another' organization had killed the man. The Duffy the regiment did claim that year was Patrick, an IRA quartermaster aged fifty, father of six and an unemployed fitter. He was killed by fourteen bullets as he checked firearms in a deserted house in Derry, his daughter and grandchild waiting for him in a car parked just outside. He was given a VIP funeral by the IRA.

This was a controversial year for the SAS in Ireland. Just before midnight on 21 June, five soldiers from G (for Guards) squadron and a captain, armed with Armalites, waited for three IRA bombers on their way to hit a government engineering depot with satchel bombs. 'We thought Christmas had arrived,' one of them said of this ambush. The three were killed in a hail of gunfire. Two of the bodies were finished off, as a precaution, with shots to the head. The gang's getaway driver escaped with the car. An innocent Protestant, William Hanna, aged twenty-eight, was shot in his stead. In the darkness he died wearing his Loyalist tam-o'-shanter. Two weeks later a youth aged sixteen, John Boyle, reported finding an IRA arms cache beneath a tombstone in a derelict cemetery near his family's farm at Dunloy, Antrim. The RUC called in the SAS which sent a two-man team to wait for the IRA. John Boyle returned to the scene, unaware of the ambush, and was shot dead. The soldiers were tried for murder and acquitted, but were denounced by the judge.

In the mid-1980s, arms cargoes from Libya gave a huge boost to IRA operations. These were Libya's revenge for the demonstration outside the Libyan People's Bureau in London which ended with the murder of Woman Police Constable Yvonne Fletcher and the expulsion of Libyan diplomats in April 1984. With the additional arms came a new, bold IRA style that played into the hands of the SAS, reminiscent of the heyday of the Anglo-Irish War in the spring of 1920. During the first six months of that year, sixteen defended police barracks were destroyed and twenty-nine damaged. On the evening of Friday 8 May 1987, in daylight, the Provisionals decided to show that they, too, could destroy such targets. A 200lb bomb was loaded on to a mechanical digger and driven nine miles along country roads to the RUC police barracks at Loughgall, County Tyrone.

The digger was driven by Declan Arthurs, aged twenty-one, with five years' IRA service; accompanied by Gerard O'Callaghan, aged twenty-nine, twelve years' IRA service and released from prison in 1983 after which he immediately returned to guerrilla warfare; and Tony Gormley, aged twenty-four, with six years' IRA service. A back-up van joined the digger at a rendezvous. At the wheel of this vehicle was Seamus Donnelly, aged nineteen, with three years' IRA service already behind him. Hidden behind black balaclavas and wearing boiler suits, his passengers were some of the movement's hardest men: Patrick Kelly, aged thirty, commander of the operation as well as East Tyrone Pira; Jim Lynagh, aged thirty-one, undeterred by the experience of being almost killed by his own bomb fourteen years earlier; Padraig McKearney, aged thirty-two, with fifteen years' IRA service; and Eugene Kelly, aged twenty-five, with five years' IRA service. Kelly was believed to have murdered two RUC officers. Lynagh, a former Sinn Fein councillor, had killed Sir Norman Stronge, former Speaker of the Stormont Parliament, among others. McKearney was an escapee from the Maze prison and, said *Republican News*, 'a key figure in daring and innovative missions'. They were, in a word, the cream of the Provisional IRA, entrusted with a mission of great symbolic importance.

The operation had also been totally compromised by an informer. As a result, the resident SAS team in Northern Ireland had been reinforced well in advance and smuggled into the target building to replace the police officers. On Thursday 7 May, the day before the attack, almost forty SAS soldiers plus signals and others specialists had been briefed about the likely route the terrorists would take and the composition of the bomb and back-up teams. The use of lethal force as a response, according to one of those involved, was personally authorized by Prime Minister Thatcher. It is not implausible. The tiny War Cabinet she dominated during the Falklands conflict approved the sinking of an Argentine warship, the *General Belgrano* the day before the event, in May 1982. Aboard the *Belgrano* a thousand lives were at risk and 350 were lost. Another, special, factor was the use of the SAS. She had personally authorized, by car telephone, the regiment's onslaught against Iraqi terrorists at the Iranian embassy siege in 1980. The outcome was a spectacular political success. She and her husband joined the SAS celebration party after the killing was done and the hostages set free. Mrs Thatcher became as fascinated with the SAS as they were with her. Her combative spirit was exactly what they demanded of a leader. She was a regular visitor to the regiment's home base at Hereford and a presence even when not there in person.

The day before Loughgall, British Intelligence officers also knew the likely arms to be carried by Lynagh's men. These were three Heckler & Koch 7.62mm army assault rifles, two 5.56mm FN automatic rifles, a shotgun and a Ruger revolver, hidden in an arms cache and kept under constant surveillance by an undercover RUC team for days before. The SAS tooled up with belt-fed machine-guns and Armalite automatic rifles. One machine-gun team waited in a copse overlooking the target. The other was sited inside the building, at some risk from bomb damage if the IRA attack were pressed home successfully, and thereby satisfying the legalities of this war. That detail apart, this could have been Dhofar or Malaya so far as the SAS was concerned. Other, small teams were hidden on either side of the approach road, ready to close any escape routes. What was not known was the precise time at which the attack might come in. The SAS settled down to wait in its feline way for hours, or days if necessary. Lynagh, they knew, was a man who kept his own counsel.

The IRA van, a stolen blue Toyota, cruised cautiously downhill into Loughgall village at 7.15 p.m., passed the police barracks, turned around and passed it again. The machine-gunners lined up their sights, eased the safety-catches off, their ear-pieces telling them softly, 'Wait . . . Not yet . . . Wait.' The van disappeared, then returned, followed by the digger, carrying the bomb in its excavator, covered by a screen of bricks. The machine stopped near the police station. So did the van. Still the SAS waited. There was to be no pre-emptive shooting. The van door slid open and Patrick Kelly stepped out, automatic rifle in hand, followed by two other IRA men. Kelly opened the proceedings with a gesture: a futile burst of automatic fire aimed at the wall and windows of the build-ing. The SAS took that as their cue. Two machine-guns scythed through the men in the open and through the van itself. Lynagh and McKearney, wearing flack-jackets, died in the back of the van.

The bomb depended on an old-fashioned cigarette lighter to be detonated. Gormley lit the fuse, then tried to escape, the lighter still in his hand. He took cover behind a wall and then, as the shooting eased, tried to run for it. Another burst of fire brought him down. O'Callaghan, his companion on the digger, was cut down as he ran across the road away from the barracks, rifle in hand. The bomb demolished part of the target building and a telephone exchange adjoining it. There were no SAS casualties but two brothers – Oliver and Anthony Hughes – driving into Loughgall as the shooting started, were shot as they tried to reverse to avoid trouble. Anthony, aged thirty-six and the father of three children, was killed. His widow received 'substantial' compensation. The SAS also fired at another car being driven away by a woman with her young daughter as passenger. The NCO commanding one of the stop groups risked his own life to rescue her and was awarded a Military Medal.

The decision to let the bombers, while under surveillance, drive their unstable device unimpeded into an SAS killing ground foreshadowed the strategy adopted less than a year later at Gibraltar, where the three IRA terrorists were shot and killed by men of B squadron, SAS. In that case, the authorities confirmed that a suspected car-bomb had been allowed to pass through a crowded frontier post and through a busy shopping district, to be parked in preparation for an explosion forty-eight hours later. To the embarrassment of the security forces, the terrorists were found to be unarmed. The car they parked contained no bomb, though one was discovered subsequently, parked in Spain. A senior SAS officer, who dismissed the affair as 'the Gibraltar cull', had also, at an earlier stage of the regiment's involvement in Ireland, when Cleary was killed, told his men: 'I want to ensure that the IRA are dead. We are in this business to shoot them.'

The cull continued. Just after midnight on 30 June 1988, an IRA team hit a police station in North Queen Street, Belfast, with an RPG-7 anti-tank missile supplied by Libya. This was fired from the top of a saloon car. The SAS, waiting inside the building, fired back. They never discovered who owned the blood-stained jacket left at the scene. One casualty was identified, however. That was an uninvolved taxi driver, Ken Stronge, driving past as the shooting started. Stronge died three days later.

On 30 August that year Gerard Harte, aged twenty-nine, his brother Martin, aged twenty-two, and Brian Mullan, aged twenty-five, stalked a lorry driver who served in the Ulster Defence Regiment. An SAS decoy replaced the intended victim in the lorry cab. The IRA group died with Kalashnikovs in hand.

The list of IRA and other Republican terrorists killed in this now not-so-secret war lengthened steadily over the next two years: Martin Corrigan, aged twenty-five, at Kinnego, Armagh, on 18

April 1990; Desmond Grew, aged thirty-seven, and Martin McCaughey, aged twenty-three, shot while moving rifles to a new hide at Loughgall (increasing to ten the number of Republicans killed by the SAS in this village); Alexander Patterson, aged thirty-one, of the INLA at Strabane, 12 November 1990; Peter Ryan, aged thirty-seven, close-quarter assassin; Lawrence McNally, aged thirty-nine, and Tony Doris, aged twenty-one, intercepted at Coagh, Tyrone, on their way to a rendezvous with someone else's death; and Kevin Barry O'Donnell, aged twenty-one, at Clonoe, Coalisland, on 16 February 1992.

O'Donnell was determined to die for the cause. He was a student of agriculture in Shropshire when police found Kalashnikov rifles in his car in London. He persuaded a gullible English jury of his innocence. ('I don't support the IRA. I came from a devout Catholic family . . . they do not support the taking of life,' he claimed.) When the SAS killed him he was helping to fire a Russian armour-piercing Degtyarev heavy machine-gun (also from Libya), bolted on to the back of a lorry, at Coalisland police station. O'Donnell's former schoolfriend Sean O'Farrell, aged twenty-two, died with him as did Patrick Vincent, aged twenty, and Peter Clancy, aged twenty-one.

The loss of these young lives grieved their former headmaster, the priest Father Denis Faul. 'The IRA', he said, 'is a crazy outfit and should be disbanded.'

During the years that followed this waste of life, until the 1997 ceasefire, another five IRA deaths occurred at SAS hands. In 1997, an officer with long SAS service explained:

> From the outset, 22 SAS saw the Irish situation as 'A Terrorist Scenario', since that was our other role in the UK, as a counter-terrorist force. This blinkered our thinking and still does. The SAS is currently used as a hit squad, using counter-terrorist tactics superior to anything a Regular army or police unit can produce. The trouble is that this is a particularly ruthless policy. You go for 'bursts' at a body target on the premise that he/she could be wearing body armour. We failed to see that the principles we had used in Dhofar – hearts-and-minds – could have been applied equally in

Northern Ireland. To this day I do not think the SAS has seen parallels between Dhofar and Northern Ireland and by now, with the protagonists set in their ways, it is irrelevant. From the start, the directive was 'to start nailing some of those bandits especially in South Armagh, to capture or, if necessary kill them, within the rules of law applied in Northern Ireland'. The upper echelons of the Regiment appreciated the delicacy of this. The soldiers did not. Coming from Dhofar and trained to shoot on sight or be shot, the limitations of the Yellow Card in the Province were to rankle. Later, many of the men left in disgust.

This did not mean that the SAS took no prisoners, as Sean McKenna learned when he was woken up to be told: 'I want to explain the case to you. Do you realize that I could have shot you? If you want to put up a struggle or if you don't want to come, say so. I will have no hesitation about shooting you now.' ('I said that I would go with them,' McKenna admitted later.) When the SAS took control of a siege, as it did after the murder of Richard Westmacott in Belfast in 1980, then it accepted a clearly signalled, unambiguous surrender. This consistent history of taking prisoners when that could be done without risk suggests that Peter Cleary – the first man to be killed by the SAS in Ireland – was, in truth, shot while trying to escape. The unofficial motto of the regiment, however was: 'I do not believe in dying for my country: I help the other guy to die for his.' No other SAS soldier was willing to take the deadly risk to which one of their team, Lance-Corporal Al Slater, exposed himself on a quiet road in Fermanagh on a December night in 1984. Slater, thanks to a signals intercept, knew that the IRA was close by. A man strolled towards him, acting as decoy. Slater asked him a question. As he did so an IRA team shot Slater from a roadside ditch. Mortally wounded, Slater fired back, killing the decoy, a long-standing IRA man and Irish army deserter named Tony MacBride. SAS flares lit the scene and MacBride's companions fled. One of them, Kieran Fleming, drowned in the river Bannagh as he tried to swim to sanctuary across the border. Operations such as Loughgall, 1987, and Gibraltar, 1988,

reflected the growing strength of Intelligence and surveillance operations directed at the IRA after the latter's high-profile successes
over almost ten years. The IRA, since 1979, had murdered Lord
Mountbatten; slaughtered eighteen Paras at Warrenpoint; run a
successful bombing campaign in Britain, including the Brighton
attack; killed eleven people at the Enniskillen Remembrance Day
service; and acquired huge supplies of arms and explosives from
Libya. With enhanced Intelligence – and the seeming control over
events that that gave to military commanders – civilians were
increasingly in the firing line as a result of ambush operations.
Compensation was invariably awarded, but the deaths of civilians
ensnared by an undeclared war with no front-lines were perceived
(to borrow a phrase from the Sinn Fein leader Ruairi O'Bradaigh)
to be 'one of the hazards of urban guerrilla warfare'. The death
O'Bradaigh had in mind was that of Angela Gallagher, a Catholic,
killed on Iveagh Street, Belfast, on 3 September 1971. She was hit
by a badly directed burst of automatic fire from an IRA weapon.
She was just seventeen months old. As the American author and
authority on the IRA J. Bowyer Bell put it: 'War, any war, is not
tidy. Mistakes killed the transient and unlucky. Mistakes seemed
integral to the armed struggle.'

Coherently organized military Intelligence proved to be the most
pervasive influence that the SAS brought to bear in Ireland, a more
potent weapon than its formidable firepower, skill-at-arms and
courage. The process was controlled by an elite officer-group within
the regiment, running the Intelligence and Security Group and
much else. In time, some of its offspring would outgrow and out-
match the regiment in the Intelligence-gathering game. A coalition
of Intelligence agencies, sometimes working uneasily together,
sometimes engaged in internecine warfare, emerged.

British civilian agencies included the Security Service, MI5; the
Secret Intelligence Service, MI6; GCHQ; and the National Criminal Intelligence Service. Military teams, working under the Intelligence and Security Group, were the SAS troop posted to the
Province; 14 Intelligence Company; the Field Reconnaissance Unit,
running its informers in competition with the RUC Special Branch;
various other arms of the Intelligence Corps such as the Weapons

Intelligence Unit and the computer experts of 12 Intelligence Company. The RAF provided aerial photography for Intelligence officers via its Reconnaissance Interpretation Centre, flying Canberras and other aircraft while using long-range Nimrods on tracking missions against IRA arms smugglers in international waters. The Army Air Corps flew Beavers carrying infra-red and thermal imagery gear to identify buried 'treasure'.

The theoretical leader in the war against terrorism in Northern Ireland after 1976 was the Royal Ulster Constabulary, whose Special Branch ran the most complete network of informer-agents (for the good reason that the RUC's personnel were not posted to the Province for two or three years; they were there permanently). The RUC had its own surveillance experts of E4A; its own 'hit squad' of Headquarters Mobile Support Units and – when it came to terrorist crime – the world's best forensic science department. In Britain, co-ordination of police and military activity to halt IRA attacks was left to the Special Branch, itself a loosely organized entity, until 1992, when MI5 took over that task.

What all these agencies shared, learning from the SAS as well as their own experience, was high morale. The army's role in the years after Operation Motorman and the end of an army-led war, stripped to its essentials, was reactive and bad for morale. The army's street patrols offered ready targets to snipers. Terrorist bombs, cunningly booby-trapped, killed and maimed ordnance teams sent to defuse them. In the countryside, where it was still a soldiers' war, military vehicles were shredded in the sudden mayhem of culvert bombs triggered remotely. When the troops moved by helicopter to evade that threat, they were at risk from cones of fire directed at airspace above military bases by IRA machine-guns. Even behind the wire at fortified bases in Germany as well as Ireland, the soldiers were not safe from mortar attack.

The Intelligence elite and the SAS hit squad, by contrast, were licensed to take the war to the enemy. They were not victims. By 1996, the new culture of directed Intelligence had proliferated like some exotic plant inside a greenhouse in Bedfordshire, new home of the Defence Intelligence and Security School. The system could run effective surveillance on an entire population and, through the use of psychological warfare (reserved, so far, for use in Bosnia), shape popular perceptions of events to suit a military strategy. It gave enormous power to those in charge of the system in Northern Ireland, free from most constraints. As Michael Mates put it, reflecting on his period as Northern Ireland Secretary in 1991–92:

> I never had to go looking for power. This is where Northern Ireland is different. You had more than you could use. If I thought the Security Forces needed an extra £10 millions, I could give it to them. That's power. I had power to let prisoners out of prison; power to keep them in; power to stop their visits and change their conditions: to put a glass panel between them and others. I didn't have to go to Parliament for these . . . There's no bloody democracy down there. That's why it works so well. I've never been happier. I had power. But one keeps very quiet about it.

Having served its purpose across the water, could this Security-coalition machine be employed at home? It is a plausible nightmare scenario, and not just one dreamed up by the British Left, or what remains of it. That it is not much misused has everything to do with the conservatism (with a small 'c') of the British officer corps and the army's policy of moving on key people at regular intervals, even at the risk of reduced efficiency following a change of command. The turnover of ministers within governments and of governments themselves has also checked potential abuse of an Orwellian creation, the monster created to contain the IRA. Yet it remains a creature more dangerous than anything to emerge from the monster-rich culture of Irish mythology and, like nuclear weaponry, it cannot be uninvented.

9

The Eyeball, the Eavesdrop and the Judas Kiss

There are two ways to penetrate an army that wears no uniform. One route is from within, using informers and planted double-agents, adding worms to a wormhole, as it were. The other is external, like the early bird waiting for the worm to surface. The first depends almost entirely on human beings. The second employs eavesdropping and other surveillance gear from cameras the size of a pinhead to satellites. In practice, a combination of all means of Intelligence-gathering is used to track suspected terrorists.

In Northern Ireland, where around 3,000 killers are thought to be at large among a population of 1.5 million people, at least 1 million names are now on some security agency's computer. In Britain, the total number of suspects stored in the databanks of MI5's Branch (through its Joint Computer Bureau), the Special Branch, the National Criminal Intelligence Service and the rest, is around 2 million. Merely calling at the 'wrong' address at a time when it is under surveillance is sufficient to earn a place as an 'associate' of a suspect group on, say, the Special Branch computer, not only in the war-torn Province but also in the Home Counties. Innocently storing a package for a friend can lead to a long prison sentence on both sides of the Irish Sea. The figures quoted above, unofficially provided by army and civilian Intelligence officers of various kinds, represent only a fraction of the effort now invested in the silent war.

Only rarely does this lead to an SAS ambush; or a sectarian assassination by Protestant ultras doubling as members of the Security Forces; or the 'own-goal' bomb that explodes prematurely;

or the doctored bullet that blows up in the barrel of the IRA gun, killing the gunman. All these are very high-risk strategies, mostly deniable, usually unauthorized. More commonly, the result is to put a terrorist into the Maze prison for years, using forensic evidence that can be exposed to the enemy – such as a tell-tale fibre or bloodstain – rather than the whispered word that really started the chain of evidence. The Intelligence orchestra created by the British since 1969 is unique. Its time came, internationally, with the end of the Cold War. The 'New World Order' diplomacy, made in Washington, depended upon identifying charismatic 'bad guys' and arresting them, alive or dead. It was the strategy of the Hollywood western, enforced globally. In dealing with terrorists, the Federal Bureau of Investigation claimed worldwide jurisdiction. As a result of the Irish War, the British could, and did, deliver the necessary skills in places such as Bosnia.

What could never be achieved was a totally unified Intelligence Command. The IRA took the war to England, to Germany and Holland and to the Irish Republic itself. The War of the Four Campaigns was born and each spawned its own Intelligence teams. Where a synthesis did happen it was usually due to one or two army units. These were the SAS regiment and the Intelligence Corps. On the main battleground of the Six Counties, the SAS formed links with both MI5 and the Ulster Special Branch.

In the late 1970s, Sergeant Alan Brewer (a *nom de guerre*), an SAS soldier known to his friends as the Snake, took part in a pioneering exercise of this synthesis of stealthy Intelligence and military initiative. 'I find myself yomping across fields in South Armagh, carrying this bloody great ladder, with this geezer from Box Five Hundred.' (Box Five Hundred is the Post Office box number for MI5 and a thinly disguised code among insiders to refer to the Security Service. Sometimes it is abbreviated simply to 'Box', though since the Secret Intelligence Service, MI6, is known as Box Eight Fifty, for similar reasons, there can be confusion unless the context is clear.) 'We were going to a house owned by a leading Pira target. Usually, we watched the place from a distance. I couldn't understand why we were just going to walk in there with the ladder, screw the place, bug it with electronics and walk away again.'

What Brewer was about to learn was that Box had tricks which even the SAS would not consider employing. One in particular, used in Britain as well as Ireland, was to entice a target away from his house through the offer of a lavish holiday in the sun, all expenses paid. The target was persuaded that he, or she, had won the holiday by chance in a competition to promote a breakfast food. The agency took care to confirm that a real competition existed and that a real prize was on offer. The agency's lookalike holiday was also real and paid for from MI5's secret budget. While the target was away, the Security Service would plant a host of listening devices. In time, it was even possible to install a miniaturized video camera inside a domestic light switch.

A former officer of the Security Service confirmed that the decoy holiday (the 'dodgy holiday') was a standard part of its repertoire: 'We only had trouble once in persuading a Republican family to go away. The father was an IRA quartermaster in Luton. He was happy to take the bait. It was his wife who was really suspicious.'

In theory, Intelligence flowed from the Joint Intelligence Committee and Directorate of Military Intelligence in London through the Northern Ireland Office to Stormont in one direction and the military Intelligence cell at HQ Northern Ireland (the Intelligence and Security Group) in another, down two parallel ladders belonging, respectively, to the RUC and the army. In practice, the system was a dynamic, organic, devious beast which reflected shifting personalities, priorities, rivalries and loyalties. The RUC's special firearms Headquarters Mobile Support Unit involved in controversial 'shoot-to-kill' episodes was SAS-trained. The RUC's surveillance experts of E4A were trained by MI5 and the army's own Watchers, 14 Intelligence Company and its front-line detachments (the 'Dets'). In its turn, 14 Company was originally invented by an SAS officer who had also served in SIS. Such convolutions give depth to the phrase 'the Intelligence Community'.

The Intelligence war against the IRA got off to a bad start. Although an MI6 assessment in 1966 concluded that the Republicans, half a century after the Dublin rebellion, were a serious threat, the movement's deception plan, concealing its renewed campaign beneath a cloak of civil rights, worked well enough to deceive the

RUC Special Branch, the leading agency involved between 1968 and the early 1970s. As someone with access to Special Branch assessments at the time later admitted: 'They were unreal. They never predicted anything but a campaign similar to the fifties campaign, which had been easily contained.' The fact that Protestant ultras such as Ian Paisley claimed that the civil rights movement was really a front for the IRA in itself served only to convince many people that this was not the case; that the IRA truly was a lifeless fossil.

When the army arrived on the scene in 1969, it perceived the RUC as a busted, discredited force. Intelligence was not to be shared with the police. Classified documents, even at Stormont Castle, were for years to come designated 'UK Eyes Only: Not for RUC'. The RUC's monumental failure to identify current, as distinct from long-retired, IRA men when the army, pressured by Stormont, interned 1,576 people in 1971, confirmed the impression that the local police were inept. Of 342 suspects picked up in the first twenty-four hours, 115 were released within two days.

Prior to the decision to give back primacy for security to the police in 1977, the use and misuse of Intelligence by the army reflected the adoption of an old-fashioned strategy of counter-insurgency generally: a heavy-booted policy of military repression. The Province was also a new, fertile hunting ground for ambitious men and women from both box numbers. The Chief of Intelligence at Stormont Castle after direct rule was Craig Smellie of MI6; his successor, Ian Cameron of MI5. From 1971 to 1977, MI6 had its own headquarters in a large suburban house at Laneside, on the shores of Belfast Lough, where paramilitaries and British officials could meet on safe ground. To impose order and dampen rivalries which often led to the compromise (and death of) agents of one agency by another, Prime Minister Thatcher appointed Sir Maurice Oldfield, an old MI6 hand now in retirement, as security co-ordinator. In time he was exposed by his RUC protection team as a homosexual who consorted with rent-boys. Nevertheless, secret political contacts were maintained, through MI6 'back-channels' for most of the war between successive British governments and the IRA. Political Intelligence and Military Intelligence are not the same thing and so, regardless of the temperature of the war or the state of the ceasefire, the war of Military Intelligence continued. So did the whispered political exchanges. Usually the two processes worked against each other.

The army did not wish to talk to terrorists, but to kill them. Brigadier Frank Kitson, the guru of covert penetration and commander of British forces in Belfast, following his successes with 'counter-gangs' during the Kenya Mau-Mau campaign, argued: 'We beat terrorists before we negotiate with them.' An SAS commander had told his team in 1976: 'We are in business to shoot them.'

The counter-gang philosophy became blood brother of the army's Intelligence game in a series of near-private wars between 1971 and 1976. At the base of the pyramid were the uniformed battalions, on tours lasting a few months. These carried out mass arrests so as to identify potential informers and to provide a safe cover within which to talk to a single, known source. Lieutenant-Colonel Robin Evelegh, commanding the Royal Green Jackets in Belfast in 1972, revealed that to speak safely to a single informer it might be necessary to 'talk compulsorily' to fifty people. In 1980, the Royal Scots, seeking the gunman who shot a soldier in West Belfast, raided 604 homes to question local people. Such activities were a gift to IRA propagandists. They also turned some Republicans into informers, through the simple process of planting weapons or ammunition and following that up with the threat of life imprisonment for possession. Such freelance activities did not always go unnoticed. In 1976 five soldiers of the Black Watch regiment were themselves imprisoned for planting ammunition on people in the Republican Andersonstown district of Belfast. But some people were 'turned' by this means and, when they were, they were recruited to a typical counter-gang, the Mobile Reconnaissance Force, a military team in civilian dress created by Brigadier Kitson.

As it happened, the SAS, fighting a secret war against communist guerrillas in Oman, was following a similar path, using former enemies as *their* native guides. In Oman, these units were known as 'firqas'. In Belfast, they were 'freds'. With the help of the freds, the MRF identified active Provisionals, then shot them, usually from moving, unmarked cars, using the IRA's own gangster weapon, the Thompson sub-machine-gun. Random casualties who once included a man in bed near the scene, might have been forgiven for concluding that the bullets they picked out of their bodies were fired by one faction or another of the IRA. The leader of one MRF gun team, having admitted in court what he had done, was not convicted of any offence. Ian Gilmour, Minister of State for Defence, questioned in Parliament about the MRF's activities, said: 'Intelligence is vital in dealing with terrorism. The whole House will be grateful for and surprised by the restraint and care the Army uses in dealing with terrorists.'

The freds were at risk from both sides. A deserter from the Royal Irish Rangers joined the Provisionals' 1st battalion in Andersonstown, was arrested by the army and recruited to the freds. An influential Intelligence officer in those days recalled:

> While he was with the MRF he continued feeding information back to the IRA about the MRF. We intercepted the information he was sending, changed it and fed false information back to the Provos. Eventually the Provos got to him. He was shot outside the Royal Victoria Hospital, Belfast. He was a remarkable character. He lived in a house under Army guard yet he arranged to send out details of MRF vehicles, their registration numbers and the people MRF worked with.
>
> His dead letter box was like something out of James Bond. He extracted a brick from a wall at a house in Broadway. He would put a note in there while on patrol; then put a chalk mark or a scratch to signal that there was a message. The Provos left a different mark when they collected it.

The army did not share Ian Gilmour's sunny view of the MRF, disbanded it and for a time relied upon its own two-tier Intelligence structure at its Lisburn headquarters, where a faceless SAS officer ran the 'dirty raincoat brigade' along the corridor from the orthodox staff officer known as G2 (Int), who conducted briefings. (G2 would intercept his counterpart to ask: 'When you come in from your Dirty Mac operations, could you pop in and give us a bit of pepper-and-salt for the morning briefing?'). But as violence exploded in

England as well as the Province, there was a vacuum where there should have been Intelligence. The experimental use of the SAS in 1974 to fill the gap left by the MRF was a messy failure.

Nevertheless, the regiment provided some of the most innovative minds in the Intelligence game, usually in command of the Intelligence & Security Group controlling other more shadowy teams. Members of the group included Captain Robert Nairac, who should have remained at his desk but preferred to pass himself off as a hard Belfast man in the deadly territory of South Armagh. He was snatched from the Three Steps pub at Forkhill after singing an Irish ballad or two, taken away and assassinated simply on suspicion of being 'not right' by the border team of the IRA. His body was never found. Intelligence officers working with him concluded that it had been carved up and fed to pigs in the Irish Republic.

Groups controlled by Int & Sy Gp, as it was known, included a new military reconnaissance team, first known as '4 Field Survey Troop' of the Royal Engineers or the Northern Ireland Training and Tactics Team (NITAT). Later it was '14 Int Company'. This team's front-line soldiers – women as well as men – wore civilian clothes to conceal weapons ranging from a fighting knife to a sub-machine-gun. They served with sub-units known as the 'Dets' from secret bases serviced directly by air from Britain. A senior SAS officer is credited with creating this stand-off surveillance team in 1974. Its people were chosen for a combination of physical endurance, good judgement and quick wits. They had to be capable of hiding out for long periods in cramped attics, derelict barns or even the boots of cars; mentally agile enough to use the mind as a camera in a brief glimpse of an IRA home while camouflaged in civilian clothes; and be skilled in driving Q cars which could dispense a barrage of exploding stun grenades, like a man-o'-war of Nelson's day firing a broadside, if that were needed to clear a way through a hostile crowd. As 'courting couples', women and men of the Dets learned to pick the locks of doorways where, to the casual observer, they were making love, not war. In some senses they reflected the deep reconnaissance, high-risk life of the Long Range Desert Group, on which the pioneers of the 1st SAS depended so much in the Second World War.

The price of compromise was life itself; the risks recognized by the very high number of bravery awards, such as the Queen's Gallantry Medal, made to men and women serving with the Dets; more, certainly, than were won by the SAS and probably exceeding the number won by any other group. The unit suffered its first loss in April 1974 when Captain Anthony Pollen, Coldstream Guards, was spotted by Republican 'dickers' (lookouts), surrounded and shot dead in hostile Bogside. In 1981, a young officer of 14 Company, driving alone in Derry in an Opel Q car, was stopped abruptly by an Escort which cut in front of him. Two IRA heavies, George McBrearty and Charles Maguire, stepped out of the blocking car, armed with Armalites. One guarded each end of the Opel. With his foot, the officer hit a secret communication button hidden on the floor to summon help and eased his pistol from beneath his thigh. As McBrearty approached him, he shot him through the window, four times. From the rear, Maguire shot into the car but missed as the British agent swung his door open and rolled out, turned and fired into his adversary's head. The other two members of the IRA team were still in their car. The officer jumped back into his vehicle and fired at the Escort, using the driver's door as a defensive shield before reversing away and swinging out of trouble in a fast J-turn, followed by more IRA bullets. He left two terrorists dead and a third wounded. The IRA, embarrassed, falsely claimed that this had been an SAS ambush in which they were outgunned and outnumbered. It was this experience that prompted 14 Int Company to fit to its Q cars the extra refinement of stun grenades.

From the mid 1970s, orthodox regiments were also learning the ways of this new, covert warfare, dropping reconnaissance teams unseen into ditches after dark, resupplying them and collecting their ordure as opportunity arose. In 1977, Major-General Dick Trent, Commander of Land Forces in the Province, raised the Close Observation Platoons, teams of thirty men from infantry battalions who were given advanced tuition in the sort of work 14 Int Company and the SAS were doing at close quarters in high-risk areas. There was much cross-fertilization. The first boss of 4 Field Survey Troop was Tony Ball, a former Parachute regiment and SAS corporal, ultimately promoted to lieutenant-colonel. Commissioned into the King's Own Scottish Borderers, he ran his regiment's reconnaissance platoon in 1972 and created the army's first covert observation post in Republican Belfast. One of his friends said: 'Tony actually enjoyed risk.' Ball's progress in the Irish conflict was later to take a sinister turn. In time he left the British army to join the Sultan's Special Force in Oman as a mercenary, and died in a high-speed desert road accident.

In 1973, yet another group was hatched within the army's Intelligence centre at Ashford, Kent, home of the Intelligence Corps. Founded in 1940, the Corps was the prep school for grandees of British Intelligence, ranging from the novelist John Le Carré (as Captain David Cornwell) to Maurice Oldfield. Its other stars included a Foreign Secretary (Michael Stewart), actors (Michael Denison and Leonard Rossiter), academics (Correlli Barnett and Lord Dacre) and the Queen's dressmaker, Sir Hardy Amies. The Corps was also the training ground for thousands of soldiers never formally 'badged' as Intelligence operatives, but sent on high-risk assignments behind the Iron Curtain to work with the Brixmis spy mission at Potsdam. In 1972, Ashford invited volunteers to act as Military Intelligence officers and Military Intelligence Liaison officers. The three-month training course was a novel one. As well as covert photography, volunteers learned to handle a variety of weapons known to be in IRA hands but not issued to the British army. Even more extraordinary, they were taught to make terrorist devices, including a petrol-bomb ignited by chemical means, and advanced guerrilla warfare techniques including the conversion of a wine bottle into a shaped explosive charge capable of cutting through three inches of mild steel. This was hardly the stuff of defensive strategy. One reason for such lessons became apparent, according to one graduate, when 'in our practical test we used this technique to blow out the dial combination lock on a safe'. Lock-picking was also on the Intelligence school's curriculum. The Dets' favourite burglary tool was a hooked instrument known as Slim Jim, used for car thefts. (Average time for this operation: three seconds.)

One aspect of Det training was unique. A memoir by one of the team, Captain 'James Rennie', reveals that they learned to speak with a variety of Irish accents (a skill that did not save Nairac's life):

To operate effectively we had to be able to hold our own in everyday conversations in the different areas that we would deploy to, and to achieve this we had been voice-coached regularly by a charming retired Irish actor and his wife. They played us tapes of the different regional accents, from the relatively soft lilt of South Armagh, with its galloping delivery, to the harsher, slightly clipped, but more measured tones of North Belfast. Now they led us in conversation classes, taking the opportunity to instruct us in certain cultural aspects of Irish life.

The training of both groups suggested an illegal, short-cut to Intelligence-gathering by men and women who went armed with IRA weapons which, if used to kill someone, would not point too obviously to a British undercover unit. Only half of the volunteers passed the Ashford course. Those who did went on to work alongside the Royal Ulster Constabulary as police liaison officers, serving in a Special Military Intelligence Unit. As an SAS officer explained his links with the RUC after 1976: 'They had the knowledge. We could do their dirty work.' One officer stretched the dubious ethics of this odd liaison by burglarizing the secret files of the RUC unit to which he was attached. He was caught and sent home. Mutual animosities between most Military Intelligence officers and their RUC counterparts continued through the next twenty years or so.

Two styles of external surveillance – bird watching worm, as distinct from worm watching worm – were now emerging. One was military reconnaissance, favoured by the SAS and Close Observation Platoons (COPs) standing off at a distance and remaining undetected. Sometimes this meant that when sudden intervention was needed to save lives – assassination attempts against Bernadette Devlin (Mrs McAliskey) and the first plot against Gerry Adams were examples – help came almost too late. The other method used by MI5 and the Dets, was to get in close and think of a plausible cover story to explain away any accident or compromise that resulted.

When MI5 and the special army units worked together in Ireland, it was usually because the Security Service operator was a technician, wiring a terrorist suspect's home with concealed cameras and microphones. As one MI5 operator put it: 'There are homes in this Blessed Isle where the occupant sits to watch his television, which we have rigged so that the television is watching him.' In time, the IRA's bombing campaigns in England and the run-down of the Cold War led to increasing involvement by Box Five Hundred in the Irish War. In October 1992, it became the leading Intelligence agency against Republican terrorism in Britain. In Northern Ireland, the RUC kept theoretical control, led by a tiny elite of thirty Special Branch officers, ten of whom were lost in a helicopter crash in June 1994.

At 6 p.m. on 2 June that year an RAF Chinook helicopter struck a cliff on the Mull of Kintyre, Western Scotland. Among the twenty-nine dead were six senior MI5 officers, including its Director and Co-ordinator of Intelligence; ten of the RUC Special Branch, including the Boss, whose combined experience represented 246 years of intelligence-gathering; and nine Army Intelligence officers, including a full colonel who was the head of military intelligence in the Province. The victims were on their way to an annual intelligence junket.

The RAF attributed the crash to 'pilot error' in spite of the machine's history of chronic technical problems, the absence of a radar system or flight recorder. In the preceding decade, six of the RAF's Chinook fleet of only forty-one machines had crashed.

The damage to Intelligence was contained, thanks to the computerised logs of every agent-informer 'transaction'. This was not Dublin 1920, when Michael Collins's assassination 'squad' could blind official intelligence at a single stroke. Nonetheless the loss was grievous. As one RUC source put it: 'The bare facts may be on computer, but computers don't have judgement, understanding. These guys knew the psychology of the people they were dealing with, they knew the political nuances; the body language. No computer can give you that.'

After the crash, MI5 sent its men and women on operations not only to the Province but to the Irish Republic also, without mentioning this to its own Directorate of Counter-Intelligence in Ulster. Box's methods of surveillance and counter-surveillance were also taught, if clumsily, to the Ashford graduates by the SMIU group. The remorseless advance of MI5 worried some people. John Alderson, adviser on law and order to the Council of Europe, said: 'MI5 is not under the same restraints as the police. They infiltrate organisations, people's jobs and lives. They operate almost like a cancer, infiltrating and destroying trust. The acorn of a *Stasi* has been planted. It is there for future governments to build on.' By contrast, Stella Rimington, Director-General of MI5, could claim in 1994 that the agency had foiled 80 per cent of attempted terrorist attacks in Northern Ireland and that it now devoted nearly half its resources, including 2,000 agents, to the Irish War.

The branch of MI5 in charge of static and mobile surveillance was and is A4, part of A branch (Operations & Intelligence) in a fast-growing empire that has at least fourteen main departments and many sub-units. The field officers of A4 are dedicated expert people who are often treated as a lesser breed by the desk analysts and policy-makers. Foot surveillance is taught to students of MI5 and military Intelligence officers using a drill known as the A-B-C system. At least three people are used to follow the target: A (for Adjacent, also known as the 'Eyeball') is nearest; B (Back-up) is further back, preferably concealed from the quarry. Both usually stick to the same side of the road. C (Control) has a wide field of vision on the opposite side of the road, guiding the other two with concealed throat microphone and/or discreet hand signals. A guide for novice trackers suggests: 'Behave naturally; have a purpose for being there; be prepared with a cover story (ensure that it fits the situation); remember you are most vulnerable when coming from cover.' The guidance deals with distance from the target, anticipation, body language, local knowledge, concentration and teamwork.

Means by which the target is kept off-guard include 'boxing' and 'paralleling'. 'The subject is allowed to proceed on a route where there are a minimal number of surveillance officers. The idea is to let the subject "run" from point to point to be checked at various places by surveillance officers on parallel routes or ahead.' Even if new faces are introduced into the surveillance team, close control deteriorates in this form of play. However, 'the most important factor about surveillance is the need to be honest about exposure.

It is better to have a controlled loss rather than to hang on to the subject too long.'

The MI5 technique is manpower-intensive. Up to fifty Watchers might be needed to maintain twenty-four-hour cover on a single target. The result was a drive to recruit a large number of officers in a short time.

Ashford's graduates and MI5 Watchers discovered there was a big difference between running surveillance exercises in suburban shops around Kent or inner London pubs, and the Republican ghettos of Ireland where children absorb in their pushchairs a wariness of new faces, where women hammer the pavement with bin lids as a warning of strangers at the door.

There is one door the IRA cannot guard. This is the gateway to the next world, the Republican funeral. It is more than a burial ritual as other soldiers understand it. It follows the tradition of that ancient Celtic warrior caste, the *fianna*, a caste 'subject only to the authority of their leaders and standing apart from and largely independent of normal society'. The *fianna* claim their own at the moment of departure, regardless of the wishes of lawful next-of-kin. This was true of the hunger-striker Frank Stagg in 1976 and the Aldwych bus bomber Edward O'Brien in 1996. As the *Daily Telegraph* reported: 'Appeals by the family of Edward O'Brien . . . to be allowed to bury their son in peace were ignored as prominent members of the IRA and Sinn Fein arrived at his funeral. There was no gun salute . . . but the presence of the republican terrorists was unmistakable when O'Brien, aged 21, was interred in his native town of Gorey.' Those attending included Willie McGuinness, brother of Martin, the ex-IRA chieftain and Sinn Fein negotiator.

Such gatherings were usually impossible to conceal and provided the Watchers of MI5 and others with the perfect opportunity to target an individual terrorist, photograph him, tail him and learn more about his associates and current base. It was no surprise to SAS insiders to spot, among Republican mourners at a televised funeral, one of their officers in civilian dress, mingling with the press and carrying his reporter's notebook.

Mobile surveillance is a variant of that old Hollywood movie favourite, the car chase. MI5 regards a convoy of four to five cars plus a motorcycle outrider as normal for the pursuit of a single target. It will also use an aircraft such as an Islander – hired from a civilian contractor – in rural areas where 'heel clipping' by a car would be too obvious. Car drills include paralleling as well as boxing and following but at night, on a long chase, they are not always sufficient. The agency's field officers chasing an IRA car from Cricklewood to Stranraer overnight knew that their quarry was carrying weapons when he began his journey. They lost him briefly at a motorway halt and, many hours later, the target was clean when arrested.

Technology has made life easier. Pinhead-sized cameras can be concealed inside car wing-mirrors and controlled remotely. Suspect homes on both sides of the Irish Sea are now watched, twenty-four hours a day, by not one but an array of hidden cameras monitored at a distant control room. Tracing devices have been miniaturized since the clumsy transmitter known as 'The Brick', with its long spike-antenna, was attached to the cars of Iraqi officials in London in 1991. ('We thought they were going to poison one of London's water supply reservoirs,' one officer said later.) At that time, MI5 Watchers could be identified by the patch of sticking plaster worn on the palm of the hand to cover the wound inflicted by the spike as they hurriedly attached it to the target. Stratagems used to attach the brick to a target vehicle, even when the scene was under closed-circuit television watch, included staging a fake road accident along-side the target to set up a 'casualty'. The casualty would be an MI5 field officer who would roll under the target car, now stationary, to do what had to be done. This sort of street theatre is anathema to SAS reconnaissance artists, who regard it as too flamboyant and probably ineffective.

In the late 1990s, tracing devices came as small, compact packages slipped under a bumper, transmitting to a GPS satellite and broadcasting the location of the target on to a map projected on to the screen of a portable computer. At £13,000 per unit, however, the system is not yet in wide circulation among Intelligence agencies. As a cheap alternative form of surveillance, MI5 or 14 Company will steal a targeted vehicle in the early hours, or while the owner is on a 'dodgy holiday' (see page 135) to wire it for sound, with miniature microphones and transmitters. Both tricks work only so long as the human quarry continues to use the same car. IRA veterans, wise in the ways of counter-surveillance, change their cars as often as they can steal or hijack them.

Robert Cross (*nom de guerre*) has long experience of this sort of work as an MI5 field officer. He has worked under so many aliases as to require a series of 'alias-keepers'. The alias-keeper accepts mail and inquiries addressed to the alias and provides convincing responses. If the alias has adopted the guise of a pork butcher, his alias-keeper is a real pork butcher who has been positively vetted by MI5 to do that job unpaid, for the honour of serving Queen and Country. As a bogus motorcycle courier, Cross stayed close to an IRA suspect driving a battered van in north London. The IRA man suddenly pulled to the kerb. Cross allowed the collision to occur, leapt off his machine and invited the van driver to get out and settle this small difference with his fists. The terrorist was now convinced that no real secret agent would behave like this. Not wishing to be further exposed he declined the offer of a street brawl. It was the sort of performance that would make the stealthy footpads of army Intelligence shudder, but it worked. MI5 now had a shrewd idea which scrap yard was being used as a workshop to build lorry bombs and mortars.

The work is enormously stressful. Cross, after an exacting day's work in London, changed identity to run a safe-house for an IRA bodyguard who had been turned and was now being debriefed. His alias required a totally separate set of credit cards and a new driving licence.

I had a van in the livery of my non-existent business. I had to infiltrate the village to make myself known and live a 'normal life'. The whole thing became a nightmare. I couldn't have any personal mail sent to me. My real domestic life was in chaos. In the safe-house, the television concealed a video camera facing the sofa. The IRA man made love on that. I had to ask him to move the television away when he was entertaining his girlfriend.

In Operation Flavius in Gibraltar in 1988, when three IRA

soldiers, including Mairead Farrell, were shot dead by the SAS, more than thirty Watchers from Box were involved for weeks beforehand. Some of them, simply by being voyeurs, acquired some degree of empathy with their targets. 'When we heard the SAS were being brought in, we knew how it would end,' one of them said later. 'It felt very doomy.' The whole thing was traumatic for one of the women on the team, who was just a few feet from Sean Savage when he died. He had been under surveillance even before he left Belfast, telling his mother that he was off for a healthy, cultural weekend in the *Gaeltacht* in Galway. 'When the shooting happened,' an MI5 source revealed, 'it should have come as no surprise, but it did.'

The Watcher identified at the Gibraltar inquest as Miss J said that Savage was 15 feet in front of her when he spun round in response to the sound of shots fired at the other two, some distance away. With two SAS soldiers she was in a narrow, tree-lined passageway, approaching a pedestrian underpass. The soldiers drew their guns and fired. One of them was closing in on Savage when a woman got between them. 'With one arm', said the soldier, 'I had to move the female away and with my other arm I drew my pistol and engaged Savage.' He fired nine shots. 'I fired the first round and carried on firing, very rapid, right into Savage's body as he was turning and fell away to the ground. The last two rounds were aimed at his head. This was possibly inches away from the ground, just before he became still.'

What of Miss J? She did not confirm that she was the woman who had tried to interpose her body between the soldier and his target, though no other woman was called to give evidence along those lines. She told the inquest that she was 'petrified' and terrified Savage might trigger a bomb or fire a gun. She continued: 'I felt Savage knew in an instant what was happening. I did not see him after that. I turned around immediately. I did not want to have eyeball contact . . . When I turned away from Savage I did not see anything. I heard a police siren still going. There was a lot of noise in my right ear through my earpiece from the radio.'

MI5 sources who have helped prepare this chapter knew members of the Gibraltar team. They assert that one of them, a woman, was so badly affected by the experience that she resigned from the agency and emigrated to Australia once the inquest was over. The SAS hit team, less unhappy, held a celebratory party at a restaurant on their return to Hereford.

Not all assignments ended so violently. The Birmingham-born Felim Hamill, an apparently gentle doctor of philosophy who rendered his name in Gaelic as O'Hadhmaill, had moved with his parents to Northern Ireland as a child. In 1978, a charge against him of murdering a special constable had been dropped for lack of evidence. In January 1994 – fourteen months after the Warrington bomb had killed two children – O'Hadhmaill moved to England, tracked by the Watchers, to a rented home in Accrington, Lancashire. They followed him to Preston, were surprised when he walked into the University of Central Lancashire, then discovered he had joined its staff. He was there just six weeks, commuting by train, sharing the same carriage with the same regular travellers. Some grumbled with him as they waited for the train that was always late. They, like the young couple so often holding hands in the train when it arrived, were all from MI5. O'Hadhmaill was under surveillance by teams following the A-B-C drill.

One day they watched as he returned home carrying a large plastic container, apparently part of a beer-making kit. He carefully unpacked and repacked the contents on the near-empty train. The Watcher leaning over the seat behind him noted that he wore gloves for this job. Then he unwrapped cigarette papers on which he had made notes, smiling as he did so. O'Hadhmaill's beer-making box was in reality part of his Sinn Fein Conjuror's Outfit and the notes were lists of targets: 'A' for military, 'P' for political and 'S' for strategic. They included, in code, details of senior politicians connected with the Province, oil and gas installations in Britain, prominent buildings, events such as Cruft's dog show and the date of a Royal Marines Band concert.

What he did not yet have was the Semtex. Across the water, RUC Special Branch learned from one of its informers that the IRA was shipping a car containing explosives to England. The Watchers picked it up as it was unloaded as part of a consignment carried by a car transporter at Fleetwood, Lancashire, on 13

February. The car, a silver Datsun, was taken south, unloaded and left in a car park at West Thurrock, Essex. After waiting several days, O'Hadhmaill travelled to London by train and then by cab to South Mimms motorway service station on the M25, where he waited for hours, only to return home. The Watchers at first believed that this was deliberate counter-surveillance on his part. As one officer explained: 'IRA suspects sometimes made a meal of counter-surveillance. I remember tailing a Provo car in London. It roared several times round the same roundabout while the driver wound down his window and lifted two fingers.' In fact, the same terrorist did this routinely, as prescribed by his trainers, with no knowledge of whether or not he was being followed. The Watchers did not think much of that. As one of them said: 'The KGB were real professionals. They never went in for that sort of thing. If they knew they were being followed they never "showed out".'

O'Hadhmaill was having trouble with his own people. Arrangements made for him to pick up the Datsun did not match the instructions he had been given. MI5 knew where the car was, he did not. Three times in five days he made the trip south by train and cab. Finally he went to Blackpool, then Bolton, to make telephone calls using code-words found in his wallet. This was an emergency procedure. Total silence was expected once an operation was up and running.

The Datsun was moved to a west London street, then to South Mimms service area. On 20 February, O' Hadhmaill returned there for the fourth time. The car's ignition key was concealed where only he would find it. He drove home to Accrington, followed by teams of Watchers. Two days later, he dismantled the seats of the car in a garage. The building was surrounded. Armed Special Branch officers, with MI5 men, stormed in to arrest him. 'He was a scared man,' one said later, 'so scared that he filled his pants.'

The Datsun was an arsenal on wheels. It contained 37lb (17kg) of Semtex, fifteen of the latest Mk-17 IRA time/power units, one for each bomb; seventeen detonators; two magnetic booby-trap bombs to be attached to the underside of cars driven by potential victims of assassination; a pistol and ammunition; all hidden in the seats and beneath the wheel arches.

O'Hadhmaill, when he had changed his underwear, did not contest the evidence against him, to the surprise of the police who now had to process the case. He described himself as a political prisoner. When he came to trial in November 1994 his defence counsel tried to claim that the IRA was moving towards peace when O'Hadhmaill was lifted. On 31 October, the movement had declared its 'complete ceasefire', encouraging many IRA prisoners to believe that their release was imminent. In truth, the war was not over. The trial judge, Mr Justice Rougier, did not believe it either, though he prayed that the peace initiative would ultimately succeed. He added that he could not understand how someone with O'Hadhmaill's philosophical background could reconcile himself 'with the killing of men, women and children whom you have no personal quarrel with. I do not know how you managed to persuade yourself that the end justifies the means.' O'Hadhmaill said he had started his trial 'unbowed and unbroken and I will be going out the same way'. He was sentenced to twenty-five years' imprisonment.

If O'Hadhmaill – a reconstructed expatriate Irishman in search of roots – was one stock figure on the landscape of this war, then the informer was another. Every agency – MI5, MI6, British Special Branch, RUC Special Branch, Gardai Special Branch and the army's agent-handling Field Reconnaissance Unit (FRU) – ran its network of spies and sleepers inside the various Republican organizations. It was a job that sometimes paid well, until the informer was caught by the IRA and executed summarily. The Swiss numbered bank account and the hooded body, a single shot in the brain, arms pinioned, dumped like garbage in a rain-ditch in South Armagh were all part of the culture. Some informers served up the same information to different Intelligence agencies, like a freelance journalist recycling the same story for different editors. Desk collators might discover that the collateral cover (confirmation) of the information supplied by one agent about another's input was, in fact, all from a single source.

Patrick Daly, a left-wing Irish activist living in the Bristol area in the 1970s, was a spectacularly successful informer. In 1974 he was one of the first to be arrested under the Prevention of Terrorism Act and threatened with deportation. He was a trusted political supporter of the political wing of the Irish National Liberation Army (INLA), a Republican splinter group specializing in VIP assassination. One of its victims, in 1979, was Airey Neave MP. Another, in 1990, was Ian Gow, whose murder led to the loss of a key parliamentary seat and, indirectly, to the sacking of Margaret Thatcher, who was increasingly perceived by her party as an electoral liability.

Daly was happily settled and married and disinclined to return to the old country when he was lifted. He agreed to become a Special Branch informer. Later he would also serve MI5 from a base in the Irish Republic. His first scalp was that of Peter Jordan, a retired schoolteacher and a neighbour in Bristol. Jordan seems to have had no Irish blood, just a bloody-minded dislike of English attitudes to the Irish. He went on a one-man crusade to do something about it. One day he spotted an item in the Engagements listings in a newspaper. It concerned the forthcoming marriage of the daughter of an SAS lieutenant-colonel. The wedding was to take place in a Herefordshire hamlet. With Daly as his driver, Jordan went to the village church, studied the list of churchwardens and others posted at the church door and suggested the target to INLA, which sent a team to England to kill the officer.

By this time, Daly was being paid £100 each month by the Special Branch, when he was not carrying banners in support of the Troops Out movement. He tipped off the Branch about Jordan's assassination scheme. The Branch tracked the INLA hit team members as they spent a carefree night in Liverpool, where a woman officer danced with one of them at a disco. The assassination squad was then arrested. So was Jordan, who went to prison for fourteen years. He was still unaware that Daly had informed on him. Daly wrote more than fifty letters to Jordan in prison, offering support, reminding him, 'Always remember you have friends and comrades outside to help you . . . Just say what you want and we will do it, whether it's pickets or MPs.' He didn't mean it, of course. It was that classic double-cross of the Intelligence game, the 'Judas Kiss' (also known as the 'Rubber Dick'), which Daly regarded as just another aspect of his cover.

In 1989, Daly moved to Galway in the Irish Republic and started a driving school. He was now run by MI5. It was a good time to work for Box, which was about to take over the leading Intelligence role in the war against the IRA. Special Branch's golden handshake was £2,180. 'I don't think it was big money,' he said. 'I was risking my life.' INLA was planning a bombing campaign in England. Daly was recruited to return to the area he knew – Bristol and the Mendips – where MI5 provided him with a safe-house. They also identified the stone quarry which the INLA sought, complete with an explosives store. Unlike the IRA, the INLA did not have Semtex. Nor did they seem to have sufficient knowledge to build effective HME bombs from fertilizer. Box put together an impressive-looking package of 'explosive' and 'detonators', all harmless. The trap (codenamed Operation Breaksea) was now baited.

The INLA sent three of its best operators to England, guided by Daly. Martin McMonagle from Limerick, Liam Heffernan from Belfast and Anthony Gorman, another Belfast man wanted for the 1992 murder of an army recruiting sergeant in Derby. Within the bugged safe-house, the three were heard discussing their tactics if they were compromised. According to one of the MI5 team, they swore a death-pact. None proposed to be taken alive. Police marksmen were advised accordingly. The process had something in common with Gibraltar, where a senior MI5 officer's briefing of the SAS hit squad convinced the soldiers that it would make sense to shoot first and ask questions afterwards. The INLA team sent to Somerset were luckier than the IRA three in Gibraltar. The ambush into which they walked was manned by armed police officers, who prefer arrest to killing. On his way to the explosives store, McMonagle tripped over one of the police and a struggle began. Gorman raced away to a successful escape, eluding search dogs and helicopters. The other two were arrested. Heffernan was sentenced to twenty-three years' imprisonment and McMonagle to twenty-five years.

Throughout their trial, the defence constantly challenged the role of the informer Daly. Was he merely an informer or an *agent-provocateur*? Was MI5 defending the realm or its own political position in Whitehall, setting up a 'sting' operation, illegally planning a crime which it could then solve at a time when it needed a spectacular success to justify its new prominence in the Irish War? Daly's controller, 'C', described him as 'an outstanding agent' whose cover was now blown. He and his family were given new identities and a payment of £400,000. But as Mr Nigel Sweeney, crown prosecutor, put it: 'He has in effect put himself in prison for the rest of his life. If he had been discovered there would not have been for him a three-week trial at the Old Bailey, just a quick bullet in the back of the head.' Another MI5 officer, 'A', was asked whether his organization had needed 'a considerable Intelligence coup' during discussions with Special Branch about their Intelligence roles. 'A' agreed, but added: 'That did not manifest itself to people on the ground.' He denied that the INLA bomb plot was instigated by MI5. The jury believed him.

In England by the mid-1990s, the IRA was feeling the heat. Communication was a major headache. No army, not even a secret army, can function without good 'coms'. For the Republicans, there was a limit to the number of contacts that could be made in person, though this was the only certain way to avoid the pervasive, baleful presence of Box. Coded signals in newspaper small-ads lacked the flexibility of two-way conversation. The terrorists learned not to write letters, even in code. The agency would stake out the likely letter box as well as the target's home, then follow a well-rehearsed drill to intercept the target's mail. As one field officer explained: 'One of us would address a letter to himself and stamp it. As soon as the target had posted his letter, we would do the same. We would have authority to order the postman or sorter to hand over all the mail. The letter we wanted was immediately beneath our dummy letter, or very close to it.' As an alternative the IRA tried pagers, but British cryptologists broke the codes being used.

With American help, the Republicans experimented with e-mail. It is theoretically possible to relay a message from, say, Belfast to London via Tokyo and Anchorage while concealing the sender's identity and address. The expert advice was: 'Don't do anything silly like planning to assassinate the President. *They* have ways of finding you.' The US National Security Agency, the world's biggest eavesdropper, has always had close links with Britain's GCHQ. Instead of secret communications on the net, the Republicans went public, with websites to seek popular support. But this was no way to run a war. By 1997, contact between an IRA bomb team in England and its controllers in the Irish Republic were sustained only by telephone calls at pre-arranged times between public telephones in bars or on the street in both countries. Even then the English end of the contact was often compromised by the Watchers.

MI5 was to have its failures as well as its successes after establishing its leading role. For a time its agent force was boosted by soldiers from the SAS, the Det, Intelligence Corps and elsewhere on temporary attachment after a short orientation course. During the IRA's 'complete' seventeen-month ceasefire from August 1994, a total of forty of these auxiliary full-time agents were sent back to the army. The SAS, in particular, was not impressed. One officer revealed: 'Details of further cuts were passed to us by MI5 the same day – Friday 9 February 1996 – that the Canary Wharf bomb shattered the ceasefire.' That miscalculation was not made by the front-line field officers of Box Five Hundred, working in a high-risk environment without firearms for their own protection. It was a policy decision taken at the highest echelons of an Intelligence agency misled by the latest IRA deception, even though it was known that, throughout the spurious ceasefire, weapons and explosives were being stockpiled for the next phase of the campaign. 'You could also say', one source suggested, 'that, like some second marriages, it was a triumph of optimism over experience.'

The army also had its little problems from time to time in the treacherous game of agent-handling. In the late 1970s, at Ashford, it created an Intelligence Corps team dedicated to the task. The team was the Field Reconnaissance Unit, or FRU, which became the third arm – alongside 14 Int Company and the SAS detachment – of the army's Intelligence & Security Group empire. In theory, the FRU, like the rest of the army in Northern Ireland, was working in support of the RUC, particularly that force's Special Branch. In practice, it ran its own parallel and independent Intelligence system. It provided the RUC with a token amount of its product to cover the political niceties. It acted upon the wisdom of General Sir James Glover, a mandarin of military Intelligence in the early 1980s, that there are as many ways to persuade an opponent to change sides as there are human motives: politics, jealousy, a desire to get even and settle old scores, even a quarrel about who owns an interesting firearm will do, sex, the good life. One of its agents stopped Stephen Lambert, an IRA Volunteer who had served his time, and handed him a brown envelope containing an unsolicited £200. With the money came 'a wee note'. Lambert met his contact as proposed, having first alerted Martin McGuinness. The conversation was covertly recorded. The English voice was unmistakably that of an NCO; the message, both avuncular and sinister:

> From now on, you are under my protection. It's the rest of them who can worry now. What you tell me is very tight ... We work to the government. You'll get a really good service from us. We go to the highest ... We run professional agents ... I'm not interested in collecting evidence so I can stand you up in a court ... I use evidence so we can put people away, get them off the scene whether to discredit them or if they are beyond help then we can always set them up and do anything like that.

In the late 1980s, pressured by the Thatcher administration to produce more dramatic results in reaction to the IRA's heavy bombing campaign, it took a pro-active role in the dirty war between Protestant terrorists and Republicans, with disastrous results. Brian Nelson, a failed Black Watch soldier from Belfast, was recruited by the FRU in 1987 to penetrate the Loyalist Ulster Defence Association. He soon became the UDA Intelligence chief, steering assassins towards their Republican targets. At least sixteen UDA murders were carried out while he was in place, in spite of his efforts to warn the security authorities of what was about to happen. He was put on trial in January 1992. He admitted twenty charges, including five of conspiracy to murder, fourteen of having information of use of terrorists, and one of possessing a sub-machine-gun. The prosecution did not proceed with fifteen other charges including two of murder. Nelson emerged as a hero in the eyes of his army handlers as well as a criminal. The lieutenant-colonel commanding the FRU at the time described him as 'a very courageous man whose mistakes were all very understandable'. The officer, Colonel J, revealed that no guidelines existed for running agents who, in Northern Ireland, were bound to become involved in criminality. Nelson was sentenced to ten years' imprisonment.

The case sent shockwaves through the Intelligence establishment in the Province, prompting suspicions that although Nelson had done his best to alert the authorities to impending murders, this information was not always passed on, as it should have been, to the RUC or the victim in time to stop the killings. The job of running agents took its toll of those involved. Just before the 1997 ceasefire, officers and NCOs serving with FRU admitted privately that the stress was such that one of their operators could not be expected to function efficiently for more than two years. Like MI5 front-liners living with the problems of multiple aliases, they were discovering that the stress was cumulative. The best informers, by contrast, thrived on the double or triple life. It was a source of adrenalin-driven excitement. Nelson certainly enjoyed his work. He wrote in his prison journal: 'Pitting your wits against those who you seek to compromise acts like a drug. The more you experience it the more you want it, regardless of the moments of intense fear.'

The RUC, meanwhile, continued to draw much of its Intelligence from its own Special Branch informers within the IRA – of whom there were probably hundreds – and from Watchers of E4A. The joint RUC/army Intelligence war against the Provisionals was a world of shifting loyalties. In the 1980s, the RUC's top informer within the IRA was Brendan Davison. He was in charge of the IRA unit responsible for detecting informants and agents infiltrating the movement. Professionally, Davison and Nelson were mirror-images of one another. Nelson's reports often referred to Davison. One source said Nelson behaved 'as if he was waging a war' against the other man. In fact, Nelson warned his army handlers that Davison was heavily targeted for assassination by the UDA's military arm, the UVF. It is questionable whether the army passed on Nelson's warnings in sufficient detail, or at all. Davison was murdered by the IRA and the RUC lost its best source at the time. The veteran correspondent David McKittrick wrote four years later: 'Senior RUC detectives still suspect that the Army played an under-hand role in the events which led to Davison's death. Antipathy between the two intelligence agencies reached such a pitch that, at a social function police and Army handlers nearly came to blows.'

A similar ambiguity surrounds the fate of the informer whose tip-off in 1987 gave the SAS its chance at Loughgall to kill eight Provisionals (see Chapter 8). The IRA ran a fanatical molehunt to find the source, who was being run by the RUC Special Branch. Suspicion fell upon a local woman, Colette O'Neill, from whose home telephone confirmation had been given for the attack to proceed. She was briefly abducted and questioned. The RUC unsuccessfully attempted to prosecute her abductors. The IRA investigation exonerated her, even though she was saved by a tiny transmitter which sent an SOS to Special Branch when she was abducted. The IRA never forgives informers, particularly when the betrayal has caused the loss of eight fighting men. So why was Mrs O'Neill let off the hook? The truth, as relayed by one of the SAS ambush team, was stranger than fiction, but it was a truth recognized by the IRA.

'The fact of the matter is that the informer was one of the eight people attacking us that day,' an SAS Intelligence source explained. 'He should not have been "slotted". We were supposed to identify him quite easily because he would be wearing a red woolly hat or a scarf. He was not wearing either.'

How did it come about that an informer set himself up for a lethal trap of this sort? It still puzzles the SAS, but there is an intelligent guess to be made in place of hard information: 'The Loughgall team leader, Jim Lynagh, was a sharp operator. When he called a Volunteer in, that man never knew whether it was to be court-martialled, congratulated or told, "Get the overalls on: we're going to war." The informer was probably caught on the hop. He wasn't carrying his little red marker.'

Second only to the informer is the computer or, rather, the array of computers which act as the collating brains of this new style of warfare. In Northern Ireland, for example, the army uses two systems: 'Vengeful', dedicated to vehicles, and 'Crucible', for people. Crucible, one source explained, 'will hold a personal file containing a map/picture showing this is where a suspect lives as well as details of family and past'. Vengeful is linked to the Northern

Ireland vehicle licensing office. The two systems provide total cover of a largely innocent population, the sea within which the terrorist fish still swim. Information management is handled by yet another Intelligence Corps team, the Joint Surveillance Group. Intelligence data are graded from a basic, 'Green Army' Level III, available to ordinary line battalions, to Level V (brigade headquarters and above) to a level of joint Intelligence which, in theory at least, holds the crown jewels of sensitive information provided by 14 Company, MI5 and Special Branch. The lowest level information would note that 'Sean Kelly and Seamus Maguire met in a certain pub and had three pints of Guinness'. At a higher level, Sean Kelly would be spotted in a Republican neighbourhood which is off his usual operational area. Top-level data, handled by the Joint Action Unit, Northern Ireland (JACUNI), would cover such cases as the Loughgall operation before it happened. As a secret army Intelligence analysis pointed out, 'the Approach' phase of a terrorist attack 'is the terrorist's most vulnerable stage as he can be directly linked to incriminating evidence', though 'in the aftermath of any Security Forces or terrorist action – "the Escape" phase – valuable information can be gained by both overt and covert surveillance assets.'

Throughout the IRA ceasefires of 1995 and 1997–98, the British army energetically modernized its armoury of computers. The scale and cost of this programme reflected the army's belief that it would continue to fight an Intelligence war in Northern Ireland for many years ahead and that the surveillance war would increasingly become part of normal life in England. The object was to unify vehicle data in Vengeful with cameras able to read vehicle number plates at many locations and link those to the personal computer data held on terrorist suspects: the open, invisible, electronic prison concept. The automatic number plate registration cameras were code-named 'Glutton'. During 1997, eighty overt Glutton cameras were to be switched on at unidentified but public sites in Northern Ireland. Another twenty would be covert. As a secret military paper noted: ' "Vengeful" data is collected overtly. Suspect terrorists use routes that are unlikely to attract the deployment of vehicle checkpoints. Therefore it is difficult to detect vehicle movements of interest.'

The sites where Glutton would operate in England included many ports on the east and west coasts. The resulting Intelligence was to be categorized as 'coarse-grain', defined as 'overt framework operations which record terrorist movements through associates and any suspicious activity'; and 'fine-grain', that is, 'covert, point-targeted, as tasked by the RUC'.

Another new Intelligence computer was 'Caister', a knowledge-based system (KBS) to replace the earlier Crucible in sifting personal information about terrorists and their associates. Caister or its later variant 'Calshot', it was hoped, would be part of a process of analysis where the computer, rather than the human mind, identified significant links between one suspect and another. The generic name given to this technique is Artificial Intelligence. Laden with personal files Caister, according to one document, would 'provide dual central processing suites at Thiepval [military HQ] and Knock [RUC HQ] interconnected by megastream support up to 350 terminals over secure communications bearers. Data up to "Secret". Average response time of ten seconds for a single enquiry with 192 concurrent references.'

Artificial Intelligence was trialled and failed at an earlier stage under the code-name 'Effigy', but by 1997, under the code-name 'Mannequin', plans were virtually complete to have a second shot at this project, regarded as vital to a successful counter-terrorist campaign in the future. The key was integration, and an electronic spring-clean of the Military Intelligence cupboard in which, in 1994, there were no fewer than thirty-seven separate computer programs, virtually none of which was compatible with any other. As one document put it:

> Vengeful and Mannequin need to be integrated to ensure we derive maximum operational benefit from the information they hold. A single intelligence data base with KBS (knowledge-based system) is considered the key to successful intelligence analysis in support of Army and RUC counter-terrorist operations. The system will provide . . . support for up to six hundred terminals over secure bearers [ie, communication links] . . . up to [category] Secret with real-time response to users. Estimated In-Service Date: 1998.

As the new systems were being trialled, the army suffered a propaganda blow on the computer front. A Welsh Guards sergeant, his battalion's Intelligence officer, or someone acting on his behalf, dumped his unwanted secret papers in an unclassified dustbin instead of the shredder at the end of his tour of duty in South Armagh in September 1997. The documents, together with computer disks, were taken to a civilian garbage-disposal dump where someone spotted them and handed them over to the IRA. In January 1998 the Provisionals' newspaper, *Republican News*, exposed the material including aerial photographs and maps showing the homes of twenty-one alleged IRA suspects and details of Vengeful. One of the suspects was Pat McNamee, a Sinn Fein councillor in Crossmaglen. He said the documents showed that the army had never called a ceasefire and had exploited the IRA's truce to infiltrate nationalist areas. He added:

> This calls into question the commitment of the British Government to the peace process. The really scary thing from a personal point of view is that these documents could have fallen into the hands of Loyalist assassins. Given the history of collusion between British forces and Loyalist killers, there is obvious concern that this material could have fallen into the hands of loyalist killers . . . A ready-made kit to bring killers to people's doors.

In practice, the documents did little more than confirm that the army used computer systems as an aid to Intelligence analysis. The upgraded program points to a different order of commitment, in which the computer takes over the functions of the human analyst.

As an extensive, five-part paper aimed at co-ordinating Northern Ireland surveillance strategy (the *G3 Military Surveillance Strategy Northern Ireland*), prepared for the GoC, noted in November 1997:

> The use of ever-increasing emerging technologies requires us to disguise the true nature of the devices. This should be done using decoys, camouflage, deception and by constantly reviewing the signature of our active systems . . . Operational

security – opsec – is of paramount importance particularly for covert operations but programme cost realities dictate there will be increasing reliance on shared systems . . . Integral to surveillance is monitoring and *manipulating* all terrorist communication and information systems. In Northern Ireland this is conducted by special troops and controlled at strategic level.

Equally revealing of the army's pessimism about an end to hostilities, regardless of ceasefires, was the strategy document's perception of the legal framework for running future covert operations. It suggested: 'Working within the law is an essential element . . . We are entitled to use a variety of means and devices and under certain circumstances to enter private property.' Additional contributors to this secret analysis disagreed. One noted that working within the law was a constraint on rather than an element of surveillance, while the Ministry of Defence's expert in MO (Military Operations) 2 demonstrated a chilling knowledge of legislation as yet not tabled in the House of Commons. He, or she, wrote: 'While current military surveillance is protected within current law it is worth noting that particular care must be taken to ensure that the proposed legislation which will eventually replace EPA [Emergency Powers Act] and PTA [Prevention of Terrorism Act] should safeguard military surveillance rights.'

The view implied by this – that the long war was set to continue, even as three governments placed their faith in peace talks – was confirmed by a GoC Directive reminding senior officers serving in Northern Ireland in 1997 that the army's objectives for the next four years assumed that military strength in the Province would be maintained at six resident battalions, with one garrison on the mainland; six Royal Irish Rangers battalions; a constant level of force troops; six roulement infantry battalions (serving on rotation for short periods); one roulement engineer squadron and one roulement transport battalion. In effect, according to one source, the plans indicated a standing army in Northern Ireland comprising three brigades and a headquarters; that is, a complete division of 10,000 troops or more, for the foreseeable future. In December

1997 the total army garrison in the Province was 15,097; the RAF, 1,164 and the Royal Navy, 321.

Meanwhile in Britain, the growth of computerized Intelligence was also exponential, thanks to Irish terrorism. In the early 1990s it was limited by lack of funding and incompatibility between police systems. While Kent spent £4,005 on information technology for every officer, Durham spent £641. But £20 million was invested in the Metropolitan Police Crime Report Information System, CRIS, while HOLMES (Home Office Large Major Enquiry System) was in use in both London and Manchester, major target areas for the IRA. Surveillance cameras around sensitive areas such as the City of London, linked to computers which will automatically identify suspect vehicles within four seconds, evolved into computerized, digital maps of human faces. These have the potential to alert supermarkets to the presence of known shoplifters as well as MI5's Watchers to the movement of terrorists. Among the first terrorists to be detected as a result of such techniques were the Harrods bombers, Jan Taylor, aged fifty-one, former army corporal, and Patrick Hayes, aged forty-one, a computer programer with a degree in business studies. Neither man was Irish. Hayes told the Court: 'I am proud of everything I have done.' Police discovered that both progressed from 'weekend Socialist Workers' in the 1970s to IRA terrorists in the 1990s.

Hayes and Taylor were sentenced to thirty years' imprisonment in May 1994. The damage their war did to freedom of movement in Britain without close, intrusive state surveillance was permanent.

Their secrets compromised by electronic eavesdrop and Watchers, their bombs intercepted, the IRA made plans in 1997 to attack their favourite prestige target, the City. This time they would fight fire with fire. In a world where weapons and battlefield control depend on computers, soldiers took a close interest in paralysing an opponent's system and protecting their own. One method was to hack into the opposition's computer and fill it with viruses. Another was to disrupt the enemy computer from a distance by hitting it with high-energy radio frequency ('Herf') guns to project a pulse of electro-magnetic radiation similar to that given off in a nuclear explosion.

Dr Matt Warren, an expert in the field at Plymouth Business School, learned of the IRA's interest, which is assisted by Irish-America. He explained that much of the extraordinarily high £1.8 billion cost of the Baltic Exchange bomb in 1992 was due to lost economic activity. Herf attacks could achieve the same result without the physical damage or odium attached to killing civilians. The implications for public safety were even more sombre, given the vulnerability of air traffic control and flood control systems (to take just two examples) to computer failure. This would be exotic, but not fantasy, warfare. Major Nick Chantler, an Intelligence officer in Australia's military reserve as well as assistant professor at the University of Technology, Queensland, noted: 'There is nothing to stop anyone generating radio frequencies and firing them at computers. This technology is available to the person in the street. You can just buy it off the shelf. There is surplus ex-military stuff around that the resourceful person can dig up.'

Whatever else, the IRA had proved resourceful.

PART III

The Irish Hard-War Machine

10

The Armalite
and Other Theologies

The Irish Republican Army, as even sympathetic observers have noted, is long on violence and short on political awareness. In 1972, the year which saw more deaths than any other in the renewed Troubles, the writer Richard Trench, working for the socialist journal 7 *Days*, interviewed a young Provo warrior named Liam who believed that 'somehow, by some miraculous process, sectarianism and exploitation will disappear when "The Republic" is formed. Ask him how it will happen and he will scratch his head and say: "The boys with the brains will work that out. I'm not much of one for big ideas."' The reason why the physical force tradition (see Chapter 5) is the continuing thread in this history is that the Republicans, and their predecessors, nourish a simple, three-item agenda to embrace all political and economic problems. It is the reunification of Ireland, expulsion of the British, and reorganization of the country by reference to Ireland's four 'green fields', the ancient provinces of Leinster, Munster, Connaught and Ulster, to create a loose federation run by worker-control.

Resistance strategy has been shaped not so much by military analysis as extemporization, using whatever weapons come to hand. This was as true in 1997 as in 1691. As a consequence, the weaponry dictates the tactics, in turn creating a style and finally a philosophy of violence that is self-perpetuating and self-justifying. As a Belfast graffito-philosopher put it: 'God made the Catholics, but the Armalite made them equal.'

Co-ordination of IRA operations was always a loose, decentralized business depending on local, even family links. The exception came during the spring and summer of 1969, when weapons which might have been available to defend the Catholic ghettos of Belfast and Derry were withheld by the IRA. At that time, even the emerging Provisionals were heavily influenced by the siren call of the People's Democracy, with whom Pira formed a joint organization, the Northern Resistance Movement, after the IRA split. Confirming its change of direction, the PD quit the Northern Ireland Civil Rights Association, which had now served its purpose.

People's Democracy, as Lord Cameron noted, adopted 'calculated martyrdom' as a key weapon of street protest. As a political and propaganda tool, it worked brilliantly. Northern Ireland's Catholics had to be seen as victims if the sympathy of expatriate Irish communities in America, as well as uncommitted Catholic populations in France and elsewhere, was to be won. In a long war of insurgency and counter-insurgency, the ultimate battlefield was public opinion. The idea was to provoke the British into over-reaction. In practice, for most of the thirty years after 1968, it was the British who were obliged, by public sentiment, to limit the firepower they brought to bear. Only once were tracked vehicles used – for a matter of a few hours – to demolish barricades at Free Derry, pre-empting any journalist from using the word 'tank' in the context of this 'police' action. Automatic weapons, particularly belt-fed machine-guns, were rarely used.

Security Forces, by contrast, were soon exposed to heavy machine-gun fire, anti-tank missiles and mines as they moved around in unprotected vehicles. The IRA imposed no inhibition on the weight of explosive it directed against the enemy, often in civilian areas which included hospitals and places of worship in defiance of the accepted rules of war. Yet, throughout the conflict, much of world opinion remained convinced that the IRA was the underdog. This success was largely due to the perception created in 1969 that the Catholics were victims. So they were. The question was, whose victims?

Republican arms to defend them *were* available, though these were not held on the Lower Falls or in Bogside (as Cathal Goulding admitted later). Gerry Adams later asserted that a mere three revolvers were available to the Belfast IRA in August 1969, which he further claimed consisted of just twenty-four members. The IRA were assuredly outgunned and outnumbered at that time, but not to this extent. The American writer J. Bowyer Bell confirmed: 'a small IRA group with only petrol bombs for weapons was joined by several older IRA men from the 1940s who were armed with a Thompson, a .303 rifle and four pistols. Together for ninety minutes firing into the street, they kept the loyalists back, wounding as many as eight.' (In some versions, the automatic weapon at St Comgall's was not a Thompson but a German Schmeisser).

An early raid on the Falls Road, towards the end of 1969, uncovered 13,000 rounds of 9mm ammunition in one house plus smaller consignments of similar ammunition in neighbouring houses. These contained a mixed bag of Swedish Karlsborg bullets made in 1951 and 1952, British Kynoch bullets made in 1956 and 1958 and a large collection of Second World War ammunition, probably made for the Sten gun. To one British expert, Lieutenant-Colonel George Styles GC, the find announced that 'an organisation, a terrorist cell', was well established in the area.

Styles was not the only one to notice what was going on. The distinguished Irish journalist Andrew Boyd wrote at that time:

Today, only a few days before Christmas 1969, Northern Ireland is in a state of distress. British soldiers are still on the barricades as darkness falls and man checkpoints on the main roads into Belfast and Derry. They face an icy hard winter with often only the empty factories and empty schools as quarters. All around them arms and explosives are accumulating in the hands of fanatical civilians. British military intelligence officers, with little co-operation from either the Stormont Government or the RUC, comb the place for evidence that will lead to the arrest of terrorists.

George Styles's forecasts of doom in the officers' mess at the army's Lisburn headquarters, he wrote, 'were still a standing joke. "All this talk of impending disaster, George, is just your way of empire building",' his brother officers told him. Styles's vocation was bomb disposal and he had fought a terrorist campaign in Malaya. In his mess, as in my newspaper, any suggestions at that time that the IRA was still a force to be reckoned with were derided. By the following July, as Styles noted, the arms search that was used to justify the Falls Road curfew uncovered fifty-two pistols, thirty-five rifles, six automatic weapons, fourteen shotguns, 100 bombs, 250lb of high explosive, 21,000 rounds of ammunition and eight two-way radio sets.

From a standing start – if Republican propaganda was to be believed about the state of its arms in 1969 – this was an astonishing achievement, one which suggests a mismatch between the cover story and the physical evidence. British government representatives in the Province were apparently unaware of these developments. Nor, as it later transpired, did they know that an Intelligence officer of the Dublin government was active in Northern Ireland to promote a clandestine supply of firearms to the 'defence committees'. The IRA was still coy, twenty-eight years later, about the condition of its armoury at that early stage, though as early as May 1970 a BBC television team was permitted to film IRA men training in house-clearance techniques armed with Thompsons. The setting for that, as later events suggested, might have been in a camp run by the regular Irish Army. Another film, of earlier vintage, revealed that the IRA was able to draw on its stock of .303 Bren machine-guns so as to run weapons training classes. In 1997 Billy McKee, a Belfast IRA veteran of the 1960s, smiled when he was asked: 'What did the Provisional IRA do for weapons?' He replied: 'Weapons! Went out and looked for them. Stole them. Begged them and bought them. It didn't care where they bought them.'

In 1969 and long before, there were many more IRA weapons across the border, concealed in barns in Kerry and elsewhere. More guns were brandished by the IRA as they provided an overnight guard for Bernadette Devlin and other PD marchers on their way to Burntollet seven months before the Catholics of Derry and Belfast came under concerted attack in August. There were even more weapons in the United States which could be supplied, subject to one fundamental condition. That they were not supplied (see Chapter 1) was because US sympathy had to be engaged by a pogrom of the Catholics in Northern Ireland. Until such sources could be tapped systematically, the Republicans of Ulster did what they do best: they extemporized and, as a result, began a long, remarkably effective process of manufacturing their own weapons as well as buying them. So rapidly did the armoury grow that British Intelligence found it necessary to print, and update regularly, a classified document entitled *The Northern Terrorist Arsenal*. As the March 1980 edition explained: 'The need has been recognised despite extensive reference books of firearms for a simple, concise guide to weapons used by terrorists in Northern Ireland.'

Between 1 January and 7 April 1970, well before the Falls Road curfew turned the Catholic population towards the IRA, there had been twenty-nine explosions in the Province. Most of the raw material was made in England and sold to dealers in the Irish Republic for use in quarrying and civil engineering. An early example was a collection of mines contained in boxes as they floated ashore at St John's Point, County Down. Military Intelligence concluded that they were landed by ship on a beach where 'someone got his tide tables wrong'. They were taken out by the tide and spotted by RUC officers as they came back inshore. As Styles reported: 'Explosives and detonators were ludicrously easy to obtain [in 1970] under the 1875 Explosives Act. We wrote to agents in Northern Ireland asking for their catalogues and price lists for explosives. This way we identified the types that were freely available in the Province.' Forensic evidence confirmed the source of much of the material. What the bombers did not appreciate was that commercial explosive did not have the prolonged shelf-life of military HE, nor was it as stable. Soon the bombers were blowing themselves up. The attrition rate against the bomber was seven-to-one in favour of the soldiers dismantling them. In spite of that, the 100th IRA bomb was detonated at an electricity transformer near Bogside on 15 September 1970.

As the bombers developed their techniques, the IRA trawled its network of contacts for more firearms. Though Thompson sub-machine-guns were available, the .45 calibre ammunition they used was hard to get. The Republicans turned, not surprisingly, to the Clan na Gael, in particular to its old quartermaster and supplier in New York, George Harrison. Harrison was a native of Mayo. When the Troubles resumed he was aged fifty-four, an insular bachelor who earned his living as a security guard. There is no evidence that he ever exposed himself to the risk of front-line action but he did supply many of the weapons used by the IRA in its abortive 1950s campaign. In 1969, the movement resurrected him. Harrison in turn went to the American black market. In a gun-culture, there is little need for a clandestine supplier. When that is what is wanted, the source is the Mafia.

Writing for *Jane's Intelligence Review*, the Dublin journalist Sean Boyle estimated that, in 1969, the Harrison network smuggled seventy firearms to Northern Ireland including Second World War M-1 self-loading rifles, M-3 sub-machine-guns, pistols and 60,000 rounds of ammunition. Another security specialist, Ian Greig, suggested: 'Normally, the weapons arrived only three or four at a time, by air or ship freight, packed in false-bottomed crates.' The luxury liner the QE2 was used by Irish crew members as a Republican delivery vehicle. The Harrison network enjoyed a charmed existence until the FBI smashed it in the early 1980s.

What the Mob could not supply was stolen from ill-guarded armouries, notably those of the military reserve, the National Guard, near such Irish American centres as Boston. A US Army report quoted by Congressman Les Aspin on 2 September 1975 concluded that, between 1971 and 1974, 'extremist groups' including the IRA had stolen sufficient arms and ammunition from US armouries 'to arm ten battalions or 8,000 men'. The assessment was clearly an exaggeration and is not reflected in the pattern of weapons recovered in Northern Ireland, but it is undoubtedly the case that National Guard armouries were targeted for such modern weapons as the M-60 machine-gun, ammunition for which – in 7.62mm calibre – was plentiful since it is a standard Nato bullet. This weapon, with an effective range of 1,200 yards, killed, among others, Captain Richard Westmacott, SAS, in 1980.

In 1969, the most surprising arms smuggling operation run on behalf of the IRA (though no one conceded that at the time) was one involving senior ministers of the Dublin government and officers of the Irish Military Intelligence service. A key player was Captain James Kelly, whose secret trips to Northern Ireland that year worried his bosses in Dublin. As the Irish Defence Minister, James Gibbons, later admitted:

I was not as immediately concerned about the arms smuggling content of Captain Kelly's activities as much as what I regarded as the dire danger of his capture by the North of Ireland Police Authority or Security Authorities and, in those circumstances, I had a very serious fear that if these authorities captured Captain Kelly – as an Intelligence Officer of the Irish Army – and if they put him through the wringer, that they would extract every possible iota of Irish Army intelligence information from him, to the detriment of national security.

This operation, ostensibly run on behalf of the so-called 'defence committees' in the North, was halted after a personal intervention by the Prime Minister, Jack Lynch. As a result, in May 1970, two Irish Cabinet ministers were sacked and arrested. With three others – the Intelligence officer, a Belgian-born Dublin businessman and a Belfast IRA veteran – they were charged with conspiring to import arms and ammunition illegally into the Irish Republic. One of the ministers, Charles Haughey, and the other three accused were put on trial and acquitted. Haughey re-entered public life, became Prime Minister from 1979 to 1992 and resigned amid a row over a ten-year-old telephone-tapping scandal. In 1997 Haughey, aged seventy-two, admitted that while he was Prime Minister he had received gifts worth £1.3 million from the millionaire proprietor of Dunne's Stores, Ben Dunne, after earlier denying all knowledge of them. A new tribunal was then appointed to probe other sources of funds paid into secret bank accounts from which Haughey had benefited.

The Irish arms trial shed much light on the willingness of senior political figures in the Republic to provide arms, funds and military training for Ulster Catholics who were under threat. A total of 500 rifles was moved from the defence force store to Dundalk, on the border, following an appeal from, among others, John Kelly of the IRA in Belfast. James Gibbons, the Irish Defence Minister at the time, gave evidence and was pressed about 'contingency plans towards possible future events in the North of Ireland'. Gibbons replied: 'I did get such instructions and passed them on to the

173

Army.' He refused to confirm that the weapons might have been for distribution into the North of Ireland but a later witness, Colonel Michael Hefferon, Ireland's Director of Intelligence, did so. As he put it: 'The rifles had been moved very quickly because of the decision that it would be better to have them nearer the Border than Dublin if it was necessary for them to be distributed to civilians in the North of Ireland.' (Two years later, in January 1972, the journal 7 *Days* claimed: 'Dundalk is an old smuggling centre and in 1969 was the distribution point for the Dublin Government's 500 Spring-Enfield rifles that eventually got into the hands of the CCDCs in the North.') Hefferon revealed that other weapons – an arsenal of 500 pistols and 180,000 bullets – were to have been imported from Austria 'for the Northern Defence Committees, in the event that a situation would arise where the Government would agree to them going to them'. Meanwhile, this consignment would be stored 'in a safe place . . . in a monastery in Cavan'.

Not only were plans made to distribute arms to IRA front organizations in the North; in the autumn of 1969, following the breakdown of order in August, nine men from the Catholic Bogside area of Derry received firearms training at a fort in Donegal, having been enrolled for just a week as members of the Irish Territorial Army, the *Forsa Cosanta Aitiuil*, or FCA. Gibbons confirmed under cross-examination that he had authorized this. He said this was a pilot scheme, 'making use of the Defence Forces so as to assist the minority in Derry to be in a position to defend themselves', though the function of the FCA was home defence of the twenty-six counties, not Free Derry in the North.

There is some evidence, slender though it is, that the IRA had other military training even before the civil rights campaign had run its course. The right-wing, London-based Institute for the Study of Terrorism asserts: 'IRA gunmen did, in fact, train at some Palestinian Liberation Organisation terrorist bases in Jordan in the summers of 1968 and 1969 before the Official–Provisional split.' Tim Pat Coogan, writing of 1969–79, says, without elaboration: 'The obvious analogies between the situation of Irish Catholics and of the Palestinians (whose poverty and lack of opportunity provide a continuing stream of recruits to the PLO) have meant inevitable contact between the IRA, the PLO and other organisations.' In 1971, as the Provos started killing British soldiers, the secretary of Provisional Sinn Fein, Maria de Burca, attended a Fatah conference in Kuwait. 'Sinn Fein are not gun-running,' she said, 'but I can only speak for Sinn Fein.'

As well as efforts to import firearms and to provide military training, Captain Kelly's friends in the North were given a bank account in Dublin, opened in two false names at Christmas 1969. Kelly reminded the barrister cross-examining him that, while one of the bogus signatories lived in Northern Ireland, 'I think we claim jurisdiction over the thirty-two counties.' The funds came from 'legitimate charitable collections' for the Relief of Distress in the North and monies made available from the government through the Irish Red Cross. The money, he said, 'was under the control of the Northern Ireland Defence Committees. These were the people who controlled the money.' A total of £15,000 was paid for the Austrian pistols and ammunition. This was a fraction of the £100,000 originally put into the fund for the Relief of Distress in the North.

According to Mr Haughey, who was Minister of Finance at the time, the funds used to open the bank account in 1969 were not voted on in the Dail Eireann until April 1970. By then 'somewhat over £90,000 had been spent'. Haughey claimed: '£20,000, as far as I know, went to a housing group.'

He was asked: 'Did you use the Red Cross as a cloak and a blind to conceal the fact that this money was being paid to the Defence Committees?' He replied:

No, I was very much aware of the role which the Defence Committees were playing inside Belfast City, where they were responsible for policing large areas, for feeding people, for the organisation of all sorts of humanitarian activities. These people would normally be assisted directly by the Irish Red Cross. In the circumstances, the Irish Red Cross could not do that, and, therefore, as I say, we established a Committee for the Relief of Distress in the North, through which these monies would be handled.

Where some of the funds finally went and for what purpose remains unresolved though a knowledgeable Dublin journalist, reflecting on Haughey's disgrace, commented:

Every deal which Haughey as prime minister authorised is under scrutiny as the biggest financial scandal in Irish history unfolds. What is known for sure is that the man who twenty-seven years ago chaired a committee that leaked the money that started the Provisional IRA is now doomed to end his years in ignominy because of that very act.

In the dark days of August 1969, the Dublin government had one option other than co-operation with the IRA; this was to use its own regular army to move into the Six Counties. It did not do this. It established five field hospitals and two refugee centres near the border, which the troops might have to defend. The nearest it came to direct intervention in the North was a contingency plan 'for the defence of the threatened population . . . the disposition of small arms where they could most readily be made available to recognised representatives of those under attack'.

Trevor C. Salmon, a specialist in international relations who has studied the curious history of Irish 'neutrality', concluded:

Although no invasion *per se* was planned, a contingency plan for helping Northern nationalists did exist and that may have involved some incursions, if these were ultimately deemed necessary. The intervention would be to 'save' the nationalist population, not to bring about unity, which the Irish lacked the power to do . . . It is significant that the [Irish] Army's own assessment stressed its weakness. Although some politicians wished, in effect, to go to war, a neutral state can hardly voluntarily do so.

The miasma of false identities and bank accounts for siphoning funds from government coffers through the Irish Red Cross into a slush fund for arms purchases to help representatives of defence committees who were, invariably, members of one arm or other of the IRA in the Six Counties, was familiar territory to an organization intent on concealing its true intentions. What was clear was that, at the time, significant parts of the Dublin government and its Military Intelligence were convinced, as were journalists and others, that the Northern Catholics were victims of a Unionist pogrom for which no remedy existed other than the armed struggle.

For the first three years of the renewed Troubles, until 1972, modest but useful supplies of firearms continued to reach the IRA from overseas. Those which were uncovered hint at what was escaping detection at the time. They included the first consignment of Armalites, lightweight, automatic weapons developed for the Vietnam War. The Armalite, also known as the M-16, was superior to any equivalent weapon carried by either the British or Irish army. Its capabilities included a muzzle velocity of 1,000 metres per second, a maximum range of over 2,000 metres, a lethal range of 400 metres (at which it would penetrate a steel helmet) and a rate of fire of up to 950 bullets per minute. As the AR-15 it was available as a hunting rifle in US gunshops. These weapons were supplied not only from America but also from Japan, where the guns were built under licence, though, as *Jane's* editor noted, 'Japanese law requires that their rifles be sold only to non-combatant nations and Japan would not countenance export to the USA during the Vietnam war.' Britain did not start making the Armalite until the mid-1970s; by then it had long been part of the IRA's armoury.

In 1971, 4.5 tons of small arms purchased for the IRA from the Czech arms manufacturer Omnipol was seized at Schipol airport, Holland. This was not the only link between the Republicans and the Warsaw Pact that year. Boris Shtern, a Soviet journalist on an assignment with the Russian fishing fleet, saw a crate handed over at sea off the Irish coast from one of the trawlers to an inshore vessel. Shtern, in an interview with Canadian Broadcasting after his defection, said: 'At two o'clock at night my ship came near Ireland. Two boats with Irish people came to the ship and the KGB officer on our boat, Misha Boulanger, gave them a big box, we think of arms.'

Elsewhere in 1971, the Republicans were playing the brotherhood card with Basque Separatists in Spain and Breton nationalists in France. An IRA apostate, Maria Maguire, revealed in her memoirs that the Basque ETA terrorist movement had supplied the Provisionals with fifty revolvers in exchange for training in the use of explosives. Spanish police subsequently claimed that the IRA had provided the raw material used to blow up the Spanish Prime Minister, Admiral Luis Carrera Blanco, in December 1973. In 1972, meanwhile, two Breton nationalist groups – the Breton Liberation Front and the Breton Republican Army – opened a joint liaison mission in Bray, near Dublin, to forge links with the IRA. By 1975, when transnational terrorism was becoming an international menace, sponsored by the Warsaw Pact, PLO terrorists obtained arms from East Germany and Czechoslovakia which they shipped through Syria to Montreal. There, French Canadian extremists of the Front de Liberation de Quebec acted as agents to pass them on to Breton nationalists who transferred them to an Irish fishing vessel off Cork.

There was nothing the Dublin government could do to arrest this traffic, even if it wished to do so. In 1969 and the spring of 1970, for example, not one Irish Naval Service vessel was seaworthy. The Irish government expressed concern about this, in the light of British, not IRA, incursions into Irish sea, air and land space. Brian Lenihan, Ireland's Transport Minister, confirmed in a Dail debate in 1972 that, in the two years ending in February that year, there were twenty-seven confirmed British overflights and eighty-eight known border incursions by the British army. During 1970–71, the British had boarded a number of Irish vessels in Carlingford Lough, looking for arms. Irish MPs were outraged. As one of them put it, Irish vessels were 'entitled to the full protection of the military forces of the State'. What no one noticed was that Ireland's inshore waters had become the IRA's equivalent of the Ho Chi Minh trail which, in Vietnam, was being energetically bombed by the US Air Force to halt supplies to Vietminh terrorists.

The beneficiaries of Eire's failure to guard its borders were the two IRA factions, both now engaged in a renewed war. The year 1970 saw two RUC men killed among twenty fatalities. Arms searches uncovered 11 machine-guns, 104 rifles, 47 shotguns and 162 hand-guns. In 1971, prior to internment and Bloody Sunday, terrorism exploded in the province as if in response to a well-prepared strategy. In that year, the Security Forces logged 6,948 incidents of all types, including more than 1,000 bomb explosions that killed fifty people. There were 261 attacks on police stations. The army was fired at on 1,500 occasions. The Security Forces lost fifty-nine dead out of a total of 180 violent deaths. Arms searches uncovered more than 700 weapons – 28 machine-guns, 279 rifles, 136 shotguns, 273 hand-guns – as well as 1,681 grenades and blast-bombs. The most significant find was a single rocket-launcher, precursor of the RPG-7 anti-tank rocket copied from the original Soviet weapon and built by Fatah in Egypt from 1970. By 1972, the most fatal year of the renewed Troubles, violence claimed 478 lives of whom 146 were members of the Security Forces; weapon finds of all kinds also soared. What was largely missing from this inventory was the mortar, a weapon the IRA would soon begin to manufacture itself (see Chapter 11). Most of the war *matériel* came from elsewhere.

Even when allowance is made for Irish ingenuity and energy in arms smuggling and arms manufacture, such an offensive is hard to explain without the additional ingredient of external help, operating both outside and within Northern Ireland. The experience of guerrilla armies elsewhere was that years of slow, patient preparation were required to mount an offensive of the sort the IRA and its splinter groups launched in the two years after August 1969.

Who these shadowy advisers and marksmen were is still a subject for speculation but their existence may be inferred, like that of astronomical black holes, from the effects they produced. The leaders of the Provisional IRA in its early phase were dedicated zealots but not people of the calibre required to carry off an international arms trade from Eastern Europe to the USA by way of the Middle East. Leaders of the IRA delegation that met the British government secretly in 1972 included one butcher's assistant (Martin McGuinness), one street bookmaker (Seamus Twomey), a former barman (Gerry Adams), a mechanic (Ivor Bell), a professional, English-born railway shunter and ex-RAF corporal (Sean McStiofain, born John Stephenson) plus two trained professional minds, Daithi O'Conaill (teacher) and Miles Shevlin (solicitor). Even the professionals were military incompetents. O'Conaill negotiated the early American supplies and in 1971 took Maria Maguire with him to Amsterdam. She, as Tim Pat Coogan observed, 'was the type of university-educated, politically-minded type which the movement was then trying to attract'. Within a year she had quit the Provisionals and told her story to the London *Observer*.

The IRA could draw upon other university-educated, politically-minded and sophisticated allies. The journal 7 *Days* noted in January 1972: 'the People's Democracy, although a small group, have filled in part of the Provisional's ideological void and have broken from NICRA to form, together with the Provisionals, a Northern Resistance Movement to co-ordinate the Civil Disobedience campaign.' Cathal Goulding, Chief of Staff of the Official IRA, characterized PD as 'a bunch of left-wing sectarian students . . . an elitist socialist group, just as the Provisionals are an elitist nationalist group'. Provisional Sinn Fein President, Ruari O'Bradaigh, conceded: 'Each has their own house to live in, but we can be good neighbours.'

Bernadette Devlin told the same journal: 'The Provisionals are essentially an alliance. I know many of them personally . . . The main problem of the Provisional campaign is not its "terrorism", but that there is no education to go with it, no one understands what on earth the Provisionals are blowing up buildings for.'

The machine that was to provide the most valuable supply of arms and explosives was the international force built around the Palestinian resistance movement, armed as part of the Cold War by the Soviet Union and its allies, bankrolled by the Arab oil states. The thrust of that campaign – ironically, in view of Irish America's support of the IRA – was anti-American. During the Cold War, as in the Second World War, the Western Approaches and the Irish ports were of huge strategic importance to the USA to resupply its army in Europe and to the Soviets who might wish to cut that link. By 1972 arms cargoes were flowing into Ireland from Libya. The discovery of three RPG-7 rocket-launchers in 1972 and seven in 1973 offered one of the first clues to this traffic. In 1972 a letter addressed to the Provisionals in Ballymurphy signed by Atef Matouk, a Syrian who ran the Irish–Arab Society in Dublin, was intercepted by British Intelligence. It gave details of assistance on offer from the Palestinians. In parallel with aid from the PLO, the Libyan government publicly affirmed its support for the Irish. In

June 1972, the Libyan leader Colonel Gadaffi, proclaimed: 'We support the revolutionaries of Ireland. We have stood by them . . . There are arms and there is support for the revolutionaries of Ireland . . . We have decided to move to the offensive, to fight Britain in her own home.' The IRA's bombing campaign in England was about to be renewed and the scene was set for the most complex, elaborate surveillance operation of the Irish War.

On 28 March 1973, the Irish Navy, seaworthy at last, intercepted the Cypriot vessel *Claudia* and found 4 tons of Libyan arms and six prominent Provisionals led by the veteran Joe Cahill. The shipment had been watched from the air by RAF Nimrod reconnaissance aircraft and from below by submarines of the Royal Navy. The cargo comprised 250 Kalashnikov AK-M assault rifles, 500 grenades and 100 anti-tank mines.

Over the next twenty-four years, the IRA acquired a unique experience of and contact with clandestine arms suppliers. Throughout that time, three main sources kept the Provisionals' war machine going. Those were the USA, the Middle East and home-made weapons and explosives. The imports included thefts from isolated, unguarded and insecure weapons stores in Norway, held for that country's Home Guard, and regularly pillaged by extremists, including neo-Nazis. All of these were dwarfed by the series of cargoes delivered from Libya between 1985 and 1987 by the trawler skipper Adam Hopkins and others.

As FBI 'sting' operations disrupted the flow of weapons from America, the Provos turned again to Libya. Two incidents drove Libya's unstable leader to take up arms against Britain, using the IRA as proxies. On 17 April 1984, when someone inside the Libyan People's Bureau in London started shooting at Libyan dissidents demonstrating outside the building, Woman Police Constable Yvonne Fletcher was killed. The entire Libyan team was expelled from Britain. During the diplomatic stand-off that followed, five bombs were planted in London by Gadaffi's agents. In 1986, after Libyan agents were blamed for a bomb attack on American soldiers in Berlin, the US Air Force bombed the Libyan capital, Tripoli, as a reprisal. The raid was launched from Upper Heyford, Oxfordshire. Gadaffi was lucky to survive. His daughter Hanna, aged sixteen months, was killed. The *Belfast Telegraph*, on 16 April that year, quoted Gerry Adams on the subject. He accused the US of 'an act of international terrorism'. Another IRA leader, Danny Morrison, said that 'the Libyan people . . . the Palestine Liberation Organisation and the IRA are not the terrorists. The real terrorists are the governments of Britain and the United States.'

Between 1985 and 1987, four shipments of arms and explosives from Libya were successfully landed in gun-running epics reminiscent of Erskine Childers' exploits in 1914. For some parts of the operation the same port (Howth) was employed. The first of the Hopkins cargoes, in August 1985, was hidden aboard a 65-foot fishing boat, the *Casmara*, later renamed the *Kula*, and contained 10 tonnes of weapons including rifles, pistols and seven RPG rockets. This was modest compared with what soon followed. Two months later the *Kula* smuggled in machine-guns used by the IRA against army helicopters. Another 14 tonnes was carried by the *Villa*, once an oil-rig replenisher, and a vessel twice the size of *Kula*, on 10 July 1986. Two months later the same ship was back with 80 tonnes, including a tonne of Semtex plastic explosive and SAM-7 anti-aircraft missiles.

The last big cargo – 150 tonnes – was uncovered by French Customs men off the coast of Brittany in November 1987 as Hopkins and his crew aboard the trawler *Eksund* prepared to scuttle and abandon ship. The *Eksund* cargo included twenty SAM-7s, ten heavy 12.7mm Degtyarev machine-guns and 2 tonnes of Semtex. Over the next two years the Irish Republic, sensing a threat to its own stability, raided IRA arsenals to recover 200 rifles, 20 RPGs, 5 machine-guns and 650lb of Semtex. This was a small proportion of the whole. Meanwhile, the new weapons were being brought to bear. A Degtyarev bullet sliced through the armour of an RUC car in South Armagh, blowing up the petrol tank and killing Constable Michael Marshall. It also brought down a British army Lynx helicopter.

An even more fearsome addition to this new armoury was the Warsaw Pact's portable flame-thrower. As an army weapons expert said, this is 'as easy to use as a garden spray; as refillable as a gas lighter'. It could hurl a jet of flame 80 yards and generate a temperature of 1,200 degrees Fahrenheit. Security Forces found it in October 1988, before it could be used. It was hidden in the outhouse of an old people's home in Catholic West Belfast, possibly with the connivance of someone linked to the home.

The presence of such horrific weapons was serious enough. Worse was the realization of a failure by British Intelligence – led in this case by MI6 to notice the traffic from Libya in the decade after its success, acknowledged by Garret Fitzgerald, in tracking the *Claudia* in 1973. The *Casmara* was on an international Customs target list of ships suspected to be drug-running and had been searched for that reason by Irish excisemen. The Intelligence services of the USA as well as Britain were obsessively interested in Libya during the years of the Hopkins cargoes, using every means available to a modern, high-tech state including signals intercepts to keep Gadaffi under control. Dublin's Intelligence services, ultimately responsible to Charles Haughey, seem to have been as unaware of those of Washington and London. The success of the Libyan supply operation was a defeat for British Intelligence on the same scale as Britain's failure to react to Argentine preparations to seize British territory in South Georgia and the Falklands in 1982. The whole period was overshadowed by Margaret Thatcher's strident triumphalism over real and perceived enemies including the IRA hunger-strikers in 1981 and the coalminers of Britain in 1984–85. In such a climate, it is possible that all Intelligence services were overstretched in their search for the enemy within. Whatever the reason, the Libyan supplies marked a turning-point in the Irish War. Towards the late 1970s, Irish Republican violence had been falling sharply. In 1979, the body count in the Province was thirteen, the lowest ever. A cornucopia of weapons from Libya – so lavish that they could not all be employed – empowered the physical force tradition with massive political credibility as well as military clout.

The variety of IRA weaponry was outlined in the 1993 edition of the British weapons Intelligence handbook, *The Terrorist Arsenal.* It listed eight types of pistol, nine rifles, four machine-guns and two missile systems and even then, as it admitted, it covered 'only those that are more commonly encountered'. In July 1994 the

Libyan Foreign Minister, Said Mujbar, claimed in a newspaper interview that his government no longer assisted the IRA. He said:

> We supported Ireland at the beginning as a national liberation movement. Until the Irish people, Irish movement or the IRA went into a bombing spree in London, then we stopped. We stopped because of two reasons, one moral, one selfish. The moral one is that we cannot agree that we be helpers of those who go out and kill people indiscriminately . . . to go to London which is not in Ireland and to start killing people, this is something we can never condone . . . The selfish reason is that we have thousands of Libyan students in the UK.

He confirmed that arms supplies restarted after the American bombing of Tripoli in 1986, in which more than thirty Libyans had died. He added: 'You can be certain that at no point in the future will we support the IRA militarily.'

During the 1990s, one weapon in particular, a late arrival from America, sent a frisson of fear through soldiers and RUC officers manning the border. This was the Barrett Light 50 sniper rifle, firing a bullet half an inch in diameter at 2,000 mph over 1,000 yards. Its victims looked in some cases as if a shell had hit them. The firing point was usually in the Republic, the target in South Armagh. The first to be killed by this weapon, in August 1992, was Private Paul Turner, aged eighteen, hit by a single shot at Crossmaglen. RUC officers Alan Corbett, aged twenty-five and John Reid, aged thirty, were killed in November 1992 and March 1993. Lance-Corporal Lawrence Dickson, aged twenty-six, also died in March 1993 to be followed by Private John Randall, aged nineteen, in June 1993 and Lance-Corporal Kevin Pullin. By 1994, the sniper's body-count had risen to nine. In February 1997 Lance-Bombardier Stephen Restorick, manning a roadblock, paused to smile at a woman motorist and both were hit. He was killed. A massive surveillance and entrapment operation was mounted in 1994 using the resources of MI5 and the SAS. This finally succeeded in April 1997 when five members of the South Armagh IRA – an army within an army – were captured by an SAS team after a struggle in a barn near the village of Cullyhanna. They were found with an armour-plated hatchback car and the Barrett. A British officer asserted that it was 'the single biggest success in South Armagh in the past ten years'. The weapon, manufactured in Tennessee, was issued to the US Army.

The SAS, on this occasion, was under strict orders to take the sniper, or snipers, alive. According to an officer involved, this was because the regiment's heavy use of firepower at Loughgall had to be offset against a success that more closely followed the police primacy policy linked to criminalization of the IRA.

The Barrett, as well as machine-guns up to calibre .5, have been used against military helicopters landing in Crossmaglen. Between 1977 and 1993 at least twelve aircraft were hit and four brought down. The IRA have sometimes placed a circle of guns around the helicopter landing zone to put up a cone of fire, usually after dark. In September 1993, a Puma troop-carrying helicopter was hit several times as it took off. It chased the Mercedes flat-bed truck mounting a heavy machine-gun and for some time a bizarre duel continued between the two. Paddy Short, a local publican, said that villagers took cover as an intense gun battle went on for ten minutes. He added: 'We have had gun battles here before but this must have been one of the longest.' The Mercedes finally escaped across the border.

With the end of the Cold War, the vast arsenals of the Warsaw Pact were opened for business. As well as the criminal underworld, the IRA was in the market. In May 1996, Intelligence reports suggested that the terrorists had obtained a Russian sniper weapon similar to the Barrett. This was the gas-operated V-94. It was purchased during the IRA ceasefire of 1994 following negotiations with an Estonian extremist group. Lady Thatcher was said to be at the top of the sniper's target list in Britain.

The IRA's trip round the world's armaments markets, though hugely successful, did not exhaust its capacity for making war, but it did imply a political irony not present in the earlier phases of the Irish struggle. Earlier campaigns had lasted no more than three years. One reason why the Troubles were able to run for thirty years or so after 1969 was that the world was awash with the tools of warfare. While the Cold War froze warfare as well as history for forty-six years, the conflict was fought for real by surrogates, many of which were profitable markets for arms manufacturers. One of the leading exporters of weaponry was the UK itself, together with its closest ally, the United States.

11

Mortars, PRIGs and Mortality

In any other guerrilla army, supplies on the scale of those reaching the IRA from the USA, the Arab nations and Eastern Europe would have been enough to keep a war going indefinitely. The IRA, as ever, was different. Following the philosophy of 'Sinn Fein: Ourselves Alone', it has developed a home-made, do-it-yourself capability for arms manufacture which makes any effort to achieve weapons-control a doomed enterprise. The story of the IRA mortar – or, rather, the series of mortars up to the Mark 17 at the time of the last weapons Intelligence analysis – is a cautionary one for anyone who hopes that the surrender of Kalashnikovs and Armalites could be anything more than a gesture of peace. The roosting dove of peace, palm-leaf in beak, could be knocked off its perch in Dublin, Belfast or London at any time by an incoming bomb rather than a sniper round.

Ever since the Battle of Derry, when petrol-bombs destroyed the RUC's street credibility, the IRA had been working on what military professionals call 'stand-off' weapons, devices able to deliver a lethal, controlled punch from a safe distance in the concealment of dead ground or the far side of the wire. The petrol-bomb, hurled by catapult from a rooftop, was overtaken in 1972 by cans of explosive attached to the ends of arrows or lengths of dowel rod, with a safety fuse to delay ignition before the missile was fired from a bow or a shotgun. A forensic Intelligence report comments: 'Because of the unreliability of this weapon it is hardly surprising that its use was limited.'

In 1972 the IRA turned its mind towards a form of artillery

almost as venerable as the ballista and the bow-and-arrow. Starting from first principles, it considered the merits of the mortar. The mortar was used by Muhammad II in a siege of Constantinople in 1451–53 which destroyed the last remnants of the Roman Empire. As Istanbul, Constantinople has been a Muslim city ever since. The mortar then as now had a drawback: it could kill friend and foe indiscriminately. It was not much in favour until the First World War yet, as the Serbs demonstrated in grisly fashion at Sarajevo, it is the perfect weapon of terror. It enjoys only approximate accuracy and rains explosive death from the sky without warning by telephone or otherwise. Risk to the mortarman, properly managed, is nil. The weapon is simple and cheap, has a high rate of fire, is mobile, easily concealed and, as *Jane's* notes, 'fires a bomb with excellent anti-personnel characteristics'. IRA engineers seem to have taken some of their design ideas from this and other standard works on the weapon.

The first IRA mortar was used in May 1972. Technical Intelligence documents reveal:

> the bomb consisted of a length of 50mm copper pipe filled with ten ounces of commercial plastic explosive and propelled to the target by a .303 cartridge inserted into the end of a steel tube tail section. The impact [achieved by dropping the bomb into the launch tube] drove a pointed striker against a .22 cartridge and ignited the detonator. The mortar tube was trigger operated and hand held . . . It has not been used since late 1972.

The Republicans learned fast after that.

> In December 1972 a concerted wave of attacks against targets in four county towns in Northern Ireland heralded the arrival of the Mk-2 mortar. This bomb was constructed from an eight-inch length of 57mm steel pipe filled with one to two pounds of commercial explosive and propelled by a 12-bore cartridge containing ninety grains of propellant . . . A short length of split fuse provided a five-second delay between impact and ignition. This was presumably to allow

penetration of the roof of the target building before explosion in the room below.

The IRA used the Mk-3 mortar in attacks on Creggan Camp, Londonderry, and Lisanelly barracks, Omagh, in 1973. In these the bomb was dropped into the 60mm mortar barrel where the launch cartridge struck a static firing-pin on the base-plate. This ignited a J-cloth which had been soaked in sodium chlorate and then dried. This exploded to hurl the bomb 260 yards. The bomb itself depended on a mixture of ammonium nitrate. For once this was not extracted from legally available fertilizer but was high-grade crystalline ammonium nitrate. The weapon was volatile and dangerous to the user. On 16 August 1973 two IRA mortarmen were killed when their bomb exploded prematurely in the barrel during an attack on Pomeroy RUC barracks. On 9 December that year, an unexploded Mk-3 bomb was found after an attack on Aldergrove airfield, Belfast.

The Mk-4, used to attack a base at Strabane on 22 February 1974, extended the range to 400 yards using additional J-cloth/ sodium chlorate as the propellant. The explosive charge was '1lb ammonium nitrate/aluminium powder of very high purity which contained calcium carbonate, indicating it had been recovered from a local fertilizer'. Forensic scientists noted that 'all three possible [design] areas that failed during the attack on Pomeroy police station, which may have caused the accident, were redesigned'. All these mortars were produced by the same team. Even the base-plates had been cut from a single sheet of metal. Intelligence documents reported:

> Only one type of explosive has been used: an ammonium nitrate/aluminium powder mix, containing seven to fifteen per cent of aluminium. This is similar to explosive used in grenades in attacks limited to Belfast, Down and Armagh areas. In all cases the propellant was a J-cloth impregnated with sodium chlorate, between 75 and 80 per cent of the total propellant weight . . . dipping the J-cloth into a warm, saturated solution of sodium chlorate and water and hanging up to dry.

News of the Mk-5 reached the Security Forces thanks to the discovery of an IRA arms factory at Cushendall, Antrim, in May 1974. By then, the IRA was experimenting with a primitive cannon based on its mortar technology, known as a 'bombard': 'The range of this weapon is claimed in recovered terrorist literature to be 25 yds but to date no field trials have been carried out to authenticate this.'

The Mk-6 mortar – built in a conventional calibre of 60mm with a standard launch tube, bi-pod and base-plate – probably took years and several IRA lives to develop but it became a classic of the Republicans' arsenal. As Weapons Intelligence analysis reveals, it was first used on 28 September 1974, when thirty bombs were fired in one attack.

> All thirty bombs exploded and later trials on mortars recovered in finds proved that Pira had at last developed a safe, reliable and accurate mortar system . . . Operation is simple and involves only the dropping of the bomb down the launch tube onto a fixed firing pin. When the bomb reaches the bottom of the tube, the .22 cartridge initiates a plain detonator which in turn initiates the main filling.

A later version was fired electrically from a timer/power unit using a photographic flash-bulb instead of the percussion cap. Electrical ignition makes life easier and safer for the terrorist. The bomb is pre-loaded and fired remotely. Combined with a timer (as at Heathrow airport), the weapon gives the terrorist an opportunity to escape, as well as enabling several bombs to be launched simultaneously. By 1993, analysts studying the Mk-6 could report: 'The latest single tube base plates are extremely well made and may easily be mistaken for military models.'

Once in the air, the bomb 'arms itself by means of a wind-driven propeller, which is an integral part of the striker'. The front of the bomb carried a .22 percussion cap which, on impact, triggered the main charge, 3lb of Semtex H high explosive.

The IRA now had 'a sophisticated and reasonably accurate weapon system, used successfully against Security Forces bases in urban areas of Northern Ireland. Targets have been engaged at short range to minimise possible collateral damage to adjacent civilian housing. (In Germany, greater areas are possible.)' For some IRA warriors, however, it was too sophisticated. They discarded the launcher and delivered the bomb by hand. Sometimes they scored. In March 1987 a Mk-6 mortar bomb was dropped by hand from the top of Divis Flats in Belfast on to a Security Forces vehicle, penetrating the vehicle's roof armour with devastating results.

The Mk-6, trialled in Eire, had a maximum range of 1,200 yards 'which might mean that preparations for an attack may not be easily detected and that military installations can be engaged from areas of dead ground outwith [beyond] the arcs of observation of sentries or prowler guards'.

In 1978–79, as military bases were strengthened against attacks by the Mk-6, the terrorists adopted a new design philosophy, one which increased the throw-weight of the bomb while disregarding the risk to civilians living near military targets.

Many of these weapons failed during the trial period, but the IRA doggedly continued to develop new mortars. As the defences around security bases improved, so a bigger bomb was needed to penetrate these. In an effort to increase the explosive payload the guerrillas created the Mk-7 and Mk-8, first used in 1976 against the combined army/RUC barracks at Crossmaglen, South Armagh. It was made from 4 feet of steel tubing and has been described as a 'stretched' Mk-6. The bomb it fired was an aerodynamic disaster, too long to be stable in flight. Of the first ten bombs fired in an initial operation, only four detonated. On 23 October 1976 the Mark 9 launched a shorter, fatter bomb, created from a cut-down gas cylinder, from an array of ten tubes against an army base at Crossmaglen. Seven penetrated the target area and all exploded. The weapon which took this deadly process a stage further was the Mk-10 mortar, first used in March 1979, and able to hurl a bomb devised from steel tubing 1.4m long, 165mm in diameter, over a distance of 200 metres with a 40lb warhead of home-made explosive. The bomb, usually fabricated from an oxy-acetyline gas cylinder with the ends trimmed off, was pre-loaded into the barrel and detonated electrically. The IRA design used not one launcher tube but up to ten in one unit, each tube angled differently from the others in the array so as to widen the potential target area. Many of these weapons failed during the trial period. Between 1973 and early 1978, the Provisionals made seventy-one mortar attacks against the Security Forces without causing a single death. In the two years 1981–82 there were nine mortar attacks on Security Force bases throughout the Province, causing just ten minor military casualties and wounding one civilian. But as the IRA said of its attempts to assassinate Margaret Thatcher: 'We only have to get lucky once.' In guerrilla warfare, persistence always pays off eventually. That happened with the Mk-10 mortar on 28 February 1985 when nine RUC officers were killed as they relaxed within the false security of their fortified canteen at Newry.

Meanwhile, as an additional twist to its policy of making an acceptable level of violence less acceptable to the British, the IRA was preparing to return to the offensive in the British capital. In December 1988, a Provisional IRA bomb factory was uncovered in Battersea, South London. Items related to the Mk-10 mortar were found there, the harbinger of heavy mortar attacks on Downing Street and Heathrow Airport. The find also confirmed other Intelligence about IRA strategy pointing to 'a three-pronged campaign involving attacks in Northern Ireland, mainland UK and the Continent'. By the late 1990s, Security Forces were confronting the 'war of four campaigns'. The fourth was the Irish Republic.

By 1989, the IRA's armourers had built the Mk-11 mortar with a range of up to 550 yards, first used to attack an army observation post at Glassdumman, South Armagh, on 13 May 1989. The main explosive charge was a mixture of nitrobenzene and ammonium nitrate known in the trade as 'Annie'. In February 1991, with Annie as its warhead, the Mk-10 mortar was used to strike at Downing Street from a Transit van parked almost opposite the Ministry of Defence in Whitehall, in a propaganda spectacular as effective, in its way, as the Brighton bomb of 1984. John Major's War Cabinet, discussing its next move in the Gulf conflict, was obliged to dive for cover under furniture as an enemy nearer home than Iraq blasted the walls of the building.

Further expensive fortification ('hardening') of police and army barracks had followed the Mk-10 mortar attack on Newry. As one expert put it: 'It's like the Maginot Line in some bases. In 1971 the Crossmaglen RUC barracks in South Armagh was a brick-built house with wire mesh on the windows and nothing more. By 1997 it had walls 7ft thick and a top floor kept empty as a unit of "space armour".'

The IRA response to harder targets was bigger bombs. The movement developed the Mk-13 spigot mortar. The bomb for this device was a recycled 45-gallon oil drum able to deliver 800lb of home-made explosive lobbed from the back of a pick-up truck. Its drawback was its short range – as little as 60 yards – making it easy for Security Forces to identify potential launch sites. The terrorists' first answer to that problem was greater mobility. The launch platform was a heavy vehicle, such as a tipper lorry or tractor, as a mobile firing point first used at Dungannon on 22 May 1990. An Intelligence report on this ferocious weapon commented drily: 'The device is simply constructed and has none of the tolerances or engineering problems associated with the Mk-10 mortar production.'

In 1992, the South Armagh Pira moved on to build, with mixed results, two mortar bombs – the Mk-14 and Mk-15 – using gas cylinders filled with home-made explosive. Weapons Intelligence officers noted: 'The complete assembly, disguised as a cylindrical hay bale, has even been transported to the firing point attached to the hydraulic hoist at the rear of a tractor'.

The IRA wanted a weapon that combined the heavyweight punch of the Mk-13 with the range and flexibility of the Mark 10. The result was the Mark 15, 'the Barrackbuster', a bomb 1m long by 36cm diameter, delivering more than 70kg (154lb) of home-made explosive over a distance of 150 metres. The bomb was built by adapting domestic gas cylinders (Kosangas) used in remote rural areas on both sides of the border for heating and cooking. The Mk-15 bomb was used against police and army bases in Ballygawley (February 1993), Crossmaglen, Newry and the British base at Osnabruck in June 1996.

For any civilian in the area, the risk of an accidental explosion was enormous. As one official report put it:

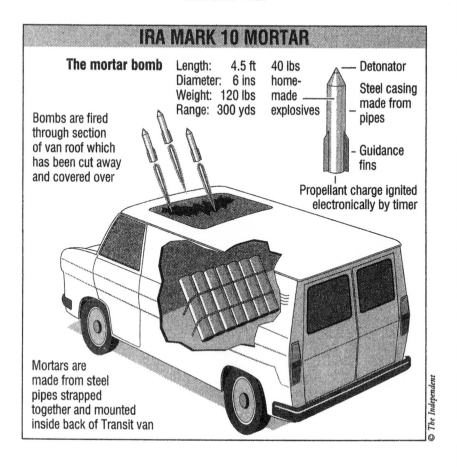

IRA MARK 10 MORTAR

The mortar bomb

Length: 4.5 ft
Diameter: 6 ins
Weight: 120 lbs
Range: 300 yds

40 lbs home-made explosives

Bombs are fired through section of van roof which has been cut away and covered over

— Detonator

Steel casing made from pipes

- Guidance fins

Propellant charge ignited electronically by timer

Mortars are made from steel pipes strapped together and mounted inside back of Transit van

© *The Independent*

The IRA's Mk-10 mortar. At Newry on 28 February 1985 just one of its bombs hit a police canteen, killing nine officers, the biggest single loss of life from this type of weapon. At Whitehall in 1991, some bombs exploded in the tube, threatening the nearby civilian population.

The bombs are not point-detonated, having to rely on the delay caused by the burning of the safety fuse. They often air-burst, fail to launch and explode in the tube or fail completely ... If they land on target they can cause devastating

Mortar was fired from a farmyard 150 yards from the base.

Tractor launched 'barrack buster' mortar

RUC ARMY BASE

Lynx helicopter hit in the tail while coming in to resupply the base.

© Solo Syndication

GRAPHIC: Chris Cherry and David Ace

South Armagh PIRA conceals a Mk-15 'Barrackbuster' mortar (throw-weight of 250 lbs of explosive) inside a haybale on the back of a tractor to make a close-quarter attack on Crossmaglen fortress. The bomb hit an Army Lynx helicopter.

damage and widespread casualties ... In vehicle-borne attacks, the Mk-10 mortar is concealed within the body of a van or in some form of camouflage such as straw bales in the back of a flatbed truck ... Aiming the system is simply done by aligning the vehicle with a permanent landscape feature in the target area such as a radio mast.

The IRA did not consider using a compass to enhance accuracy. Instead, it reduced the risk to its own men by firing the weapon remotely with a command wire, a radio control or timers.

In 1985 yet another new weapon rolled off the terrorist production line. This was the Improvised Projected Grenade, a grenade fired directly at the target from a specially constructed launcher. The IPG carried 115g (4oz) of Semtex and TNT high explosive to its target. A Weapons Intelligence report noted:

This first appeared in Strabane in 1985 [during an incident in which three terrorists were killed]. Since then it has been used either in its direct role, e.g. against mobile patrols, or as a stand-off weapon in which the grenade is lobbed over perimeter fences. Whilst the launcher itself may look crude, the projectile is made of a number of components which require a high standard of machine manufacturing.

In March 1986, after an IRA volunteer killed himself through reckless handling of a loaded launcher, additional safety features were built into the system. However, it suffered from the disadvantage that its recoil left a huge bruise on the shoulder of the operator. Then, as one Intelligence officer recalled with a grin, 'We could round up the usual suspects, remove their shirts and look for the bruise.'

The IPG was succeeded by the Pira Projected Recoilless Improvised Grenade (PRIG) first used in an attack on an RUC Hotspur armoured vehicle in Belfast on 20 May 1991. This was essentially a home-made version of the Russian rocket-propelled grenade, the RPG-7. One Intelligence source believed that the basic design for PRIG was copied from a diagram for the German *Armbrust* (Crossbow) missile, published by a standard reference book. Traditionally, such weapons carry with them the danger of casualties caused by the flash from the rear of the launcher as the missile is fired. But, as *Jane's* commented: 'Unlike many modern recoilless weapons, which rely . . . on the rearward expulsion of a large volume of high velocity gas, *Armbrust* balances the forward momentum of the projectile by ejecting a counter-mass to the rear.' The military advantage of this, to the guerrilla, is that 'it can be safely fired from a small enclosed space with a wall as close as 80 centimetres behind the firer'. A firer lying prone 'presents no better target than does a rifleman'. Equally useful is 'the absence of flash, smoke and blast when fired and a firing noise similar in type and intensity to a pistol shot'. It is the ideal weapon for urban warfare.

In the IRA version, the grenade is made from a 1lb food tin

filled with 600g of Semtex. The launcher is a length of steel tube with a propellant chamber added to it. The design reveals a scientific mind capable of lateral thinking. The professionally made *Armbrust* depends for its counter-mass on 5,000 small plastic flakes which fan out as they leave the launch tube and fall harmlessly to the ground about 10 metres behind it. The IRA system also uses a counter-balance in the rear of the launch tube that is the same weight as the grenade. An Intelligence analysis revealed: 'Normally this is two packets of digestive biscuits wrapped in J-cloths. The J-cloths increase the external diameter of the biscuits to match the internal diameter of the launch tube, thereby achieving a limited amount of rearward obturation.'

Forensic teams crawling over the suspected IRA firing points learned to watch out for remnants of biscuit wrappers and J-cloths as well as other clues to the weapon used against them. The synthesis of high-tech knowledge quarried out of standard reference books on military technology with what is known in the Third World as 'intermediate' (or bicycle) technology is what makes Irish disarmament unlikely in the foreseeable future . . .

The PRIG had another major advantage which added enormously to its destructive, armour-piercing power. Its design incorporated the shaped charge principle known as HEAT (for High Energy Anti-Tank). In this design the explosive charge is in the rear of the warhead, formed round a hollow cone. On impact the hollow portion crumples, bringing the base of the explosive cone to the surface of the armour. At the same time the fuse ignites the charge at the rear. The conical shape of the front of the charge focuses the explosive into a high-velocity, high-temperature gas jet. As *Jane's* commented: 'Such a jet will penetrate solid armour plate to a depth typically, for a large projectile of 30cm or more; and if this amounts to perforation [of the armour] a jet of hot gas and molten metal is squirted into the interior of the tank.' Design of the PRIG warhead embodies exactly these principles, as does the terrorists' Mk-12 mortar bomb. An Intelligence officer explained: 'If the main explosive charge is home-made rather than Semtex or TNT, then the additional energy resulting from the shaped charge design will make HME [home-made explosive] an equally formidable weapon.'

Meanwhile, the IRA continued to use the existing instruments in its deadly orchestra. The Mk-6, its most conventional mortar array, armed with Semtex warheads, was used in a blitz against London's Heathrow airport in March 1994. After a mere fifty-two-minute telephone warning, an array of five mortar tubes in the back of a stolen Nissan car parked at an airport hotel lofted bombs over Heathrow police station and the airport perimeter fence to land without exploding on a 20m-wide apron at the edge of the 45m-wide north runway. During the next forty-three minutes, twenty-three aircraft took off from the runway. Gerry Adams added his own contribution to the attack, launched as the Commons routinely renewed the Prevention of Terrorism Act. Adams told an Irish Radio interviewer: 'The conflict is ongoing. Every so often, there will be something spectacular to remind the outside world. This attack is in the middle of stalemate. I would now ask John Major to end the stalemate.'

Two more, similar, attacks were made within three days. The second and third were launched from camouflaged pits in scrubland. One put a bomb on the roof of Terminal 4 while 4,000 people were inside. Only good luck prevented its detonation, with a massive number of deaths. IRA engineers were more concerned with the reason why twelve of their mortar bombs did not explode. The answer was that they were often unstable in flight. The detonating mechanism had to hit the target at an angle of 90 degrees. The engineers were working on that. In May 1990, Security Forces uncovered a home-made gyroscope in a Provo arms cache designed to overcome the problem.

Eight days after the Heathrow attack, a mortar team lobbed a big Mk-10 from the back of a tractor into the Crossmaglen army base as a Lynx helicopter was landing. The shot damaged the helicopter's tail unit. The machine was 100 feet above the ground and started to spin uncontrollably. The army pilot, using 'exceptional skill and clear thinking', succeeded in landing the machine inside the base. The crew of three ran clear, then realized that their passenger, an RUC officer, was still inside. They ran back and dragged him out just before the Lynx and its fuel tanks exploded. So did ammunition aboard the helicopter. The attack was made from farmland 150 yards from the target, at the extreme edge of the Mark 10's range. A local non-Unionist MP, Seamus Mallon, said: 'God knows how many people could have been killed. When you realise this mortar was lobbed over a number of houses it brings home the enormity of the danger so many people faced. Yet again you have Sinn Fein talking peace in the morning and carrying out these murderous attacks through the IRA in the evening.' A local SDLP (nationalist) councillor, John Fee, described the attack as 'an act of lunacy'. Mr Fee's criticism provoked a beating by two men outside his home in the darkness. His ribs were broken and face smashed in what was clearly a planned attack carried out by thugs well practised in such business. Fee commented: 'The IRA, I believe, felt they had to create a very high-profile way of telling people, "Keep your mouth shut."' The IRA denied responsibility, but few people regarded the denials as credible.

Three months later, in July 1994, the IRA mortar team again demonstrated their indifference to local, civilian, opinion. This time, the attack vehicle carrying the mortar tubes was left in the car park of a Roman Catholic church – St Bridgid's, in the Malone Road area of South Belfast – as a wedding ceremony was taking place inside the building. One bomb struck the roof of a block of flats adjoining a base held by the Royal Irish Regiment. No soldiers were hurt but the driver of a bus waiting nearby was gravely injured. Guests were arriving for a second wedding when the explosions occurred.

Undeterred, a team belonging to South Amagh IRA parked a red Leyland tipper truck converted into a mobile firing point for the Mark 10 on a building site 100 yards from Newry police station, scene of the 1985 attack. They left three mortars to be triggered by a timing device, which lobbed the bombs over a main street, shops and houses. Anthony McCabe, who was opening a shop alongside the station, described what happened.

> We heard a dull thud. Next minute the ground lifted and shook. We shouted to everyone to get out. As we went through the door the second went off. There was a hail of glass and stones. We kept running towards the bottom of the street. A couple of nuns were badly shaken. Then the third went off and the whole place was raining with glass. One fellow was running and his hand was open like a book. Blood was running down his arm.

More than forty civilians were injured in this attack as were three of the Security Forces. Civilians wounded by flying glass, masonry and shrapnel included a girl aged two and several old people. The IRA team were not among the casualties. Having activated the timers, they scurried away in Renault 21 cars.

Such operations reflected the same morality that justified the use of Whiterock College of Further Education in Republican West Belfast as a hiding place for 2lb of Semtex, an improvised grenade, a bomb, an AK47 rifle and .38 revolver. The cache was uncovered as the mortar attacks were made on Heathrow. It was concealed in the roof space of a boiler room directly below a classroom. It also contained detonators, a pressure plate for a booby trap, 1,500 bullets and a timer/power unit. Someone was using the college as a bomb factory.

During the IRA ceasefire later that year, the movement's engineering department continued to work energetically on mortar technology. They had a special target in mind. In February 1996, after Edward O'Brien blew himself up on a bus in London, police found among his belongings a plan to attack Downing Street or Parliament from a barge on the Thames. The police increased their waterborne patrols with six fast inflatable patrol craft.

Meanwhile, possibly because of the adverse publicity resulting from the use of clumsy, blockbusting weapons such as the Mk-10, the IRA developed a new light mortar system with a range – up to 1,200 yards – comparable to that of the

Mk-6, but adapted as a rocket-propelled missile for direct, aimed attack rather than a bomb lobbed into the air in the general area of a target. As an Intelligence report put it: 'Pira has developed a new light system that is compact, portable, easily concealed and may be designed to fire a mobile version of the PRIG round.' British security forces were alerted to the new threat by the Republic's Gardai, who uncovered an IRA engineering department factory at Clonaslee, County Laois, in June.

The Gardai had a score to settle with the IRA. For years, the Republicans had honoured an unwritten agreement not to attack Security Forces in the South. In June 1996, Garda (Constable) Jerry McCabe was shot dead by an IRA team trying to rob a postal van in the Republic. Ballistic tests on the fatal bullets confirmed that they came from a Kalashnikov assault rifle used in an IRA raid two years earlier. Public outrage at this murder drew 25,000 people to McCabe's funeral in Limerick, turning it into a demonstration against terrorism. It was – in that over-worked phrase – a turning-point in the conflict. The Gardai appealed to the Irish public for information. As if by magic, the force started uncovering IRA arms factories. Little more than two weeks after McCabe's death, the Irish police raided a farm near Clonaslee in County Laois and caught two senior members of the movement's Southern Command (a quartermaster and an engineer) in a bunker 14 feet by 8 feet at the end of a tunnel leading from a concealed entrance in a garden. They were making mortar bombs. The tunnel might have been used as a range for test firing. The bunker yielded the full range of explosives components: forty mortar tubes, Semtex, ammonia and nitrate used in home-made explosives, switches, timers, detonators, guns, tail fins and other mortar parts. Sixteen more tubes were found in a workshop above ground.

Four months later, the Gardai discovered a new type of mortar launch frame at Ballybinaby near Hackballscross in County Louth, for use with the new system. It had three tubes. In all, eight frames were found. The implication was that a multi-barrel attack could be mounted. The expert assessment was that the weapon could hurl twice the weight of the Mk-6 mortar (600g of Semtex rather than 300g), but, as an Intelligence report also concluded:

> The short launch tube of the new weapon will affect its accuracy and it is possible it will be used more effectively at the shorter end of this range scale [of 100m to 1,000m]. The main operational advantages of the system to Pira will be its portability and comparatively easy handling. It is therefore a suitable weapon for mounting attacks on large targets in NI and the mainland or overseas.

In February 1996, when a massive lorry bomb at Canary Wharf ended the spurious IRA truce that year, warnings sent to military bases in Britain stressed the risk of 'stand-off' attacks as well as close-quarter assassination, sleeper bombs and vehicle bombs. The fabrication of mortars was one example of the IRA's formidable skills in building a war machine without outside help. (So, too, for simple street fighting was the grenade which, by the 1990s, had evolved into the Mk-14, filled with ball bearings or steel rings as the lethal component, or the Mk-15, the coffee-jar grenade, in which 1p coins were used to create shrapnel.) The mortar and PRIG were also valuable propaganda weapons, symbols of serious, professional military status, but they lacked the strategic impact of big bombs, which the Provisionals' engineering department built on an ever grander scale, some exceeding 8,000lb in explosive weight.

Through two world wars, high-explosive bombs had failed to fulfil the expectations of the air generals from Lord Trenchard to Bomber Harris to deliver a decisive, strategic, knock-out blow. The resistance of civilians subject to blitzkrieg usually hardened. Only the use of atomic weapons secured something like that result in Japan in 1945. Yet the IRA, bombing economic targets in London at ground level rather than from the air, came close to realizing the airmen's dream. There was never a hope that the IRA could destroy the British economy – such destruction could not be achieved by the RAF in

Germany or the USAF in Vietnam – but in a peacetime culture that shrank from casualties, it could cause some expensive dents.

12

'Me Owld Alarram Clock'
(the Sinn Fein Conjuror's Outfit)

In song, it was celebrated by the Dubliners in a chirpy number about something called 'jelliganite', attached to 'me owld alarram clock'. Brendan Behan, playwright and failed terrorist, gaily described it in the 1940s as his 'Sinn Fein conjuror's outfit'. In 1992, after a century of lethal experiment, the Bomb finally came right for the IRA. The path of this perverse love affair with explosive (low explosive as well as high) did not run smooth. From 1970–71, Republican bomb construction had been a process of reinventing the wheel, not only in the manufacture of explosive material but in devising ever more novel methods of triggering the stuff on command. After almost three more decades, Irish Republicans were the world's leaders in the design of Improvised Explosive Devices (IEDs, in military shorthand).

Between 1969 and February 1996, the IRA lost approximately 120 of its own due to premature explosions. Thousands more, overwhelmingly innocent civilians, were also killed along the way. A minority of the 'own-goal' casualties were key players. Brendan Burns, aged thirty-three, was the bomber who slaughtered eighteen Parachute regiment soldiers at Warrenpoint in 1979 and another five at Camlough in 1981, as well as Lord Chief Justice Gibson in 1987. The reputed lover of Mairead Farrell, his life ended as he built a bomb a few days before she was shot dead in Gibraltar by the SAS in 1988. Thomas Begley, a Belfast Catholic who liquidized himself with a bomb on the Protestant Shankill Road in 1993, was specially favoured: his pall-bearers included Gerry Adams.

However, most of the own-goalers were disposable IRA mules,

inexperienced nonentities and wannabe terrorists ready, as one cynical veteran put it, 'to go to England and plant a bomb for Owld Oireland'. Some did not have far to go. Frank Ryan, railway labourer and failed British soldier from Harlow, Essex, killed himself with a bomb at St Albans, Hertfordshire, in 1991. His teammate, Patricia Black-Donnelly, from an embattled Belfast council estate, was aged eighteen, with less than a year's experience of active service before, as the movement put it, 'dying on a foreign street'. Both were victims not only of the bomb they prematurely primed but also the naivety – emotional as well as political – required by the godfathers who half-trained them. Edward O'Brien, aged twenty-one, whose bomb destroyed him on a London bus in February 1996, was an ex-altar boy of poor intelligence from Gorey, County Wexford.

One of the first IRA own-goals was at a house in Bogside, Derry, in 1971 where three IRA men blew themselves up along with two women in the house. Another early casualty was Jack McCabe, an IRA veteran of the 1940s campaign who had smuggled weapons including a Schmeisser sub-machine-gun into Republican Belfast. He was mixing ingredients for a home-made bomb in December 1971, using a metal shovel on a concrete garage floor. The predictable result was a spark and a premature explosion. In spite of his years in terrorism, McCabe had ignored, or did not know, Rule No. 2 (out of eight basic rules) for bomb-makers: DO NOT *stir mixture with metal object.* McCabe's bomb removed his testicles and blinded him before he died a lingering death. By then – in this first year of internment – there had been more than 1,000 explosions in Northern Ireland. Other bomb-makers, such as Shane Paul O'Doherty of Derry, suffered nothing worse than a 'gelignite headache' as they constructed their devices in back kitchens and garden sheds. The first IRA man to kill himself in Britain in the latest campaign was James McDade, who blew himself up in November 1974 while planting his bomb at Coventry telephone exchange. The local IRA unit responded to his death with the notorious Birmingham pub bombings. Those, in turn, prompted the Prevention of Terrorism Act.

By the late 1970s, the IRA had learned to build safety features into its bombs. By the 1990s, aided by the Intelligence of, among others, a former priest named Patrick Ryan who became a specialist in timing devices, IRA technology improved to the point where own-goal deaths were rare. This experience was obtained, on the whole, at the expense of civilians of both communities and all ages in Northern Ireland, particularly during the first two years (1971 and 1972) of the renewed IRA offensive. Of the forty-eight soldiers killed in Northern Ireland during 1971, just six were murdered by bombers. The first was Sergeant Michael Willets of the Parachute regiment, who died a hero's death on 5 May 1971 when he used his body to shield two children from a no-warning suitcase bomb hurled into the entrance of a Belfast police station. Two other soldiers killed by bombs were explosive specialists – Ammunition Technical Officers – of the Royal Army Ordnance Corps, which soon suffered a twenty per cent casualty rate.

The civilians were not at war with anyone. On 9 February 1971, five engineers on their way to service a remote BBC transmitter in Tyrone were blown up and killed. Bars, usually Protestant, hit in Belfast that year included the Four Step Inn (two killed, twenty-seven injured), the Red Lion, Ormeau Road (two killed, thirty-six injured), and McGurk's (fifteen killed, thirteen injured). As part of a campaign of economic warfare, the IRA bombed a furniture showroom on the Protestant Shankill Road on 11 December. The dead included Colin Nicholl, aged seven months and Tracy Munn, aged two. Two adults were also killed.

As part of the same attrition, shops and offices were attacked throughout the Province. The Provisionals gloated. The front page of *Republican News* on 12 December, under the headline '£1,000,000 up in smoke' described the destruction of a linoleum factory and assured readers that a £50 million grant from the London government to aid Northern Ireland's economy 'will soon be swallowed up'.

In March 1972, two months after Bloody Sunday, IRA bombs in the Abercorn Restaurant and at a Belfast car park killed eight people and injured 276. In July, the Bloody Friday blitz on Belfast's main bus station employed 26 bombs to kill nine people. By the end of 1972, a total of 468 people had been killed by terrorism, of whom the great majority (323) were civilians murdered by IRA bombs. The total number of soldiers killed in this way was just thirty. By 1992 the total number of explosions, most of them the work of the IRA, had passed 10,000. The IRA's body-count was still dominated by innocent civilians. In 1989 John Hume, leader of the predominantly Catholic Social Democratic and Labour Party, calculated that more than half of the 2,667 people killed during the first twenty years of conflict had been non-combatants. As *Time* magazine also noted: 'a total 58 per cent perished at the hands of the IRA and other Irish Republican terrorist groups, while 25 per cent fell to the Protestant extremists and 11 per cent to British security forces.' It was due to the IRA's manipulative skill during those twenty years that the memory of civilians shot dead on Bloody Sunday was kept green while the greater number of innocents killed by the IRA were discreetly forgotten.

Beneath the mayhem, a technical war was emerging between the bomb-makers and the men responsible for detecting or dismantling the bombs before they could cause more pain. When commercial explosive supplies – frangex, opencast gelignite, gelamex or plaster gelatine – ran short, the terrorists' engineering department created at least six different types of explosive or incendiary mixtures from home-made recipes. 'Co-op Mix' was a yellowish-white blend of sodium chlorate and nitrobenzene, little used after 1977. ANFO, the most popular heavy filling in big bombs, combined ammonium nitrate with fuel oil: a simple can of petrol was converted into a deadly fuel-air explosive weapon generating a terrifying blast. Fire-bombs were constructed using a simple mixture of sodium chlorate and sugar, in transparent cassette containers. Often one type of explosive was used to detonate the heavier, slower charge of another.

To give the bomber a chance to escape, the IRA developed Timing and Power Units (TPUs) ranging from a simple clothes peg or acid-filled condom to a linked array of electronic timers taken from washing machines or videos. As a sub-discipline, the IRA created bombs specifically tailored to ambush soldiers and police officers, lured by bogus calls for emergency help, or by a separate, 'come-on' bomb. Ambush IEDs used command wires in the early part of the campaign. These were often buried, but even then they were frequently visible to British air reconnaissance teams. The explosive charge could be buried inside a house, a car, or a wall. One Intelligence source revealed:

> It has been known for the terrorist to use a baby alarm to listen in to what is happening at the ambush contact point. No visual contact with the target was necessary. Or the bomber might use an observer 'off-set' from the bomb command position to give a signal when the target was at the contact point. This signal has been by radio as well as a visual one.

The first bomb triggered remotely by radio command, in January 1972, a month before Bloody Sunday, was adapted from a model aircraft guidance system. By the mid-1970s the IRA was using sophisticated electronic switches as detonators to try to prevent premature detonation of the bombs by army operators jamming the air-waves. As an Intelligence report put it:

> Aero-modelling equipment proved to have too many drawbacks . . . subject to many spurious signals emanating from a multitude of sources which put the terrorist at greater risk than the target. Over the years the terrorist has managed to refine his RC [radio controlled] capability and incorporate encoding/decoding devices in the system which make the device less susceptible to initiation by stray signals.

By the early 1980s, the authorities had uncovered detonation systems adapted from radios used to monitor weather forecasts and by 1986 the electro-magnetic booby trap was in use. An Intelligence report told the story:

> During a recovery operation in South Armagh a search dog showed an interest in a dry stone wall 30 metres from a derelict building. Remote investigation of the wall revealed that part of it had been rebuilt with clean stones. Further investigation was carried out with a clearance charge. This caused partial detonation of a booby trap device concealed in the wall. A device with a coil of wire was dug into the

ground at the base of the wall . . . The bomb was activated when an electromagnetic field of sufficient force intercepted the coil . . . In the late seventies it was thought that Pira were intending to use a similar type of circuit to offset SF [Security Forces] successes with metal detection equipment. Then a list of electronic components under the heading 'AMD' was found. This was believed to represent 'Anti-Metal Detector'. It was shown that these components could be wired into a circuit and when used in conjunction with a coil, would cause a switch [on the bomb] to change state in response to the sweeping motion of the metal detection equipment.

Another type of booby trap, most frequently used in assassinations, was the mercury tilt switch. Airey Neave MP was murdered by such a bomb, attached to the underside of his car, in 1979. As he drove up the ramp from the House of Commons underground car park, the tilt switch did its deadly work. By 1993 the IRA was using a Mk-17 TPU incorporating a time delay and a mercury tilt switch glued to the outside of the bomb container. Magnets were used to attach such bombs to cars and two-hour Memopark timers (designed to remind motorists that it was time to feed the parking meter) ensured a punctual explosion. In this design, the tilt switch was an anti-handling device intended to kill anyone trying to remove the bomb.

Radar detectors bought from the USA were also a late innovation, first found by Security Forces in 1988. Used legitimately by police forces to enforce speed limits on motorists, an electronic gun is aimed at the target vehicle from half a mile away. The smart motorist's counter to that is a radar detector, fitted on the dashboard to warn him that his vehicle is being 'painted' by the police radar. As converted by the IRA with some simple rewiring, the radar detector is attached to a detonator. As the beam of the radar gun hits the radar detector in the car, the car-bomb explodes. In the USA in 1990, FBI agents working against the IRA in an undercover 'sting' operation brought to justice several American scientists in this field, one of whom had top secret US government clearance when he was arrested. The case was another reminder of widespread public support for the IRA in the USA.

The war of the air-waves continued right up to the 1997 ceasefire. As one Intelligence report observed:

> The distinct advantage of the RC [radio control] over the CWIED [command wire improvised explosive device] is the absence of the tell-tale wire. The RCIED field is constantly changing with technical developments brought about mainly by the legalisation of CB radios in the UK. This has prompted an increase in equipment available and the number of frequency bands and channels which they operate on.

Yet another design, though a distinctly hit-and-miss system, was the Projectile Command IED. With the explosive, two sheets of copper were used which, when brought into contact with one another, started the detonation cycle. The novelty lay in the means by which that contact was made. It was done with a rifle bullet fired from a safe distance. It meant that the IRA's favourite mobile attack weapon, the car-bomb, could be rigged in advance, parked at the target and detonated at any time by a marksman.

Equally ingenious was the use of a camera flashlight fired from 100 yards away to strike a light-sensitive cell that then triggered a bomb or Mk-12 mortar hidden in a parked car. The bomb was fired directly at its target, horizontally. At Newry it was used to attack a police vehicle driving out of its barracks on a road flanking a canal. The police driver died instantly. The IRA trigger man, with flash gun, was safely tucked away on the other side of the canal, 100 feet away. The advantage of this system, and a similar one employing infra-red sensors designed to operate garage doors remotely, was that it left no tell-tale chemical stain or fibre on the body or clothes of the operator to assist a Diplock Court with forensic evidence.

Attacks on civilian targets led to a different type of bomb-making technology. Shane O'Doherty, a prominent IRA bomb-maker before he underwent a change of heart, sent dozens of letter-bombs to human targets in England between 1973 and 1974. Like mortar attacks and assassination machines, letter-bombs come with no warning.

For attacks on political leaders and holiday resorts alike, the Republicans refined their timing systems to a remarkable degree. When police raided the Glasgow apartment used by the Brighton bomber Patrick Magee, they discovered a bomb cache containing 140lb of commercial gelignite. Timer/power units, not yet installed in bombs, were set to run for forty-eight days. Home Office scientists checked the accuracy of these. The worst was inaccurate by just a few minutes. One of the bombs was already planted in room 112 of the Rubens Hotel, London, as part of an attack on the British tourist industry. Searchers knew it had to be there yet it was not uncovered for three hours. The bomb that nearly wiped out the British Cabinet at the Grand Hotel, Brighton, in 1984 was never detected. Even if the entire building, and many like it, were paralysed for months by search parties, the bombers could still deliver their attack by bicycle or on foot. This type of bomb, in a normal, civilian environment not under military surveillance, was virtually invisible as well as undetectable.

Another factor was at work in this war as in any other prolonged armed conflict. Time and battle coarsened everyone, shaping their perceptions to accept the abnormal as routine. The Europa Hotel in Belfast, a honeypot for visiting journalists and repeatedly attacked, staged a party to 'celebrate' its twenty-fifth bomb. At the grand piano on the first floor, a pianist played 'Look For The Silver Lining', a serenade that drifted through net curtains into the street below, for the room, once again, was without windows. Next day, the glazier's van arrived to make good the damage. That was the good news. The bad news was that the IRA had hijacked the vehicle. It now came with Bomb no. 26.

The most vivid example of a coarsening spirit during the Republican blitz of the late 1980s/early 1990s was the IRA's habit of taking children as hostages, so as to force the owner of a car or lorry – usually the child's father – to drive the bomb to its target as a proxy 'Volunteer'. Five soldiers and a civilian lost their lives as a result. Unlike Muslim fundamentalists, IRA Volunteers were not prepared to be used as human bombs, though the effectiveness of this form of attack could not have been lost upon them. Meanwhile in the back rooms, Republican war scientists pursued their deadly vocation. As the 1997 ceasefire took effect, an arms find in the Republic revealed that prolonged terrorist experiments with the satellite-navigation aid GPS had at last produced a vehicle bomb that could be guided to its target remotely, somewhat like a pilotless Cruise missile. Six years earlier, in 1991, the idea was mooted by the *Sunday Telegraph* whose electronics expert noted that the use of GPS in the Gulf War that year made it 'comparatively simple to adapt the system to feed into a light plane's autopilot or steer a lorry bomb to the target'. The IRA took note.

On 1 May 1992, the Provisionals adapted a van so that it could run on a railway. The van was then loaded with explosives. From the back of the unmanned vehicle, a long command wire paid out as the bomb, engine running and in second gear, moved steadily down the line. Alongside the command wire a rope also trailed from the van, marking the distance travelled, like a horizontal plumb-line. When the rope uncoiled to reveal a large knot, the bombers knew that the van was now at a point opposite an army PVCP (permanent vehicle checkpoint) at Killeen. There, a Fusilier on guard had enough time to warn his comrades, and save their lives, before the explosion killed him.

Over the years it also became clear that IRA bombers, like the Security Forces, were fighting a war of short-term, often reactive tactics without any long-term strategy except, perhaps, attrition. Attacks that wiped out substantial numbers of soldiers – such as Warrenpoint in 1979 (when eighteen Paras were killed) or Bally-gawley, Antrim (eight soldiers blown up in their bus), burnished the IRA's reputation as a big boy's guerrilla army. Prestige assassin-ations had the same impact, though it was the dissident INLA that was the more effective in this department.

With explosives outstripping military strategy – almost 10 tonnes were found in 1988, for example – the Republican bombing cam-paign in practice was not coherent. There were sudden switches of priority, from hits against British army bases in England and Ger-many to attacks on rail commuters; from small incendiaries planted in Manchester shops by the *Cumann na mBan*'s own 'petroleuses' to a farm trailer hostage-bomb laden with 8,500lb of mixed explo-sives in Fermanagh. (The *Cumann na mBan* is the women's section of the IRA – illegal in Northern Ireland and the Republic – used to gather Intelligence, provide safe accommodation and to make and place bombs, especially fire-bombs, in shops.)

Republican pronouncements about bombing reflected this essential lack of direction. When the Official IRA killed five women cleaners and a Catholic army padre at the Parachute regiment mess in 1972, Bernadette Devlin denounced it as 'horrifically wrong' because it strengthened the political credibility of the opposition. In February 1991, when another blast killed a traveller at Victoria station, London, the Sinn Fein spokesman Mitchel McLaughlin described it as catastrophic. He also saw it as 'a tragedy for the Republican struggle . . . It provides opportunity for fudging issues . . . If we are into a situation where the IRA deliberately went out and killed civilians then we are into serious problems.' Murdering a Protestant plumber, Robin Hanna, along with his wife Maureen and their six-year-old son David, with a roadside bomb meant for someone else in 1987 was clinically tagged, 'a tragic error'. In the same year, a long burst of machine-gun fire aimed at a woman and her boyfriend in a car outside her home in Fermanagh, intended for the woman's brother, was 'badly carried out'. In July 1989, a bomb that killed an elderly woman and a youth outside a swimming pool in West Belfast instead of soldiers prompted Gerry Adams, the local MP, to suggest that the IRA 'must get its house in order'.

In practice, the IRA was becoming more, rather than less, sectarian with the passage of time as well as deliberately targeting civilians. In January 1992 seven civilians were murdered and seven others grievously injured when their bus was blown up near Carrickmore, a Republican stronghold. The casualties were builders working on an army base, cause enough, in IRA eyes, to kill them. In the preceding six years, thirty civilians had been murdered on the pretext that they were part of the British armed forces.

Usually, however, the movement said nothing or adopted the safe moral cover of a pious statement that all violent deaths were regrettable, or blamed the Security Forces for their 'failure' to react to IRA warnings. In some cases the text used was similar to that used by O'Bradaigh after the killing of seventeen-month-old Angela Gallagher: 'One of the hazards of urban guerrilla warfare.' The slaughter of Jonathan Ball, aged three, and Tim Parry, aged twelve, in Warrington in 1993 prompted the admission that this episode 'did not serve the interests of the IRA'. One source told Mary Holland of the *Observer*: 'We are not at war with the British population.'

At an IRA extradition hearing in the United States soon after this attack Bernadette Devlin (Mrs McAliskey) refused to condemn the Warrington bombers. She said: 'It was a terrible action, but then the American War of Independence was not won with feather dusters either . . . I refuse to condemn those who are forced by the system to resort to violence, but if I actually supported violence I would use it.' By implication, the end justified the means.

Such comments smothered the guilt that should attach to child murder with Irish fatalism and a token shrug of regret. The same fatalism, expressed as a sort of historical determinism over-riding the right to life, was a postscript to the bombing of civilians at prayer at Enniskillen war memorial in 1987. Eleven people, mainly old people and children, lost their lives. Gordon Wilson, whose daughter died as she lay with him beneath the rubble, holding his hand, tried to engage in human dialogue with the Provisionals. He also prayed that their God might forgive them. But as he put it before he also died prematurely: 'They told me that history is on their side.' It was ten years before Gerry Adams said: 'I hope there will be no more Enniskillens and I am deeply sorry about what happened in Enniskillen.'

Cases where the movement apologized publicly were rare and as unpredictable as the bombers' own actions. One such case, followed the deaths of Sean Dalton, a fifty-five-year-old taxi driver, and Sheila Lewis, aged sixty, checking a friend's empty apartment in Derry when an IRA booby trap blew them up. As Martin McGuinness conceded: 'These accidents are very damaging to the armed struggle. If they continued, they would cut into our support.' A public apology was also offered after the death of Roger Elwood, aged twenty-five, knocked down by an IRA bomb team's stolen getaway car in Dunmurry, South Belfast, in October 1991. That apology, for once, dispensed with the usual political sermon and reflected the essentially parochial minds of many IRA terrorists. Insularity in itself may be no bad thing but as the Anglican envoy Terry Waite has suggested: 'The terrible thing about terrorism is that ultimately it destroys those who practise it. Slowly but surely, as they try to extinguish life in others, the light within them dies.'

This corrosive process of denying a common humanity, which the IRA has to accept as necessary political armour, would explain the absence of recognizable grief among Republicans and their sympathizers, such as the actor Mickey Rourke, about the human cost of the campaign. Learning of Mr Rourke's financial support and empathy for the IRA, the Unionist MP William McCrea wrote about the murder of his cousins Rachel and Robert McLernon, aged sixteen and twenty-one, in a 1976 bomb attack. The two were waved down by a stranger near Cookstown, Tyrone, as they drove happily to show relatives Rachel's engagement ring.

A car had gone over a hedge, and Rachel and her friends went to help whoever was inside. But there was nobody, and somebody immediately shouted: 'Watch, maybe there's a bomb.' They climbed back onto the road, and Rachel and Robert pointed to something in the field. At that moment an IRA bomb exploded and Rachel and Robert were blown to bits. I remember the face of Rachel in the mortuary when I went to identify her. She had become engaged to be married that day and she was a beauty queen. I looked down upon her and saw half of her face blown off. Her brother lay to the right-hand side. He was in a small plastic bag stacked against a table. He didn't even get onto the table, because there wasn't sufficient of him left. As I looked upon them I can assure you there was nothing glorious and nothing beautiful about the handiwork of terrorism . . . Two years later their mother Shirley died of a broken heart at the age of forty-three. I was with her right up until the minute she died. She kept saying to me: 'William, two of my children left me one night and I have waited for them to return every day since then.' She saw the two coffins. They were sealed. They had to be. I was the only one who saw them and so she didn't accept their deaths. Her death, Mr Rourke, is not to be found in the statistics listing the victims of violence.

Northern Ireland is not a normal, civilian environment. There, the Security Forces were able to create counter-strategies which worked just well enough to make it impossible for the IRA to bomb the population into acceptance of their form of Irish unity. The counter-strategies employed ranged from simple, remotely-controlled or long-armed mechanical devices such as the mini-tractor, Wheelbarrow, used to disrupt bombs from a safe distance, to advanced electronics combined with RAF aircraft, including the Canberra, an old reconnaissance machine still employed by the Dublin government to make mapping flights over the Republic.

The army learned new tricks and codified search techniques in *Volume on Counter-Terrorist Search (CTS), Military Engineering, Vol. II*, which ranged from the inner recesses of the human body to outdoor searches. The body search is limited.

> Except in very exceptional circumstances intimate body searches may only be carried out by a medical practitioner or registered nurse after authority of a police superintendent or his like has been obtained. There are four categories: a Quick Body Search (in the public eye); Detailed Body Search (out of the public eye); Strip Search (in a place of custody); Intimate Body Search (by a medical practitioner) . . . [However,] Customs & Excise have separate powers.

The reason for such detail had to do with the fact that IRA women – such as the seventeen-year-old concealing a Semtex bomb strapped to her stomach under maternity clothes, on her way by bus to Belfast airport in April 1990 – were happy to exploit the traditional courtesy accorded by civilized society to females. In this case, the trick, already employed with success by woman terrorists from Algeria to Vietnam, resulted in a ten-year prison sentence.

Outdoor search techniques taught soldiers to identify 'hide locations' for weapons, masks, maps and other war *matériel*. 'Markers might include a distinctive tree in the corner of a field; a telegraph pole in a hedge; a distinctive natural object or set of objects.' Added to this, the reconnaissance teams were instructed: 'Use air photography to identify areas of recent digging.'

Vehicle and house searches required special training courses as hundreds of thousands of cars and homes were checked for hidden explosives and booby traps. Devices ranging from X-rays and chemical sniffers to closed-circuit television were deployed, linked to elaborate computer systems creating a new security industry.

Meanwhile, in the English bombing campaign the IRA repeated many of the mistakes made in Northern Ireland, resulting in some of the worst atrocities. Aldershot, Guildford, Birmingham, War-rington and Manchester, among others, constitute a litany of cruelty, pain and horror. There was no clearly discernible, consist-ent advantage obtained as a result of most of these bombings. Some events, such as the mortar attacks on Downing Street and Heathrow airport, were deliberately staged political spectaculars (to use Gerry Adams's definition). Some were macabre exercises in propaganda amounting to a theatre of cruelty. These included slaying of cere-monial troops on horseback, their horses and military musicians. Its purpose was to shock and it succeeded, but it prompted an equally strong reaction against the Irish as a race. The Warrington murders were so counter-productive to the IRA's political aims that according to some British Military Intelligence officers, they contributed to the movement's decision to call its 1994 ceasefire.

If there was a link between the targets and bombs used, other than those directed precisely against soldiers, it constituted a *laissez-faire* approach to warfare amounting in practice to trial-and-error. The terrorists finally got lucky in April 1992 when a huge lorry-bomb shredded two office tower blocks in the City of London. These were the Baltic Exchange, home of the world's leading shipping market, and the Commercial Union. In Northern Ireland, claims for bomb damage were met by the British taxpayer, a total of £657 million since 1969. In London, the commercial insurance industry carried the risk.

Treasury and underwriters both paled when the compensation bill was presented for just two buildings. It was almost £800 million or equal to half a penny in the pound on income tax; such was the price of London's reputation as a world financial centre. Equally intimidating was the knowledge that the explosive used to do such damage was not military or commercial plastic but one of the IRA's home-made mixtures. The implication was that, even without external help, the terrorists now had a war machine capable of bankrupting the City. Later bombings produced equally daunting costs. The attack on Manchester's retail shopping centre in 1996 cost around £400 million.

The Association of British Insurers, representing Britain's leading underwriters, decided that, in future, it could not afford to provide cover for businesses suffering terrorist losses. As one report explained: 'They were forced into the move because international re-insurance companies refused to underwrite the risk.' Philip Marcell, chairman of the London Insurance and Reinsurance Market Association, said: 'Most people are just not prepared to expose themselves to the risk . . . The reinsurance market has only a limited amount of capital to risk.'

This was language which a monetarist government understood. So did the IRA. When its men returned to the City the following April to park a 1,000lb lorry bomb, the back-up team telephoned eight warnings of 'a massive bomb . . . Clear a wide area'. Sure enough, the Stock Exchange was blasted, along with Wren's church of St Ethelburga. The NatWest tower, formerly a City landmark, was now a City eyesore. As the *Daily Mail* put it: 'Black gaps punched its fifty-two floors like a mouth full of bad teeth.' The cost was estimated at £1 billion. The Lord Mayor of London telephoned the Prime Minister, John Major, to remind him, pointedly: 'The City of London earned £17 billion last year for the nation as a whole. Its operating environment and future must be preserved.'

The Warrington bomb, which had taken the lives of two children, had exploded a month earlier. The *Daily Express* recognized a brutal truth. Comparing the two outrages, it commented:

> Granted, the Warrington bomb took more human life . . . but the sight of hundreds of wrecked or damaged buildings also chills the heart. Buildings are symbols of settled society, of civilisation itself . . . That is why the City blast disturbs us almost as much as an atrocity exacting a greater toll in human life. And why a bomb meant, primarily, to damage property is no less an attack on society than one meant to kill and maim men, women and children.

The IRA campaign was now becoming a matter of financial arithmetic as well as body-count. The *Express* went on: 'The bill for damages has been set as high as £1 billion, with the taxpayer having to foot £800 millions of it . . . We can afford no more City bombings, no more Warringtons, no more Enniskillens . . . We must start to land some blows of our own.'

In a speech at the Guildhall, near the scene of the City bombings, on 15 November the same year, John Major offered talks with Sinn Fein if the IRA ended its campaign of violence. The IRA had already received dovelike overtures in public to reinforce the secret negotiations going on with Whitehall. The terrorists' heavy bombing campaign, starting with the murder of eleven Royal Marine musicians at Deal, Kent, in 1989, had moved on to an experimental shot at the Stock Exchange in July the following year. In October 1990, the first unofficial contact was made with Sinn Fein, according to Martin McGuinness. A month later, with the backing of the British government, Northern Ireland Secretary Peter Brooke made a breathtaking disclaimer.'The British government', he affirmed, 'has no selfish strategic or economic interest in Northern Ireland.' As the Northern Ireland Office source confirmed privately in 1996:

The interpretations placed on this phrase suggest it has been widely misunderstood . . . The British government did *not* claim to have no strategic interest in Northern Ireland . . . The government may have strategic, economic as well as political interests in Northern Ireland. What it is saying is that it will not *selfishly* allow these to override the views of the majority of people in Northern Ireland.

Britain, it would seem, was committed to a unique military plan: an unselfish strategy. Didn't this deny the experience of history? Not at all, according to the NIO. Recalling the Second World War as well as the Cold War, its spokesman said that Ireland, North and South, had been of key strategic importance:

The British government would not seek to impose a presence in the absence of democratic support, as was shown by the unilateral surrender of the Treaty ports in the Irish Free

State in the 1930s, ports which could have been extremely valuable in the battle of the Atlantic [against U-boat attacks on Allied convoys] allowing the Royal Navy to keep open for longer the Western Approaches, thus shortening supply lines to the UK.

This was not the whole truth. From 1941, London had made it brutally clear to Dublin that 'in a war like this it is impossible to foresee what might develop. A situation of life and death might arise in which it might be essential, in our view, to the survival of the liberties of Britain and Southern Ireland too that we should have use of the ports.'

The expectations raised in Republican minds by British ambiguity led to more bombing, not less, for the IRA was not in the business of semantics but war, the continuation of political dialogue by means other than dialogue. The blitz of the early 1990s, using ever-bigger bombs, had its precedents. As Conor Cruise O'Brien argued, firm and fair government in the Province, not attached to some vague search for 'agreed solutions' politically, was accompanied, coincidentally or not, by reduced loss of life through terrorism. During Roy Mason's tough rule of the Province, the death tolls (1976 to 1979) fell from 297 per year to thirteen.

Towards the end of 1979, a new wave of searching for 'agreed solutions' began when Mason's Conservative successor, Humphrey Atkins, proposed a 'conference for political settlement'. The death toll in the following year was 76, and 101 in the year after ... The Anglo Irish agreement was concluded in November 1985. In the two following years the death toll rose from 61 to 93 ... Every new initiative, and the disappointments that follow, stimulates the IRA by conveying that the British are at their wits' end and that withdrawal is around the corner.

That analysis, written in August 1989, looks like inspired precognition in the light of the experience of the years that followed. The lorry bomb that wrecked newspaper offices at Canary Wharf, East London, on 9 February 1996, signalled the end of a spurious seventeen-month 'complete cessation' of IRA warfare and ended the 'initiative' that persuaded most people that the violence was really over. The 100 wounded included a girl aged seventeen and her unborn child. Two people were killed. The cost was assessed at £80 million. A political scramble began to find a lollipop for the IRA. Suddenly the long stalemate in the argument about the terms on which the IRA's political twin, Sinn Fein, could be admitted to talks with the British government was seen to soften. The British government changed its hardline stance on a negotiating timetable and arms decommissioning. 'Not since Hiroshima has a single bomb achieved the dramatic political effect of the IRA's strike against the London Docklands,' affirmed the *Independent on Sunday*.

Four months later, five days after 'peace talks' began, excluding Sinn Fein, the IRA blew up the Arndale shopping centre in Manchester, injuring 200 people including another pregnant woman. ('The baby's heart is still beating but the mother has severe abdominal pain and is very shocked', said her consultant surgeon, Dr Kevin Mackway Jones.) As usual, civilians were the ones who suffered. The cost of the damage was estimated at £150 million. On behalf of Sinn Fein, Gerry Adams said: 'If this bomb explosion ... is linked to the conflict here in Ireland, obviously I regret it and I sympathise with those who have been injured.' A former, now-repentant, IRA bomber, Shane O'Doherty, described the attack as 'a triumph of ignorance over experience ... It undermines the nobility and morality of the cause of Ireland's freedom'.

Twelve months later, following the election of a New Labour government in Britain, the IRA concluded that, for the time being, there was more to be gained from talking than bombing. It announced on 20 July 1997: 'We have ordered the unequivocal restoration of the ceasefire of August 1994. All IRA units have been instructed accordingly.' Democrats noted the absence of a single, vital word from the terrorists' offer: the ceasefire was not permanent. When the Sinn Fein came to the conference table a few weeks later, the IRA arsenal was still intact. Martin McGuinness could announce that the intention of his team was to 'smash the Union' in the knowledge that the IRA was still the military tail that wagged the political dog.

Throughout the bombing years, as politicians fiddled, the Security Forces got on with the war. The British response to IRA brute force was increasingly war by stealth and cunning (see Chapter 9), employing silent weapons that combined to produce a machine almost as sinister as the IRA's bomb teams.

The armistice that accompanied the 1998 Good Friday peace deal and was endorsed by a huge majority of Irish civilians provoked a new split within the IRA, one which left the breakaway groups in possession of most of the movement's Semtex and many of its firearms. Like the Arimaspi – those one-eyed northern warriors described by Herodotus as perpetually fighting a mythical opponent – they continued to do 'what we do best'. For them, the only solution was a military one, win or lose. They might have learned from Shane O'Doherty, one of their own. As he once explained, the Irish Republican's 'imagination' – in which he relives the heroics of 1916 – 'doesn't allow for victims; doesn't allow for civil rights and human rights'. But then, O'Doherty is the only IRA bomber to have written letters of apology to each of his victims while he was in prison.

Theobald Wolfe Tone (1763–98), revolutionary leader, restless romantic and military incompetent, built his own myth as a
symbol of Irish Republicanism. (Original
print in Mary Evans Picture Library)

Lord Edward Fitzgerald, one of the few military professionals among the United Irishmen, was shot while resisting arrest on 19 May 1798 and died of his wounds two weeks later. He represented the move of Irish resistance 'from Jacobites to Jacobins.' (Original print in Mary Evans Picture Library)

The age of the terrorist bomb arrives: Clerkenwell, London, 13 December 1867.
Fenians trying to blast a way out of gaol for their quartermaster destroyed a row
of houses, killing twelve innocent civilians, including one child. (Original print in
Mary Evans Picture Library)

The most momentous Irish assassination of the nineteenth century: newly appointed Irish Secretary Lord Frederick Cavendish and his assistant, Thomas Burke, were stabbed with twelve-inch knives in Phoenix Park, Dublin, 6 May 1882. (Original print in Mary Evans Picture Library)

FACING PAGE: The Anglo-Irish War, 1920. 'Black and Tans' – armed, short-service irregulars – searched and shot at random anyone they suspected of terrorism. Lloyd George and Churchill supported them. (Original photograph, Hulton Getty)

SAS soldiers, openly wearing their regimental cap badges and berets, on patrol in
Antrim, 1969. At that time they were searching for Loyalist arms.
(Private collection)

The chokepoint of Burntollet Bridge, January 1969. Left-wing 'civil rights' agitators seek a 'calculated martyrdom' and a propaganda victory. They are duly ambushed by a Protestant mob including police reservists. (*Belfast Telegraph*)

Bogside, August 1969. Petrol bombs, soon to pour a firestorm onto the heads of the RUC, stockpiled on the roof of Rossville Street flats alongside the Irish tricolour. (*Belfast Telegraph*)

Belfast, August 1969. Catholic families, burned out of their homes by Protestant neighbours, move deeper into the security of the Falls Road ghetto. But who is to protect them there? (*Belfast Telegraph*)

The father of Angela Gallagher, sorrow etched on his face, prepares to bury the girl, who died in an IRA attack in 1971. (Broadside, Northern Ireland Government, ca. 1972)

FACING PAGE: 'Justice, IRA Style,' read the caption to these images, published in an anti-IRA sheet. 'A bucket of tar, a cluster of feathers and a pair of scissors – the implements of IRA "justice." On the night of 9 November 1971, the mediaeval practice of tarring, feathering and hair-cutting was applied to 19-year-old Marta Doherty, a Roman Catholic from Londonderry's Bogside, who was then tied to a lamp-post. Marta's "crime"? She had fallen in love with a soldier. In 1971 alone, twenty-six men and women were tarred and feathered. Still more were badly beaten up. Others had arms and legs broken or were shot and wounded – as a warning.' (Broadside, Northern Ireland Government, ca. 1972)

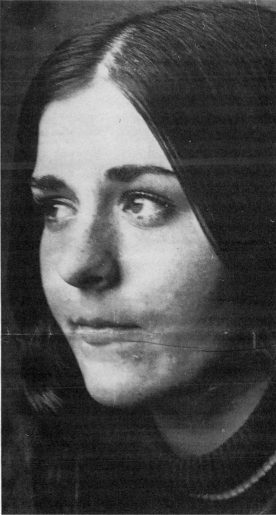

JUSTICE
IRA STYLE

A bucket of tar, a cluster of feathers and a pair of scissors—the implements of IRA "justice".

On the night of November 9/10, 1971, the mediaeval practice of tarring, feathering and hair-cutting was applied to 19-year-old Marta Doherty, a Roman Catholic from Londonderry's Bogside, who was then tied to a lamp-post.

Marta's "crime"—she had fallen in love with a soldier.

In 1971, alone, 26 men and women were tarred and feathered. Still more were badly beaten up. Others had arms and legs broken or were shot and wounded—as a warning.

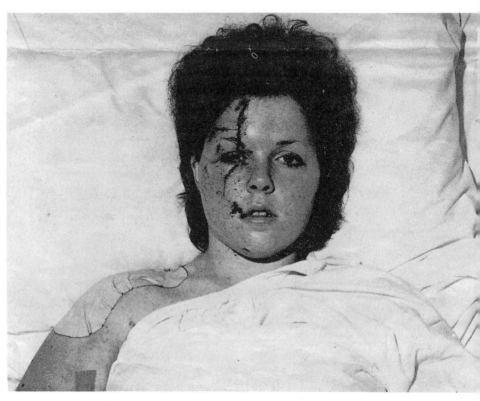

On 25 August 1971 hundreds of people were at work at the headquarters of the Electricity Board for Northern Ireland in Belfast. Just before 11 a.m., an anonymous caller warned the switchboard operator that there was a bomb in the building. An alarm sounded, but before the building emptied an explosion killed one man and injured thirty-five others so badly that they required emergency medical treatment. 'Many of them were teenage girls,' reported the government, 'some bleeding profusely from severe gashes to their faces – the effects of which may in some cases be permanent.' (Broadside, Northern Ireland Government, ca. 1972)

The scene after the Aldershot explosion, 22 February 1972. Five women, a Roman
Catholic priest and a gardener died and seventeen other persons were injured by
an IRA bomb that destroyed the officers' mess of the 16th Parachute Brigade at
Aldershot, southwest of London. 'This demonstrates the madness of the IRA in
horrifying fashion,' the *Daily Express* commented. 'We are facing nothing less than
Murder Incorporated.' 'The atrocity brings home to England in a particularly
horrible way,' said the London *Times*, 'what Northern Ireland has been subject to
for months and months and months.' (Broadside, Northern Ireland
Government, ca. 1972)

Bloody Sunday, Bogside, 1972. This episode, which resulted in the killing of fourteen unarmed persons, followed the logic of the 1970 Falls Road Curfew doctrine, which permitted paramilitary units to use 'every means' to suppress riots. (*Belfast Telegraph*)

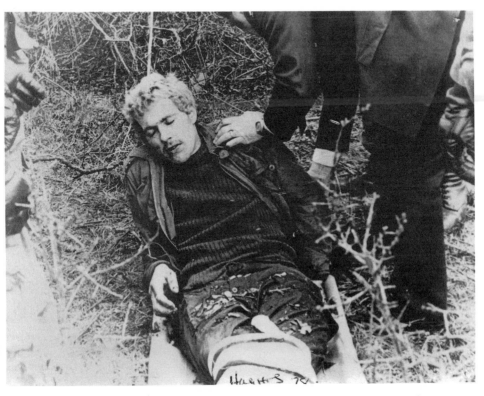

IRA hard-man Francis Hughes in 1978, found by soldiers thirteen hours after crawling away, seriously wounded by the SAS. He died in 1981 in prison on a hunger strike, believing that his death would help unify Ireland.
(Private collection)

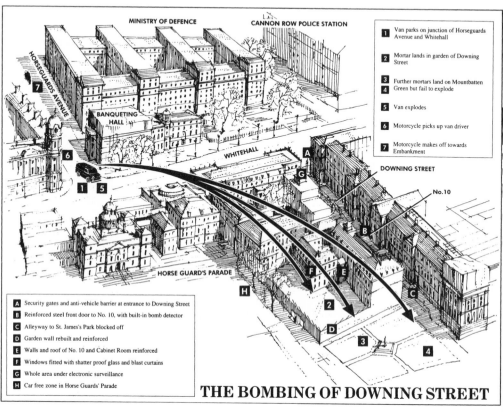

THE BOMBING OF DOWNING STREET

The most audacious mortar attack of the war: an IRA mortar-tube array, aimed by pointing a van at the precise angle, comes within a few feet of killing John Major's Gulf War Cabinet. (*Independent* / Terry Sullivan / Brian Green)

13

A Darker Shade of Red

In a dirty war, moral shades of grey – or, in this case, red – seem irrelevant to appalled spectators. The throat that is cut bleeds just as profusely regardless of the owner's religion. Yet distinctions between levels of personal violence do matter, even in Ireland, where precisely-directed political assassination can be screened by the horrors of sectarian murder.

Most soldiers, however irregular – even those who are 'beasted' before joining the Paras – are not psychopaths. Yet it is also the case that Loyalist/Protestant terror groups, unlike Republicans, have always contained a significant proportion of volunteers who come armed with serious criminal records before they discover the joys of sectarian murder. When Republicans behave as psychopaths, it is usually as a result of the coarsening effect of their armed struggle. They do not have previous 'form' outside terrorism, which makes their capacity to insulate themselves from normal human feelings the more surprising. The Republican claim that their violence is not sectarian (derided by some who have served in their ranks) leads, on occasion, to a double-standard of culpability that enables the political Left in Britain to be more ready to make excuses for Republican atrocities than for the Loyalist equivalents. There is another significant difference. Loyalists, because of their blunt-instrument approach to the use of force and lack of political ingenuity, have had little effect on the outcome of the Irish War. What effect there is (discussed below) results from the use made of them by elements of the Security Forces as deniable instruments of extra-judicial homicide. At that point, Loyalists, from merely reacting violently to a changing world, become proactive agents in an attempt to turn the clock back to 1690.

For the first twenty years of the renewed Troubles, Loyalists targeted civilians for no reason other than that they were born into the wrong religion. Behind the trappings of the Union Flag, the bowler hat, the rolled umbrella and the sash, they turned John Bull's Other Island into Britain's Bosnia. Killing '*taigs*' (Catholics) had long been regarded with a degree of indulgence in a Protestant land for a Protestant people. This was a culture with which the Ku Klux Klan would have felt comfortable, as anyone (including the author) who has been beaten up by respectable-seeming, middle-aged men at a Paisleyite rally can confirm. On a really bad day in the early 1970s it was possible to be used as a punchbag by officers of the Royal Ulster Constabulary immediately after Paisley's supporters had had their fun. But in the gentler times of the mid-1960s, the two communities, in general, had learned to respect at least the other's right to life. The communities mingled increasingly in mixed pubs, betting shops, dance halls, military service, at university and through membership of the Northern Ireland Labour Party. At its peak in 1962, the NILP vote in sixteen Belfast constituencies was 58,811. The total Unionist vote in those same constituencies was 69,096. As Paul Bew, Professor of Irish Politics at Queen's University, Belfast, has pointed out: 'The NILP, which had both Catholic and Protestant activists, was torn apart by the stresses of the Troubles.'

The limited, though traumatic, sectarianism of 1968–69 was followed by an upsurge of sectarian murders by Protestants in mid-1972 after the abolition of the Stormont Parliament. The Shankill Butchers – a gang of eleven men who preferred to kill slowly – murdered at least seventeen people. They dragged a Catholic road-sweeper into a taxi, beat him with a wheelbrace so hard that they fractured his skull, then cut his throat so as to expose his spinal column. It was the sort of killing that French survivors of Algerian massacres describe as 'the Berber smile'. By 1993 one of the leaders, Robert 'Basher' Bates, was a born-again Christian permitted home leave from his fourteen life sentences. At the time the Butchers were busy, other Loyalists bombed Catholic pubs without the formality of a warning. In just one such attack, fifteen people were killed.

By the mid-1980s, Loyalist violence touched the lowest level with a mere twenty murders in a three-year period. (The SAS graph was moving in the other direction, though on a more modest scale.) It was a time of attrition involving, mostly, just the major players, the IRA and the Security Forces. The 1985 Anglo-Irish Agreement, establishing a new relationship between Britain and constitutional Irish nationalists, inflamed Loyalist terrorism and prompted a widespread belief, even among non-violent Protestants, that violence pays. Soon, 42 per cent of that community were ready to express support for their paramilitaries. By April 1989, the Irish Information Partnership concluded that 90 per cent of people killed by Loyalists were civilians. The total Loyalist body-count was 610, compared with 325 civilians killed by the IRA and 178 civilian victims of Security Forces' violence through the use of rubber bullets, badly aimed gunfire, accurate gunfire which killed at least a dozen delinquent 'joy-riders', and aggressive driving. By 1993 the number of civilians murdered by Loyalists had risen to 800, or about fifty per year compared with seven prior to 1985. The IRA, however, was still the most efficient killing-machine overall, responsible for more than half the 3,000-plus violent deaths of this campaign.

During the twelve years between the Anglo-Irish Agreement and the 1997 ceasefires by both Republicans and Loyalists, the cruelties multiplied, as if terrorists on both sides were competing for some terrible trophy. Although ministers of religion of all persuasions seemed unable to control the process, a crude 'Law of Political Effectiveness' did start to emerge from the mayhem. Sectarian killings spread fear throughout entire communities and thereby made normal political life less viable. Well targeted political assassinations usually had a direct, immediate and dramatic political impact. Three categories of murder could be identified: unvarnished ('mindless') sectarian killing; tit-for-tat homicidal competition; and effective political assassination. The first category included the most macabre crimes which, apart from their ability first to shock then to numb normal minds, had the least effect on the outcome of the war. No orthodox weapons of war were required: any blunt instrument would serve the purpose. The second category was a form of gang warfare disguised as serious armed conflict, and continued after the ceasefires, between competing drugs barons, often from within the same community. This type of conflict did require access to firearms and explosives. The effect of the crime barons' political atrocities was to polarize opinion. The third type of killing was the stuff of serious warfare, employing all the weapons and expertise of this conflict, of which the most lethal was accurate Intelligence.

The following examples among thousands of Categories I and II may be safely passed over by the reader who prefers military history to the techniques of psychopathic murder.

1. February 1992: Ann Marie Smyth, aged twenty-five, from Armagh. Lured from a football supporters' club in East Belfast after an incautious remark identified her as a Catholic in a Protestant area, she was taken to a back bedroom nearby and strangled. Her throat was cut after her corpse was dumped on waste land. The strangler, Samuel Cooke, threatened Justice Higgins after being sentenced: 'No doubt we'll win our appeal, then we'll come to see you.' Cooke's appeal failed in March 1997.

2. September 1993: Michael Edwards, aged thirty-nine. A Catholic sweetshop owner living in a mixed area of South Belfast, he had no links with Sinn Fein or the IRA. Ulster Defence Association gunmen shot him repeatedly as he lay in bed beside his wife. Some of his six children held him as he expired, saying: 'Don't die, Daddy. Don't die, Daddy.'

3. April 1994: Margaret Wright, aged thirty-one. An epileptic Protestant misidentified as a Catholic, she was stripped, beaten, tortured and shot four times in the head in a sadistic orgy at a Loyalist band hall in South Belfast by the Red Hand Commandos (a paramilitary group, occasionally linked to the UVF, declared illegal in 1973). Her 'crime', apart from her suspected Catholicism, was that 'she asked questions in the band hall that were completely innocent' (as Lord Justice Nicholson put it). This was not the public Loyalist image of the neatly rolled umbrella and family Bible, but

the tattooed forearm and fist, the beer belly and tobacco-stained teeth. Miss Wright's naked body was thrust into a mobile rubbish bin and trundled away to a derelict house. There it was dumped over a wall, into a back yard, to lie among the litter, the dog dung and broken bottles. Two of the gang were murdered by their own people for having made the wrong guess about Miss Wright's religion. Six others, including one woman, went to prison.

The dynamics of reprisal attacks, though less cold-blooded than most solo murders, were no less shocking. In March 1991 the IRA shot and wounded the widow of a murdered RUC officer who now worked as a civilian employee of the force. In response, Ulster Volunteer Force gunmen murdered three Catholics – a girl of sixteen, a nineteen-year-old woman and a man aged twenty-nine – in a mobile shop. The terrorist group responsible, Portadown UVF, had murdered nineteen Catholics (some of them Republicans) during the preceding three years. In November the same year, the IRA planted a bomb in the military wing of Musgrave Park Hospital, Belfast. No warning was given. Two soldiers were killed. Other casualties included a girl aged seven. A few days later, among other violent events, a Catholic woman and her teenage son were burned to death in a Loyalist petrol-bombing in North Belfast.

Such wickedness was not unique to Ireland. It formed part of a globally reported phenomenon in which armed men, usually young, got their kicks out of killing unarmed, usually vulnerable groups under the guise of politically-directed warfare. Ireland, however, was the place where that tradition had been long established, though overlaid by a veil of myth, legend and song. Ireland was the place where irregular guerrilla warfare and terrorism, as understood in modern times, was invented and then sanctified as the physical force tradition.

To have military impact it was necessary to kill the right people. Terrorists in both camps trawled the public record to identify their key enemies. Catholics bold enough to work openly for Sinn Fein were soft targets on both sides of the border (just like Unionist politicians in the North). Between October 1988 and August 1993, for example, approximately twenty members of Sinn Fein, or their close relatives selected as proxy victims, were shot dead by Loyalists in close-quarter, selective assassinations. Gerry Adams proclaimed, 'Membership of Sinn Fein should not mean the death penalty', while simultaneously upholding the right of the Irish people to their armed struggle.

More serious for the credibility of the official Security Forces on both sides of the border was a growing pile of evidence and corpses that stank of collusion with terrorists. From the outset, a few maverick spirits in the British regular army were prepared to step over the line between lawful and criminal force, using official Intelligence. Some describe it as the Dirty Harry syndrome, the licence an unbalanced policeman gives himself to play avenging angel. On 10 January 1975 a freelance team shot dead the North Armagh Provisional leader, John Francis Green. The Provisionals had called one of their tactical ceasefires and Green was resting in the illusory sanctuary of Monaghan, just inside the Republic. The consensus among some SAS veterans is that Green was murdered by Tony Ball, the colourful ex-Para and SAS man (see Chapter 9).

Major André Dennison, another SAS veteran, served with 6th Battalion of the Ulster Defence Regiment from 1972 to 1975. His friend and biographer, Johan Meiring, wrote that Dennison spoke of his wars as little as he did of his women,

> but there were unguarded moments when Dennison hinted of dark deeds, like the elusive IRA leader holed up in his Londonderry 'safe house' where the frustrated SAS could not 'legally' reach him for months on end. Then the mysterious, never-explained shotgun blast in the dark of the night, snuffing out the IRA man on his own doorstep when he answered the coded knock known only to his mistress.

In 1975 Dennison moved on, like others, from the Province to Rhodesia, where assassination of political enemies, including Herbert Chitepo, ZANU chairman, by ex-British special forces soldiers on behalf of the Rhodesian Central Intelligence Organization, was commonplace.

Ball and Dennison operated before London's adoption of 'police primacy' in containing terrorism in Ulster in 1976, at a time when a colonial-style counter-insurgency war strategy could turn a blind eye to 'dirty tricks'. These included doctoring IRA ammunition so as to make it blow up in the user's face. The IRA got wise to this and other signs of tampering with its hidden armouries by simply attaching hairs to places which would be disrupted by an intruder. Dirty tricks, in themselves, did not have a significant effect upon the war.

The UDR, with which Dennison served as a training major, was raised in 1970 to ease the burden of internal security duties in Northern Ireland from the regular British army. It included a part-time reserve element which promptly attracted veterans of the disbanded and discredited Ulster Special Constabulary (B Specials). In 1991 the UDR – then 6,100 strong – was merged with the Royal Irish Rangers, a regular unit with a fair number of Catholics from both sides of the border. The part-time element remained. During its twenty-one years, the UDR lost 240 people to terrorism. There was another, less noble side to this sacrifice. By 1989 sixteen UDR soldiers were serving prison sentences for murder and another seven for manslaughter. Their victims were, almost without exception, Catholics. One of the Shankill Butchers was a UDR soldier. Two other members of the regiment were part of the team that slaughtered the Miami Showband. Many more killers in UDR ranks doubling for one of the Loyalist gangs, went undetected. Yet others opened up their armouries to Loyalist groups to await Doomsday, the moment when, it was feared, Britain would desert the Loyalist cause.

The 'Ulsterization' of the conflict, led by the RUC, tightened the grip of Protestants on many military operations and the Intelligence needed to make them succeed. That process in turn led to a massive leak of personal dossiers about Republicans to their Loyalist opponents. More than 60 per cent of all Security Forces in the Province were locally recruited by the 1990s, while more than 70 per cent of those killed were RUC or UDR/RIR personnel. As David McKittrick once put it: 'The war against the IRA is carried out by Protestants in uniform.' In a country where the Union Flag flies over 200 police stations on 12 July (the Boyne anniversary and an occasion of drum-beating Orange Order triumphalism three centuries later), this was not surprising. The anniversary is one of nineteen such days each year when, according to the RUC Code, the flag must be flown from sunrise to sunset.

What was singular and outside the Code was the use of official files to target Republicans for illegal homicide, a practice ignored by British governments until 25 August 1989. On that day, Loughlin Maginn was shot dead by the UDA as he sat in his front lounge watching television. His family disputed Loyalist claims that the victim was an IRA Volunteer. Piqued by the denial, the UDA released Maginn's personal file, compiled by British Military Intelligence and leaked by two UDR men: Andrew Browne (ex-Gordon Highlander) and Andrew Smith (ex-Devon & Dorset regiment). Both men were imprisoned for life in 1992. The Maginn file was followed by a veritable library of other, similar, secret documents – an assassin's compendium. A local newspaper, the *Antrim Guardian*, received – anonymously – details of twenty Republican suspects in September 1992. An inquiry into the Maginn case and others by Mr John Stevens, Deputy Chief Constable of Cambridgeshire, found that collusion was 'neither widespread nor institutionalised'.

The real issue was not whether there was collusion (which there was) but whether the lethal information that leaked was based on sound, accurate Intelligence. In November 1988, a UDR woman was imprisoned for six months for passing classified information to the UDA, and in May 1989, another UDR female received an eighteen-month suspended sentence, with a British soldier, for passing personal files and photographs to the Ulster Volunteer Force. The difficulty facing Stevens was that out of thirty-seven people murdered by Loyalists through 1988 and August 1989, only three were IRA members. Most were innocent civilians. As Father Denis Faul pointed out, the leaked list contained names of people whose only offence was to support Sinn Fein. He thundered: 'The consequences of this are devastating. Who is going to do anything to protect the Catholic community? Upon whom can they rely? It is also devastating for the ordinary, decent RUC man who is trying to work impartially and compassionately. No-one is going to trust them now.'

The Security Forces of the North were not the only people in the business of leaking personal records. On 13 April 1991 the IRA shot dead Ian Sproule, a Protestant aged twenty-three, as he parked his car at his parents' home at Castlederg, Tyrone. A joiner by trade, he had recently returned to the Province from England. The IRA asserted that he was a UVF terrorist who had fire-bombed premises in County Donegal, across the border, in February 1987. To prove its point, the IRA produced a confidential Intelligence bulletin circulated by the Republic's police force, the Garda. The Northern Ireland Office, among others, deplored this. As it said, 'Attempts by terrorists to use such material to lend respectability to their evil crimes are particularly obnoxious: murder is murder.'

The Loyalist Ulster Freedom Fighters murdered in their turn Edward Fullerton, aged fifty-six, a Sinn Fein councillor living at Buncrana, Donegal. He was shot dead on 25 May 1991 after his front door had been smashed in. The Combined Loyalist Military Command said that Mr Fullerton had been killed 'in retaliation for the supplying of information to the Provisional IRA about Ian Sproule'.

The response of Loyalist terror groups and their allies within the Security Forces was to sharpen up their act after Stevens' inquiry, and strike more precisely at genuine IRA targets or, and this suited them just as well, close proxies in the form of parents, children and siblings of Republican terrorists. On the night of Sunday, 6 September 1992, Charlie Fox, aged sixty-three and his wife Teresa, aged fifty-three, were shot dead in their home near Moy, County Tyrone. Mrs Fox, wearing outdoor clothes, lay in the kitchen; her husband, dressed for bed, lay in an adjoining room. The bodies were found next morning by their daughters. The murders were condemned by community leaders including the Unionist MP Ken Maginnis, who denounced the crime as 'a blasphemy before God'.

The house was examined by Military Intelligence officers as well as forensic scientists. An MIO later told me:

The style of this attack was extremely professional, cool, almost clinical. Usually UVF assassins spray the windows with gunfire. They don't like close, eye-to-eye contact. This one was different. They broke into and cleared the house, moving methodically through each room. We could reconstruct what had happened. We know from boot marks on the doors and the bullets they had made a room-by-room clearance. The latch was blown on one door. Every single room in the house had been cleared in a military-style operation.

Why should an inoffensive, elderly Catholic couple merit the attention of a highly-trained military assassination squad? Theirs was what is known as 'a Republican family'. Nine days before the murders, their son Patrick Daniel Fox, aged twenty-three, was imprisoned for twelve years having admitted possessing a 1,250lb bomb. An earlier court hearing had been told that he had been a member of an IRA active service unit in continental Europe. The Fox's son-in-law, Kevin McKearney, had been shot dead a few weeks before at his butcher's shop in Moy. Two of McKearney's brothers were killed during IRA operations. One was among the men killed by the SAS at Loughgall in 1987.

One evening in May 1994, two boys playing near a derelict building at Dungannon, Tyrone, stumbled upon four or five camouflaged gunmen. They ran to a nearby house, occupied by Brigid Mallon, aged sixty, and her sister-in-law Roseanne, aged seventy-six. Both women were Catholics. Brigid's sons Martin, aged thirty-seven, and Christopher, aged thirty-two, had served terms of imprisonment for alleged paramilitary offences. Two weeks earlier, said Martin, 'some Special Branch men told a friend of mine that they were going to shoot some of my family to see how I liked it'. Christopher Mallon told the boys to report what they had seen to the police. He said later that the police told the boys that regular army personnel were in the area. Dungannon is a centre of Republican activity and that seemed plausible. But at 3 p.m. a civilian Nissan Stanza halted outside Mrs Mallon's house. A man stared at the property and drove away. Just before midnight, the car was back again. Three people got out and ran to the back of the house. Living across the street, Brigid Mallon's daughter saw what was happening and tried to telephone a warning to her mother. As Mrs

Mallon answered the call, gunmen opened fire through the window, killing Roseanne and wounding Brigid.

Two months later, a friend of Martin Mallon was checking farmland he had rented. The land overlooked the rear of Mrs Mallon's house. He discovered surveillance cameras hidden in bushes, pointing towards the house and took them away. Minutes later army helicopters landed in the field. According to an investigation by the Dublin newspaper the *Sunday Business Post* and the London Sunday the *Observer*, the Mallon brothers met RUC detectives. They claimed that they had the cameras and invited the police to ascertain whether it could help to identify Roseanne's murderers. 'The officers confirmed the equipment belonged to the Ministry of Defence but refused to answer further questions.' Later, a journalist taped a conversation with the detective leading the inquiry who said, 'You are talking about two different organisations . . . you are talking about Special Branch or indeed perhaps Military Intelligence. I am CID.' The army claimed that 'all operations are in support of the RUC'. Martin Mallon was convinced that, at some level, collusion was at work. 'I have no doubt that what is on the tapes is entirely relevant to the murder,' he said. 'The whole thing shows why the RUC can have no credibility with Nationalists.'

On Saturday night, 6 August 1994, Mrs Kathleen O'Hagan, aged thirty-eight, was murdered by UVF gunmen who used a sledgehammer to smash their way into her isolated bungalow south of Omagh, Tyrone. She was seven months pregnant. With her were her five other children. One of these, baby Thomas, aged eighteen months, was in a cot in her bedroom. The assassins fired at her repeatedly as she cowered in a corner. Her husband, Patrick, found the couple's older sons, aged between eight and four, cradling their mother's body when he returned home in the early hours from a family reunion. A priest, Father John Ryder, visited the scene and reported: 'They came up to her bedroom and shot her there in front of one of the children. Some of the bullet marks struck the wall above the baby's cot. She was huddled there on the floor in the corner of the bedroom.'

The UVF issued a statement claiming the murder, adding that Mr O'Hagan – convicted of possessing arms and explosives during the mid-1970s – would have been killed also had he been at home. The Loyalist statement said: 'We in the UVF will show republicans how hard it is to listen to a diet of peace [*sic*] while they wage the deadly deed of war. Brace yourselves for death because you are going to see plenty of it.'

Soon after Mrs O'Hagan's murder, the Provisional IRA proclaimed a ceasefire. Experts quarrel about the reasons why the movement did so at the time; why the violence resumed with the Canary Wharf bomb in February 1996 and why the violence went on hold once again. Like the mechanisms used to renew the revolution with public support in 1969, the process by which the finger comes off the IRA's trigger is carefully concealed from public scrutiny. There are two apparently opposed explanations which are compatible if it is the case that the Republicans were finally worn down, after twenty-five years, by a combination of carrot as well as stick. Theory No. 1 is that the Loyalist assassination offensive had pushed the Republicans to a position where they needed some respite. There was, perhaps, a hint of this in the pained remark of Gerry Adams at Sinn Fein's 1992 conference: 'The British government should learn republicans will not be assassinated out of existence.' It is a view shared by some British Intelligence officers. Colonel Michael Mates MP put it like this:

> A bunch of loyalists came out of gaol where they had been serving life sentences, during which time they had found out a helluva lot about how Pira worked, and they said to themselves: 'There must be a better way than filling a bar with bullets. We need to knock off major players.' The 'selection committee' were sitting in the place where all the best candidates were. Among those who were assassinated between the Downing Street Declaration [December 1993] and the declaration of peace [August 1994] were about fifteen top people. The IRA were taking a hell of a pasting. The hard men agreed to a ceasefire as a tactical pause. They said, 'We can't go on taking casualties at this rate.' That's exactly what it was, a tactical pause. They carried on moving their stuff around and training. They took over lock-up garages

in London [to store arms and explosives] six weeks after the ceasefire. They didn't have a ceasefire. They just ceased firing.

IRA veterans reject that reasoning. They point to their own impressive body-count between 1986 and the ceasefire of 1994: forty-five or so Loyalist leaders, many of them people who had been acquitted of crimes by British virtual justice, but were executed all the same by the IRA. They ranged from John Bingham, UVF leader in North Belfast in September 1986 – who would have lived had he stayed in prison for the whole of a twenty-year sentence – to Ray Smallwoods, in July 1994. Smallwoods was the man who shot Bernadette McAliskey (formerly Devlin) in July 1980. Just before the IRA murdered him outside his Lisburn home, he said:

Killing is terrible. But I have no regrets, no remorse about what I did. You have to understand that she treated the British people of Ulster with contempt. To this day she, and people like Adams … want a deal with Westminster over the heads of the British people who live here. This is our country and we have nowhere else to go. We are the most loyal citizens of Britain, but we would not be welcome in the mainland UK. That is why we have to fight.

The opposite view is that the IRA had agreed, reluctantly, to a trial ceasefire ('complete' but not 'permanent') not from a position of weakness but of strength, in the belief that, at long last, victory was within its grasp. The Downing Street Declaration repeated the British government's promise that it had 'no selfish, strategic, or economic interest in Northern Ireland'. It imposed no demand on the IRA to hand over weapons or identify arms dumps. It left unchallenged Dublin's claims to the Province, while giving the Republic a continuing role in the future of the North. The British would 'uphold the democratic wish of *a greater number of the people of Northern Ireland* on the issue of whether they prefer to support the Union or a sovereign, united Ireland'. This phrase, instead of the usual genuflection towards the *majority* (i.e. Protestant) community implicitly recognized that the Catholic population in the

North was growing fast, from 37 per cent of the population in 1971 to 43 per cent in 1991 and would in time constitute the 'greater number'.

One sentence in the declaration glittered like the Holy Grail in Republican eyes. It said: 'The British Government agrees that it is for the people of the island of Ireland alone, by agreement between the two parts respectively, to exercise their right of self-determination on the basis of consent, freely and concurrently given, North and South, to bring about a united Ireland, if that is their wish.' As the astute Conor Cruise O'Brien noted: 'That sentence, issued officially on behalf of the British government, conveys to them the message that the IRA is winning. Hence the euphoria.'

Added to what was on the public record were the unattributable briefings, such as the Downing Street guidance given in November 1993 to Anthony Bevins, political editor of the *Observer*:

> The view was formed that if enough economic and political progress was made in Northern Ireland, the terrorists might conclude that the results of violence were no longer worth the risks involved ... A key British source said that the Provisional IRA was imbued with an ideology and a theology. He then added the breathtaking statement that its ideology included an 'ethical dimension', that members would not continue killing for the sake of it.

Remove the cause, went the argument, and the killing would cease.

The IRA's belief that British resolve to oppose change was crumbling was further enhanced by secret 'back-channel' contacts between the two sides. This dialogue had stuttered on since the beginning of the renewed Troubles. From 1989, position papers were exchanged through 'deniable heroes' including clergymen, businessmen and professionals. A British civil servant met Martin McGuinness two days after the Warrington bomb atrocity in March 1993. (Interestingly, a senior member of the agent-handling Intelligence group, the FRU, when asked as part of the research for this history, stated his belief that the IRA ceasefire was prompted directly by the bad publicity provoked by Warrington. If true, it would reflect unusual sensitivity on the part of the Republicans to outside opinion. That theory says much about the opinion of the cream of British Military Intelligence of their adversaries' motivation.) McGuinness claimed that the British representative had said that 'the eventual outcome of all that Britain was trying to do would be that the island would be as one'.

The British emphasis throughout was on gradualism; the key word, *eventual.* But the credibility of Sinn Fein's leaders among their own hard men, particularly the culturally frozen South Armagh IRA units and the East Tyrone brigade, depended on a *prompt* British surrender, ditching the Loyalists. In February 1994, six months before the ceasefire took effect, a Sinn Fein debate about the Downing Street Declaration smouldered with defiance of threats of a British crackdown if the party rejected the terms implied by the Declaration. McGuinness was applauded deliriously when he said: 'What are they going to do? Are they going to murder us? We've had that. Are they going to intern us? We've had that. Are they going to use supergrasses against us? We've had that, too. We've had it all and we're not afraid of it.' Rory Dougan, from the Republican 'cowboy' border town of Dundalk, was cheered as he said: 'It was a direct result of IRA operations in England . . . that forced the British government into the position in which they now find themselves. What shook the British government to its foundations were the vibrations of IRA bombs exploding in the City of London.' This was echoed by the right-wing London *Sunday Telegraph* two years later: 'The Downing Street Declaration of 1993 which launched the peace process would not have been signed by John Major without the Baltic Exchange and Bishopsgate bombs.' At the convention, old men 'stripped their sleeves' to talk of a Republicans' St Crispin Day. Like Jim Gibney of Belfast, they acknowledged that 'the struggle had entered a new phase, pregnant with possibilities'. In prisons throughout the UK, Republicans prepared to throw away the calendar, convinced that freedom would be granted tomorrow, or the day after at the latest.

Some sophisticated minds even glimpsed hope in the end of the Cold War and collapse of the Warsaw Pact. Perhaps it was true. Perhaps the British not only had no *selfish* strategic or economic interest in Ireland, but no strategic interest at all.

It was all talk, of course: a dream of peace beyond fulfilment, a poisoned gift. British gradualism, based on a superior Catholic birth-rate in Northern Ireland, contained a deadly pill for Republican aspirations, for it carried with it a loss of momentum and, with that, fading commitment to the physical force tradition as young guerrillas discovered that there was a life outside the movement. If it all depended upon the birth-rate, then they could make love rather than war as a road to reunification. The Republicans had been here before. In December 1974 the Provisional IRA declared a ceasefire that lasted for seven months. The Loyalists cut loose with a new round of sectarian murders. In London, a Cabinet sub-committee, part of a Labour administration, 'seriously considered' withdrawal from the Province, according to the then-Home Secretary, Merlyn Rees. But the effect on the Provisionals was disastrous. As Gerry Adams put it, 'The British government probably came as near at that time to defeating the Republican struggle as at any time during the last fourteen years.'

The ceasefire that lasted from August 1994 to February 1996 was always a shaky structure in spite of a public guarantee by Martin McGuinness on 1 September that year: 'The ceasefire will hold in all circumstances.' A few weeks before it began, the RUC Chief Constable Hugh Annesley acknowledged: 'There is a genuine debate about peace within republican circles . . . Those who favour moving in that direction are probably, just probably, in the ascendancy.' Five months later he believed that the ceasefire had a 60:40 chance of surviving until the following Easter. By then, the most martial spirits of the Belfast Falls Road were warning Gerry Adams through street graffiti: *Adams – Remember Collins 1922*. It was brilliant shorthand to define the growing gulf between the Sinn Fein political leadership – assumed by British Intelligence to be synonymous with leadership of the Provisional IRA – and the people truly in charge of the guerrilla army. In January 1995, some of the South Armagh irreconcilables even went so far as to prepare Adams's assassination. MI5 intervened to warn Adams and the assassination team was arrested just before its plan was to be put into effect. There were official Whitehall denials but Michael Mates, among others, denied the denials. He told me:

It really was the case that people were discovered within the IRA with a plan, *Take Out Adams.* We told Adams what he might do to put these fellows right. As it happened we then lifted the leader of that thing in connection with a quite separate incident some months later, so he was out of circulation. Whether that was planned by the hardline Pira who didn't want a ceasefire I am not sure.

The Republicans made good use of the ceasefire. In the USA, President Clinton and the Friends of Sinn Fein helped Gerry Adams to raise £840,000. In the Catholic ghettos of the North, the Provisionals blooded new Volunteers by murdering seven alleged drug-dealers with shotguns: a messy process but one that left no ballistic evidence to link the so-called Direct Action Against Drugs movement with the IRA. The IRA, after all, was publicly committed to a 'complete cessation' of violence. The killings reminded the Catholics who their masters were. As Adams himself acknowledged: 'They [the IRA] have never gone away, you know.' Even more valuable to the Provisionals was the opportunity to move not one but probably half-a-dozen bomb teams into Britain. Bernadette Hyland, on behalf of the Irish in Britain Representation Group, Manchester, complained that '20,000 Irish people were stopped as they travelled home' during the ceasefire. This intensive screening was insufficient to identify the Provo 'Lily-whites' (people, such as the Aldwych own-goal bomber Edward O'Brien, with no criminal or political history) now being set in place for the next offensive along with safe-houses and storage depots.

Other warriors were less easy to conceal from MI5. In July 1997 a six-man Active Service Unit was convicted of plotting to bomb electricity supply stations around the Home Counties and plunge much of Southeast England into darkness. Each of the team was sentenced to thirty-five years' imprisonment. Two of the terrorists – Gerard Hanratty and John Crawley, a former US Marine – had been released from prison during the ceasefire. Another member, Donal Gannon, a bomb engineer tracked by MI5 under their code-name for him, 'Paradise News', had left his fingerprints on a Clapham, South London, bomb factory in 1988, but had no previous convictions. More than 300 detectives and MI5 agents tracked the gang around London and on reconnaissance trips to six national grid sub-stations during Operation Airlines. This was not overkill. According to Commander John Grieve, head of Scotland Yard's anti-terrorist branch, they were six 'of the most dangerous men ever gathered in one place'.

Thanks to the 1998 Good Friday peace deal, they would qualify for release by the year 2000, along with James McArdle from Crossmaglen, 'sentenced' to twenty-five years' imprisonment on 25 June that year. McArdle was the man who drove the lorry bomb that ended the IRA 'ceasefire' in 1996 most of the way to London. The blast killed a newsagent and his assistant. McArdle, said one report, 'looked on emotionless' as he was convicted. He probably knew that an earlier bomber, Patrick Magee (Brighton, 1984), already enjoyed occasional home leave in spite of a thirty-five year sentence (as a welcome change from his PhD studies in 'Troubles Fiction').

Meanwhile, two Scots Guards soldiers, Jim Fisher and Mark Wright (see Chapter 7), continued serving prison time. As the journalist Martin Bell MP noted, 'It is unthinkable that convicted terrorists may be released yet these two soldiers, who were serving their country, can still be held in prison.'

Such was the realpolitik underlying the peace deal.

When the bombing resumed, in 1996, it was a sign that the bombers within the Republican movement rather than Sinn Fein politicians, whose credibility had shrunk with every day of stalemate, were in control. Adams had acknowledged during the ceasefire that neither side was capable of military victory. MI5, taking him at his word, stood down the temporary agents it had borrowed from the army and briefed journalists that 'there was little danger of the IRA's calling off the ceasefire'. The IRA was about to prove Adams and MI5 wrong. The Docklands bomb of 9 February 1996 killed two innocents and sent a fresh shudder through the City, even though its most sensitive computer operations had been moved to its own safe-house. Following that explosion, the British government of John Major dropped its demand for paramilitary disarmament before talks with Sinn

Fein could happen and instead proposed a date for talks so long as the violence ceased. The IRA had no intention of giving up the arms it would need for the war against the Unionists once the British pulled out of Ulster. For this reason the Provos, in a public statement twelve weeks earlier, had described the notion of surrendering arms as 'ludicrous'. After 9 February, Downing Street recognized the strength of the physical force tradition. As one London newspaper put it: 'For seventeen months the guns were silent and the bombers lay low: the peace process moved at a snail's pace. Then a half-ton of fertiliser, 100 injuries, two deaths, £80 millions of damage: within nineteen days we are within sight of the negotiating table. Why does anybody bother to say that violence must always be resisted, that it will never work?'

Other big bombs followed in Britain, identified by Military Intelligence officers as 'strategic', not only in their physical effect but also because of the sense that the IRA was co-ordinating them from Ireland instead of following its usual policy of equipping its Active Service Units and then leaving them to make their own tactical, front-line decisions. A separate 'chaos strategy', disrupting the 1997 Grand National, alienated the Irish on both sides of the water. An Irish jockey won the delayed race.

The Provisionals' high-profile attacks in Britain were paralleled by the use of the Barrett Light sniper rifle to kill Lance-Bombardier Stephen Restorick in Bessbrook village, South Armagh. Other 'spectaculars' included the bomb planted inside the British army headquarters at Lisburn in October 1996 and the provocative assassination attempt just before Christmas against Nigel Dodds, secretary of Ian Paisley's Democratic Unionist Party. The toxin of that attack lay not only in its attempt to murder an orthodox politician but in its manner and timing: in a children's ward of a hospital where Dodds was visiting his sick son. The killing of RUC officers and the style of some attacks on police barracks, experts noted, reflected a similar pattern of warfare then being waged by Basque ETA terrorists in Spain. More important, the IRA's targeting was restricted to 'hard' military and police targets rather than civilian shopping centres in the Province.

Selective or not, renewed IRA violence came with a political price tag, imposing new, surprising limitations on the bombers. Most Catholics in the North wanted peace. They voted in a newspaper poll against reunification of Ireland, if that meant a Provo Republic, as had an earlier generation in the twenty-six counties. Alienated by Provo brutalities, ordinary people – not professional informers – started to tip off the authorities about suspicious activities in their back alleys. The Provisionals had to issue a warning to the public not to use the Security Forces' anonymous 'hot line'. This did not halt a stream of denunciations from every quarter of normal Irish opinion. Cardinal Cahal Daly departed from public life into retirement, at seventy-nine, with the observation that the IRA was 'politically inept and morally wrong'. The Irish Republic's Garda, angered by the murder of one of its detectives during an IRA post office robbery in June, sharpened up assistance to British Intelligence and uncovered obscure arms dumps in remote Donegal. Even worse for the Provisionals, some of their own started to compromise operations. Bombs mysteriously failed to detonate as the renewed campaign continued into the winter of 1996. Others, such as two lorry bombs on their way from Ireland to Britain in November, were intercepted by MI5 officers.

The IRA waited for a change of government at Westminster before announcing an 'unequivocal restoration of the ceasefire' to take effect on 20 July 1997. Britain's New Labour leadership moved fast to respond to this olive branch, even though it barely concealed a loaded gun. Public opinion, this time, was distinctly underwhelmed. There were no street parties to celebrate the peace; just scepticism. The sceptics were vindicated a few weeks later. As efforts to make political bedfellows out of two irreconcilable forces inched arthritically forwards, Republican guerrillas were increasingly unhappy. Paramilitaries of both communities pursued ethnic cleansing programmes, programmes of terror that did nothing to build confidence at the Stormont talks. Families Against Intimidation and Terror (FAIT) learned that twenty families each month were being ordered out of their homes by the IRA. There was a 'continuous stream' of refugees from Loyalist areas also. Known cases, said FAIT, were 'a fraction of the whole'.

The Provisionals spelled out the brutal reality of real politics two days after Gerry Adams affirmed Sinn Fein's commitment to the non-violent Mitchell Principles. They reminded the world, through their tame newspaper *An Phoblacht*, that 'the IRA would have problems with sections of the Mitchell Principles, but then the IRA is not a participant in these talks'. Gerry Adams, putting a brave face on a political disaster, thought the timing of this pronouncement was 'unfortunate'. But then, as he and his fellow Westminster MP Martin McGuinness had often reminded journalists during their recent and successful campaign to win seats in the British Parliament, 'Sinn Fein is not the IRA; the IRA is not Sinn Fein.'

The ancient fault-line within Irish nationalism between the men of force and the men of persuasion and ideas was now about to reopen. When key leaders of the Provisionals walked away from the movement in November 1997, they took with them details of the movement's hidden Libyan armouries, the very sinews of war. Waiting to welcome them a hundred thousand times were the antique veterans of the old War Party, now known as the Continuity Army Council. The CAC had been in business since the last split in 1986, a split about the doctrine of non-recognition of the orthodox processes of politics. It represented a simple, fundamentalist agenda of *force majeur*, expressed militarily through the bombing of tourist hotels in the North. As a distinguished Dublin journalist, Kevin Myers, put it:

> The IRA is bound by its constitution, first drafted in 1917, as vital today in the minds of IRA members. It requires the IRA to bring about a British withdrawal from Ireland and only then to seek the opinion of the electorate about the institutions of state they might wish to create . . . The IRA is an absolutist organisation commanded by the terms of its existence to achieve a British withdrawal from Ireland, regardless of the wishes of the Irish people. To expect the IRA to be or to do other than to seek a British withdrawal is like expecting a consistory of cardinals to abandon their interest in Christ and to take up water polo instead.

For the War Party, the dual doctrine of Armalite and ballot box had served a useful purpose in unifying the two wings of the Republican movement, but the ballot box to decide the main issue was never intended to be taken seriously. Now that it had become serious, it was repudiated. Yet again, the governments of London and Dublin as well as the leadership of the Republican and nationalist movement faced hard choices. One was to return to the war of attrition, something with which the professional warriors of all groups could live, and die, indefinitely; it was their *raison d'être* and, equally important, their main source of income. But if the Irish War was not to continue indefinitely, then the obvious precedent was internment of all terrorists, Loyalists as well as Republican, on both sides of the Irish border as well as in Great Britain. That weapon, however, had been renounced by Blair's optimistic new team almost as soon as it took office, in the fond belief that it could obtain a political settlement of the Irish Question by May 1998, twelve months after its election. Appraising the shape of things to come, Unionists could be forgiven for suspecting that a sell-out was on the way and, with it, the indiscriminate civil war for which they had prepared since 1921.

As the IRA ceasefire stretched from July 1997 into the autumn of 1999, a few Republicans, following Joe Cahill's lead, *did* declare themselves in favour of peaceful politics. Micky McMullan – IRA veteran and former editor of Sinn Fein's *Republican News* – said: 'I believe [arms] decommissioning . . . should happen because Republicanism is not militarism. It is political. The political battle is there to be won.' Such words were music to the ears of the War Party, whose support was quietly growing.

Winning the worst of both worlds, the Provisional IRA's refusal to hand over a single, symbolic rifle – 'Not One Bullet!' as the graffiti put it – paralysed politics. Even worse, as *The Times* noted, Ireland's referendum vote to abolish its claim to Northern Ireland could lapse if the Belfast Agreement failed. But if the peace remained unconvincing there could be no return to the sort of war it had been prior to 1998, if only because Loyalist whistle-blowers such as Bobby Phillpot had confirmed that their activities had enjoyed the complicity of Britain's regular army. Deniable, surrogate death squads – Britain's most potent weapon in the war against the IRA – had had their day.

PART IV

A Nation Once Again?

14

The End of Chivalry, 1691

The well-intentioned efforts of politicians in 1998 rested upon the belief that the Irish Problem could be settled by men of good-will in the context of a modern world. When did that world begin? Republicans argued that it was with Partition in 1921, a process which created a continued, unwanted British presence on Irish soil. Gerry Adams, on his way to Downing Street in December 1997, said he was going to conclude 'unfinished business', to end 'all the hurt and grief and division which has come from British involvement in our affairs'.

If challenged further about its political antecedents, the Republican Publicity Bureau will almost certainly flick back the Irish calendar to 1798 and the republicanism of Wolfe Tone. But nowhere in the ocean of Republican literature, among the mounds of garish pamphlets and political ephemera, does one encounter the ghosts of Irish resistance fighters who were not Republicans. Some, like Patrick Sarsfield, first Earl of Lucan, were members of the English as well as the Irish aristocracy. Some were professional soldiers who became mercenaries in a foreign army without ever giving up hope of winning freedom for the homeland which, for the most part, they would never see again. This was the Army of the Diaspora. More numerous were those who remained in Ireland to wage the war of the flea against the elephant, a nocturnal style of resistance that combined terrorism and guerrilla tactics with economic boycott, social ostracism, tar-and-feather. Theirs was, by necessity, a very dirty war indeed. What follows, in outline, is their story from the departure of Sarsfield from Ireland in 1691.

*　　*　　*

Irish chivalry died on 22 December 1691. On that day Patrick Sarsfield, first Earl of Lucan, sailed into permanent exile with the remnants of his defeated army, from the deep, deadly cold waters of Cork harbour. Sarsfield was a sort of Irish Fluellen, quick to take offence against jokes about his race. He was also a superb professional cavalry soldier, accustomed to a war of movement, rather than a static effort to hold ground. He was a natural guerrilla. Had the French high command taken his advice or better, left it to him to run their war after the defeat on the Boyne the year before, Irish history would not have continued to fester into the late twentieth century.

Sarsfield's parting was macabre, even by Irish standards. Women unwilling to be left to their fate walked into the harbour to drown themselves as the fleet sailed. Some carried their babies with them. As Macaulay described it:

> After the soldiers had embarked, room was found for the families of many. But still there remained on the waterside a great multitude clamouring piteously to be taken on board. As the last boats put off there was a rush into the surf. Some women caught hold of the ropes, were dragged out of their depth, clung till their fingers were cut through, and perished in the waves. The ships began to move. A wild and terrible wail rose from the shore, and excited unwonted compassion in hearts steeled by hatred of the Irish race and of the Romish faith.
>
> Even the stern Cromwellian, now at length after a desperate struggle of three years, left the undisputed lord of the bloodstained and devastated island, could not hear unmoved that bitter cry, in which was poured forth all the rage and all the sorrow of a conquered nation.
>
> The sails disappeared. The emaciated and brokenhearted crowd . . . dispersed, to beg their way home through a wasted land, or to lie down and die by the roadside of grief and hunger . . . In Ireland, there was peace.

English intervention in Ireland had started in 1155 in a curiously oblique fashion, via Rome. The only English Pope, Adrian IV (originally Nicholas Breakspear), invited Henry II to impose order on the Celtic church in Ireland. He did so in a papal letter, a bull entitled *Laudabiliter*, 'to the King of the English approving of the said king's intentions to enter Ireland to improve the state of the Church there'.

From the dawn of Christendom Ireland had been a case apart, untamed by the order of the Roman Empire or Viking settlements. St Patrick's predecessor as the Christian missionary to Ireland, Palladius, and Patrick himself, visited themselves upon Hibernia long before the schism that divided Christians in 1054. This history prompted a rare joke 1,500 years later, by the Revd Ian Paisley in the House of Commons: that St Patrick's Day should be a universal public holiday, since 'that would please the nationalists because they think Saint Patrick was a Roman Catholic and it would please Protestants because they know he was a "protestant" [that is, a Celtic Christian] and a Briton'.

By the time Henry VIII broke with Rome and appointed himself Head of the Church, many of the Anglo-Norman aristocrats imposed on Ireland after Adrian's bull had been assimilated to become Norman Irish. English control barely existed beyond the Pale, the perimeter defence around Dublin. Beyond that a tribal system of shared landownership – which appealed to the Utopian Socialists of a later generation, such as James Connolly – was still intact, as was a native system of justice known as Brehon. According to one estimate, Ireland had some 200 kings during this Utopian period in which, Connolly asserted, the Irish peasant was 'a free clansman owning his tribelands and controlling its administration in common with his fellows'.

This decentralized arrangement suited the anarchic Celts. For Henry VIII it was a challenge to his authority and a security threat. The Scots and English had accepted Reformation. The Irish remained obstinately, dangerously Catholic. Ireland's political status was changed to that of a kingdom, subject to the monarch's direct control, from 1541. The Gaelic kings soon sold out to the English king. As the historian Brendan Fitzpatrick noted: 'When asked to sign away their Gaelic power base in return for a state guarantee of private ownership, not one of the great Gaelic chiefs preserved his people's land at the expense of his own aggrandisement. In doing so, they abandoned the very essence of the Gaelic culture which had put them there in the first place.'

Betrayal of the original Irish by the clan chiefs – as James Connolly pointed out before he died in front of an English firing-squad in 1916 – was followed by a second betrayal on the part of the Norman Irish aristocracy. These so-called 'Old English' acquired from their own diaspora 'a foreign schooling to discredit Gaelic ideas of equality and democracy' and a papal policy 'which looks upon Catholic Ireland simply as a tool to be used for the spiritual reconquest of England to Catholicity'.

The destructive century following Henry VIII's claim to Ireland was essentially one in which dissident Irish aristocrats, whether Celt or Norman by blood, sought to defend or enhance their power: Yellow Ford, near Armagh, in August 1598, when Queen Elizabeth's army was defeated in open battle by Hugh O'Neill's superior use of cavalry and infantry; Kinsale, 1601, when O'Neill and his Spanish allies were finally beaten by crop-burning and food denial (a technique used by the British in South Africa and elsewhere, somewhat later). O'Neill's defeat opened the way for the settlement of English and Scottish Protestants in Ireland on estates abandoned by the Ulster earls when they fled to Rome in 1607.

The landless Irish now had a colonial stockade on which to focus resentment. In 1641, as the crypto-Catholic Stuart monarchy drifted helplessly towards civil war against its own Parliament, 10,000 Protestant settlers were massacred. Cromwell, victor in the English Civil War, exacted his revenge eleven years later. A basic theme of modern Irish history had emerged: robbed of their native leaders and identity an increasingly degenerate people were united only in their hatred of England.

In spite of Protestant mythology, the campaign fought between the exiled Catholic King James II and his son-in-law William of Orange from 1689 to 1691 was not primarily about Irish independence or even Catholicism. James was a political client of France's 'Sun King', Louis XIV, who was then engaged in an expansionist European war against Spain, the Holy Roman Empire, the Netherlands, Sweden, Denmark, Bavaria, Brandenburg and Savoy. The

nominally Catholic Louis had been excommunicated by Pope Innocent XI. At the Boyne, the Pope's money was on the Protestant
King William. James, having fled to France from England after
William's landing at Brixham on 5 November 1688, sailed reluctantly to Ireland the following year in a final, desperate attempt to
recover the throne and convert the English to Catholicism. That,
at any rate, was the theory.

In reality, the most important function of James and his French
generals in Ireland was not to liberate the Irish or eliminate Protestant settlements in Ulster but to entice a massive diversion of
anti-French military resources away from the more important
battleground of Continental Europe. James's function, in tying up
15,000 English and Dutch soldiers, 10,000 horses and 500 ships,
was similar to that of the Yugoslav leader, General Tito, as he
opposed the Wehrmacht during the Second World War. As Har-
man Murtagh has observed:

> Louis's intervention on behalf of James focused William's
> attention on Ireland as nothing else would have done . . . In
> May 1689, England at last declared war on France . . . The
> Irish adventure was highly successful for the French. The
> cost was comparatively light; certainly it was only a fraction
> of the cost to William of containing it. In 1690, for example,
> the only year that Louis sent troops, his commitment was
> about one fifth of the number William brought in from
> outside. And at the end Louis received a handsome dividend
> of trained Irish soldiers to support his war-effort on the
> Continent . . . Throughout the Irish war, the French navy
> sailed the high seas with impunity, a foretaste of the coming
> French interest in expansion overseas.

At the beginning of this French campaign in Ireland, James's
French–Irish force had besieged Londonderry for fifteen weeks
but failed to crack the city's resistance. After Londonderry, the
French King Louis – through his devious adviser on James's staff,
the Comte de Lauzun – tried to persuade James to retreat all the
way to Dublin, to burn the city down and then keep marching west.
That way, Lauzun believed, dysentery and the Irish fever that was

prevalent in the Williamite ranks would take care of the enemy more effectively than Jacobite arms.

The stand, if that is what it was, by King James at the Boyne on 1 July 1690 was an ill-considered compromise between two opposed strategies. It was an encounter in which Sarsfield came close to killing King William and in which James fled from easily defended high ground as his adversary waded across a river to attack. James's adversary was his own son-in-law, an underweight, gauche, tuberculose asthmatic with a perpetual cough, yet a man of restless energy and action who hunted wild boar when he was not at war.

James hastened away and did not pause until he reached Dublin, where he blamed the Irish for his defeat.

Next day James was up by 5 a.m. to resume his flight. He rode for almost twenty-four hours, pistols dangerously cocked all the way, until he reached the south-east tip of Ireland, more than a hundred miles from the Boyne. A few hours later he was aboard ship, sailing swiftly to Kinsale, where he transferred to a French man-o'-war. At noon on Friday 4 July he sailed to France, never to return.

Resistance to English rule was now to slip increasingly into the hands of irregulars, many of them of doubtful legitimacy except in one matter: they were determined to continue the fight. For the remaining miserable eighteen months of this campaign the two idioms of conflict – orthodox and guerrilla – were to be found in resistance to William. The orthodox strategy was French. The war of mobility and the guerrilla was led by Sarsfield.

James's Irish army – 20,000 infantry and 3,500 cavalry – retreated to the sanctuary of solid Norman walls around Limerick, on the Shannon. King William, with his fellow Dutchman General Ginkel, led a force up to the city walls to besiege it. They could not breach the walls without heavy artillery, but that was on its way. Or so they thought.

After dark, early in the siege, Sarsfield and a raiding force of 800 cavalry left by the back door, crossed the Shannon to County Clare, recrossed at a ford to avoid the guard on Killaloe bridge and moved stealthily forward into the Tipperary wilderness of Silvermines Mountains. Half a century earlier, during a massacre of Protestants,

the mines had been destroyed. Now mountain and mine were perceived as haunted places, unvisited at night except by those with
murder in mind. Sarsfield and his men lay up there through the
day. A local spy told them where to find William's artillery convoy,
as it, too, rested. In Macaulay's account:

> Sarsfield learned in the evening that the detachment which
> guarded the English artillery had halted for the night, seven
> miles from William's camp, on a pleasant carpet of green
> turf, and under the ruined walls of an old castle; that officers
> and men seemed to think themselves perfectly secure; that
> the beasts [oxen] had been turned loose to graze and that
> even the sentinels were dozing. When it was dark the Irish
> horsemen quitted their hiding place, and were conducted by
> the people of the country to the spot where the escort lay
> sleeping round the guns. The surprise was complete.

This was what the Gaelic soldier was good at: the war of the
nocturnal bandit. William, learning from his spies that Sarsfield
was on the hunt, correctly guessed the target and despatched Sir
John Lanier with a force to guard the guns, but it was too late.
Throats were cut silently; pistols put to sleeping heads; an alarm
raised. For sixty men with the convoy their sleep was permanent.
The rest disappeared into the darkness. One lieutenant, Sarsfield's
prisoner, watched as the Irishmen systematically stuffed each big
gun with powder, fixed its mouth to the ground and then fired the
touch-charge at the breech so that the gun's destructive force was
turned upon itself. Sarsfield, nodding with satisfaction, told his
prisoner: 'If I had failed in this attempt I should have been off to
France.'

Lanier, with 500 horsemen, saw the flash on the horizon, heard the
explosions and knew that he was too late. In spite of that, the siege of
Limerick went ahead but without conviction. A few artillery pieces
were found but the rains came and the besieging army were mired in
the mud. The fever returned. Five hundred English grenadiers tried
to storm the city in mid-afternoon on 27 August but (Macaulay
again): 'the very women of Limerick mingled in the combat, stood
firmly under the hottest fire and flung stones and broken bottles at

the enemy. In the moment when the conflict was fiercest a mine exploded, and hurled a fine German battalion into the air.'

William's soldiers fell back, ostensibly to plan another attack next day but they were all but out of gunpowder and the Irish rain lashed them into weariness. They clawed their way out of the mud and withdrew. For the Irish, it seemed, the fight was at last for their country rather than a part of some grand design handed down from the Vatican, the Palace of Versailles or Westminster, but it was not to be. The French sent a new general to take charge. This was the Marquis de St Ruth, also known as 'The Hangman' because of his way with critics. St Ruth, against Sarsfield's advice, took on Ginkel's army in open combat at Aughrim, a desolate bog west of Athlone. St Ruth was decapitated there by a cannonball. Then around 7,000 Irish Infantry were hacked to death after the cavalry had fled, led in their panic by the gentry. Looters stripped the corpses of clothing so that, from the top of nearby Kilcommedon Hill, the landscape appeared at first sight to be one great pasture covered by grazing sheep. This was an illusion. The 'sheep' were naked, dead soldiers.

'Soon', Macaulay noted, 'a multitude of dogs came to feast on the carnage. These beasts became so fierce, and acquired such a taste for human flesh, that it was long dangerous for men to travel that road otherwise than in companies.'

A contemporary writer, Diarmuid Murtagh, concluded:

> It was of the Catholic aristocracy that the battle had taken its heaviest toll. There was scarce a noble family, whether Gaelic or Anglo-Norman, that did not mourn a son. One family mourned seven. Aughrim was more fatal to the old aristocracy of Ireland than Flodden had been to the knighthood of Scotland, or Agincourt to the chivalry of France . . . The Catholic aristocracy disappeared from the Irish scene, and the political leadership of the Irish people passed into other hands.

Fitzpatrick, another contemporary historian, said:

> Who these men were and what they thought they were being killed for will never be known. They were not dying for

Louis XIV or James II, both of whom had now lost interest. Nor were they dying as property-owning Old English [that is, Norman Irish] for these had fled with the cavalry. They were not dying as Catholics, because the papacy had not supported the war. They were not 'dying for Ireland' because there was as yet no romantic myth to die for. It is hard to avoid the conclusion that they died for nothing at all.

The campaign limped on until the autumn. From the wild hills of Kerry to the Atlantic offshore islands, a defeated people submitted to the inevitability of an English, Protestant victory. Only Limerick held out, with Sarsfield prominent in its defence. This time, there were no night rides to ambush an advancing enemy. Ginkel knew he had to choke the last resistance, or do a deal with the Irish commander, before the winter and its rain returned, bringing the usual epidemics of fever and dysentery.

For a time, Irish irregulars known as 'rapparees', inspired by Sarsfield, had slipped into the Williamite territory to run a guerrilla and terrorist campaign. As supplies in Jacobite Ireland dried up, the rapparee raids became looting expeditions by hungry men whose armour was made of twisted straw. As the situation tightened during the winter of 1690–91, the difference between regular infantry and rapparees all but vanished. Pursuit of these human foxes was usually a waste of time. It was said that the rapparee, lying in the long grass of the bog, was harder to spot than the sitting hare; that he could spring into a stream and vanish, lying like an otter with only his nose exposed to the air.

Nay, [affirmed one source] a whole gang of banditti would, in the twinkling of an eye, transform itself into a crowd of harmless labourers. Every man took his gun to pieces, hid the lock in his clothes, stuck a cork in the muzzle, stopped the touch hole with a quill and threw the weapon into the next pond. Nothing was to be seen but a train of poor rustics who had not so much as a cudgel among them and whose humble look and crouching walk seemed to show that their spirit was thoroughly broken to slavery.

Until, that is, darkness descended. Occasionally, Williamite militiamen picked up the rapparees carrying their weapons, and hanged them from a convenient tree.

Unperturbed by such distractions, the Dutch general cunningly swept up what was left of the Irish cavalry on the plain of Clare, across the River Shannon, by putting his own horsemen over the river in 'tin boats'. When all hope was extinguished, Sarsfield negotiated the surrender. Talking to English officers, he asked: 'Has not this last campaign raised your opinion of Irish soldiers?'

'To tell the truth,' one of them replied, 'we think of them much as we always did.'

Sarsfield gave a reply that echoed round Europe for long afterwards: 'As low as we are now, change kings with us and we will willingly try our luck with you again.'

A parade was held on the field across the Shannon from which Ginkel had driven the last organized resistance. Those troops who wished to go into permanent exile, to France, were to march before Ginkel and Sarsfield one way, past a mark that was the point of no return. Those who were willing to swear allegiance to William were to halt at the mark. The scene anticipated a similar choice made in 1940 by soldiers of the French Foreign Legion: one parade area for those loyal to Vichy, another for those prepared to fight in exile with de Gaulle and the Allies. All but seven of the first regiment that paraded at Limerick chose to stay with the Jacobites, though many deserted when the moment of parting came. The Catholic natives of Ulster, almost to a man, switched their allegiance and went home. Another 2,000 accepted safe passes to quit soldiering completely. They, too, returned home.

The greatest number, around 12,000, threw in their lot with Sarsfield and exile. Those who possessed property in Ireland lost everything. They became the Wild Geese, part of a military diaspora that produced the best fighting formations in Spain, where three regimental banners bore the Irish harp; others fought in France and in Austria. Some individuals and their descendants did spectacularly well: one became a Marshal of France; another, Prime Minister of Spain.

Most of those who marched with Sarsfield did not believe, as they stepped forward in Clare, that their exile would last for ever. Within a year, Sarsfield promised, the French would invade Ireland and they would return home victorious. Such an invasion was to have been staged in May 1692 but nothing came of it. Sarsfield was fatally wounded in a battle at Landen, in Holland, on 19 August 1693. As he died he murmured, 'If only it was for Ireland.' It was, in its own way, the first declaration of an ideal of Irish nationhood divorced from Catholicism or class, or even professed loyalty to the English crown. It was to be taken up later by others who sacrificed their lives for an ideal shared by few of their fellow countrymen.

One of those who had switched sides to join William was Henry Luttrell, an officer who had led the panic flight of cavalry from the field at Aughrim. (The Irish, with their long memories, still remember the spot; it is called Luttrell's Pass.) Luttrell had been also engaged in secret negotiations with the English during the siege of Limerick. With Sarsfield gone, Luttrell was awarded the estate confiscated from his brother Simon, who went into exile, and a pension of £500 a year from England. After twenty-five years the Celts caught up with him. He was murdered in his sedan chair in Dublin. Another eighty years passed and his remains were dug up and the skull smashed with a pickaxe.

The Limerick treaty Sarsfield negotiated with Ginkel was betrayed. Promises of security of tenure were over-ridden by a new colonization scheme through which 1.5 million acres of land were confiscated. William's biggest beneficiary, Lord Bentinck, was given 135,000 acres while a certain Sir T. Prendergast had to make do with a mere 7,083. None of the twelve biggest land-grabbers was prominent in the risky business of actual warfare. In a further betrayal, religious discrimination was restored. Presbyterians as well as Catholics suffered fines and imprisonment for practising their religion. As a result, 250,000 Ulster Protestants migrated to America between 1717 and 1776. They arrived in time to fight against England in the American War of Independence.

Sarsfield's bequest belonged to those often nameless people who fought the war of the weak against the strong. Orthodox history relates that Irish resistance was extinguished for a century after

Sarsfield's departure, until the French Revolution stirred the waters of Bantry Bay. In practice, the conflict smouldered on for the simple reason that it was effectively a crime to be an Irishman under English rule. It was not just a matter of religious and political discrimination or the theft of land. The Penal Laws even outlawed Gaelic names. Prefixes such as 'Mac' or 'Mag' were erased. The Irish handled that by eliding the last letter of the illegal prefix on to the rest of the name, so that MacOrmac (Ormac's son, or kin) became Cormac (with variations) as did MagOrman and MagEraghty. The gentry, what was left of it, was whipped if any of its number owned a horse worth more than £5. Catholic priests, ministering secretly as 'hedge priests', risked being hanged, drawn and quartered.

The criminalized, leaderless but energetic and nocturnal Irish were natural terrorists. It was another sixty years – not long in Irish history – before the 'criminals' gathered in such strength as to be identifiable as a political group. The story of the secret societies known as Whiteboys was to prove as brutal as any other chapter in the Irish War.

15

Enlightenment and Terror, 1798

The peace imposed upon Ireland for sixty years after Sarsfield camouflaged a threat to English security which, finally, could be resolved only by recruiting Catholic Irish soldiers to fight rebellious colonists in America and the French army on both sides of the Atlantic. The camouflaged threat was that skilled Irish warriors were now formed up as a permanent, professional Irish Brigade in the service of France as part of an enemy coalition still discreetly recruiting new blood in Ireland. Within a short time after Sarsfield left, 20,000 Irish Jacobites had joined the Catholic armies of Spain, Naples and the Habsburg Empire as well as that of France.

While the Stuart campaigns of 1715 and 1745 in Scotland found no obvious support in Ireland as such, the expatriate Wild Geese relished a new way to attack the Dutch–German dynasty in England. Charles Wogan, born in Rathcoffee, Kildare, in 1689, was an aide-de-camp to the Jacobite General Foster in 1715. He was taken prisoner during that rebellion and escaped from Newgate Prison, London. Thereafter he acted as a secret agent for Prince James Stuart, Catholic claimant to the British and Irish crowns. James, in Rome, was without an heir. It was, in its day, a political question of the first magnitude. Without issue, the Stuart dynasty could not sustain its claim to the British crown. Wogan was turned loose upon the European courts to find a suitable bride. In 1717 he discovered the beautiful, fifteen-year-old Clementina Sobieksa, daughter of the claimant to the Polish throne. She was now living under the protection of her cousin, the German emperor Charles VI. Clementina was related to many of Europe's royal houses.

A bizarre struggle now began. The British government persuaded the German emperor to put Clementina under house arrest at Innsbruck. Simultaneously the English king, George I, waved a bribe of £100,000 at the Prince of Baden to marry Clementina before James got there. The lady herself rejected this second suitor. Wogan, with a team of Irishmen serving with Dillon's regiment, part of the Irish Brigade, sprang his prisoner by smuggling secret notes to her and substituting a maid for Clementina under the noses of her guards. Their escape, in a snowstorm across the Alps, had the gallant absurdity of a Rossini opera. Clementina fell into a stream soon after escaping from the house. She forgot her jewels, part of a Stuart inheritance and therefore politically important. Captain Lucius O'Toole was sent back to retrieve them, and succeeded. The party resumed its flight towards the Italian border. Their horses exhausted, their carriage disabled, they had to make the final dash across the frontier on foot in the snow, through a mountain pass. The escape made the English king a fool throughout Europe. The Polish princess married her Jacobite prince amid great pomp and soon presented the Stuarts with a child who would grow into legend as Bonny Prince Charlie, focus of the 1745 Rebellion. Wogan was appointed a senator of Rome, a baronet and a colonel. He ended his life as governor of La Mancha, Spain.

Outside Europe, England's need for military manpower grew as the pace of colonial wars quickened around much of the northern hemisphere. Fighting men were needed to oppose a French army in North America from 1755 and rebellious Americans after 1776. The East India Company, with a commercial empire to protect in India, signed up 10,000 fighting Irish Catholics from within Ireland itself. France, its spirit renewed by the ritual blood sacrifice of the anti-monarchist revolution of 1789, now posed a threat to Britain's home defence requiring a home guard in Ireland. The effect of wars on both sides of the Atlantic focused attention on Ireland's strategic importance to Continental Europe. For the first time this was not only a question of a Spanish or French Catholic threat to a Protestant England, but a maritime issue that would remain current almost to the end of the Cold War two hundred years later. As the French writer Le Biez put it: 'The independence of Ireland is necessary for the world. The French Revolution spread the seeds of liberty throughout the Continent of Europe. Perhaps the Irish Revolution will soon provide us with the liberty of the seas.'

The logic of these pressures on English military manpower, to the dismay of a protected, privileged Protestant elite in Ireland, was a series of Catholic Relief bills to reverse the cruelties of the Penal Laws passed after the Boyne. As the Irish historian Thomas Bartlett noted, the Relief Act of 1778 'firmly established the principle of Catholic relief as a key element of war-time strategy'. That suited the Catholic hierarchy in Ireland, which perceived the American rebel colonists as 'Puritan . . . Calvinistic and republican'.

So it was that Irish Catholics were officially rearmed and trained again as regular soldiers. In 1793, as royal heads rolled in Paris, the passage through the Irish Parliament in Dublin of the latest Catholic Relief bill was matched by a Militia bill to raise a force of 20,000 to defend Ireland from France. Prime Minister William Pitt even granted regular commissions to suitably qualified Irish Catholics. As Bartlett argued: 'Within a generation the British state had gone from a policy of firm exclusion of Catholic soldiers to one of forced inclusion; from fear of Catholic numbers to reliance on them to meet the needs of war.'

Just beneath the surface of such stirring events, in the isolation of Ireland beyond the Pale, native resistance smouldered on. The polite description of the terrorist groups of the time was that they were 'agrarian secret societies'. From 1759, the Whiteboys (so-called because of their 'uniform' of white sheets or shirts over their clothes) took to the countryside at night, as many as 500 at a time, to burn out those now occupying their former homes and land. They were the products of their time, protesting that they were not enemies of the Crown. In 1762 as a group of Whiteboys was about to be despatched, they declared from the scaffold that 'it never entered into our thoughts to do anything against the King and Government'.

They were not sectarian in their choice of victims. Catholic Relief, in time, created Catholic landowners who were as likely to suffer the Whiteboy punishment as any Protestant incomer. The historian W. E. H. Lecky recorded:

one of the mildest punishments was to drag a man at midnight from his bed, often in midwinter, beat him and leave him bound and naked in a ditch by the roadside ... Not infrequently they carried their victim to a newly-dug grave and left him, sometimes with his ears cut off, buried up to the chin in earth, or in thorns or furze. Men were placed naked on horseback on saddles covered with thorns, or with a hedgehog's skin.

This was not warfare as the professionals understood it. It did reflect the cruel humour of a rural community that hunted non-human as well as human quarry. It was the badger-baiting, fox-hunting culture with political and cultural overtones. Adding more fuel to the bonfire was the sectarian bush war that developed between working-class Protestants and Catholics from 1785. Protestant thugs in Ulster raided Catholic homes, ostensibly in search of illegal weapons. Such attacks were usually made at dawn. The attackers deodorized their activities with the title Peep-o'-Day Boys. They were the direct progenitors of the Orange Order. A Catholic counterpart, to fight off such attacks, soon emerged. It called itself the Defenders.

Defender operations became pre-emptive. They did not warm to their co-religionists' newly granted 'right' – if conscription to military service is a right – to join the official militia. It was only a matter of time before, in 1793, the Defenders were at war with the militia as well as with the Peep-o'-Day Boys. In January, eighteen Defenders were killed by fellow Catholics of the militia at Kells, County Meath. In the spring, sixty-eight Defenders were sentenced to death and seventy-seven to transportation. In July, fifty militiamen armed with muskets confronted 2,000 Defenders near Wexford. The militia commander, Major Valloton, tried negotiating with his opponents and was struck down. The militia instantly opened fire, killing eighty Defenders. Such reverses, following a pattern of Irish resistance, generated more trouble. Lecky concluded:

> Defenderism soon ceased to be either a league for mutual protection or a mere system of religious riot. It assumed the

usual Irish form of a secret and permanent organisation, held together by oaths, moving under a hidden direction, attracting to itself all kinds of criminals, and making itself the organ of all kinds of discontent. It became to a great extent a new Whiteboy movement, aiming specially at the reduction and abolition of tithes and redress of agrarian grievances, and in this form it passed rapidly into counties where the poorer population were exclusively Catholic, and where there was little or no religious animosity. It was also early noticed that it was accompanied by nightly meetings for the purpose of drill.

The illegal drills were often conducted with bravura. Sir George Hill, a magistrate in Derry, watched with interest as 6,000 'clean, well-appointed men from many quarters' assembled with spades carried like muskets, ostensibly to dig the potatoes of a prisoner.

They marched with an erect and defiant mien; but when ordered by the soldiers to disperse, they at once obeyed, saying with an affected humility, that it was hard to be impeded in their charitable purpose 'of digging a forlorn woman's potatoes and asking if they were allowed to dig their own.' No other provocation was given. About 1,500 men had crossed the mountains during the night to be present at the meeting.

Sir George was particularly alarmed by the calmness and self-control of these people 'under invisible guidance'. He asked some of them if they would resist the French in case of an invasion: 'They answered, in a tone that was impossible either to resent or misunderstand: "Our arms have been taken away . . . we must not talk politics; we pay dearly for the Militia; Government has taken everything into its own hand; if the French come, we cannot resist; we are good Christians, resigned to our fate."'

One who was not resigned to his fate was Theobald Wolfe Tone, a revolutionary leader who was to become an icon of the IRA in the twentieth century. Tone, the son of a well-heeled Protestant, wanted adventure in the British army but his family insisted he complete his law studies at Trinity College, Dublin. His restless, romantic spirit scanned the political horizon to identify a stirring cause. One of these, he thought, was the expansion of the British Empire into the South Seas to confound Spain. Later, the success of the French Revolution in melting down the old order had on him the effect it had on many others. It was the dawning of a new age in which anything was possible. Tone fell in love with an ideal of Irish nationhood that defied political reality. It was the romantic attachment of the medieval knight for his distant lady: perfect as long as it was for ever unconsummated.

Backed by Protestant dissenters and Catholic intellectuals he formed the Society of United Irishmen, a movement ostensibly seeking reform of the Irish Parliament in Dublin and to reduce English influence in Irish affairs. Tone, in private, was more radical. He believed in Irish independence and more: if only the French would invade Ireland, 'there is scarcely an army in the country and the militia, the bulk of whom are Catholics, would . . . refuse to act if they saw such a force as they could look to for support'.

The implicit admission in this statement – written to a French emissary in 1793, as the Terror raged and war began between France and England – was that a successful Irish revolution required the professional leadership of a French army for it to succeed. It conveyed a naive belief that a French army of occupation, even a republican army, would more readily acknowledge Irish self-determination than the British. The French, like the English, had a selfish, strategic interest in an island that commanded the western approaches to the Atlantic. Tone's letter contained two fatal misjudgements about Ireland itself. The first was that a majority of Irishmen would rise up to the sound of the Marseillaise. The second was that the Catholics serving in His Majesty's forces would mutiny. Added to Tone's conviction that there really existed an Irish political consensus able to absorb the stresses of sectarianism, his was an agenda for heroic defeat. Pursuing his dream, Tone went to America, then to France to join its army and prepare for the great invasion. He was promoted from lieutenant to general in less than a year.

A tattered French fleet did put in a brief appearance in Bantry

Bay, at the farthest south-westerly corner of Ireland, in December 1796. The operation was ineffectual. Its main effect was to promote a massive backlash upon the Irish civilian community by their rulers, Irish as well as British, and to renew the dialogue of violence between the two. The French were not entirely to blame for the débâcle. Their sailing ships were battered by easterly gales which blew them back out to sea, while their political navigation was cruelly miscued by the optimism of Tone and other United Irishmen. Tone believed that a successful rebellion triggered by a French invasion would 'knock England out of the war' against France.

The French fleet was spotted as it came over the westerly horizon on 21 December. A lone horseman rode forty miles through snow in four hours to raise the alarm in Cork. Soon, 400 soldiers of the Galway militia were assembled on the beach to repel the invaders. The gale did the job for them. Of 14,000 men in the original French task force, only half reached Ireland. Of those, only a handful landed on an offshore island, where their officer was taken prisoner.

Wolfe Tone was with the fleet but he did not set foot on his native soil. As he sailed back to France, he reflected that the British had not had such an escape since the Spanish Armada in 1588. The British agreed. Elsewhere in Europe, Napoleon's armies were picking off foreign rulers – in Poland, Italy and Austria – like chickens for the pot. Even the Royal Navy's victory over a Spanish fleet supporting France off Cape St Vincent in February 1797 was soon robbed of its gloss by the Royal Navy's own mutiny three months later, a rebellion stirred by former Defenders who, on suspicion and without trial, had been dumped illegally to serve unpaid aboard British warships.

Fear of France after Bantry Bay fuelled English paranoia in its efforts to suppress Irish rebellion, real or imagined. In Ulster the British commander, General Gerard Lake, was instructed to disarm the North. Lake's concept of counter-insurgency, like that of many regular soldiers who followed him, was Cromwellian in its use of terror to suppress terror. The troops under his command, mostly Catholic militiamen, burned homes, flogged and murdered the occupants regardless of whether arms were found or not. As the

English version of the Terror spread, public tortures used to break Irish resistance included the use of a cap filled with molten pitch, which was placed on the victim's head and ignited, with horrific results.

Intelligent British soldiers were appalled by this travesty of military strategy against an entire civilian population. Sir Ralph Abercromby, the new Commander-in-Chief of the army in Ireland, resigned after noting in a letter home that 'every crime, every cruelty that could be committed by Cossacks or Calmucks, has been transacted here'.

The 1798 Rebellion that followed was fatally flawed, thanks to the saturation of the rebel movement at all levels by government spies. It lacked the massive popular support that Tone had predicted. Without those elements it became a doomed, inept, bloodstained and chaotic episode of Irish history which Irish bards transmuted into a hardy, long-lived myth. The leaders of the United Irishmen were a social elite, unfamiliar with the ruffianly Defenders who now formed the largest part of their guerrilla army. The elite were either Protestant dissenters or 'Horse' Catholics: prosperous intellectuals influenced by the Utopian egalitarianism of the French Revolution. In that they were not unique. Such works as Mozart's *Marriage of Figaro*, based on a Beaumarchais play which the French government censored, owed their existence to the ideas that came from the philosophical fountain of the Enlightenment.

With the Enlightenment came the bloodshed. As amateur revolutionaries, the United Irishmen did not understand the imperative need for secrecy in plotting a coup. So it came about that on 12 March 1798 most of the movement's 'Supreme National Directory' – using jargon borrowed from the Jacobins – were gathered in the home of Oliver Bond in Leinster. Aptly, in view of the group's lack of clear thought, their host was a wool merchant. They still nourished hopes of a new French invasion, though just a week earlier – in spite of Wolfe Tone's continued presence in Paris – the French government had decided to set aside a plan to invade England and to attack Egypt instead. That adventure would be led by Bonaparte, taking with him the best of the French armed forces. Bonaparte had decided against invading the British Isles for the good reason that the Royal Navy had command of the seas there and far beyond.

The Directory's meeting was betrayed to the authorities in advance by one of its own members, the informer 'Colonel' Thomas Reynolds. The gathering was raided and fifteen key people seized. Their arrests convinced the British that a new French invasion was imminent and, on 30 March, martial law was imposed on much of Ireland. The security forces – Catholic militia, Protestant yeomanry, Welsh irregulars and German mercenaries from Hesse (a state that had supplied men to help the British make war on their American colony twenty years earlier) – were free to billet themselves on any town or village they chose and to root out revolution by any means. Areas which had been, by Irish standards, comparatively peaceful hitherto were plunged into a nightmare of smashed doors and screams as random victims were tied down to be flayed alive in public. Many villagers preferred the comparative safety of the fields rather than the dangers of home.

Despite the fact that the game was up, the rebellion proceeded. In many places, local people who had handed over their pikes and sworn peaceful allegiance to the government, discovered that such gestures won them no favours. The innocent were punished with the guilty. As a result, the rebellion that followed outside Dublin was not the popular uprising of Irish myth so much as a desperate effort to defend isolated communities by force of arms against marauding bands of cavalry. The majority of ordinary folk – as one of their leaders later admitted to a Dublin parliamentary inquiry – cared nothing for the cause of Irish nationalism. They simply sought security and redress of grievances.

The outcome might yet have been different had even one of the self-proclaimed leaders of the rebellion eluded capture long enough to make some sort of impact. Tone, Napper Tandy and others were still enjoying the good life in France. (Tone wrote at this time about having 'a delicious time with my family' in Paris.) One who resisted bravely was Lord Edward Fitzgerald, younger brother of the Duke of Leinster.

Fitzgerald was one of the very few military professionals among the United Irishmen. As an officer in the British army, he had 'served with heroism in action against the American colonies' before being dismissed for his undisguised sympathy for the French Revolution. Sir Richard Musgrave, who detested Republicans, acknowledged that:

> Lord Edward had served with reputation in the fifteenth regiment, during a great part of the American war and on many occasions had displayed great valour and considerable abilities as an officer. When in the army, he was considered a man of honour and humanity, and was much esteemed by his brother officers for his frankness, courage and good nature; qualities which he was supposed to possess in a very high degree.

Fitzgerald was not a typical officer, but he was not without ambition. In November 1791 his regiment landed at Portsmouth. Soon afterwards, Fitzgerald's hopes of promotion were dashed. He took off to Paris where he became 'from disgust, an enthusiastic admirer of the extravagant political theories of the French'.

In fact, Fitzgerald's radicalism came with his mother's milk. Mama was the Duchess of Leinster, a great-granddaughter of Charles II, a believer in Rousseau, sea-bathing and adultery. As a reviewer of a biography of Fitzgerald said of his career:

> [it] encompasses the sort of adventures and coincidences normally only found in the racier Flashman novels ... Returning to Europe, Fitzgerald carouses with Charles James Fox; cuckolds the playwright Sheridan; and breakfasts in revolutionary Paris with the arch-radical Tom Paine. There he falls in love with one of the most celebrated beauties of the day, Pamela, the daughter of Madam de Genlis ... Pamela and Lord Edward marry, with the future King Louis-Philippe of France among the witnesses.

Fitzgerald was driven by more than disgust about his failure to get promoted. Lecky believed he had 'all the temperament of a sentimentalist and an enthusiast. To such men the new lights which had arisen in France were as fatally attractive as the candle to the moth.' In the autumn of 1792, in company with Paine, he publicly toasted an end to hereditary titles and feudal distinctions. Word of the party got back to London, where Fitzgerald was cashiered. Back in Ireland, he took his seat in the Dublin Parliament and created uproar with an interjection favouring rebellion. In fact, according to Lecky: 'he alone in the Irish Parliament represented sentiments which were spreading widely throughout the country.'

By 1798, Fitzgerald was the rebels' leading strategist. In British eyes he was the Most Wanted rebel. His eyes were on Dublin. On 18 May, a group of soldiers waited for him at Watling Street, near the city. Shots were exchanged with Fitzgerald's advance guard. Fitzgerald escaped to a safe-house in Dublin but was soon traced. Next day,

> government having received positive information that he had arrived in Dublin and was lodged at the house of one Murphy . . . sent major Sirr [the town major] to arrest him. He, accompanied by captain Swan of the Revenue corps, and captain Ryan of the Sepulchre's, and eight soldiers disguised, about five o'clock in the evening repaired in coaches to Murphy's house. While they were posting the soldiers in such a manner as to prevent the possibility of an escape, captain Swan, perceiving a woman run hastily upstairs for the purpose, as he supposed, of alarming lord Edward, followed her with utmost speed; and, on entering an apartment, found lord Edward lying on a bed, in his dressing jacket. He approached the bed and informed his lordship that he had a warrant against him, and that resistance would be vain; and he assured him, at the same time, that he would treat him with the utmost respect.
>
> On that, lord Edward sprang from the bed, and snapped a pistol, which missed fire, at captain Swan. He then closed with him, drew a dagger, gave him a wound in the hand and different wounds in the body; one of them under the ribs was deep and dangerous, and bled most copiously.
>
> At the moment captain Ryan entered, and missed fire at lord Edward with a pocket pistol, on which he made a lunge at him with a sword cane, which bent on his ribs; but affected him so much, that he threw himself on the bed, and captain

Ryan having thrown himself on him, a violent scuffle ensued, during which lord Edward drew a dagger and plunged it into his side. They then fell on the ground, where captain Ryan received many desperate wounds; one of which in the lower part of his belly was so large, that his bowels fell out on the floor. Major Sirr, having entered the room, saw captain Swan bleeding very much and lord Edward advancing towards the door, while captain Ryan, on the floor and in the woeful state which I described, was holding him by one leg and captain Swan by the other, he therefore fired at lord Edward with a pistol and wounded him in the shoulder, on which he cried out for mercy and surrendered himself. His lordship was then conveyed to the castle.

News of Fitzgerald's arrest travelled fast. The rebels' hopes 'of getting possession of the metropolis . . . rested much on his valour . . . Numbers of them were seen going from one part of the town to the other with quick pace and serious countenance. Others were perceived in small parties, conversing with that seriousness of countenance and energy of gesticulation which strongly indicated the agitation of their minds.'

The rebels could and should have guessed that plans for the rising would be discovered somewhere among Fitzgerald's possessions. Sure enough, in his writing box and his pockets was 'the plan for taking a city . . . Dublin, [which] shews the bold designs of the rebels and how terrifick the insurrection would have been'.

On 21 May, two more leaders of the unconsummated revolution were arrested. The brothers John and Henry Sheares had a plan to seize a military barracks at Loughlinstown and take Dublin. They took into their confidence a militia officer who promptly betrayed them. For the rebels, there were other portents of trouble. Justice Drury in Dublin 'seized a blacksmith in Thomas Street at noonday, in the act of forging pikes; and he led him through the streets to the Castle, with his head and shoulders garnished with a number of them, and thence with his two assistants to prison.' In raids elsewhere, weapons including cannon, several six-pounder and four-pounder guns were uncovered.

An uprising against established, armed forces depends above all else upon the element of surprise. This was lost utterly with the capture of the Directory team, Fitzgerald and the Sheares brothers. The United Irishmen's attempt went ahead anyway. In many areas, this was an act of desperation, because there was no alternative. The signal for rebellion in many areas was to be the non-arrival of the Dublin mail coaches, to be ambushed soon after leaving the city. Some of them were; some were not. The confusion was total. There was still time to halt the assault on Dublin, but in spite of the arrest of their leaders, the rebels brought their pikes out of hiding anyway and marched on the night of 23 May. The capital feared that the Paris Terror was about to be re-enacted on the streets of Dublin for, after Fitzgerald's arrest, wrote Musgrave, government and loyal subjects 'continued in a woeful state of suspense'. The Loyalists knew an attack was imminent but they did not know when it would come.

Three miles from Dublin, in the village (as it then was) of Rathfarnham, an officer of the yeomanry was tipped off by a government agent that the rebels were gathering in the mountains nearby. The Viceroy, Lord Camden, asked to be kept informed of any rebel march towards the city. Later, Samuel Bennet, a young yeomanry private saw 'a great concourse of rebels armed with muskets, pikes and pistols'. He mounted his horse and galloped through the dusk to alert the Viceroy. His message was bleak:

> The rebels in great numbers were risen and were in the road and adjacent fields as he went to Dublin. In the city, particularly in the suburbs, he saw a great number of rebels with pikes in gateways, alleys and stable lanes, waiting the beat of their drums and the approach of rebel columns from the country ... As he passed they frequently cried out, animating each other, 'Come on boys! Who's afraid?'

Alerted by Trooper Bennet, the drums of the City of Cork regiment thundered out their call to arms and took up positions at Stephen's Green, then on the city outskirts, just an hour before the rebel drums were to have sounded their signal to attack. Other yeomanry, well briefed, seized the rendezvous earmarked by the rebels as their assembly points. As a result, the rebel assault went off at half-cock and its warriors melted away. Those who were taken prisoner revealed that the heart of the operation was a projected attack on Dublin Castle, the Viceroy's headquarters,

> by two desperate bands of ruffians armed with pikes and cutlasses. A select band was to have ascended with long ladders into the bed-chambers of the principal members of government and to have murdered them or carried them off as hostages. The city was to have been set on fire in different places; and the basin which supplied it with water, and the pipes through which it was conveyed were to have been destroyed.

Dublin was to have been cut off from external aid by a great cordon of United Irishmen in counties surrounding the city. They would then have advanced on Dublin to link up with their comrades within the city. The yeomanry's pre-emptive attack halted that strategy. Meanwhile, Fitzgerald's papers were shedding light on a new threat: a note suggesting that the French might use Wexford harbour as a better place to disembark an expeditionary force than the hostile west coast. The government's basilisk eye turned towards Wexford and the notorious North Cork militia were earmarked for operations there. Units of the United Irishmen in Wexford were also preparing for battle. Their purpose, as Professor Daniel Gahan has shown, was not to join the assault on Dublin but to seize control of their own county. This would make good sense if Fitzgerald had hopes of creating a safe beachhead for a French army.

The signal for the Wexford rising seems to have been an uprising on 25 May at Carlow, north-west of Wexford. There the government forces – yeomanry, militia and the 9th Dragoons – opened fire on the United Irishmen, who lost their nerve and fled. A grim pursuit killed some 400 rebels. The leader, Heydon – like many rebels, doubling as a yeomanry soldier – was hanged. Worse was to come. As Robert Kee described it: 'Men were stripped and flogged and their flesh cut to shreds by the cat-o'-nine tails in attempts to extract information from them. Some who refused to talk

were finally hanged, naked, bleeding and insensible as they were.'
News of the Carlow rising reached Wexford on the afternoon
of 26 May and was taken by the Wexford men as a signal to start
their rebellion also. That night, by the rising of the moon, thousands of men slipped out of their homes in parishes to the north
and centre of the county. They gathered in a crescent of forces
from the border with Carlow to the east coast, first in bands of
twenty to thirty, then by quick march to larger assembly areas. A
study by Daniel Gahan suggested: 'It had all the hallmarks of a
well-planned operation; when examined closely it shows few signs
of being a spontaneous popular response to a "great fear".' Certainly in an age when military movements could not be co-ordinated
except by word-of-mouth or letter, it was an impressive demonstration of military planning.

If, indeed, the United Irishmen of Wexford were well organized
and led, it sheds light on the controversial role of a Catholic curate,
the Seville-educated Father John Murphy of Boulavogue. On 25
May, a troop of yeomanry rode menacingly into the village and
rode out again. The young priest, who had persuaded his flock to
forswear violence, advised them to stay at home out of sight. Next
day the cavalry were back to demand that arms be surrendered.
Murphy was with a group gathered in front of a local farm. Murphy's people stoned the horsemen; an unwise provocation. The
officer commanding the yeomanry, Lieutenant Bookey, rode
through the crowd and torched the farm, whose thatch blazed high
in the hot sun. Murphy's people mobbed Bookey and his small
bodyguard. Bookey was piked through the neck and dismounted,
before being chopped to pieces. Yeomanry vengeance was exacted
next day, when farms over a wide area were burned down, as was
the Catholic chapel at Boulavogue.

Subsequent partisan histories make irreconcilable claims. The
Catholic Edward Hay, writing in 1803, concluded that Murphy,
'impressed with horror at the desolation around him, took up arms
with the people, representing to them that they had better die
courageously in the field than be butchered in their houses'. According to the Protestant Musgrave, writing three years later, Murphy
had greeted a Protestant neighbour named Webster on the road

in friendly fashion on 25 May, a Saturday, 'and yet, in about three hours after, was at the head of a numerous party of rebels who burned the houses of Webster and his brother and many of his protestant neighbours'. Musgrave was well aware that his version was challenged for he added:

> Some persons have asserted that the yeomen were the aggressors on this occasion and that father Murphy would not have embarked in the rebellion, if he had not been provoked by the burning of his house and his chapel; but the facts which I have related are a sufficient refutation of this; and the affidavits of rebel leaders of the names of Rossiter and Crawley, remove all doubts on it.

Recent scholarship has concluded that the Wexford Rebellion was the result of careful planning and not a fearful response to a rumour (cultivated, say some sources, by the United Irishmen) that Catholics were to be massacred by Orangemen. If that is so, then Murphy, in spite of his cloth, was an acknowledged leader of the rebellion before his village was attacked. Whatever the reason, Murphy now became a warlord as well as a priest. (In the Irish tradition, the one occupation does not necessarily preclude the other.) With 1,000 men, Murphy camped on nearby Oulart Hill on 27 May, where they combined with another rebel force. They came under attack from a company of the North Cork militia, a regiment of torturers. Murphy's people stood their ground and beat the militia, who were outnumbered.

An English officer in the battle, Lieutenant-Colonel Foote, recounted in a letter to a friend:

> I marched to a hill called Oulart, where between four and five thousand rebels were posted. From their great superiority of numbers, it was not my intention to have attacked them, unless some unforeseen favourable circumstances should warrant that measure; however, my officers were of contrary opinion. I met here part of a yeoman cavalry corps, about sixteen; the remainder, with their sergeant, having that morning joined the rebels.

Foote, knowing he was outnumbered, sent for reinforcements but

> afterwards, when I joined the party, I found that they were moved forward by the officer next in command; and the soldiers cried out that they would beat the rebels out of the field. By this movement we were immediately engaged with the rebels, who fired from behind hedges, without shewing any regular front. We beat their advanced party from one hedge to another . . . killing great numbers of them, till they retreated in great disorder to the main body, which consisted mostly of pikemen.
>
> [Again Foote tried to disengage his men] . . . but unfortunately the too great ardour of the men and officers could not be restrained. They rushed forward, were surrounded and overpowered by numbers. They displayed great valour and intrepidity, and killed a great number of rebels. Of this detachment none have as yet returned to Wexford but myself, a serjeant and three privates. I received a wound from a pike in my breast, a slight one in my arm and several bruises and contusions.

What was new was that the local people were now fighting as a coherent force. As they surrendered, the militiamen held up their Catholic breviaries to beg mercy of their co-religionists. They received no quarter. The market town of Enniscorthy was now at the mercy of the rebels who advanced behind a screen of cattle. As W. E. H. Lecky explained:

> Adopting a rude but not ineffectual strategy, which they more than once repeated in the course of the rebellion, and which is said to have been practised in Ireland as far back as the days of Strongbow, the rebels broke the ranks of the soldiers by driving into them a number of horses and cattle, which were goaded on by pikemen.

According to Musgrave, the rebels were as adept with guns as pikes that day. A veteran of the American war, Captain Drury, 'declared he had never experienced a heavier or better-directed fire. As the county of Wexford abounds with water fowl, the occupation of a fowler is so profitable that numbers of the lower class of people are not only expert in the use of fire arms, but excellent marksmen.'

A new camp was set up next day at nearby Vinegar Hill and rapidly became a focus for the United Irishmen throughout much of Wexford, a place where little order prevailed. In fine, hot weather, sheets and carpets looted from Protestant homes were spread as soft furnishings. Cattle were butchered and cooked in the open. An angry hunger for vengeance upon real and perceived enemies had to be satisfied and sufficient liquor drunk to loosen inhibitions. So the United Irishmen turned their attention to the thirty-five Enniscorthy Protestant prisoners, all civilians, they held in a derelict windmill. In groups of up to fifteen people, they were butchered in the space before the windmill, with pikes and guns. The bodies were then crudely buried, some still alive. A few survived to tell the tale.

As the slow massacre kept their troops happy and occupied, the leaders on Vinegar Hill discussed their next strategic move. The new thrust could have gone south-west, towards the town of New Ross, or south-east, towards the coast and the town of Wexford. Wexford was chosen, probably because of its importance as a port and landing site. On 29 May the rebel army, now numbered in thousands, streamed ten miles down to Forth Mountain, a high point just outside the town. Next day, the fourth of the rising, they occupied the town itself. Meanwhile, as Gahan noted, independently of this marching army, 'the rebellion spread into the far south-east and far south-west of the county both *before* government forces drove the people to rebel by their atrocities and *before* insurgent armies had the chance to intimidate people into joining'.

The only resistance, by a party of Meath militia, was ineffectual. With Wexford in their hands the rebels put two Protestant radicals – prototype Utopian United Irishmen – in nominal charge of a guerrilla army of 16,000 bloodthirsty Catholic Defenders. A former British army officer, Matthew Keogh, became local town governor. The Commander-in-Chief was a landowner named Beauchamp Bagenal Harvey. His army separated into three columns. One returned to Vinegar Hill before an assault on the town of New-townbarry in the north. A second marched to Carrigrew Hill over-looking the town of Gorey, to the north-east. A third column, led by Harvey, moved west to seize New Ross. That, at least, was the plan. All three objectives were about twenty-five miles from Wexford.

On 1 June the first two columns were forced back to lick their wounds at Vinegar Hill. This seems to have been the first intimation to reach the Wexford rebels that the Dublin rising, key to the whole revolution, had not gone according to plan. One of the northern columns finally made a reckless frontal assault on the seaside town of Arklow on 9 June, led by another priest, Michael Murphy. The attackers were cut to pieces by grapeshot aimed from well-prepared defences.

Musgrave carefully listed the forces involved in this key battle. As well as local yeomanry, a defending force totalling 1,137 was overwhelmingly made up of Irish militiamen from Cavan, Tyrone, Armagh and North Cork, as well as a Londonderry company of grenadiers. Regular units included the 4th and 5th Royal Irish Dragoon Guards, the Ancient British Fencible Light Dragoons – a Welsh contingent noted for its cruelty – the Suffolk Fencibles and Dunbarton infantry. Finally there were 300 men of the Durham Fencibles, 'a very fine regiment' which arrived at lunchtime, 'with-out whose assistance the little garrison would not probably have been able to withstand the superior numbers of the enemy'.

Musgrave calculated that the attacking rebel force numbered 25,000 with six-pounder guns, with a front rank of infantry sharp-shooters skilled at shooting down geese. 'They were covered in the rear by the pikemen, many deep, and at certain intervals their line was strengthened by numerous masses of men, who were ready to supply the places of those who fell.'

Kee showed that the heavy guns fired wide of the mark and that, aside from one successful ambush, the rebels made insufficient use of cover and probably depended upon weight of numbers to win the day in a frontal assault. A ratio of attackers to defenders of around 12:1 should have given them victory. That it did not demon-strated the hard reality of what happens when a guerrilla army makes the mistake of fighting a regular army in open, orthodox combat. Fitzgerald, the only professional soldier among the leader-ship, had wisely concluded that his countrymen were best used in harassing, guerrilla operations backed by a regular French army.

Harvey's force now paused about eight miles short of its objective at New Ross and spent the next two vital days (2 and 3 June) drilling. In prison in Dublin, meanwhile, the rebellion's lost general, Fitzgerald, was dying a lingering death from the wound he had suffered in resisting arrest on 19 May. His aunt, Lady Louisa Con-nolly, and the Earl of Clare visited him on 3 June to find him delirious, convinced that any sudden noise was the first explosion of the revolution. He died on 4 June, only hours before the rebellion suffered a decisive defeat at New Ross. For the assault on the town on 5 June, Harvey's column stampeded a herd of cattle as a screen behind which to overrun the outer defences of the town, as at Enniscorthy. Having reached the fixed guns defending the town, the rebels made a brave but foolhardy frontal assault. As Musgrave noted:

> One rebel, emboldened by fanaticism and drunkenness, advanced before his comrades, seized a gun, crammed his hat and wig into it and cried out, 'Come on, boys! Her mouth is stopped.' At that instant the gunner laid the match to the gun and blew the unfortunate savage to atoms. This fact has been verified by the affidavit of a person who saw it from a window.

Once in New Ross the rebels found themselves locked into a savage, close-quarter street battle that ended, after thirteen hours, in withdrawal. Most of them fought bravely, if without co-ordination. Some of them hit the liquor stores and died in their cups.

These reverses triggered the usual atrocities against unarmed Protestant captives and civilian hostages. At Scullabogue, a barn crowded with 200 people, including children, was torched. The barn was 34 feet long and 15 feet wide with walls a mere 12 feet high. Those not suffocated in the heat or burned alive were slaugh-tered by pikemen. The stink of roasting flesh hung over the scene.

Musgrave, piecing the evidence together three years later, con-cluded that 184 Protestant prisoners were burned inside the barn and thirty-seven shot in front of it. Quoting a witness at a subsequent trial of one of those responsible, he wrote:

> He then attended [accompanied] the rebels to the barn, in which there was a great number of men, women and children; and that the rebels were endeavouring to set fire to it, while the poor prisoners, shrieking and crying out for mercy, crowded to the back door of the barn, which they forced open for the purpose of admitting air: That for some time they continued to put the door between them and the rebels, who were piking or shooting them: That in attempting to do so, their hands or fingers were cut off: That the rebels continued to force into the barn bundles of straw to encrease the fire. At last, the prisoners having been overcome by the flame and smoke, their moans and cries gradually died away in the silence of death . . .

> No less than twenty-four protestants were taken from the village of Tintern, about eight miles distant, many of them old and feeble, and were in one drove to the barn, where they perished. Thomas Shee and Patrick Prendergast, both Romanists, were burnt in the barn because they would not consent to the massacre of their protestant masters . . .

> The witness, during this terrible scene, saw a child who got under the door and was likely to escape, but much hurt and bruised; when a rebel perceiving it, darted his pike through it and threw it into the flames.

The Wexford rebels were now running out of steam and out of ideas. As government forces prepared to march south, the rebels passed two weeks, from 6 to 19 June, moving in an aimless, circular fashion from one hill to another around territory they controlled. Professor Gahan suggested they did this because they still expected to receive news that Dublin had been taken by the United Irishmen after all. A priest named John Martin of Drogheda, a messenger from rebels further east in the Irish Midlands, had told them this was so.

Bagenal Harvey was sacked when he tried to halt the massacre of fellow Protestants. He now acknowledged that his army was in practice 'a set of savages exceeding all description'. Worse was to come. With the rebels in retreat, they had to abandon the town of Wexford. Their parting gesture was a massacre on the bridge across the River Slaney, near its estuary, on 20 June. The river was already bloody from massacres upstream. The war criminals in this episode were led by Thomas Dixon and his wife, who ignored instructions from the rebel Protestant town governor, Keogh, not to molest prisoners. The historian Lecky (supported independently by Musgrave) concluded that ninety-seven people died, stabbed with pikes and flung into the river. He added: 'So much blood covered the bridge, that it is related that, when Dixon and his wife endeavoured to ride over it, their frightened horses refused to proceed and they were obliged to dismount, Mrs Dixon holding up her riding habit lest it should be reddened in the stream.'

The Dixons escaped when the rebellion was finally put down and were never traced.

Musgrave recounted that the Wexford City prison was full of Protestants. Between 4 p.m. and 7 p.m., parties of ten to twenty prisoners were taken from the prison in a macabre procession headed by someone carrying a black flag, escorted by pikemen. On the bridge they were slaughtered, one by one.

> The mob, consisting of more women than men, expressed their savage joy on the immolation of each of the victims, by loud huzzas. The manner, in general, of putting them to death was thus: 'Two rebels pushed their pikes into the breast of the victim, and two into his back; and in that state (writhing with torture) they held him suspended, till dead, and then threw him over the bridge into the water.

The massacre halted suddenly, when a cry went up that reinforcements were needed at Vinegar Hill, now threatened by advancing government forces. Another hundred or so of the Wexford prisoners would have been put to death but for the arrival of regular soldiers commanded by Sir John Moore, who was later to die at Corunna.

The main rebel base at Vinegar Hill was lost on 21 June as government troops under General Lake moved in. Their battle-cry was long-winded if politically sound: 'Long live King George! Down with Republicanism!' The rebel forces broke and fled east in small armed bands, to be hunted down over the next six weeks. The reckoning followed. As Lord Cornwallis put it, the yeomanry had 'saved the country but ... now take the lead in rapine and murder'. Cornwallis wanted to try a gentler form of pacification. He created certificates of pardon (known as 'Cornys') to be given to rebels who surrendered their weapons. His army had other ideas. The reprisals that followed, a few of which were given an official gloss, added another twist to the dialogue of violence in which Irish patriots would be trapped for long afterwards. One estimate suggests that 25,000 people were put to death after the United Irishmen were beaten, sixty-five of them hanged on Wexford bridge.

Lecky concluded: 'Discipline had almost wholly gone. Military licence was perfectly unrestrained and the massacres which had taken place [during the Rebellion] – magnified a hundredfold by report – had produced a savage thirst for blood.' He quoted another observer, Gordon, as follows: 'I have reason to think that more men than fell in battle were slain in cold blood. No quarter was given to persons taken prisoner as rebels, with or without arms ... The Hessians exceeded any other troops in the business of depredation and many loyalists who had escaped from the rebels were put to death by these foreigners.'

Lecky, reviewing the evidence, found 'little or no difference in point of ferocity between the Irish yeomanry, who were chiefly Protestant, and the Irish militia, who were chiefly Catholic'. He added, however, that many of the worst excesses were attributed by opposed Catholic and Protestant writers to foreigners, the Welsh 'Ancient Britons' and regiments from Hesse. The German mercenaries might have fought on the other side if Tone, the absentee moral and political leader of the rebellion, had followed his plan to include them in an invading army to expel the English. Tone probably knew that Hessians fighting for the English king against his American colonists from 1777 to 1779 had been bribed by Jefferson and Franklin to change sides. The bribe was citizenship and land formerly occupied by Native Americans. A private soldier who turned coat was rewarded with 50 acres. The price of a full colonel was 1,000 acres. About 6,000 Germans accepted and settled permanently in the New World. The Irish, a decade or so later, did not have land to spare.

In time, most of the Republicans prominent in the rebellion were brought to trial. The Protestant leaders in Wexford, Beauchamp Bagenal Harvey and Matthew Keogh, were hanged from the bridge there on 1 July. General Moore, who was present, sought clemency for Keogh who had risked his life in trying to put the brake on rebel atrocities. General Lake rejected Moore's request, dramatically made as Keogh was on the gallows.

Meanwhile, seventy of the movement's political grandfathers, including members of the Supreme National Directory, seized in the raid on Oliver Bond's house four months earlier, were still in custody in Dublin. Their cause lost, key members of the Directory – Arthur O'Connor, Thomas Emmet and William MacNeven – agreed to reveal everything about their movement except the identities of others involved. In return they were permitted to go unscathed into exile in a country of their own choice.

By 1802, when the Treaty of Amiens brought the Anglo-French war to a halt, the rebel VIPs were sent to France and liberty. Emmet and MacNeven, among others, later settled in the United States. Rank-and-file rebels who had been lucky enough to avoid a death sentence were transported to Australian penal colonies or to Hesse, to become slaves of the King of Prussia. Their fate was probably no less harsh than the total number of innocents still serving as slaves of the Royal Navy. As in Cromwell's time, Ireland was now a place stripped of natural justice, where the guilty and innocent were punished alike simply for being available as fodder for an angry government. It was not a prescription for stability.

Meanwhile, with calamitous timing, spurred on by Tone's optimism, the French were about to try, yet again, to land in Ireland. The force that came ashore at Killala, County Mayo, on 22 August was a mere token: 1,000 officers led by General Humbert, outnumbered twenty-to-one by Cornwallis's well-rested army. The French had been persuaded that, in this case, an absence of equality, fraternity and liberty would not matter because their arrival would prompt a popular, massive uprising of the natives. They were wrong. By 8 September, Humbert's force had surrendered.

Another reason why it had been unrealistic to hope that an invasion would succeed where rebellion from within had failed was the Royal Navy's control of the seas. The first task facing any invasion fleet was to avoid destruction just beyond the harbour bar. Humbert's tiny expedition sailed aboard a mere three frigates. It did well to dodge the British squadron prowling around the approaches to Rochefort. The rest of the trip and the landing in Mayo relied upon Humbert's use of the Royal Navy white ensign as part of a deception plan.

Ignoring the danger signs, the French tried yet again in late September. This time, they brought Wolfe Tone along. He was a VIP passenger aboard the seventy-four-gun battleship *Hoche*, leading a fleet of nine other vessels of which eight were twelve-gun or twenty-four-gun frigates. On 12 October, twenty-three days later, this fleet was intercepted off Horn Head, Donegal, by a smaller Royal Navy squadron. The encounter that followed was a reprise, in miniature, of the Cape St Vincent battle twenty months earlier. There, the British had also smashed an invasion fleet against the odds, thanks to superior speed, co-ordination, gunnery and an unsporting 'wolf pack' tactic: the Royal Navy would attack a single ship, bringing concentrated firepower to bear locally at virtually point-blank range. Having destroyed one target, they reformed to co-ordinate a similar attack on the next. As one British captain put it: 'We flew to them like a hawk to his prey.'

At Horn Head the French battleship survived for just four hours before she struck her colours. Only three of this fleet escaped the onslaught. The prisoners included Tone, resplendent in a French uniform of blue and gold. It was another three weeks before the prisoners were landed at Lough Swilly, a mere 15 miles away. Tone, like a fading actor still seeking recognition, greeted an old acquaintance among the spectators watching the disembarkation. On 10 November, after a short trial at Dublin, he was sentenced to death by hanging as a felon, rather than the honourable soldier's end he requested, by firing squad. In his death cell, he used a concealed knife to hack his throat open. He was still alive next morning. Death on the scaffold was deferred as he passed his last week on earth in agony. When he did finally expire it was, after all, by his own hand.

Tone had dedicated himself to an illusion about the nature of Ireland. This was that the nation's route to independence required violent Republican revolution on the French model. A military incompetent, he refreshed British paranoia about the Irish at a point in time when Ireland's opportunity clearly lay – through Catholic Relief – in supporting England against its enemies rather than exploiting England's danger. Yet in most Irish eyes, Tone's restless, romantic life and melodramatic death retrieved the failures. His success was posthumous. He became a greater threat as a dead, non-sectarian symbol of Irish republicanism than he ever could be as a living, dilettante general. He built his own myth for a culture that renews itself by reference to mythology. In that sense at least, he did not fool himself.

16

The Silent Massacre, 1845

Two gallows, one in Dublin, the second in Manchester, separated in time by sixty-four years, were the next major milestones in the Irish War. In August 1803 Robert Emmet was hanged after writing from the condemned cell a celebrated political obituary: 'Let no man write my epitaph . . . When my country takes her place among the nations of the earth then, and not till then, let my epitaph be written.'

On the second scaffold in 1867, William Allen, Philip Larkin and Michael O'Brien were executed for raiding a prison van to rescue fellow Fenians, killing a police sergeant in the process.

These sixty-four years were ones in which, having defeated France at Waterloo in 1815, Britain enjoyed a unique period of expansion: industrially at home and acquiring an empire overseas. Many perceived this as a period of sylvan peace, apart from an inept Crimean campaign in the 1850s and a mutiny in India. Ireland, however, was not at peace. Absorbed into the English parliamentary system in 1803, Ireland was technically not a colony but the natives were treated – in Kipling's words – as lesser breeds without the law. Republicans inspired by Tone's and Emmet's belief in political independence were able to create a political empire of their own overseas – an empire of belief and aspiration – thanks to the penal exile of Irishmen in Australia or their political exile in France and America; and later through the deliberate recruitment of expatriate Irishmen to the Fenians in the United States. In Ireland as such there was no great uprising in the nineteenth century: just anger, localized terrorism, threat and counter-threat exchanged between Republicans and Orangemen.

The significant difference between Emmet's crime in 1803 and that of the 'Manchester Martyrs' in 1867 was that Emmet had tried to seize Dublin Castle, seat of government, while the Manchester men were satisfied with a street brawl on enemy soil. Emmet had an immediate strategic objective – creation of a full-blown provisional government – while the Fenians were pursuing a tactical adventure so as to spring two of their number from captivity.

There was another, more profound difference. The Fenians used international terrorism to further their cause, anticipating the revolutionary anarchists of the late nineteenth and early twentieth centuries. Though the Fenians dedicated themselves to Irish freedom as they perceived it, they also shared something of the anarchist view of life as a state of permanent revolution, a diaspora divorced from ties of family or even nationhood. They founded a tradition of terrorism-as-lifestyle which the Provisional IRA renewed in 1970; a tradition which had much in common with the dispossessed people of Palestine and their transnational terrorism after 1968. Emmet, by contrast, was in a line of resistance that accepted public self-immolation; resistance as a grand moral gesture to rouse common people to virtuous heroism. Emmet's little rebellion was the precursor of Easter 1916. His style was strong on moral virtue but short – lamentably short, in his case – on military reality and luck. Terrorism, though morally bankrupt, would get results. In time, the challenge facing Irish revolutionaries was somehow to combine the two disparate traditions so as to retain moral credibility *and* run a campaign of militarily-effective terrorism. That process would not come about for another century.

Robert Emmet and his brother Thomas (imprisoned for his part in the 1798 rebellion, but not hanged) were the high-flying sons of a prominent government doctor. In the normal course of events they should have become pillars of the Protestant establishment in Dublin. Both were lured by the excitement of the revolution in Paris where Robert represented the United Irishmen, or what was left of it, in 1801. He was still there when the war between France and Britain paused, thanks to the Treaty of Amiens. The peace would last a mere fourteen months. It ended because the British insisted on holding on to Malta, instead of handing over the island to the Knights of St John, as had been agreed. Napoleon, faced with this breach, promptly dusted down the many plans to invade England that had accumulated in French archives over the previous hundred years. He then set about creating an invasion fleet at Boulogne. That it never sailed was due to Nelson's victory over Villeneuve at Trafalgar in October 1805 but that was part of an unknown future when Napoleon's Grand Army of 167,000 veterans was assembled alongside 2,343 ships, including 700 invasion barges, at the Channel. Napoleon made no secret of his plans. As the historian Alfred Cobban has pointed out: 'The Bayeux tapestry was brought to Paris for exhibition as a reminder of a previous successful invasion of England from France.'

This should have been the stroke of fortune for which Emmet, Tone and others had been devoutly hoping. A French invasion of England on such a scale, followed by a quick strike against London, would have made it impossible for England to keep its grip on a still rebellious Ireland. In the event, Emmet did not command the degree of French support for his new Irish rebellion that he expected, due to divisions among Irish exiles in Paris. (Many years later, the playwright Brendan Behan declared that the first item on any Irish Republican agenda was 'The Split'.) Much worse, Emmet launched his attempted coup prematurely, in July 1803, at a time when the French were still putting their invasion force together.

The rebels' target, as usual, was Dublin Castle; the date set for the attack, 23 July 1803, just a few weeks after hostilities between France and England were renewed. But on 16 July, an explosives and arms factory run by Emmet's men in a Dublin back street blew up. Emmet, though he wisely limited his initial operation to Dublin, now repeated the mistake of the men of 1798 in carrying on with the attempt when it was clearly going wrong. A call to arms went to Kildare, where veterans of the earlier rebellion were scavenging for survival. On the night of 22 July a handful of warriors from Kildare who did arrive were disappointed when they learned there was to be no French invasion. Some promptly went to the pub, then home. At 9 o'clock that night, faced with this and other portents of failure, Emmet tried to call off his attack. He changed his mind again next day.

A printing press, meanwhile, was churning out copies of a proclamation for the 'Provisional Government of the Republic', ordering seizure of church land in the anti-clerical tradition of the French Revolution. The proclamation also proposed a parliament elected by universal suffrage and proportional representation. Emmet, wearing a striking green uniform and feathered cocked hat, received this paperwork as he waited for his army to rally at a depot in Thomas Street. The hours passed. The force that was to sweep the English into the sea eventually totalled fewer than a hundred. Since it was now Saturday evening, not everyone was sober.

The plan was to travel in horse-drawn carriages, so as to conceal arms and explosives and scaling ladders, to the castle walls. Someone had blundered. A single, misjudged shot panicked the horses. They bolted, carriages and all. So Emmet, sword in hand, led his men on foot towards their objective. Many of the troops, armed with blunderbusses and pikes, quietly dispersed into the side streets and went home. The rebel band, now little more than twenty strong, encountered a coach carrying a VIP passenger who was quickly identified as Lord Chief Justice Kilwarden and his son-in-law. Kilwarden, by the standards of the age, was judged 'a decent sort of fellow' by Dubliners. This did not save him. Emmet's gang hauled the two men out of the coach and piked them to death. Emmet himself claimed later – probably truthfully – that he did not know of this murder and condemned it when he did learn of it.

The killing seems to have been a catalyst for riots elsewhere that night in which thirty people died. Emmet, at last unable to deny the reality of failure, called a halt to the operation and told the handful of troops still loyal to him to disperse. He went on the run. 'Wanted' notices were posted, describing him as a man with 'an ugly, sour countenance and dirty brown complexion'.

That should have ended Emmet's place in history, but in a country where oratory, poetry and mysticism count for more than military realities, Emmet's great moment was yet to come. This was his trial, after a month in hiding, and execution. From the dock he declared his belief in an independent Irish Republic. Like the Minstrel Boy, his was one Irish (if Protestant) voice unswerving in its dedication to the cause. He was no longer an intellectual advocate of the doctrine of Rousseau and Voltaire, but a passionate patriot. The court indulged him as he delivered his own funeral oration:

> I have but one request to ask at my departure from this world. It is the charity of its silence. Let no man write my epitaph; for as no man who knows my motives dare now vindicate them, let not prejudice or ignorance asperse them. Let them rest in obscurity and peace, my memory be left in oblivion and my tomb remain uninscribed, until other times and other men can do justice to my character. When my country takes her place among the nations of the earth, then and not till then, let my epitaph be written.

Emmet's execution was a messy sacrifice: a delayed hanging, decapitation, the severed head displayed, the martyr's blood dripping from the scaffold to provide a feast for stray dogs and puddles of blood into which patriots and ghouls dipped handkerchiefs. Yet the Emmet legend became a best-seller of Irish mythology. As Robert Kee noted:

> The reason why exactly the Emmet débâcle should have become transformed into a myth of such powerful emotive force, and thus indirectly of political importance, is not immediately easy to see. His failure could hardly have been more ignominious and complete ... Why was it Robert Emmet's portrait above all others that was to go up along with the crucifix in countless small homes in Ireland for over a century and may even be seen there still?
> The proximity of the crucifix may provide a clue. The success of the Emmet myth lay in the very need to ennoble failure. For tragic failure was to become part of Ireland's identity, something almost indistinguishable from 'the cause' itself.

After the failures of Tone, Fitzgerald and Emmet in Dublin and Napoleon at Waterloo, Irish armed resistance went into one of its periods of reclusive rural throat-cutting. One night in 1811 a gang of Whiteboys broke into the home of a North Cork land agent named John Purcell. Purcell defended himself with a carving knife.

In the darkness he fatally stabbed one intruder and wounded four others. One of the Whiteboys was subsequently hanged. Purcell received a knighthood.

In the cities, political opposition was alive and well: Daniel O'Connell campaigned successfully for Catholic emancipation but the new land war, ostensibly in support of O'Connell, was less about lofty thoughts than empty bellies, fuelled by Catholic bigotry. Typical of this phase of conflict was the Terry Alt movement, active from 1829 to 1831. The real Terry Alt, it was said, was 'a most harmless and inoffensive man'. His name was misused to become an ironic battle-cry: 'Well done, Terry Alt!'

Ireland was a rural culture divided between landowners and tenants. The tenants might rent a field for just a single season, long enough to take one potato crop. Rising rents, relentless rain and harvest failures sharpened the grievances of the poor fifteen years before the nightmare of the famine. In the late 1820s many landowners preferred sheep and cattle as a resource, to human tenants. This meant evicting tenants by force, smashing ('tumbling') the hovels in which they lived.

In January 1831 William Blood, land agent for Lord Stradbroke on an estate in County Clare, was ambushed by six men and murdered. Soon another four estate employees were killed, usually at night. By May that year the number of murders among the landowner class was nineteen. Punishment beatings that stopped just short of death – a familiar part of life in the Ulster ghettos after 1970 – were rife in Clare and elsewhere. The victims were herdsmen, guards set over pastures, estate labourers or people simply identified as 'strangers'. By day the Terry Alts created another unique form of protest. They assembled hundreds of people to dig up pastures as a first step towards growing potatoes once more. Professor James Donnelly described the process in an article about the Terry Alt movement:

> The size of the crowds was certainly one of their most arresting features. Though some involved only scores of people, most crowds numbered in the hundreds and not a few included more than a thousand. They were usually mixed in

age and sex, comprising women and children as well as adult males ... In the typical case the diggers marched to their appointed work in military order, with spades and pitchforks hoisted on their shoulders, and with fifers or other musicians playing before them. Naturally, this ritual drew onlookers, who followed the marchers to the designated place and lustily cheered them on as they stripped and set to work. While some participants turned up the grass with their spades ... others broke the sods with their pitchforks ... It was a ritual to toss the sods of grass into the air and at the same time to raise a cry, such as '*Hey* for O'Connell, and *hey* for Clare.' Because the crowds were so large, it was possible to turn up a field of five or ten acres in an hour or less, and it was not unusual for one crowd to polish off several fields in a morning's work of protest, sport and conviviality. Small parties of police ... were no use ... Sizeable detachments of soldiers ... soon brought the turning up of pastures to an end.

The authorities condemned twenty-one members of the movement to death and transported fifty-eight others but, as Donnelly argued, 'judicial penalties reached only a tiny fraction of the Terry Alts and their legions of supporters ... Agrarian rebellion was a fairly low-risk strategy.'

From the autumn of 1845 effective armed resistance was defeated not by security forces but the horrors of the potato famine. The potato had nourished Ireland so well that her population exploded. More than four million people in Ireland (and two million in Britain) ate almost nothing else. Meanwhile, inefficient division of land into ever smaller plots led to dangerous over-cultivation. Together, these two factors were a demographic time-bomb waiting only for a detonator. That came from the USA. It was a fungus called *Phytophtora infestans*. In July, a hot, promising summer changed to a baleful season of driving rain and fog. Potatoes which looked normal in the ground were rotten under the skin. Over the next five years, as the crop failed again, more than a million people starved to death in Ireland amid scenes of medieval horror. As

Professor Cormac O'Grada, writing in 1994, put it: 'The Famine ranks as Europe's greatest natural disaster ... Even the most Thatcherite of European politicians today would be deemed "wet" compared with those in power and influence in Westminster during the Famine. There is some truth, then, in the claim that in the 1840s, "Ireland died of political economy."' What rubbed home this savage truth was the compensation paid to Britain's former slave-owners – twice the amount voted for Irish famine relief – and a subsequent decision to load Irish taxpayers with the bill, at a time when, constitutionally, Ireland and Britain were one nation.

It was not just the English who turned a blind eye to the silent massacre at their back door. The Irish gentry had never had it so good. The Irish racehorse and hunter, absorbing the peculiar strength that comes from pasture underpinned by limestone, developed a bone strength that made the breed fitter than any rival. From the 1843 Steeplechase de Paris (first prize, £990) to the 1847 Aintree Grand National, Irish bloodstock swept the board. Grania Willis, an equestrian historian commented, without any hint of irony: 'These were the famine years in Ireland and the performances of Irish horses both at home and abroad were the one bright spot in an otherwise desperate period.'

Initially, the British government provided £8 million for public works schemes but, following more agrarian violence in late 1847, the English public concluded that the ungrateful Irish must be taught a lesson. An English observer in Ireland concluded that surrounded by 'an abundance of cheap food ... very many have been done to death by pure tyranny'. Equally potent in shaping British policy was a banking crash in October 1847 and a campaign to cut back state spending, particularly Irish relief, which carried with it the threat of extra income tax in Britain. A cartoon of the time depicted John Bull, in the role of Sinbad carrying the Old Man of the Sea on his back. In this version, the ungrateful incubus was (who else?) Paddy.

The following year was a spectacularly successful one for Europe's continental revolutionaries. France, Austria, Italy, Hungary and Germany all felt the scourge of street violence as a way to political change. Monarchies toppled. In South London, protesting

Chartists faced armed troops and backed off. In Ireland, a Harrow-educated Liberal MP and former magistrate, William Smith O'Brien, incited the peasants of Tipperary to rise. With two pistols in his coat and escorted by two supporters, he strode into the police station at Mullinahone and asked the officers – a head constable plus five men – to surrender. The police refused and withdrew to a stronger post. O'Brien left town in a jaunty-car, smoking a cigar. A few days later police opened fire on a crowd of O'Brien's supporters, killing two of them. The crowd surrounded a policeman bringing a message and stole his horse. Later, the same policeman encountered O'Brien riding the animal. O'Brien returned it to him. Later that year, the former MP was transported to Tasmania but was eventually pardoned and allowed to return to Ireland.

By the standards of continental Europe at the time, Irish resistance was feeble. Such movements as Young Ireland and O'Brien's Irish Confederation were significant not for what they achieved at the time but because of the revolutionary careers they started. A companion of O'Brien in his small-town misadventures was a twenty-five-year-old railway worker from Kilkenny named James Stephens, later to be founding father of the Irish Republican Brotherhood and the Fenian Brotherhood. Another of the group, Thomas Meagher (pronounced 'Maher'), became a general in the Union Army that won the American Civil War. A third, John Mitchel, emerged as an influential journalist on the opposing Confederate side of that conflict.

Fuelled by emigration to the United States as thousands of Irish men, women and children sought escape from famine, the focus for resistance to English control of Ireland was shifting also to America and away from France. This harvest was a bitter one for England. Unlike the potato, the crop of new trouble never failed. One million humans had died of hunger. Two million more emigrated to the United States. Some went direct; others by way of the penal colonies of Australia and Tasmania, from which they then escaped, usually by dishonouring their parole. Many would become skilled in the arts of war in America before returning to Europe to exact their vengeance.

Even Catholic theology had a cutting edge in the New World

that it dared not speak aloud in Ireland. In 1861, one of the rebels of 1848 named Terence Bellew McManus, died in California. The veteran Fenian John O'Leary said of McManus that before his conviction for high treason he was 'little, if at all known to fame' and subsequently 'had done nothing to increase his reputation'. But there is such a thing as funereal chic in Irish culture. The Fenians and their successors developed it into an art form. McManus's body lay in state in St Patrick's Cathedral, New York, as Archbishop Hughes told the congregation that the church had sometimes found it lawful to resist and overthrow a tyranny. McManus's body was then sent home to Dublin, where another Catholic prelate, Archbishop Cullen, prohibited any lying-in-state.

James Connolly, before a British firing squad ended his life in 1916, carefully documented the political conservatism of the Roman Catholic Church in the matter of the Irish Question. From the twelfth century and Henry II onwards, he suggested, the church was lavish in its use of excommunication, or the threat of excommunication, against nationalist rebels opposed to English rule. According to Connolly, not even the victims of the famine, which is currently laid at Britain's door, were immune from priestly discipline, along with their other sufferings. In a polemic against the church published in 1910, he wrote:

> During the great Irish famine of 1845–6–7–8–9 the Irish people died in hundreds of thousands of hunger, whilst there was food enough to feed three times the population. When the starving peasantry was called upon to refuse to pay rent to idle landlords, and to rise in revolt against the system that was murdering them, the clergy commanded them to pay their rents, instructed them that they would lose their immortal souls should they refuse to do so, and threw all the weight of their position against the revolutionary movement for the freedom of Ireland.

17

Sacrificial Sons of Erin,
1860–1865

On 13 December 1862 Bill McCarter, a twenty-one-year-old Derryman, survived a desperate uphill march so as to come within musket range of the enemy a mere fifty paces away. He had almost reached the cover of a low stone wall when he and his comrades were ambushed by a hostile brigade of 2,400 who cut them to pieces as if this were a turkey shoot. McCarter stood his ground. He had fired six or seven shots when he was hit in the right arm. The blood flowed down his clothes, filling his right shoe until it overflowed. He collapsed but as he lay on the ground more bullets tore the clothes from his back or thudded into the bodies of his friends who lay within touching distance. After dark, soaked by rain but half-mad with thirst, he crawled away to the safety of dead ground where a stretcher party found him.

McCarter's enemy were not British soldiers but fellow Irishmen. His battlefield was a sacrificial one, part of the American Civil War. At Marye's Heights, Fredericksburg, Virginia, that day, he was part of the Federal army's spearhead, the Irish Brigade. The brigade was led by the Young Irelander rebel of 1848, Thomas Meagher, son of a Mayor of Waterford and educated at the exclusive Stony-hurst School in England. The brigade's green flag was decorated with the Irish harp and a Gaelic motto, *Faugh a Ballagh* (Clear the Way).

The opposition that bitterly cold day was Brigadier General Thomas Cobb's Georgia Brigade, another largely Irish unit. As Meagher's men continued their doomed march on to enemy guns, there was a brief, poignant moment of recognition as the Southern troops recognized the Green Flag. They paused in the business of killing to cheer their opponents. One of their leaders, Major-General Pickett, wrote later to his fiancée: 'Your soldier's heart almost stood still as he watched those sons of Erin fearlessly rush to their death. The brilliant assault on Marye's Heights of their Irish Brigade was beyond description. Why, my darling, we forgot they were fighting us, and cheer after cheer at their fearlessness went up along our lines.'

The sacrifice of the Irish regiments in the Civil War was to have an effect upon America's attitude to the Irish struggle which was still plain more than a century later. Not only were many of the heroes of the victorious North Irish, they were also dedicated members of the Fenian Brotherhood, the new wave of Irish resistance to English rule founded by James Stephens in Dublin on his return from exile in Paris. Stephens was already in touch with Thomas O'Mahony, another rebel who had emerged as a leader of the Irish Emigrant Aid Society in New York.

Stephens, after his life as a revolutionary émigré in Paris, was wary of his countrymen's love of gossip and 'crack'. Security would not be easy. He organized his new movement in self-contained 'circles' so that the rank-and-file would know only those within a single group, not the whole command structure. After 1970 the IRA would reorganize along similar lines. Even so, as Stephens discovered, the Irish Republican Brotherhood attracted an informer from the very beginning: a parish priest at Skibbereen. In October 1858, seven months after founding his new movement, Stephens went on a fund-raising tour of the United States and collected £600 – a substantial sum but rather less than the prize money collected by a single Irish horse in Paris at that time. While in America again in 1859, he and the exiled O'Mahony, living in New York, set up the American association which became the Fenian Brotherhood. O'Mahony it was who coined the word 'Fenian', from the *Fianna* – an elite fighting group – of the legendary warrior Finn MacCumhail. In time the word Fenian was attached to Republicans on both sides of the Atlantic and is still a term of abuse when used by extremist Ulster Protestants to describe their enemy.

At that time, shortly before the American Civil War, the Irish were not universally welcomed by earlier generations of settlers including some of the Bostonian Irish. An Irish American historian, Frank A. O'Reilly, even suggested:

Prior to the Civil War, the Irish struggled to subsist in the United States. They repeatedly felt the wrath of an isolationist, Know-Nothing society that generally despised the Irish. Often the spectre of the Irish-Catholics' paving the way for a Papal *coup d'état* sparked violent and deadly Nativist riots throughout America ... When the Civil War broke out many Irishmen viewed the conflict ambivalently as they attempted to scratch out a hand-to-mouth existence.

One emigrant broke through the barrier of prejudice that pervaded pre-1860 America. This was Matilda Tone, widow of Wolfe Tone, icon of the 1798 Rebellion with whom she had eloped at the age of fifteen. After his death in prison, Matilda made a new life in America and settled near Georgetown, Washington DC. She remarried but, far from forgetting Tone, she carefully fostered his memory and got his written work published. Tone's name became, as one observer put it, 'a mascot' for Irish American nationalism, while Matilda Tone was at the centre of the United Irish exile community in the USA from 1815 until her death. When she died in 1849 aged eighty, her funeral was attended by representatives of Irish American societies, American and French generals and – in recognition of Tone's rank in the French army – the French ambassador to the United States. She is buried in Greenwood Cemetery, Brooklyn, New York.

The flood of starving Irish refugees into America after 1841 was less acceptable to polite America than the romantic, solitary figure of Matilda Tone. The new generation of political exiles, the men of '48, were quick to recognize the gap and the means to bridge it. Colonel William Halpin, an Irish American Fenian who commanded the Kentucky regiment in the Civil War, wrote in 1864:

Nearly all the officers of General TF Meagher's original and famous Irish Brigade, as also the Corcoran Legion, were Fenians. Colonel M'Iver of the 170th New York Volunteers belongs to the Order [the Fenian Brotherhood], as does also General Gleeson of the 63rd ... In the Corcoran Legion alone last year twenty-four Fenian officers were killed, or crippled, including Colonel Murphy. The 164th New York was originally raised and officered by Fenians, who had graduated in the 99th New York State Militia, otherwise called the Phoenix or Fenian Regiment, a regiment which has educated and sent into the army three full sets of officers within the past few years, together with over 1,200 men of rank and file. In Milford, Massachusetts, out of a circle of 115 Fenians previous to the war, eighty at once enlisted in a body, under their Centre, Major Peard and of these but twenty-three are now alive. In Connecticut one whole circle [i.e., a Fenian Circle, or group] of about two hundred volunteered unanimously; but, as their State quota was full, they went off in the 10th Ohio Infantry ... Two thirds of the 9th Massachusetts Infantry were Fenians, who went off under a Fenian colonel who was shot through the head while leading his regiment. The 'Douglas Brigade' of Illinois, raised in Chicago, was in great part Fenian as was also the brigade raised by the late lamented Colonel Milligan, who was high up in the order.

Halpin's exhaustive list adds many other units including the famous 42nd New York regiment, 'chiefly organised by Lieutenant-Colonel Michael Doheny, one of the original founders of the Order'. Even this list is not complete, for it excludes the 69th New York and other Irish regiments of the Army of the Potomac. A later commentator, hostile to Fenianism, was John Rutherford who correctly concluded:

The service of the Fenians in the army of the Federal States had two purposes: to manufacture themselves into effective soldiers and to purchase the favour of the authorities. In both purposes they were successful ... It is most extraordinary that such a conspiracy should have been allowed to grow up openly, in a country at peace with the State against which it was directed. There is nothing like it in modern history ... It was encouraged in every way ... Federal officers in high command were actually allowed to absent themselves from their posts, in the heat of the strife, in order to attend to Fenian business.

The Southern army was also well penetrated by Fenians, serving in such units as the 6th Louisiana Volunteers – 'the Bloody Sixth' – part of Lee's Army of Northern Virginia. The Sixth fought at virtually every Civil War battle including Sharpsburg, Fredericksburg, Chancellorsville and Gettysburg. The South's senior officers doubling as Fenians included General 'Fighting Cleborne', a deserter from an English Guards regiment, and Gordon Massey, born in Limerick, a British army corporal in the Crimea and a leader of a Fenian operation against England in 1867. Rutherford wrote:

We know of an instance in which one of Morgan's raiders, having been captured red-handed, would have been hanged, but for his connection with the Brotherhood. At his capture the man received a wound, which for ever disabled him as a soldier. He was released immediately after his discharge from hospital, and as he was energetic, intelligent and tolerably educated, besides being a hardened soldier, he was sent across to Dublin where he became a salaried officer of the [Fenian] Conspiracy.

The most impressive testament to the Fenian penetration of both armies was the freedom allowed to the movement's co-founder James Stephens. In 1864, using the nom-de-guerre Captain Daly, 'he was passed from one end of the Northern armies to the other, examining every Circle therein as he went'. Similar indulgence was granted to Stephens's partner, John O'Mahony, whose officers obtained passes permitting them to cross the battle lines to communicate with Fenians on the Southern side of the conflict.

'There was', Rutherford continued, 'an understanding between the Fenian Head Centre on the one side, and the Executive of the Northern States on the other that when the war should be triumphantly closed, the Fenians should receive not merely countenance, but material aid in the struggle they proposed to open with England.'

So it proved. In 1886, for example, the US Senate refused to ratify a treaty with England which provided for the extradition of Irish dynamiters. In 1888, both Republican and Democratic parties included in their electoral platforms what one historian describes as 'a gratuitous pledge to Irish Home Rule', while in 1897 the Republicans, pursuing the now-valued Irish vote, stressed the hatred of England nourished by their candidate McKinley.

The price for this strategic political asset, paid between 1861 and 1865, was Irish blood at such battles as Bull Run, Antietam, Fredericksburg and Chancellorsville. Even Rutherford conceded: 'At the close of the strife, the military Fenians counted 15,000 men. And it is not too much to say that at least as many more perished on the various fields of battle, or in the hospitals. Several of the Fenian regiments were recruited bodily three times over, and yet returned from the war the merest skeletons.'

Meagher, wrote Frank A. O'Reilly,

> deliberately focused attention on his brigade's Irish heritage [though it was only one of forty similar units] so that the United States would appreciate its sacrifices as the work of a composite group of Irish-Americans ... Members of Meagher's Irish Brigade constantly crusaded to keep its name and exploits before the public ... Officers published tracts during the war ranging from newspaper articles to religious sermons on the faithfulness and integrity of the Irish.

The Irish were suddenly fashionable. They were 'not only heroes but patriots and saints as well'. They were 'fearless and peerless in battle'. A Fenian cult developed. At public auctions, bonds were sold, redeemable when the Irish Republic became a fact of life. W. D. D'Arcy found that 'Armed Fenian units paraded in American towns; Fenian periodicals and song books proliferated and there was a popular brand of Fenian tobacco.'

In spite of the indulgence of the American government and the safe haven the USA now provided for Fenian attacks on Britain, to say nothing of the $250,000 raised for the movement in America, it made little headway in its war of liberation. One reason for this was Stephens's chronic procrastination when it came to concrete military action, a habit which enraged the American Fenians. They reasoned that if they could seize territory anywhere, and hoist the Green Flag over it, then an Irish Republic would exist in deed. This confused thinking led to one plot, soon abandoned, to occupy a desolate island off the coast of New Brunswick, and an attack on British Canada which did go ahead. On the night of 31 May 1866, 600 'Amerfenians' crossed the Niagara river, not far from Buffalo. An Irish immigrant named John O'Neill, still serving in the US army, was appointed leader at the last moment. The group styled itself the 'Irish Republican Army'.

According to the contemporary Fenian historian John Savage, men and arms were towed across the river in four canal boats.

> At 4am the Irish Flag was raised on British soil by Colonel Starr. O'Neill ordered the telegraph wires to be cut down and ordered a party to destroy a railway bridge. Starr occupied a fort three miles up-river from the town of Erie. O'Neill received intelligence that a force of 5,000 with artillery was advancing in two columns.

According to the anti-Fenian writer Rutherford, the defending force were Canadian volunteers not regular soldiers and there were fewer of them on hand than the 500 invaders. What does seem clear is that the Fenians took and held Fort Erie after a brief action in which some fifteen Candians died. The handful of Fenians killed included a Union veteran named James Geraghty. Expected reinforcements from the USA did not cross the water. With no backup, O'Neill's people sailed back the way they had come, after marching 40 miles and fighting two engagements. They were subject to token arrest by the American authorities. Rutherford's assessment was that 'these six hundred Fenians crossed the Niagara to destroy a little property – their scanty strength would not allow them to destroy more – and to slay and wound some fifty or sixty Canadians who had turned out in defence of their homes against a band of raiders whom they had done nothing whatever to provoke.'

The Canadian operation was useful for morale as well as an

interesting trial run for the emerging IRA, but the action should have been in Ireland. Stephens, chief of the Brotherhood, repeatedly promised that it would be (as Zionists of the diaspora would put it) 'next year in Jerusalem' or, in this case, Dublin. When that did not happen the American Brothers deposed Stephens and appointed in his place Thomas J. Kelly, one of the Connecticut Fenians who had joined the 10th Ohio regiment. The previous year Kelly had already visited Ireland to monitor Fenian training. Stephens was there too but, unlike Stephens, Kelly had avoided capture by the British authorities. After a short time Stephens was sensationally sprung from prison by a team that included Kelly. Once back in New York after that adventure, in December 1866, Stephens again postponed a projected Irish rebellion, claiming that resources were insufficient. For the ardent American Brothers, that was the last straw since, by this time, the Fenians had about 80,000 supporters in Britain as well as tens of thousands in America and 19,000 in Ireland itself.

In practice, the Irish struggle was becoming, as so often, a war of Intelligence and intrigue which would betray the gains made by the sacrifice of Irish blood in the American Civil War. By 1866 the British Secret Service had placed agents, or bought informers, at almost every level of the Fenian movement in America as well as in Ireland. This was not new. For almost a century London had invested heavily in a Secret Service dedicated to the Irish problem, making Ireland, in General John Moore's phrase, 'the Country of Informers'. As the British Chief Secretary to the Dublin Viceroy, Lord Carlisle, put it in 1781, proposing a Secret Service fund: 'In the present state of the country the wise application of about £3,000 a year might be of a degree of importance to his Majesty's affairs beyond what words can estimate.'

The informers were drawn from every niche of Irish society. Priests such as Father Arthur O'Leary in the eighteenth century (of whom a government official wrote: 'He is willing to undertake what is wished for £100 a year') and Father John O'Sullivan of Kenmare during the Fenian years betrayed the sacramental trust of the confessional. Defence lawyers such as Leonard McNally betrayed their duty to their clients. Key members of the Fenian Brotherhood betrayed their secret oath to that organization. One of the most deadly was the red-bearded Jim MacDermott, a spy in New York for the British consul, and a member of the Fenians' inner councils for years.

As early as 20 April 1861 the American Fenian journal, the *New York Phoenix*, found it necessary to publish a blacklist of informers in Ireland and America. The list included, for example: 'Carolan, Ballynahinch, County Down. Five feet seven in height, sixty years of age; blue eyes, gray hair and long, thin features; supposed to be prowling round Belfast . . . William Everett, about forty-five years of age, five feet ten inches in height with a lank body apparently possessing the flexibility of a bamboo.'

In Dublin, Pierce Nagel was a disgraced ex-schoolteacher who wormed his way into the confidence of Stephens and became a Fenian courier. But, said Rutherford, 'from early 1864 he formed a connection with the Dublin police, from whom he received twelve shillings weekly, and various gratuities'. Nagel gave evidence at the trial of Fenians in Dublin in 1865. One of the accused, later sentenced to penal servitude, was O'Donovan Rossa. Rossa, defending himself, cross-examined Nagel. A spectator noted: 'Both of the men looked a hell of hate into each other's eyes.'

During the same year, Francis Pettit, an army pensioner, informed the War Office that he had been sworn into the Brotherhood by its members in the north of England. The Fenian historian Desmond Ryan recorded: 'He was told of the purchases of rifles in Birmingham, the recruiting among Irish soldiers [serving with the British army], wonderful stories of the arms smuggled into Ireland and the universal drillings there. He agreed to go over to Dublin and act as a military instructor.'

This was dangerous work, for the Brotherhood handed out rough justice to suspected informers. In February 1866 the Fenians committed their first murder on Irish soil. The victim, George Clark, was almost certainly innocent of anything except his work for the movement. Clark was a bricklayer who had helped build smelting furnaces in an IRB arms factory at Loftus Lane, Dublin. The Brother in charge of it, a chemist appointed as 'Chief of the Scientific Department' was the real traitor. The factory was raided by the police. The same night, an IRB committee of safety – mainly

American – was convened in a brothel where, said one account, 'courtesans and conspirators alternately sat round a large table covered with bottles, glasses, etc while the matter was discussed in slang impenetrable to the frail sisters'.

The chemist identified Clark as the spy. 'A few hours later,' Ryan recounted:

> an order written on the curl-paper of a courtesan was carried to the President of the Assassination Committee, directing him to select men for the deed. One of these men was to commit the murder, the others were to shoot their comrade should he show any token of faltering.
>
> Early on Friday evening, 17 February, the chemist met Clark, as if by chance . . . They had a drink, then the scientist asked Clark to help some other men carry some boxes. Clark agreed. They met the other men, then went by various streets, over a drawbridge and along the Grand Canal till they reached the large mills called 'Mallet's Folley' and found the way blocked up. While they were talking, poor Clark heard the rapid but stealthy tread of two others coming up. It was then quite dark . . . One of the newcomers rushed up to Clark and dealt him a heavy blow with a bludgeon on the back of the head, which stupified him. He staggered against the wall from which he rebounded, still wavering. Recovering a little, he exclaimed: 'Good god! What have I done? Murder! Murder!' Hardly was the last word uttered when a shot was fired full in his face.

Clark remained conscious in hospital for twenty-four hours. He gave a deposition but did not name names and said nothing about the arms factory. He died the following day. Meanwhile the chemist continued for years to take money as a police informer on Fenian activities in England as well as Ireland. He even impersonated James Stephens to swindle IRB sympathizers in Lancashire. His last victim was a police inspector in London who was persuaded to provide £20 to cover the costs of a trip to Paris to attend an IRB executive meeting. The chemist used the money instead to pay his fare to New York. Rutherford ends the story: 'Here our informant paused, to conclude with a significant look and in a meaning tone: "He is not likely to trouble the English Government any more." '

It is arguable that there were spies in the Fenian movement even better informed than the 'Chief of the Scientific Department'. Rutherford went so far as to allege that James Stephens himself had an 'understanding' with the authorities in Dublin Castle dating from 1864. The suspicion and its effects bore some resemblance to the paranoia within MI5 during the Cold War, when that agency's boss, Roger Hollis, was suspected of working for the KGB. The histories of both men describe careers that were, to put it mildly, accident-prone. Rutherford points to Stephens's repeated postponement of promised operations in Ireland. There were other odd episodes. In July 1865, a Fenian courier lost a highly compromising document which was passed to the authorities. Rutherford saw this as no accident but an event which provided Stephens with the latest excuse to put an operation on hold. Two months later, the police raided the Dublin offices of the IRB's newspaper, the *Irish People*, at a time when a large amount of sensitive material was to be found there. Rutherford commented: 'It is clear . . . that the police had received good information, better than any accessible to Nagle, the ostensible informer and that they had timed their visit well.'

Soon after this raid a number of Fenian leaders were arrested. Stephens avoided arrest by taking to disguise and going into hiding, but Rutherford implied that the disguise and safe-house were transparent, had the police seriously wanted to find their man. On 10 November, as it happens, Stephens was arrested, due in part to the fact that the IRB guard was drunk. A mere two weeks later Stephens was sprung from Richmond prison, Dublin, by a Fenian group including Kelly. Skeleton keys as well as a rope ladder were needed. Most important of all, the guards' attention had to be spectacularly absent. Rutherford commented: 'Somehow or other – our readers may speculate how, for themselves – the proceedings of the officials inside were precisely of the kind to facilitate the proceedings of the conspirators outside.' He concluded that 'James Stephens did not break prison in any way, but walked as quietly out of the place as if he had been released by order of the authorities'.

This, then, was the background to the American Fenian's first serious operation against the English in England. Men who had survived front-line warfare in an orthodox military conflict, now sought to become guerrillas behind enemy lines. Their organization was rotten with spies, intrigue and backbiting, but they had had enough waiting and would proceed anyway, regardless of their former leaders' inhibitions. On 11 February 1867, led by T. J. Kelly, they targeted the armoury of Chester Castle. The plan was betrayed by an informer in their ranks, John Joseph Corydon – the Brotherhood's chief transatlantic courier – but even without this setback, the plan was too complicated to work. One team, aided by the Fenians of Lancashire and elsewhere in the north of England, would seize the armoury and empty it of weapons. Meanwhile, other groups would hijack trains between Chester and Holyhead. Yet another team would deny rail and telegraphic communications to the authorities. The arms would then be rushed to Holyhead, where the mailboat was to be taken over for a fast voyage to Ireland, where a rising was to be staged by rebels waiting for news from Chester.

That afternoon, as 1,000 hard men, many carrying barely-concealed revolvers, drifted conspicuously into Chester, one of the leaders of the armoury team, Captain John McCafferty (a former Confederate soldier), was tipped off that the operation was already compromised. To a trained eye, the signs were clear. The castle guard had been doubled; the local Volunteers summoned to their barracks and a Guards regiment was despatched from London. McCafferty, before he was arrested, ordered his men to abort the operation and get back to Ireland after dumping their revolvers. For some time after, the weapons were to be found around Chester railway station. At the ports of Dublin and Dundalk, the police waited and pounced on young Irishmen who had suddenly given up well-paid work in England to return to their homeland. One of those arrested later, on 4 March, was Gordon Massey, the Limerick-born British army corporal now styled 'General' Massey and another veteran of the Southern, Confederate army in America. Massey was betrayed by Corydon and arrested in his home town. Massey in turn promptly betrayed his Brothers by turning Queen's Evidence to inform on them.

Worse was to follow. Though there were some spirited attacks on police barracks in Dublin, Limerick and Cork, they fell far short of the general uprising which had seemed, from the perspective of New York, so likely. Even as the Fenians still at large were publishing in *The Times* their proclamation of 'The Provisional Government of the Irish Republic', military flying columns were hunting down the remnants in the south and south-west of Ireland.

The Fenians of New York, who had been paying and pressing for a war of Irish independence for so long, could not believe that their rebellion had collapsed almost as soon as it had started. 'So,' wrote the Fenian historian Desmond Ryan, 'long after the last shot in Ireland had been fired, the Irish-Americans acted.' They sent a ship named the *Jackmel*, with 8,000 rifles and forty men under the command of Captain Kavanagh (a Union navy officer in the Civil War) to invade Ireland on 12 April. When the ship arrived off Ireland on Easter Sunday, 29 April, Kavanagh hoisted the Green Flag, renamed the vessel *Erin's Hope* and distributed Fenian commissions. He then spent some days dodging around the perilous west coast, looking for a suitable spot to land unobserved. Soon, rations were running out aboard *Erin's Hope*. A few men were landed to forage for food. They were arrested. One obligingly turned Queen's Evidence against his comrades. The ship then sailed back to America with the arms still on board.

T. J. Kelly, commander of the Chester operation, was now a wanted man in England. He was finally spotted and arrested in Manchester with another of his team. Seven months had passed since the Chester débâcle. A week after the arrests, a police van taking Kelly and two of his companions was ambushed by thirty armed Fenians. The prisoners were manacled inside the unescorted van, with other, non-political criminals and were guarded by Police Sergeant Brett who had keys for the van's rear doors. One of the attackers fired a shot blindly through a ventilator in the side of the van to frighten Brett into opening the vehicle. The shot killed Brett outright. Soon afterwards, Kelly and his companions were set free. They were never recaptured. The ambush party also got away from the scene undetected.

A massive, indiscriminate police trawl of Irishmen in Manchester followed. Five men were soon charged with Brett's murder, even though none of them had fired the fatal shot. One of the accused had no links with Fenians or connection with the crime. That man was granted a free pardon for a crime he did not commit. Another of the five – Edward Condon, chief architect of the rescue – was sentenced to death but reprieved. He was an American citizen and the US government successfully pressured Britain into releasing him in spite of his defiant statement from the dock: 'I have nothing to regret . . . God Save Ireland!' The other three accused – Allen, Larkin and O'Brien – were executed. From arrest, to trial, to public execution took just thirty-six days. As the three were hanged at Manchester on 24 November, riflemen of the 72nd Highland regiment stood guard around the scaffold, bayonets fixed. Irish nationalists promptly embalmed the three, politically, as the 'Manchester Martyrs' since their end implied collective justice for a crime on which they had embarked collectively, as soldiers.

One more disaster was to occur during this first phase of Fenian terrorism. Three weeks after the executions, the organization used a barrel of gunpowder to blow a huge gap in the perimeter wall of Clerkenwell prison in the centre of working-class London. The object, yet again, was to release one of its own, an arms buyer and quartermaster named Richard O'Sullivan Burke and another Fenian named Casey. The damage was appalling. Houses across the street were flattened. Twelve civilians were killed, including a girl aged seven and another aged eleven, and 120 badly injured. The age of the terrorist bomb had arrived. In taking that road the idealistic Fenians had moved a long way from the virtuous sacrifice of the Irish Brigade before a low stone wall at Marye's Heights, Virginia.

After Brett's murder in Manchester, officers of the London Metropolitan police were issued with an enhanced weapon system: the cutlass. Ground for the necessary drills was found at Wellington barracks, within sight of Buckingham Palace. After Clerkenwell, five constables from ten divisions were given two hours' revolver training, each man firing ten rounds. London, at that time, had just 8,000 officers to police a city with a population four times that of New York. For its first expedition to England, the Fenian Brotherhood had been able to deploy at least 1,000 military veterans from America.

18

A Terrible Beauty, 1882–1916

On 6 May 1882 English efforts to find an answer to local injustice in Ireland were yet again undermined by fundamentalists who regarded mere reform as a confidence trick. That was not how it had seemed during the preceding days of political sunshine or at the start of a warm, welcoming Dublin evening when a stroll in the park seemed like a good idea to Britain's newly appointed supremo in Ireland. The minister, Lord Frederick Cavendish, was a liberal young technocrat given the task of lifting the burden of unfair rents from the back of the Irish peasantry, a scheme less than popular with Tory landlords and their friends at Westminster. Cavendish sauntered past his bodyguard, unrecognized, into the vast, vulnerable space of Phoenix Park. His senior civil servant, Thomas Henry Burke, dismayed that the new minister was wandering unescorted when lesser men needed protection round the clock, hurried to catch up with him.

From the window of a grand house overlooking the park, a servant of Lord Spencer watched with wry amusement as the two men were surrounded by six or seven others and wrestled to the ground. He thought it 'merely the horseplay of a few roughs'. In fact the servant had just witnessed the most momentous Irish assassination of the century, over which the Liberal Prime Minister, William Ewart Gladstone, wept – for Cavendish was like a son to him – and about which Gladstone's Tory enemies, including Queen Victoria, exulted. Under threat of Fenian assassination herself, she was sure the Irish were 'impossible' and resented Gladstone's efforts to treat them fairly.

The Phoenix Park assassins had taken their oath to an American-led Republican splinter group calling itself the Irish National Invincibles, a title of convenience to conceal links with more mainstream protest movements including the Fenians. The weapons, smuggled from London under her skirt by the heavily pregnant wife of one of the gang, were described at the killers' trial as 'amputation knives' and had 12-inch blades. A year later, five of the group were hanged and five others imprisoned.

Though public opposition to London in Ireland had expressed outrage at the murders of Cavendish and Burke, reaction in Dublin to the hanging of the killers told a different story. 'On the day of the execution', wrote G. Locker Lampson in 1905, 'huge crowds gathered outside the prison gates, and kneeling upon the bare ground passionately prayed for the men whom they looked upon as martyrs in a noble cause. The *Irish World* . . . opened a subscription for the families of the men who had been executed for the crime, and the money thus collected became popularly known as the "Martyrs' Fund".'

James Carey, a town councillor whose raised white handkerchief had signalled the start of the murders, turned Queen's Evidence and was set free. He fled to South Africa but was stalked by a Fenian assassin named Patrick O'Donnell, who shot him dead on board the passenger ship *Melrose Castle* off Port Elizabeth in July 1883. O'Donnell in his turn was executed at Newgate prison, London, on 18 December that year, 'but his crime was no disgrace in the eyes of the Irish Fenians, and a monument was erected in the principal Catholic cemetery to Carey's murderer with an epitaph graven upon it entrusting the memory of his martyrdom to the care of his fellow-countrymen'.

The conflict which Cavendish was helping to end is known to Irish historians as the Land War. It started in Mayo in 1879. Its cause was a recession in agriculture and the imposition of increasing rack rents on tenant farmers by greedy landowners, many of them absentees who left it to their agents, backed up by the Royal Irish Constabulary or the army, to deal with the violence their policies provoked. The Land War did not start with Republicanism or abstract notions of Irish independence and when, at last, Gladstone did succeed in rectifying the worst injustices, the Land War ended. Republican extremists played upon the anger of their fellow countrymen to promote revolution and when they failed, the leaders departed to the USA. The significance of the Phoenix Park murders was the impact they had upon the peace process worked out between Gladstone and the leader of the Irish Party at Westminster, Charles Stewart Parnell. It was a perfect example of the political utility of assassination.

Parnell, appointed leader of the tenant farmers' protest movement the Land League, was arrested on 13 October 1881 on the orders of Cavendish's hard-line predecessor as Irish Secretary, W. E. Forster, and imprisoned without trial in the notorious Kilmainham prison, Dublin. Elsewhere, the internment of another 800 activists was used to stem the violence. It did not help. In January 1882, two of Lord Ardilaun's bailiffs, an old man and his grandson named Huddy, tried to collect rents in part of Connemara known as Joyce's Country. Their bodies were found in sacks, weighted with stones, at the bottom of a local lake. In February an informer named Bernard Bailey was shot dead in front of a crowd of shoppers in Skipper's Alley, Dublin. On 2 April a Westmeath landowner named Smythe was returning from church in a carriage when he was fired at by three men with blackened faces. They missed him but killed his sister-in-law. Many such crimes were now ascribed to an enigmatic, sinister leader known as 'Captain Moonlight' who, wrote Lampson, 'scoured the country by night, burning farms, mutilating cattle and committing every description of abominable crime'. Early in 1882, hundreds of soldiers were assigned as bodyguards to landowners, agents and others at risk of peasant violence. It was clear that Forster's crackdown had failed. Without the moderating influence of Parnell, Moonlight was taking over.

In prison, Parnell had other things on his mind as well as the future of Ireland. In April 1882 Katharine ('Kitty') O'Shea, Parnell's mistress, was to give birth to his first child. Her husband, Captain Willie O'Shea, was a *mari complaisant* in this affair as well as Liberal Home Rule MP for County Clare, and friend of the charismatic Parnell. Through Willie O'Shea, Parnell started negotiations with

Gladstone thanks to which he was released on parole on 2 May, four days before the Phoenix Park murders. The unwritten agreement was known as the Kilmainham Treaty, and was denounced by the Queen as 'Gladstone's most fatal move'. Parnell would call a halt to Land League violence if new legislation were introduced to ensure that tenants in arrears with their punitive rents would not be exposed to eviction. Additionally, fair rents were to be fixed by independent tribunals and pegged for fifteen years, while loans would be available to those tenants wishing to buy their farms. The bold Fenian men had more radical ideas than that. Michael Davitt, one of the founders of the Land League on 20 April 1879, and his fellow revolutionary, Devoy, a former French Foreign Legion soldier, wanted to nationalize the land. That was a prescription for war. The average peasant wanted reform not revolution, and Gladstone's new Land Act gave it to them. As Comerford put it: 'Like so many other Irish crises, the land war of 1879–82 ended with an exodus to America' on the part of the radicals of the Land League.

The murders of Cavendish and Burke were repudiated by Land League moderates including Parnell, who offered to resign his parliamentary seat to demonstrate his sincere regret. Gladstone advised against that and again incurred the Queen's displeasure. ('Surely his eyes must be opened now,' she wrote in her diary after learning of the murders.) If Parnell was not the puppet-master manipulating the Invincibles, then who was? There was an American connection. Parnell himself, son of an Anglophobic American, grandson of an American admiral who fought against Britain in 1812, had conferred with an agent of the extremist Fenian American Clan na Gael in Paris in February 1881. The agent was the dynamiter William Mackey Lomasney. The Invincibles came into being about eight months later under the leadership of another American Fenian, Captain John McCafferty, a Confederate veteran of the Civil War and leader of the aborted plan to seize Chester Castle. McCafferty enjoyed the support of Parnell's leading lieutenants in the Land League, notably the treasurer, Patrick Egan, who kept the movement's funds in Paris. Comerford concluded that the Invincibles could not have come together without outside initiative and money.

He added: 'What little is known about the initiators [of the Phoenix Park murders] is suggestive of links with the upper but non-parliamentary echelons of the Land League; and the league had very substantial funds ... There is also the possibility of direct Irish-American involvement.'

Parnell, a calculating, Cambridge-educated politician, undoubtedly courted men of violence in his ranks and beyond but he was careful not to be so involved as to be culpable of murder. It was a fine calculation for a patriot to have to make in the polarized world of Irish nationalist politics where, by day, even Captain Moonlight was probably a decent-living man who went to Mass and cared for his old mother. A parliamentary commission looked into many of the allegations against Parnell and cleared him of involvement in the Phoenix Park affair. When he was brought down, it was as a result of his liaison with Kitty O'Shea, her husband's belated claim to her when she inherited a fortune, and Catholic puritanism roused by the divorce proceedings.

The release of Parnell from Kilmainham did not of itself end the violence. Land reform achieved that, in time. In London, the American-led Fenians waged an energetic bombing campaign, using dynamite, a new instrument popular among many revolutionaries. Queen Victoria demanded restrictions on the sale of dynamite. As she pointed out: 'Just a cupful of nitrate acid and sand mixed with glycerine and you could blow up anything.' Between March 1883 and February 1885, thirteen devices exploded without warning in the British capital. Two bombs detonated on the London underground – one between Westminster and Charing Cross, the other between Praed Street and Edgware Road – injured sixty people. Railway stations were regular targets. Sixteen visitors to the Tower of London were hurt when a bomb exploded inside it. Six American Fenians were arrested at a bomb factory in London and imprisoned. Two more – one of them the ubiquitous Lomasney – killed themselves by mistake at London Bridge.

The Dynamite War, as some now called it, had one lasting effect upon British public life: it led to the creation of an Irish Special Branch within the Metropolitan police and prompted the Home Secretary, Sir William Vernon Harcourt, to make one of the few accurate British predictions about the Irish conflict. 'This is not a temporary emergency requiring a momentary remedy,' he said in a confidential memorandum. 'Fenianism is a permanent conspiracy against English rule which will last far beyond the term of my life and must be met by a permanent organisation to detect and control it.' The new unit came into being in March 1883. A year later Fenians planted a bomb in an unguarded public lavatory below Scotland Yard, destroying much of the building.

In 1886, as the Dynamite War came to an end, the USA Senate refused to ratify a treaty with Britain which provided for the extradition of dynamiters.

For two somnolent decades after Parnell's downfall, military resistance to English rule in Ireland was smothered by the authoritarian blankets of Catholicism and the Royal Irish Constabulary. The angry pressures generated by poverty were still relieved through migration to America, where old griefs were refreshed and dollars saved for remittance back home. In spite of all, most people outside Dublin were content, if in a hoggish fashion, with the *status quo*. There was good reason for this, since it seemed that independence of a sort – akin to modern devolution – was within reach. At Westminster the powerful Irish Party voted regularly to support a Liberal government's latest Irish Home Rule bill, only for the measure to be blocked by a Tory House of Lords.

In 1912, as it seemed that Home Rule might at last become a reality, the Ulster Unionists and their Tory allies at Westminster decided to take action outside the constitution. The northern Protestants had good reason to fear that their cultural identity was under threat. Only four years earlier the Vatican had imposed a new decree, binding upon all Catholics, that children of mixed Catholic and non-Catholic marriages should be brought up as Catholics. The proposal, slowly understood outside the Catholic community, was deadly for relations between the two communities in Ireland.

Matters came to a head on 27 July 1912 at Blenheim Palace, near Oxford, when the Tory Leader of the Opposition, Bonar Law, harangued a rally about the Irish Question and spoke of pushing resistance to Home Rule 'beyond the restraints of the constitution'. He added ominously: 'There are things stronger than parliamentary majorities.'

He justified this threat of force because the government, with 271 Commons seats, did not have an overall majority but depended upon the support of 84 Irish nationalist MPs to defeat the combined forces of Tories and Liberal-Unionists. They had 273 seats. 'A corrupt parliamentary bargain' had been struck, said Law. The 'corruption' – unquestionably intervention of an extra-constitutional kind – derived, yet again, from America. The Irish Party depended at critical moments, including elections, upon Irish American funds. As Tories and Unionists saw it, the Liberal government not only lacked democratic consent for what it was doing, it was beholden to foreign funding whose provenance was unclear, even as the Vatican was engaged upon a demographic offensive against a Protestant culture.

Events moved with frightening speed after Law's opening salvo. Six months after that speech, Unionists created a private army of 100,000 men, called the Ulster Volunteer Force, to defend their cultural identity. As settlers of their land since before the founding of the state of Massachusetts, they felt that they needed no lessons in attachment to the soil from the new colonialists of Irish America. One of their number, Major Fred Crawford, illegally imported thousands of rifles and machine-guns from Germany, without any effort by the RIC or the army to stop them. The Republicans responded by creating their own army, the Irish Volunteers. Between November 1913 and January 1914, around 75,000 men joined in. Though broadly based it included a small, dedicated band of socialists – the Citizen Army – led by a Utopian trade unionist and former soldier, James Connolly. Almost from the outset, however, it was penetrated secretly and taken over from within by a handful of fanatics belonging to the Fenian Irish Republican Brotherhood. That process and its outcome bore a remarkable resemblance to the IRA's penetration of the civil rights movement in the 1960s.

In 1914 the only force able to stave off a looming Irish tribal war was the army with its headquarters at the Curragh Camp near

Dublin. In murky circumstances, more than fifty cavalry officers sent General Sir Hubert Gough back to Whitehall to extract a guarantee that the government had no intention of using the army 'to crush political opposition to the policy or principles of the Home Rule Bill'. This revelation of army involvement in Irish politics, never put to a decisive test, was itself a political fact of the first magnitude, one later known to historians as the Curragh Mutiny. The Unionists now stepped up the pressure. On the night of 24 April, Crawford landed more German arms at Bangor, Larne and Donaghadee. It says everything for the tenacity of the Irish War that a British Intelligence report on terrorist weapons uncovered in March 1980 included the following:

> 7.92mm Steyr Mod 1904 rifle: As far as is known this particular model was not used by any army. Those found bore the UVF stamp. They are thought to be part of the 1914 gun running organised by Col. [sic] Crawford. They are not normally found in terrorist hands . . . Normally unworkable when found.
>
> Vetterli-Vitali: With the Italian Army, 1887–1890: Long pistol. Ammunition not made in this calibre (10.4mm) for many years. Most found in Northern Ireland bear the UVF stamp . . . thought to have been brought into the Province before 1914 by Col Crawford.

In London, meanwhile, distinguished members of the Establishment, including the former diplomat Sir Roger Casement and historian Alice Stopford Green, energetically raised funds to buy arms for the Irish Volunteers. The first major cargo – 1,500 Mauser rifles – was unloaded at Howth, near Dublin, by day on 26 July 1914. A second cargo was smuggled by the writer/sailor Erskine Childers in two yachts, in an epic of navigation to rendezvous off Wales with another yacht, for onward transshipment to County Wicklow.

The first blood was shed in Dublin as soldiers of the King's Own Scottish Borderers were marching back to barracks, having failed to halt the Howth operation. A jeering crowd followed the soldiers, then attacked them. The Lowlanders opened fire, then charged the mob using their bayonets. Three civilians were killed and thirty-eight wounded. Ireland, yet again, was becoming ungovernable. A few months earlier, the German ambassador in London had teased the Prime Minister's wife, Margot Asquith, with the notion that Ireland was on the brink of civil war and 'nothing but a miracle could prevent it'. She had replied: 'Shocking as that would be, it would not break England.' Now, as Germany and England prepared for the war to end war, it seemed as if the ambassador might have had a point.

In practice, the Irish War was delayed while the major continental powers responded to a single assassin's pistol in faraway Sarajevo. The Liberal government in London fudged the Irish Question. Prime Minister Asquith, under Unionist pressure, agreed to put the new Home Rule bill – the Government of Ireland Act – on the statute book but only on condition that it would not become effective until the war against Germany was over. Even then, there was to be further legislation to make special provision for Protestant Ulster in any devolved Ireland. Meanwhile, excited by derring-do, young Irishmen of both communities flocked to the colours – Royal Irish Rifles, Connaught Rangers, Dublin Fusiliers and the rest – in their tens of thousands, urged on by Parnell's nationalist successor John Redmond, confident that the war would be over by Christmas.

A minority chose not to go down that road. These were the irreconcilable hard core of Republicanism, men of the IRB and Sinn Fein, moving back and forth between Irish Ireland and Irish America, endlessly plotting the expulsion of the English. For them, mere Home Rule would never suffice. Following Wolfe Tone's rhetoric, they would settle for nothing less than complete independence at any cost. Their leaders had a romantic attachment to death as a consummation to be desired for its own sake. Their state of mind was far beyond the reach of normal political dialogue or even normal warfare. For them, the bloodshed was a purifying, sacramental process of mystical enlightenment, one which enchanted many international terrorists, assassins and dynamiters of that time. The death cult had its most lurid expression in the words of the half-English schoolteacher, Padraic Pearse: 'We may make mistakes in the beginning and shoot the wrong people, but bloodshed is a cleansing and sanctifying thing.' He was also to remark: 'A citizen without arms is like a priest without religion, like a woman without chastity, like a man without manhood.'

A less manic leader of the dissident Republicans was James Connolly, Edinburgh-born Marxist, a boy soldier (with the King's Liverpool regiment in 1882); deserter from the British army, and a passionate defender of Dublin's underclass. In 1915, Connolly wrote a series of studies of insurrectionary warfare for his Citizen Army of 200 men and the somewhat larger Irish Volunteers. The cases he reviewed were the Moscow insurrection of 1905; the Tyrol, 1809; Belgium, 1815; the Alamo, 1836; Paris, 1830 and 1848. Every case was linked by a common theme: the defence of a fixed position, whether a street or a narrow route through a mountain pass, where the attackers, even in superior numbers, could be attacked from the flanks and from above from people who would melt away into the surrounding area, wearing no uniform. The series is a textbook for the urban guerrilla and was reprinted as a booklet under the title *Revolutionary Warfare* in Dublin and Belfast in 1968, as the Republican movement converted the civil rights campaign into an urban war. The year was also the centenary of Connolly's birth.

Connolly's conclusion in 1915 might have been a model for what was to follow in Dublin the next year or in Derry and Belfast half a century later: He envisaged a popular guerrilla force in which even 'little boys and girls' would be enrolled (as in Moscow in 1905) to throw up barricades in side streets to hinder an invading army.

Connolly taught that a modern city, in terms of warfare, is like a mountain.

> A mountainous country has always been held to be difficult for military operations owing to its passes or glens formed by streets and lanes. Every difficulty that exists for the operation of regular troops in mountains is multiplied a hundredfold in a city ... Defence is of almost overwhelming importance in such warfare as a popular force like the Citizen Army might be called upon to participate in. Not a mere passive defence of a position valueless in itself, but the active

defence of a position whose location threatens the supremacy or existence of the enemy. The genius of the commander must find such a position, the skill of his subordinates must prepare and fortify it, the courage of all must defend it. Out of this combination of genius, skill and courage alone can grow the flower of military success.

If the apocalyptic vision of Pearse and the bleak, sacrificial strategy of Connolly were two main elements in the next Irish rising, a third was reliance upon the use of England's enemy for Ireland's tactical benefit. Enter the former British diplomat, Sir Roger Casement. Casement, another visionary, was convinced that he could recruit a brigade of Irish soldiers from German prisoner-of-war camps to fight against England. That sublimely optimistic idea – at odds with a mind trained in professional diplomacy – ignored the facts. These were that there were, and are, two Irish military traditions: that of the guerrilla and that of the professional soldier. The prisoners-of-war instinctively knew that and knew which tribe was theirs. Casement's optimism made him blind to the statistics. Of 180,000 men who had joined the Irish Volunteers in response to the creation of the UVF, around 170,000 had chosen to support Britain's war effort against Germany in 1914. Approximately 150,000 Irishmen joined the British army. The breakaway movement which would raise a new rebellion in Ireland – while it claimed the name 'Irish Volunteers' – numbered a few thousand of whom only 1,600 would take up arms against England.

In spite of that, Casement pursued his mission. He started in the USA with the extremist Fenian movement Clan na Gael headed by the veteran John Devoy. Within a month of Anglo-German hostilities in August 1914, the Clan was talking to the German ambassador to Washington, asking for German help in staging an Irish rebellion. The plan was a reworking of Wolfe Tone's operations backed by England's earlier enemy, France. Memories of German atrocities in Ireland during 1798 were suppressed in 1914. Casement met Devoy in America and they persuaded the Germans that an Irish Brigade could be raised in Germany. The Germans agreed. Casement travelled to meet the prisoners but out of 2,000

Irishmen in British uniform gathered in a camp at Limburg in 1915, he could find only ten who could be trusted to die for a Fenian Ireland. Casement was shattered by this collision with cultural and political reality and became convinced that a rising in Ireland would be 'a futile form of force . . . and a crime too so I never have and shall not counsel that'. He seems to have had some sort of nervous breakdown soon afterwards.

In parallel with Casement's ineffectual crusade, Devoy in America did a deal with the Germans whereby they would smuggle 20,000 rifles and ten machine-guns through a Royal Navy screen into Ireland to support a rising scheduled to start on Easter Sunday, 23 April 1916. The guns were to be landed shortly before at an isolated Kerry beach known as Banna Strand. On 9 April a captured British cargo ship, renamed the *Aud* and commanded by Captain Karl Spindler, sailed for Ireland. It carried no wireless. Spindler arrived off Kerry, having dodged the navy, as originally scheduled on Thursday 20 April. The coast was empty. There was no pilot to guide Spindler inshore; no reception party. But the British were stalking him. British Naval Intelligence had long since broken the German code used for wireless transmission between Washington and Berlin. Even worse for the rebels, an American police raid on a German agency in New York on 18 April had revealed the draft of a top secret signal from the Fenian leaders to Captain Spindler. This asked Spindler to hold off his Irish landfall until Sunday night, 23 April. The absence of wireless on board the ship meant that the signal could never be sent, but the existence of the signal blew apart the secrecy surrounding the whole rebellion.

The neutral Americans – angered by the sinking of two of their merchant ships by German U-boats in the North Sea as part of a blockade of Britain – promptly passed the Fenian request to British Intelligence. The *Aud* was spotted by the Royal Navy on 21 April and ordered into Queenstown harbour next day. Spindler abandoned his cover, ran up the German flag and then scuttled his ship. As the *Aud* sank out of sight so did any serious hope of a successful uprising.

What of Casement? With two companions he was put ashore by submarine and rubber dinghy at the same coast and on the same day originally chosen to land the arms, on 21 April. Soaked and exhausted, he was found shivering in the undergrowth at an ancient fort by a police search party. In his pocket he carried a German railway ticket. That night he was in the cells at Tralee, guilty of treason in British eyes and beginning a long march to the scaffold. During his trial one of his few trusted converts from the German prison camp gave evidence against him.

The proposed rising had been approved in May 1915, in absolute secrecy, by an inner circle of seven members of the Irish Republican Brotherhood. Connolly, running his own army, seemed about to compromise the Fenian operation by starting a separate revolution until, in January 1916, Pearse brought him into the bigger con-spiracy. Politically they were uneasy comrades-in-arms: Pearse the nationalist mystic in search of purifying blood sacrifice and cruci-fixion; Connolly crusading for more humane conditions in this world for working men and women. They were united, as Irishmen, by a shared hatred of the English ruling class.

The grand plan for rebellion was like that of 1798: to seize key points in Dublin and to hold them long enough for the Volunteers elsewhere to distribute the incoming German arms for national rebellion outside the capital. With the loss of those arms there was no hope of staving off the full weight of a British counter-stroke against the Dublin rebels. At the last moment the Irish Volunteer movement was split as its Chief of Staff, Eoin MacNeill, discovered that his broad-based movement had been secretly taken over from within by the Fenian Brotherhood. For good measure, Pearse's faction imprisoned a Volunteer officer whom they suspected of obstructing their suicidal march to death and glory. MacNeill used the advertising columns of the *Sunday Independent* newspaper to publish an order to his men not to fight. The men of blood were now even more isolated from the mainstream of Irish opinion. Dublin was prosperous, in an economy that boomed in time to the big guns on the Western Front. What was not needed was artillery in the streets of Dublin.

Though forewarned by many sources, the British government sat on its hands, reassured by the capture of Casement, the sinking of the *Aud* and MacNeill's public order to the Volunteers. It had not struck them, till too late, that the rising might take place anyway. When it did, on Easter Monday, the first casualty was an unarmed constable, token guardian of the seat of government, Dublin Castle. One of Connolly's men shot him down in cold blood. The Castle could have been taken, so thinly was it guarded on a day when sane men and women had gone to the races. It was not. It soon became apparent that the rebels had not studied Connolly's guerrilla warfare lessons carefully enough. They seized a series of prominent public buildings around the city and waited for the British to react. Only in one sector was Connolly's doctrine of concealment, entrapment, ambush, mobility and flight put to effect. At three buildings at Mount Street, on 26 April, a dozen Volunteers led by Michael Malone, aged twenty-eight, a carpenter, held off 2,000 Sherwood Foresters new to the city. In three separate actions the Foresters sustained almost half the total of casualties suffered throughout the week by the entire British force.

In the heart of the city the General Post Office was occupied by Pearse and Connolly and a proclamation of independence read aloud to a crowd that was already looting nearby shops. A professor of mathematics named Eamon de Valera took possession of Boland's Flour Mills on the road to Kingstown. He would survive execution in due course because he was legally stateless. Other rebels seized Ireland's judicial headquarters, the Four Courts. Constance Gore-Booth (Countess Markievicz) was with a group that occupied St Stephen's Green until it was forced to retreat to the College of Surgeons building.

Connolly – 'the guiding brain of our resistance', according to Pearse – had made a single tactical mistake. His studies of resistance discounted the effectiveness of artillery in close-quarter urban battles because they reflected an earlier, past age of artillery. By 1916, the guns' firepower and the readiness of generals to use them regardless of collateral damage had grown exponentially. What is more – as the historian F. S. L. Lyons pointed out:

> Connolly, perhaps in an effort to reassure his inexperienced men, had forecast that a capitalist–imperialist government would never turn its guns on the property of the bourgeoisie.

If he really did believe this he could not have been more wrong. Field guns were employed as early as the afternoon of Tuesday 25 April to sweep barricades off the streets. On the following morning the fishery patrol vessel Helga used her gun to help blow the empty Liberty Hall to pieces and thereafter artillery was used at each stage of the operations. The resultant damage . . . reached massive proportions.

Massive, that is, by the cultivated standards of an elegant Georgian city prior to 1916, but times had changed and minds were coarsened by the firepower being exercised on the Western Front. That Easter, the Battle of Verdun was at its height. The British were about to attack on the Somme, with an artillery barrage that reduced the very earth itself to pulp and still they suffered 57,450 casualties on the first day. Dublin was not a grand canvas in British eyes; it was a miniature.

The rebels stood their ground bravely for six days outnumbered, as British reinforcements arrived, by twenty-to-one. With Connolly wounded by a bullet that smashed an ankle, Pearse surrendered to Brigadier-General W. H. M. Lowe, commanding British forces in Dublin, by handing over his sword at 3.30 p.m. on Saturday 30 April. Nurse Elizabeth Farrell, carrying a white flag, had opened the negotiations. Now, she moved through the city to take the surrender message to rebel units still defying the British at five other strongpoints. The centre of resistance, the General Post Office, was a smouldering wreck, the twins flags of resistance – the Irish harp and the new tricolour – still flapping through the smoke.

Dubliners, appalled by the damage, were not pleased with the Fenians. Civilians had also suffered more casualties than the combatants. At least 220 innocent people were killed and 600 wounded. The crown forces lost 134 killed and 381 wounded. Of the 1,500 rebels, only 64 were killed in battle and about 200 wounded. As the survivors were marched into captivity, uncommitted spectators jeered at them. It was at this point that the British snatched political defeat from the jaws of victory: they made the monumental mistake of turning valuable live captives into dead saints. The trap had been foreseen by the sophisticated Irish Chief Secretary Augustine Birrell who, to the fury of his security chiefs, had held off action against the rebels, even to the extent of turning a blind eye to an armed demonstration by the IRB in Dublin in order to avoid dignifying the Fenians with the martyrdom they sought. The British now delivered that martyrdom by conducting a steady, grisly series of ritual executions of the rebel leaders. All except Casement were despatched by firing-squads at Kilmainham prison: the first three on Wednesday 3 May; four the next day; one on Friday. The executions paused for the weekend and were resumed with four more on Monday 8 May; one on Tuesday; two on Friday 12 May. Casement was hanged as a felon, rather than shot as a soldier, on 3 August at Pentonville prison, London.

The first to be executed was the English-born Thomas Clarke, one of Stephens's original Fenian dynamiters, serving fifteen years for his part in the bombing campaign in England in the 1880s. By 1916 he was a slight, bespectacled wisp of a man aged fifty-nine, prematurely aged by years of imprisonment in which he had seen fellow Republicans driven insane by the cruelty of their guards. Pearse died as he had wished the same day, along with the poet Thomas MacDonagh, who had thrown back at his court-martial the sentiment, ''Tis sweet and glorious to die for one's country'. On the eve of the Somme, they were doom-laden words.

Next day was the turn of, among others, Joseph Mary Plunkett, permitted – in a macabre gesture of British clemency – to marry his fiancée Grace Gifford in Kilmainham just before they marched him off, arms pinioned, to the bleak execution yard. Edward Daly, Padraic Pearse's brother Willie, and Michael O'Hanrahan went the same day, to be followed on Friday 5 May by Major John MacBride, who had led an Irish Brigade against the British in the Boer War. MacBride refused the blindfold before he was shot. As he told his priest: 'It's not the first time I looked down their guns, Father.'

So the bell tolled on, for Con Colbert, Sean Heuston, Eamonn Ceannt, Michael Mallin, Thomas Kent, Sean MacDermott and, almost the last, James Connolly. In his final statement, Connolly had claimed the moral high ground for any minority that opposed English occupation of Irish soil. He wrote: 'Believing that the British Government has no right in Ireland, never had any right in Ireland and never can have any right in Ireland, the presence in any one generation of Irishmen of even a respectable minority ready to die to affirm that truth, makes that Government for ever a usurpation and crime against human progress.' His statement was signed with his name and title: Commandant-General, Dublin Division, Army of the Irish Republic. The IRA was now a historical reality. Its Commandant-General, crippled by his wounds, was strapped to a chair for his execution. The chair toppled over before the deed could be done. They propped him up again, at an angle to the wall. Again he toppled. A stretcher was found and they tied him to it. The priest attending him, Father McCarthy, said that when they finally opened fire, the blood spurted from Connolly's body like a fountain.

In the words of W. B. Yeats, a 'terrible beauty' was born, as was a terrible religiosity. The ubiquitous, incense-laden presence of Catholicism around the death cells and execution yard was a confirmation, for some, that the Pope himself had blessed this rebellion. That, at least, was the claim made by Count Plunkett, father of Joseph Mary Plunkett. According to Brian Murphy, writing in *History Ireland*, Plunkett père, a count of the Holy Roman Empire, was already a revolutionary before Easter 1916: 'Having visited Europe on an IRB mission for his son, Joseph Mary, and having sought, and according to Plunkett himself, having secured papal blessing for the success of the Irish Volunteers in the coming Rising.'

Kilmainham was not the only human abattoir open for business that hot summer. On the Western Front, near the rural town of Bapaume, similar scenes were being enacted as the British shot their own deserters, but out of sight of independent witnesses and beyond the maternal reach of a vivid, supportive culture. The heroes of the Somme died without a priest in attendance to record their last words. Others, including my own father – one of the Mayo Garrity clan – were finally brought home, technically alive, unheralded, psychologically and emotionally destroyed by Golgothas worse even than the Dublin rebellion. Dublin, after independence, saw to it that Armistice Day commemorations were suppressed in the Republic.

In 1916, the Republicans' political wing, Sinn Fein – founded by the journalist Arthur Griffith in 1906 – made sure that the story of their people did get out, in spite of wartime censorship. On the Kerry coast at Valentia Island not far from Banna Strand, Britain had established three transatlantic telegraph cable stations, part of London's strategic communications network called the All Red Routes. This was the starting point of the hot line to neutral America in 1916 and the staff there included the Ring family, all dedicated Fenians. As the Easter Rising began, a coded Morse message – 'Tom successfully operated on today' – was sent to a private address in New York identified too late by British Intelligence as the home of John Devoy. Donard de Cogan, writing in *History Ireland*, said: 'With the publication of the news in New York, it proved impossible for the authorities to hush the matter up and America, not yet in the war, was able to focus full attention on the Irish question . . . The Ring brothers were arrested on 15 August 1916 and held under the Defence of the Realm Act.'

Over the next two years, as the great European powers became sickened by the blood-letting they had inflicted upon themselves, the IRA reaped an unexpected political harvest from its sacrificial Easter offering. The rising had been a military nonsense. Two factors transmuted it into political gold: the martyrdom of the leaders was the stuff of legend in any culture and, more important still, it occurred at a time of growing communications and literacy. Irish rhetoric, for centuries of no military utility even when it occupied columns of a Westminster parliamentary report, now acquired an effectiveness it had never known before. Popular journalism combined with government propaganda to create a public appetite for atrocity stories. The stories coming out of Dublin were not fabrications; they were to have a profound impact on Irish politics for the rest of the century and nowhere more so than upon succeeding generations of young Irishmen and women.

For many, Republicanism acquired the sacramental lustre of Catholicism, to be obeyed without question as a moral absolute and not to be examined as just another political option. Recruitment to the Fenians and the Catholic priesthood had much in common: maleness (though females were allowed a supporting role); the discovery in adolescence of a God-given vocation; induction into a mystical ruling class; celibacy; a death wish; apotheosis on the scaffold; the shedding of blood to renew the next generation; dogmatism.

Yet in spite of the undoubted heroism and self-sacrifice of the Fenians in 1916, they could not claim political legitimacy, if such a claim meant that they represented the Irish people other than by force of arms. Their Proclamation, at the outset of the rising, claimed to speak for the people. The Irish Republican Brotherhood – and therefore its offspring the IRA – had a secret constitution which asserted that the IRB's handful of insiders, the supreme council, was the sole government of the Irish Republic 'until Ireland secures absolute national independence and a permanent republican government is established'.

In the British general election of December 1918, another force within Irish nationalism, Sinn Fein, swept the board, wiped out the old Irish Party of Parnell and Redmond and promptly created its own Dublin Parliament, the Dail Eireann. The pre-war moderate nationalists would have been grateful for the diluted, devolved independence known as Home Rule had London honoured its word, but Sinn Fein went the whole way, as it said it would. Its sixty-nine MPs, many of whom were still in prison, ignored Westminster. The first Dail Eireann in Dublin, meeting illegally, proclaimed independence and staked its claim to be the lawful government of Ireland regardless of what Westminster might say. It assuredly had a popular mandate. The IRA's claim to legitimacy, by contrast, rested upon the bloodshed of Easter 1916. As Sean MacDiarmada (MacDermott), shot the same morning as Connolly, put it in a powerful last letter from the death cell: 'The cause for which I die has been rebaptised during the past week by the blood of as good men as ever trod God's earth.' This brave and noble moral gesture was without political effect, even when sanctified in Irish culture as 'the Physical Force Tradition'. Force of arms, to have political reality, has to achieve military victory.

The Republican soldiers who had survived the Easter Rising – many of whom, including de Valera and Michael Collins, were also elected members of the Dail – had taken a separate oath to the Fenian Brotherhood, recognizing that secret society as the true government. By contrast, the founder of Sinn Fein, Arthur Griffith, had left the Fenians ten years earlier because of the Brotherhood's authoritarian direction. The two strands of Irish resistance met uneasily in the first Dail. By August 1919, such was the tension between the unelected IRA and the elected Dail that the latter's Minister of Defence (Cathal Brugha) insisted that each of its members and officials should swear to 'support and defend the Irish Republic and the government of the Irish Republic, which is Dail Eireann, against all enemies, foreign and domestic'. While the Irish Volunteers (later the IRA) took this oath as individuals, their *organization* never formally ratified the change in status that the oath implied. As F. S. L. Lyons pointed out, since those members of the Dail who were also Fenians 'had already taken an oath to the latter organisation, there was obviously cause here for confusion if not for suspicion'. The IRB's successor, the IRA, had (as Robert Kee reminded us) no more than 'nominal allegiance' to the first Dail. Not until March 1921 did the Dail accept public responsibility for the IRA's next stage in the war against England, which the Dail had not formally authorized.

The relationship between the elected Dail and the unelected IRA remained a fact of the first magnitude into the late 1990s, for the Provisional IRA's claim to political legitimacy, to represent the majority in Ireland, in its split from the Officials in 1970 still rested upon its relationship with the first Dail as well as an Irish Republic proclaimed by leaders of the 1916 rising. It meant also that the warriors would never recognize a peace treaty negotiated with London which did not endorse a united Ireland totally independent of Britain, regardless of economic reality, or of the wishes of a million Ulster Protestants settled in Ireland long before Irish America existed, or of the unification of Europe through the EC.

As the survivors of the First World War came home, the scene was set in Ireland not only for a guerrilla campaign against British occupation but also for a civil war between two wings of Republicanism, the one politically legitimate, the other not; the one prepared to accept the partition of Ireland, endorsed by a massive majority of Irish voters, the other owing nothing to the popular will and everything to the Physical Force Tradition – that is, the gun as a solution to Ireland's festering problems. The British would meet brutality with brutality, ensuring that the dialectic of the dirty war that began with Sarsfield's departure in 1691 continued unabated. It would be a war from which no one would, or could, emerge with clean hands.

19

Baptism of Blood,
1919–1921

Sean MacDermott was right: it was a baptism of blood. On 21 January, during the Dail's first meeting at Dublin Mansion House, the speeches were overlayed by the message of IRA guns pronouncing death sentences on two Catholic members of the Royal Irish Constabulary. The Dail was one of two self-appointed governments of an as-yet non-existent Irish Republic. In a rhetorical flourish which some people took all too literally, the assembly that day reaffirmed an 'existing state of war between England and Ireland'. This surprised most voters who had supported Sinn Fein a month before, when party spokesmen specifically promised that no more offensive action was required to win Irish freedom.

Only the IRA could make good the threat of renewed violence. But which faction of the Republican army? The hard fact was that two 'armies' as well as two governments claimed the right to rule Ireland. One was the inner circle of the Fenian Irish Republican Brotherhood, headed by Michael Collins who manipulated the Irish Volunteers (soon renamed the IRA) from within. The other was the general body of the IRA – loyal to Sinn Fein, Arthur Griffith, the idea of moral force and the Dail – when it was not supporting the Fenians.

The Dail did not authorize its birthday bloodletting. This resulted from an ambush ostensibly approved by no one except the four participants. The gang shot dead Constables McDonnell and O'Connell as the officers escorted a cart carrying gelignite to a Tipperary quarry. The RIC men – one of them a widower with four dependent children – were given no chance to surrender and their murders provoked the usual pious outpourings of regret, echo-ing, among others, Parnell's repudiation of the Invincibles. But, by an odd coincidence, no one could be found to help identify the murderers even though a £1,000 reward was on offer. The Dail said nothing about the incident.

In such a case it is often useful to ask 'Who benefits?' In this case it was the hardline Fenians, for the operation provoked a British retaliation perfectly calculated to unite Irishmen and women behind them. One of the four Tipperary killers, Dan Breen, later wrote that the political campaign of 1918 'had had a serious effect on our army. Many had ceased to be soldiers and had become politicians. There was a danger of disintegration . . . since the threat of conscription disappeared a few months earlier.' Later he wrote that the Volunteers were in danger of becoming 'merely a political adjunct to the Sinn Fein organisation'.

As the historian Charles Townsend has noted:

> Both arguments are significant. If, as everyone was after-wards anxious to claim, the Irish Volunteers were from the start the legally-constituted army of the Republic, why was it a danger that they should be subordinated to Sinn Fein? The short answer seems to be that in 1919 the Republic served by the Volunteers was still a different thing from that represented by Dail Eireann.

Collins himself, within weeks of the Tipperary ambush, told his supporters:

> The sooner fighting is forced and a general state of disorder created . . . the better it would be for the country. Ireland is likely to get more out of a state of general disorder than from a continuance of the situation as it now stands. The proper people are . . . ready to force the issue and they are not to be deterred by weaklings and cowards.

Constables McDonnell and O'Connell were not part of a sectarian, Protestant force repressing normal human rights. They were as Irish as the communities they served and well respected within them. Most regular RIC officers were disciplined police professionals, models of respectability who went to Mass regularly. The force as a whole shrank from the use of firearms or even training with guns. As a civilian force, they relied upon policing by consent. Yet they bore the brunt of IRA terrorist attacks over the next three years of what was to be described as the Irish War of Independence. The number of RIC men killed and wounded – 1,087 – was more than double the number of British army casualties and three times the toll of civilian victims. They were singled out by IRA assassination teams precisely because they were Irishmen who knew how their communities functioned. Without their knowledge, the government lacked any grass-roots Intelligence. Facing the choice of supporting the RIC or the IRA, a majority of uncommitted civilians supported the IRA either through fear or, more probably, because of a sense of loyalty, since to back the police was to assist continued English rule in Ireland.

After fifteen months and almost twenty police dead, one atrocity was thought to deserve another and both sides abandoned any pretence of idealism. The British Prime Minister Lloyd George, heading a coalition government, became a covert proponent of tit-for-tat assassination by security forces (or 'gunning' as he preferred to call it) while holding up his hands in public dismay at more general official reprisals including arson by police officers. The creation of a special force – the infamous 'Black and Tans' – introduced counter-terror in response to IRA attacks.

The Tans were dogs of war disguised as policemen; an armed police gendarmerie and special constabulary not subject to military discipline and outside the control of Ireland's two professional police forces. The specials were recruited hastily in 1920, largely from a pool of unemployed, brutalized veterans of the Great War ready to use the bayonet if ammunition ran out. Turned loose in a hostile land where regular RIC officers locked themselves for safety in barracks, the Tans became reprisal specialists. Their uniforms – a mixture of army khaki and dark green police uniform, topped by a Tam o' Shanter – provoked comparison with a pack of Irish foxhounds named the Black and Tans. The nickname stuck.

The first 500 were ex-officers who were styled 'temporary cadets' of the RIC, enlisted for just six months with an option to extend.

The next, larger, wave belonged to the Auxiliary Division, RIC, usually rank-and-file Tommies, sometimes described as 'Auxies'. Each Tan team was led by a captain or major. Their more memorable exploits included the sacking of Balbriggan, County Dublin, on 21 September 1920. An RIC Head Constable, popular with the Tans, was shot by an IRA assassination team in the town. The Tans poured out of their training depot nearby throughout the following thirty-six hours to burn and loot the town, firing rifles and hurling hand-grenades at random. Two local men fleeing in their nightwear were bayoneted to death. It was the first of many atrocities. The word spread that the Tans were the dregs of English criminal society, recruited from prison. In the vast majority of cases this was untrue. They became criminals after they joined the Tans. As their historian Richard Bennett noted: 'Some of them later enlisted in the Palestine Police ... At least two ended their lives at the end of the hangman's rope, and another ex-Black and Tan murderer committed suicide before the police could arrest him.'

The first prominent Republican victim of counter-terror, in March 1920, was Thomas MacCurtain, Sinn Feiner and Lord Mayor of Cork. Two hours after yet another policeman was gunned down on the streets of his city, men with camouflaged faces, in civilian clothes but with military bearing, knocked on the Lord Mayor's door. They carried rifles. As the door opened they swept upstairs and into MacCurtain's bedroom, where they found Cork's leading citizen safely tucked up in bed, and shot him. The professionalism with which this was done anticipated the cool killing of other Fenian suspects, or their next-of-kin not just in this campaign but also in Northern Ireland forty years later.

The Irish situation was now well beyond salvation and had been so for some twelve months. Already, by 1919, the only effective solution was a political one but the belated decision of the London government to permit a form of Home Rule as provided for by the 1914 legislation together with devolution for a separate Protestant Ulster was too little, too late. The IRA's victory in the guerrilla war that now began was, supremely, a conquest of Irish hearts-and-minds, a collective complicity in the murders, intimidation, knee-capping, boycotts and other crimes that followed, all denounced by the Roman Catholic hierarchy. The true state of Irish sentiment, even before the British authorities' slide into counter-terror, was graphically illustrated at Fermoy, North Cork. On 7 September 1919 eighteen soldiers of the Shropshire Light Infantry attending a church parade were ambushed by the I R A. One soldier was killed, four wounded and thirteen rifles lost to the terrorists, who drove off unscathed.

A local inquest jury later concluded that the soldier was not murdered, since his death resulted from 'a regular act of war'. The soldiers went on a rampage, attacking shops owned by members of the jury. The shopkeepers did not consider this a regular act of war and felt they had grounds for complaint.

The well-tried Fenian tactics of provocation worked in spite of a British military rundown following post-war demobilization and cuts in police manpower. In London in 1919, Ireland was still perceived as a mere training ground, not a war zone. The commanders on the spot did their best to contain an increasingly unstable situation. After the gelignite raid, the Lord Lieutenant for Ireland, Lord French, declared South Tipperary a Special Military Area where meetings, fairs, markets and pub hours were rigidly limited. This was a collective punishment which hit local commerce. In some towns a curfew was imposed. The prescription had worked, up to a point, in West Cork a few months earlier, but under Collins's leadership the I R A radicals tested and disproved the government's theory that the majority of decent ordinary Catholics would put pressure on the extremists and not vice-versa.

Collins's men raised the stakes on 13 May with the rescue of one of their number (Sean Hogan) from a prison train at Knocklong Halt, Limerick. The gunplay accompanying the rescue was likened by some people to American gangsterism. (Cowboy movies about train robberies were popular.) In this confrontation, two more constables were killed. In London, there were more words, more threats which might have provoked a shrug of mild concern on the part of the IRA. The Minister for Ireland, Ian Macpherson, declared – in words that his successors were to utter several generations later – that unless the violence stopped 'We can have no parley with Sinn Fein.'

For six weeks in the spring of 1919 the British government hesitated as the forces of law and order demanded a ban on Sinn Fein, whose moderates, it was argued, included intellectuals as well as gunmen. Even the moderates, however, were already running their own courts and other arms of government in parts of Ireland beyond the control of Dublin Castle. Local councils elected Sinn Feiners and voted to recognize the Dail as their legitimate national government. Lloyd George and other senior ministers attending the Versailles peace conference could not devote enough time to the nagging Irish Question. It was tempting to procrastinate. In any case, the British coalition government was dominated by Unionists, some of whom had sworn to defend the Province by signing the Ulster Covenant, a public oath to resist Home Rule, created by Sir Edward Carson and other Loyalists in 1912.

At this point, just one more outrage was required to make nice political calculations brutally irrelevant to the outcome, and the IRA now provided it. On 23 June the movement opened a new phase of campaigning with a programme of clinically prepared, skilled assassinations that would, in time, cripple the government's Intelligence system. The first victim was District Inspector Hunt RIC, gunned down in the bustling centre of Thurles, County Tipperary. Like most of Collins's assassination targets, he was shot in the back. The killers walked calmly away like invisible men. No one saw anything. As Townsend observes: 'This was unmistakably the first blow in a methodical campaign of terrorism. Henceforth the actions of the men whom the Government labelled the "gunmen" or "the murder gang" were inseparable from those of "moderate" Sinn Fein; and before long they would eclipse them almost entirely.'

The IRA's overall strategy was a success but outside Dublin its tactical control of events was initially negligible: a decentralized, often anarchic affair in which the weapons used ranged from illegal cattle-driving, as they had in 1798, to motorized flying columns when the security forces depended, much of the time, on pedal cycles. Step by step the government retreated, closing police barracks, giving ground and credibility to the men in trenchcoats who filled the vacuum with their own police force. At an early stage

Lloyd George's trusted Cabinet Secretary Tom Jones, a fellow Welshman, concluded that 'British constitutional rule is over'. So it was. What would now follow would be outside constitutional conventions or the rule of law.

Towards the end of the year Collins's assassination specialists, The Squad, turned their attention to Ireland's other police force, the Dublin Metropolitan Police and destroyed its political section of ten men, killing or wounding five of its members. Usually the victim was shot in the back. One of them survived long enough to turn on his attackers with the words: 'You cowards!' On 21 January 1920, Assistant Commissioner Redmond, head of the Dublin Intelligence branch, was also murdered. In March, Resident Magistrate Bell, responsible for an inquiry into Sinn Fein funds, was travelling on a tram in Dublin as his killers tapped him on the shoulder and ordered him off with the words: 'Your time has come.' Bell was shot on the street and left to die.

Collins himself, by day, was a solid, respectable politician deeply immersed in agrarian loans and the new Republic's economics. His duplicity was matched, in due course, on the British side by Lloyd George's encouragement of 'unauthorized' assassination and Churchill's support of that policy. Respectable Irishmen who still dared criticize Republican terrorism made no connection between the extremist gunmen, whom some regarded as lunatics, and the IRA's Intelligence supremo, but Collins was able to nominate targets within the government's Intelligence apparatus thanks to a network of spies within that machine. The betrayals were often of a peculiarly personal nature, spreading a subtle poison through the Republican movement as well as the police. One of Collins's stars was a double agent named Edward Broy, who smuggled out carbon copies of his colleagues' Special Branch reports which then acted as their own death warrants. Broy was not the only traitor to his paymaster. Other key spies included an English officer working for Military Intelligence not in the Dublin police headquarters but Dublin Castle. Broy was special in that he later became the Irish Free State's first police chief, promoted over the heads of other senior officers. The tradition of betrayal stuck. Even after partition a spy at the highest levels of the newly created Royal Ulster Constabulary

– a Catholic veteran of the Royal Irish Rifles named Pat Stapleton of Forest Street, Belfast – stole top-secret files for Collins. From 1979 to 1985 Eamon Collins, a clerk in the Customs service at Newry, regularly passed on the names of potential victims to the IRA even before he was a member of the movement. This process of betrayal from within was used subsequently to 'justify' Ulster Protestants in the UDR or RUC who abused their knowledge of Intelligence files so as to assassinate Catholics. Tit-for-tat betrayals and the killings that followed were to be a familiar part of Ireland's inheritance from Collins.

By 1919, police morale was at its nadir. In many towns the police garrison simply locked itself into the limited security of its barracks and peered angrily out at a hostile world. It was no help. Police barracks were over-run and burned down, one after a nocturnal gun battle in which a garrison of ten RIC men were holed up, beyond help, as if it were the French Foreign Legion defending a remote fort in the Sahara. Some police regions advocated that their own force be disbanded. In January 1920, after the murder of a popular young constable in Thurles, Tipperary, the police there rioted, smashing windows indiscriminately and shooting into the homes of known Sinn Feiners. The army in Ireland, which regarded the war against the IRA as a police matter, pressured the Chief Constable of the RIC to accept ex-servicemen. The Chief, fearing dilution of a professional force by amateurs, declined and was posted elsewhere. Recruitment into the two new security teams – the Tans and the Auxiliaries – followed soon afterwards. The Tans had been Other Ranks in the British army; the 'Auxies' were ex-officers.

As well as covert public support, the IRA also benefited from the complacency of the English officer class, still living carelessly in unfortified, civilian houses in Ireland as if they were at home in Camberley. On 26 June 1920, Brigadier Lucas, commanding 16th Brigade, went fishing in North Cork with two senior staff officers, both full colonels. They were all seized by the local IRA and held for weeks. Lucas himself escaped after a month yet still the army was not placed on active service. The army learned its lesson the hard way on 21 November – the first Bloody Sunday – when Collins's squad, reinforced by other IRA men, smashed their way into eight unguarded houses in Dublin occupied by Military Intelligence officers, twelve of whom were shot dead and others wounded. Dublin District Special Branch was paralysed by this blow, which should have come as no surprise in view of the IRA's consistent attacks on police officers, suspected informers and anyone else able to supply useful information to the government.

Government forces exacerbated their failings later that day when the Tans went to a Gaelic football game at Croke Park, Dublin, to search for the assassins, driving on to the pitch heedlessly. As on another Bloody Sunday in 1972, a Republican gun opened fire and triggered off a massacre by the Security Forces who fired indiscriminately into a crowd of spectators, twelve of whom died. A week later, the IRA took its revenge as Tom Barry's West Cork Flying Column ambushed an 'Auxie' patrol, killing eighteen of its men. Barry, a former bombardier awarded campaign medals for his service with the Royal Artillery in the war against the Turks, set up an elaborate ambush to achieve this result. As a morale-boosting preliminary, he ensured that his column of forty men made confession to Father O'Connell as they paraded at 2 a.m. on Sunday 28 November 1920. Having received the blessing of the Church, the men were briefed and marched approximately fifteen miles to the chosen killing ground at Kilmichael.

They arrived there, soaked by rain, at 8.15 a.m. and had to wait until just before dusk, at 4 p.m., for an Auxie convoy of two lorries to trundle slowly round a bend, into sight. Barry, dressed in military uniform, stepped into the road. The Auxie's driver, taking him for a British officer, slowed to a crawl. Barry tossed a grenade into the cab then opened fire on the occupants with a pistol. The lorry, without a driver, continued to roll forward. Barry blew a whistle to signal the general attack from three rifle sections flanking the road.

From the leading truck nine Auxies leaped out and a hand-to-hand battle followed. Barry had told his men that this would be no hit-and-run. The IRA team was to hold its ground until its enemy was dead. The second Auxie truck halted and its occupants dived out, lying in the road, throwing their rifles aside and shouting a surrender. At this, several of the ambush party were unwise enough to stand, offering themselves as targets. The 'surrender' was a ruse. The Auxies shot three of them with pistols, unaware that Barry and his three best shots had moved behind them. Barry barked out an order: 'Rapid fire, and don't stop till I tell you!' The Auxies tried to surrender and this time they meant it, but the IRA gave them no quarter.

Twenty men lay dead and another was dying. The vehicles were set on fire. The IRA survivors were in a state of shock. Barry decided that a spell of foot-drill was the perfect antidote to lack of moral fibre, so he ordered his men to march and counter-march, their boots slipping in the blood. His final gesture was a salute to his own two dead, lying upon a rock flanking the road, illuminated by flames like heroes from a Wagnerian opera. The men then spent days and nights in hiding with little or no food but rearmed with weapons taken from their dead enemy.

For the London government, there were now two options: surrender to terror, or the imposition of martial law and an even harder retaliation. The first ten months of 1920 had witnessed a transformation of the war in favour of the IRA. The total number of political attacks rose from fifty in January to more than 400 by September.

Worse, much worse, and confirmation of the London government's loss of control, was the army's acknowledgement that reprisals by the Security Forces against possibly innocent people caught up in the trouble could not be stopped, but only categorized as 'official' or 'unofficial' reprisals. Unofficial reprisals, carried out by the Black and Tans, included burning down creameries essential to local rural economies. Official reprisals, run by the army, usually took the form of destroying buildings, including houses, from which attacks were made on soldiers or police, or from which preparations for attacks could have been observed. (The Parachute Regiment was still using this blunt instrument as late as the 1950s, in the Canal Zone of Egypt, when most of an Arab village was erased in Operation Flatten.) In Ireland in 1920, the authorities were unmoved by the knowledge that the IRA was as efficient in dealing with anyone suspected as an informer as it was in wiping out government Intelligence officers. Ordinary people, caught between two ruthless armies, kept quiet and said nothing. The unlucky ones then had to look on helplessly as British soldiers piled their belongings in the street and torched them.

Martial law was grudgingly approved by the Cabinet on 1 December 1920. Not everyone had the same conception of what it should involve. General Sir Nevil Macready, the army supremo in Ireland, expected it to over-ride the civil law throughout the whole country, all thirty-two counties. Furthermore, the death penalty, by firing-squad, would be used liberally. Macready was ready to sanction 100 executions a week. Best of all, he hoped, a unified military/police command could be forged so that all the Security Forces would work in harmony at last. (Few counter-insurgency wars have succeeded without unified command; Malaya in the 1950s proved the point.)

The London government, mortified by Macready's Cromwellian vision, faltered. Martial law would be introduced, but in just eight of the most troublesome counties. Worse, legal confusion resulted from successful appeals on behalf of condemned IRA men to the normal, civil courts outside Martial Law Areas (MLAs). Those courts claimed jurisdiction in such cases so that no commander, even in an MLA, could be sure that he was acting within the law himself. Despite that, fourteen people were executed after military trials in 1921. There was a further complication. This was that Prime Minister Lloyd George, backed by his War Minister Winston Churchill, favoured the methods of the Tans and Auxies rather than more conventional policing, even if, occasionally, their operations led to shoot-outs between the two security arms (in what later became known as 'blue-on-blue' accidents).

Martial law and the hardline regime it embodied, supported by 40,000 troops, was a disaster. Every weapon of counter-insurgency was tried and failed. The armoury included cordon-and-search in town and country; curfew; motorized convoy; RAF air patrols; stake-outs; ambushes; use of IRA prisoners as hostages on high-risk patrols; intimidation; reprisals against civilians; rigid press control; and, when all else failed, firing-squads. An exhausted British army in 1921, unlike its successor in Northern Ireland after 1970, suffered a further, deadly disadvantage: time was not on its side. It was enmeshed in a military campaign that had to achieve a political result within a few months. The Home Rule law of 1914 was at last due to take effect, creating separate local parliaments in Dublin and Belfast, effectively partitioning the country. Elections to these bodies were scheduled for 25 May 1921. The Dublin Parliament was to sit on 28 June. If it did not, then Southern Ireland would automatically become a Crown Colony, run by a governor supported by martial law if necessary.

The IRA, now 5,000 strong (with another 4,500 men interned) was itself taking much punishment but, like General Giap just before the Tet Offensive of 1968, it managed to absorb the pain, conceal the damage and win the war of perceptions. As another Lord Mayor of Cork, Terence MacSwiney, had put it before dying on hunger strike in Brixton prison a few months earlier: 'It is not those who can inflict the most but those who can suffer the most, who will conquer.' (MacSwiney was, in Richard Bennett's phrase: 'another Irish patriot born of an English mother . . . with the fanatical zeal for Irish nationalism that this mixture of blood seems so often to engender.') The guerrillas concealed their wounds behind a blitzkrieg of ambush and assassination that convinced Macready and other senior officers that the war would be a long one. Only after a treaty was agreed did Michael Collins concede: 'You had us dead beat. We could not have lasted another three weeks.'

That was not how it seemed as a bloody spring merged into a bloodier summer and the IRA received from its American allies its first consignment of Thompson sub-machine-guns, the slow-firing automatic weapons favoured by Al Capone's gang. On 24 June the British Cabinet faced up to the reality of its situation in Ireland: that it could not win militarily or politically. The most optimistic prospect was one of a war of attrition and indeterminate length. Lloyd George invited the Sinn Fein leader Eamon de Valera to take part in unconditional negotiations. De Valera graciously agreed to a truce as a prelude to talks and arranged for the American Stars and Stripes to be flown in the emerging Irish Republic in order, as he put it, to emphasize 'the principle for which we are fighting'. De Valera, born in New York of Spanish–Irish parentage, was also giving recognition to the essential support of America for Irish revolution since the Fenian Brotherhood's foundation in the USA in 1860. He was also reminding the world that he, like all the leaders of the 1916 Rising, was one of the Brotherhood. The IRA ended its latest campaign against England in characteristically bloodthirsty style. A total of twenty people were murdered during the last thirty-six hours before the truce took effect on Monday 11 July.

As if to underline the reality of the new order, General Macready was obliged to beat a path to the Dail, meeting at the Dublin Mansion House, to agree the final terms of the truce. Though he was applauded on his arrival there, he carried a pistol, just in case.

De Valera, with his usual nimble footwork, left it to others – notably Griffith and Collins – to face the heat of substantive negotiations in London, converting a military truce into a political treaty that recognized the independence of a self-governing twenty-six county Irish Free State, but not a republic 'in virtue of the common citizenship of Ireland with Great Britain'. Ulster would be allowed its own separate identity, subject to a boundary commission to define its territory. The commission, the Irish delegation was told, would ensure 'the essential unity of Ireland'. The subliminal message was that a six-county Ulster would not be viable. Though no one was indelicate enough to spell it out, demography would ensure, in time, a Catholic majority. After two months of negotiation and still no acceptance on the part of the Irish, Lloyd George imposed an ultimatum on his opponents: sign up to the terms on offer or it would be 'war within three days'. The Irish delegation accepted, though Collins, as a Fenian bound by his Brotherhood oath, seems to have sensed – accurately, it turned out – that he was signing his own death warrant.

The planned British response, had the deal been refused by Griffith and Collins, remained secret until 1993. On 21 October 1921, a War Office paper was presented to the British Cabinet proposing another 50,000 troops for Ireland – effectively an army of occupation – as well as death sentences for possession of arms; martial law throughout Southern Ireland (but not Ulster); a blockade of Irish ports; internment of 20,000 suspects; press censorship and movement of soldiers' families to England. As Macready put it in a letter to the War Minister Sir Laming Worthington-Evans: 'The only chance of avoiding a serious setback will be to strike at once with all means at my disposal.'

The Irish were also making contingency plans. One of these was to ensure that Collins escaped. As the commander of the Irish Air Corps, Colonel Patrick Quinn, revealed:

> The first aircraft purchased by the new State was a Martin-syde Type A Mk II which was obtained during the period of the truce . . . Attending the talks in London was General Michael Collins, upon whose head the British government had placed a reward of £10,000. Had the talks broken down, General Collins would immediately have become a fugitive, and it was to facilitate his escape to Ireland that the Martin-syde was purchased.

The treaty, which took effect on 4 January 1922, was popular in Ireland. On 22 June 1922, in the country's first truly democratic election, the vote in favour of it was 72 per cent or two-to-one in favour. By now Sinn Fein had divided into two factions, for and against the London agreement, but for this election they formed a common front and still lost. De Valera was opposed to the treaty but even he admitted in a revealing letter to Joe McGarrity, the IRA's boss in North America, on 10 September: 'If the Republicans stand aside and let the Treaty come into force acquiescence in it means the abandonment of National sovereignty . . . if the Republicans do not stand aside, resistance means armed opposition to what is undoubtedly the decision of the majority of the people.'

The stage was now set for a civil war within the Free State. In London that election day a retired soldier, dressed in field marshal's full dress regalia, complete with cocked hat, stepped out of a taxi a few yards from his home on the corner of Eaton Place. The old soldier, Sir Henry Wilson, had just unveiled a plaque in honour of railwaymen lost in the Great War. As he dismounted, two men in civilian clothes drew revolvers and fired into his body at close quarters. As he tried to draw his ceremonial sword they continued shooting. It took nine bullets to kill the field marshal. Though he was now an Ulster Unionist MP, Wilson, an Anglo-Irishman, was no Blimp. Ironically, it was he who had protested to Churchill that Lloyd George's approval of Black and Tan counter-assassinations ('two Sinn Fein – for every loyalist the SF murdered') was 'suicidal'. Churchill, another hawk, approved but Wilson did not. As Sir Henry had confided to his diary almost two years earlier: 'The local [RIC] police marked down certain SFs as in their opinion the actual murderers or instigators and then coolly went and shot them without question or trial.'

Wilson's assassins, Reginald Dunne and Joseph O'Sullivan – themselves veterans of the Western Front – were hanged at Wandsworth prison on 10 August. A crowd of sympathizers stood outside singing 'Wrap The Green Flag Round Me, Boys'. (The remains of Dunne and O'Sullivan, in one of the early signs of resurgent IRA activity in the 1960s, were reinterred in Dublin, attended by an IRA guard of honour, in 1967.)

Griffith, the Free State's first President, denounced Wilson's murder with words which would be heard again in Ireland: 'It is a principle of civilised government that the assassination of a political opponent cannot be justified or condoned.' Who ordered the murder? Historians including A. J. P. Taylor, Robert Kee and Tim Pat Coogan concluded that it was Michael Collins, now leader of the pro-treaty party. 'Perhaps', suggested Taylor, 'the order was given before the treaty, and Collins had forgotten to countermand it; perhaps it was given in the belief that Wilson was organizing Unionist forces in Ulster to resist Sinn Fein.' If, as seems likely, Collins was responsible then it was a betrayal of the treaty he had just signed, ensuring that the Free State, like the first Dail, was stillborn.

Such was Conservative fury at Wilson's murder that, as Taylor observed, 'the British government were driven to threaten that their troops would be used in Dublin against the republicans unless the Free State acted. The Irish civil war was thus begun on British orders. All Irishmen resented this, even when they were fighting against each other.'

It was not quite as simple as that. The Four Courts, heart of the Irish judiciary, was occupied by a battalion of the IRA on 14 April in defiance of the Free State government. The operation was not formally authorized by the IRA Executive. A two-month stand-off followed during which many Republicans joined the occupying garrison. On 26 June, Winston Churchill told the House of Commons that unless the Free State government ended the Four Courts occupation speedily, London would take it that the treaty had been breached. Britain would then reassume 'full liberty of action'.

Free State forces, using guns supplied by the British, attacked the Four Courts on 28 June. A two-day assault ended with sixty-five fatalities, 270 wounded and the destruction of sixty-five buildings. Churchill, satisfied, congratulated Collins in a message that began: 'Now all is changed. Ireland will be mistress in her own house and we over here are in a position to safeguard your Treaty rights and further your legitimate interests effectually.'

One of the first victims of Churchill's new era was Michael Collins, ambushed on a lonely road in his native West Cork on 22 August 1922. It was his first military engagement since the 1916 Rising. He survived the initial ambush but was killed by Jimmy Ormond, a rank-and-file member of the anti-treaty IRA. Father Pat Twohig of Churchtown, County Cork, researched the ambush for forty years and finally revealed, in 1996, what happened. He told a journalist:

> A group of IRA men were heading back home to Waterford from West Cork, where they had been at a training camp. Instead of driving through a skimpy barricade in his way, Collins decided they should stand and fight. It was a terrible mistake, but typical of Collins. Ormond and the rest [of the Waterford group] quite literally happened upon the ambush and joined in. Ormond hadn't a clue who he'd killed until later, but he was the only one who could have hit Collins the way he was hit.

Collins was not yet thirty-two years old.

The sixteen-month Irish Civil War, fought mercilessly between factions favouring and opposing the Treaty, does not form part of this history of an Irish war against England. For the record, it is worth noting that the new Free State government executed seventy-seven Republicans between November 1922 and May 1923. The

Free State Military Intelligence department was probably responsible for many more executions which bypassed any legal process.
On the other side of the war, the dissidents murdered its most
dedicated former leaders including Michael Collins. As Tim Pat
Coogan has noted: 'terrible things were done. Men were chained
to mined barricades and blown to pieces, interrogations were conducted with the aid of a hammer and men went mad or were found
to be castrated.' The Catholic bishops' view of the anti-Treaty
dissidents was that 'they have wrecked Ireland from end to end,
burning and destroying ... They have caused more damage to
Ireland in three months than could be laid to the charge of British
rule in so many decades.'

For the British armed forces, the campaign of 1919–21 had one
unexpected result: it converted a handful of army officers, as well
as England's colonial enemies, to the utility of guerrilla warfare.
Collins's assassination team made a particularly strong impression
on some of them, notably J. C. F. Holland, Colin Gubbins and E. E.
Mockler-Ferryman. With Churchill they emerged as architects of
the Special Operations Executive, the guerrilla force that opposed
the Third Reich in Occupied Europe from 1940 to 1945.

In later years such authorities as the military historian John
Keegan would conclude:

> We must recognise that our response to the scourge of ter-
> rorism is compromised by what we did through SOE. The
> justification ... that we had no other means of striking back
> at the enemy ... is exactly the argument used by the Red
> Brigades, the Baader-Meinhoff Gang, the PFLP, the IRA
> and every other half-articulate terrorist organisation on
> Earth. Futile to argue that we were a democracy and Hitler
> a tyrant. Means besmirch ends. SOE besmirched Britain.

That contrasts sharply with the conclusion reached by the SOE
historian M. R. D. Foot, who once told an Irish audience:

> The Irish [thanks to the example set by Collins and followed
> by SOE] can thus claim that their resistance provided an
> originating impulse for resistance to tyrannies worse than

any they had to endure themselves. And Irish resistance, as Collins led it, showed the rest of the world an economical way to fight wars, the only sane way they can be fought in the age of the nuclear bomb.

The IRA's innovative influence did not end there. The SOE tradition was carried on by the SAS as SOE veterans, still hungry for action after their organization was disbanded, became a formative influence within the post-war SAS. They included Major Dare Newell ('Mr SAS'), son of an Anglican vicar and regimental adjutant of the SAS after SOE service in Albania and Malaya. His presence was crucial in ensuring the survival of an unconventional force, the SAS, in the regular army's peacetime Order of Battle. Another influence was Brigadier Mike Calvert, whose creation of the Malayan Scouts (SAS) as a temporary special force was (as he once told me) modelled on the Black and Tans.

Then as now, the process fed upon itself. As the writer Andrew Selth has demonstrated, the success of the IRA encouraged and taught such diverse anti-colonial guerrilla movements as the Korean opposition to Japanese occupation, the Burmese nationalists, Indian patriots and the Bengali New Violence Party. There was a direct link between the IRA and a ruthless Zionist terror group, Irgun Zvai Leumi. This was made thanks to the presence of Robert Briscoe, the only Jew to serve with the Irish Volunteers, and subsequently a Lord Mayor of Dublin. Briscoe taught a Russian Zionist, Vladimir Jabotinsky 'the methods we had found so effective in the [Irish] guerrilla war'. Briscoe then assisted Jabotinsky in setting up the Irgun, later led by Menachem Begin, with the aid of training material derived from the IRA. It was the start of a process that levered the British out of Palestine, igniting a conflict in the Middle East which continues after half a century or more.

Yet, though Collins's methods were increasingly adopted by anti-colonial movements around the world, the IRA itself was eclipsed after his death for another forty years. The movement won the war for independence because it had the backing of most of the civilian population. It lost the war against the treaty because it lacked that support. If it was to survive into a world changed by a Second

World War and post-war prosperity, it had to evolve sufficiently to appear relevant to a new generation.

The Unionists of Northern Ireland tried hard to stop the clock. A Protestant majority and a Protestant ascendancy would be assured only if the Catholics, in spite of their higher birth-rate, could be discouraged from remaining in the Province once they reached voting age. It would be a long time before the pressures of the world outside burst into the hermetically sealed world of Northern Ireland to challenge that assumption. But so long as a Protestant State for a Protestant People could be sustained, so the strategically over-riding trump card of the war of the twenty-six counties – the Anglo-Irish War – would favour the *status* quo, not the revolution. That trump card, available to the Fenian Republicans for only thirty months preceding the treaty, was the unquestioning, loyal support of most civilians. The IRA's miscalculation was to believe that it could do the same thing in *Northern* Ireland without that vital ingredient.

Epilogue
1998

The unique characteristic of the Irish War over most of the last three centuries has been its capacity to defy external influences, except where these served as tools to further the conflict. In the twentieth century, three world wars – two hot, one cold – came and went. A Soviet empire was erected and demolished and, with it, a comprehensive belief system – the Marxist 'materialist conception of history' – purporting to explain all human endeavour. Popes, presiding over a declining belief system of their own, invoked the Almighty in a search for an answer to the Irish Question, without success. National boundaries within a reconstructed Europe all but vanished as old hatreds (the Balkans apart) were submerged under a tide of multinational capitalism. None of these stirring events came close to penetrating the closed minds of Irish separatism, *Ourselves Alone*.

This does not mean that Ireland remained unchanged. On the contrary. It created the first Celtic tiger economy while its professional army was usefully employed in UN peace-keeping from Zaire to Lebanon, but not within Ireland itself. Steering clear of any commitment to Nato, Ireland benefited hugely from membership of the European Community that Nato defended. The majority of comfortable, pragmatic modern Irish people did not see themselves as active warriors in the war on their doorsteps. As ever, that war was inspired and led by a self-selecting elite, the *fianna*, dedicated to an ideal beyond fulfilment in this life. The relationship of busy, businesslike contemporary Ireland to the warrior gods and goddesses of old is somewhat like that of modern Germans to the myth of the Ring Cycle: a delicate matter of *zeitgeist*, the spirit of the age, uneasily adjusted to cultural roots. As a result of that process, the *fianna* were tolerated, even respected, by all but a handful of people. True, it was quite a handful: Cardinal Cahal Daly, Monsignor Denis Faul, John Bruton, Garret Fitzgerald, Conor Cruise O'Brien and Ruth Dudley Edwards were among those who stood up in public to deny the IRA's claim to be the true guardian of Irish identity, as well as the thousands who turned out, dressed in the anonymity of the crowd, to repudiate IRA violence. But the underlying *justice* of the cause was still seen as a thing apart.

The precise nature of Irish identity is the true source of the trouble, rather than, as Sinn Fein would claim, the issue of British jurisdiction over the Six Counties. The jurisdiction debate is bogus. It ignores the fact that most inhabitants of the Six Countries wish to remain 'British'; bastard British, but British all the same. It also overlooks the fact that all Irishmen and women resident outside the Republic, including those (like myself) born of Irish parents outside the Republic's twenty-six counties are none the less twenty-four-carat Irish citizens. Irish nationhood does not depend upon thirty-two counties. Citizenship – the legal badge of Irish identity – can even be discarded through a provision in law enabling us to renounce that status by means of a 'declaration of alienage' with no loss of face, if that is what we wish. We may also choose to be citizens of Ireland and some other country.

So what is Irish identity? Since it is a diaspora capable of surviving generations of exile in America and Australia, to the discomfiture of native Americans and native Australians, it does not depend upon continued physical contact with Irish soil, even if that soil nourishes those who grew from it in a very special way, as Irish horse-breeders can confirm. The national identity survives cultural attrition as well as exile, for Irish Gaelic is spoken by only a minority, usually on reservations known in Ireland as *Gaeltachta*. Apart from a few slogans such as *Tiocfaidh Ar La* ('Our day will come', usually shouted from the dock as a life sentence is passed), it is doubtful whether many of the current Provisional leadership speak Irish. Perhaps the national identity is its distinctive political system? Apart from its belated, bolted-on claim to the North, the Republic's constitution reflects a political system not especially Irish; not so different from, say, that of Finland. Is Irishness, then, a unique economic system of decentralized worker-control, perhaps, which the IRA would impose on the country if it had its way? In a modern Ireland, farmers enjoying EC subsidies show no inclination to return to Brehon Law or to experiment with any of Sinn Fein's economic nostrums. The reason Irish Republicans enjoy the indulgence of more moderate people is that they have been able, with great ingenuity, to hijack Celtic culture and graft on to it bogus mythologies manufactured, respectively, in the 1790s in Jacobin Paris; a century later, in the salons of Victorian London; and, around the same time, courtesy of James Connolly, derived from International Marxism. The three sources were all Utopian and doomed not just to fail but to destroy themselves spectacularly. What drove Irish resistance through those years, and still does, was the dynamic of resistance itself, the 'physical force tradition'. The Republicans were not the first to steal the nation's title deeds. Sequestration of the Irish – that is, Celtic – identity had occurred twice before. After their victory at the Battle of Moyrath (or Magh Ráth) in the sixth century, the first Christians stole pagan deities (such as Brighid, recycled by the new religion as *Saint* Brigid). From 1155 the Roman Church led by an English Pope suppressed, in its turn, Celtic Christianity.

The Irish identity peddled by the IRA owes little to real Celtic culture. It is, rather, a powerful, dynamic force which politicizes the natural culture and envenoms it through an obsession not with Ireland but with England. It reflects the absolutism of the Catholic Church at its most reactionary. The quarrel with England is refreshed, artificially if necessary, by some new outrage such as the disrupted Aintree Grand National in 1996, to generate new victims who then contribute their grief to fuel English reaction and a new storm of Irish resentment. It is a cyclical process.

The Troubles that began in 1968 were a classic of Republican political deception and Irish self-deception. In 1962 the deadly Utopianism of the IRA had at last hit the buffers of credibility. The movement's Chief of Staff, Cathal Goulding, admitted: 'Without the support of the majority of the people, we just couldn't succeed.' What was needed was a relaunch under a new brand name. In August 1967, the IRA manufactured a new product. 'We would have first to work for the establishment of basic Civil Rights in order to establish democracy and abolish discrimination. This would also give us the political manoeuvrability to establish the Republican Movement openly . . .' So far, so good. But what was the movement to do for resources? Goulding went to America but 'they couldn't support us financially unless there was some form of revolutionary activity, particularly military activity, actually going on in Ireland'.

Destabilizing the brittle structure of the Stormont regime was a great success for the new form of agitprop, combining action with propaganda. The IRA, aided by the student-led People's Democracy, saw to it that the RUC reacted with lethal force. The victims were the undefended Catholics of Bogside and the Lower Falls. They were necessary victims, if the light/dark, goodness/evil Manichaean formula of journalists and the American lobby was to be satisfied. Subsequently, Goulding admitted that the ghettos could have been defended, if armed revolution was what was required at that stage.

His problem was that, in January 1969, he lost control of the monster he had created. The IRA was already split, using the People's Democracy to inflame an already dangerous situation. Some elements of PD made common cause with the Provisionals even before the split was formalized, 'parading through Protestant districts, playing on Protestant fears', as Goulding put it (in March 1972) adding, for good measure, 'It was bollocksology'. Such provocation generated a predictably violent reaction by the Unionist-run RUC, at which point the Provisionals and their People's Democracy partners in the Northern Resistance Movement spotted what Provisional Sinn Fein president Ruairi O'Bradaigh called an exploitable revolutionary situation in the North in 1969. He added: 'There is a tide in the affairs of men, that taken at the flood leads on to success . . . We recognized that this was the tide, the first real tide in fifty years.'

Had the tide turned against him so drastically as to provoke unrestrained, sectarian attacks on Catholic areas by the mass of the Protestant population as well as elements of the police and Protestant terrorist groups, then what? The IRA had a plan for that contingency, uncovered in a Security Forces' raid on a Provisional headquarters house in Belfast in 1974. Prime Minister Harold Wilson told Parliament about the plan a few weeks later. It was intended, by

> ruthless and indiscriminate violence, to foment inter-sectarian hatred and a degree of chaos with the object of enabling the IRA to achieve a position in which it could ... occupy and control certain pre-designated and densely populated areas in the city of Belfast and its suburbs ... A deliberate intention to manipulate the emotions of large sections of the people by inflicting violence and hardship on them in the hope of creating a situation in which the IRA could present itself as the protector of the Catholic popu-lation ... The IRA did not expect, even if it was initially successful, to be able to continue to hold a number of strong-points in parts of Belfast ... Its intention would have been to carry out a scorched-earth policy of burning the houses of the ordinary people as it was compelled to withdraw ... The documents include orders to battalion commanders and the outline of the general concept, with associated maps and a draft proclamation to the civilian population ... There will be an attempt to misrepresent this information – which is a genuine find by the security authorities – as a plant, as something created to discredit the IRA. I am totally satisfied, as are the security authorities, that these documents are genuine and not even put forward themselves by the IRA for any other purpose except that which it had in mind to pursue.

The Provisionals confirmed next day that the documents were indeed genuine. The best gloss they could put on them was that the plan was already two years old – drafted in 1972 when O'Bradaigh was boasting of 'the first real tide for fifty years' – and somehow irrelevant to journalists (though not historians), and in any case, essentially defensive in its intention. Some distinguished journalists were prepared to buy this. In advance of the pogrom –

which did not in fact occur over the next twenty-five years and seemed unlikely to do so thereafter – the IRA had already drafted its public explanation as part of the scorched-earth plan: 'In the emergency which has been forced upon us, the IRA has had no alternative but to employ its full resources to the defence of its people, in the face of the armed offensive against the Catholic working class.'

The revolutionary tide did not produce the quick victory the Provisionals or People's Democracy expected; it simply renewed the sectarian Irish War of attrition on a scale more painful than the nightmare of the Irish Civil War. The longer it continued, the greater was the commitment of the survivors to the moral debt they believed they owed to those who had died for the Cause. *Dulce et decorum est, pro patria mori.* What never struck most of the *fianna* was the obvious fact that the cause of the violence was the violence itself and that for the campaign to maintain momentum, an ever-growing pile of corpses was indispensable. The Irish War had become a ritualized form of human sacrifice based, like other rituals, upon an irrational faith that the magic would work. The 'ceasefire' of 1997 prompted, very quickly, a new flow of arms from the United States to the old, unreconstructed IRA in its latest reincarnation as the Continuity Army Council, or CAC. This, as they say, is where we came in. As the wise Denis Faul observed after the latest SAS cull of young Irishmen in 1992, 'The IRA is a crazy outfit and should be disbanded.'

THE IRISH WAR 1601–1998

A Military Chronology

1601–1798	Six French landings, one Spanish, in Ireland.
1609	Ulster's native earls take flight. Ulster plantation – colonization of six northern counties – by London merchants and Scots after the clearance of native Irish from the counties of Armagh, Coleraine (Derry), Cavan, Donegal, Fermanagh and Tyrone. Since the settlers are Protestants, the seeds of a new religious war are planted, following earlier conflicts to convert Celts from Paganism to Christianity, and Celtic Christians to Rome.
1641	Thousands of settlers massacred by indigenous Irish.
1649 and 1650	Cromwell's revenge upon Ireland: thousands killed or deported; new plantation.
1689	Derry Protestants successfully resist fifteen-week siege of their walled city by King James, dedicated to a policy of 'No Surrender!'
1690	Catholic King James defeated by Protestant King William at the Boyne. The Pope, among others, backed King William since James was the tool of the excommunicated French monarch Louis XIV.
1691	Sarsfield leaves Cork to fight for France; professional Irish military resistance to English rule ends.
1699	Six-sevenths of Ireland held by foreigners.
1708 onwards	England fears invasion by Jacobites.
1720	Jacobite Sir James Cotter executed.
1745	Jacobites on march in Scotland and England.
1760	Unrest in Munster, first serious outbreak of agrarian trouble.
1760s onward	Whiteboys active.

1766	Father Sheehy executed.
1775	American War of Independence.
	Catholic gentry express their loyalty to the crown on the occasion of the revolt of the American colonies.
1778	Irish Volunteers formed, originally to defend Ireland against possible French invasion after regular troops were withdrawn to fight in the American War of Independence.
1780s	Rightboys active.
1781	America wins War of Independence.
1782	Convention of Volunteers at Dungannon supports demands for an independent Irish Parliament, under the King. Also welcomes the relaxation of the Penal Laws against Catholics.
1785	In the North, development of Protestant Peep-o'-Day Boys, also known as Protestant Boys and Wreckers – agrarian movements against Catholic landlords. As a result, Catholic groups, the Defenders, form and spread south.
1789	French Revolution.
1791	14 October. Society of United Irishmen formed when Wolfe Tone visits Belfast Volunteers.
1792	Defenders become more aggressive.
1793	9 January. Defenders clash with troops at Carrickmacross.
	January. 18 Defenders killed in clash with military in Kells, Co. Meath.
	February. War between England and France.
	Soon after outbreak of war, government passes act in Irish Parliament creating an Irish militia. Rank and file to be drawn by compulsory ballot from among peasantry (i.e. mainly Catholic). English and Irish officers.
	Government suppresses what remains of Volunteer Corps.
	A secret emissary from the revolutionary government in France, Jackson, visits Ireland and meets some United Irishmen.
	March and April. 68 Defenders sentenced to death.
	June. Reports of anti-militia riots all over Ireland, by people who do not want to be conscripted.

July. Serious anti-militia riot outside Wexford. Deaths on both sides, including about 80 Defenders.

1794

The French emissary, Jackson, is arrested, tried and commits suicide in dock.
Government outlaws Society of United Irishmen.
Wolfe Tone goes to America.
Immediately, a new United Irishmen movement is formed, starting in Belfast.
March. Defenders in clash with (Catholic) Carlow Militia at Kinsale, Co. Cork. 10 Defenders killed.
21 May. 100–200 Defenders killed, Co. Cavan.
May. 70 Defenders killed at Ballina, Co. Mayo.

1795

Defenders trying to seduce Catholic militia men from their allegiance. Kildare schoolmaster Laurence O'Connor executed for administering Defender oath to a private in North Mayo militia.
21 September. Battle of the Diamond, near Armagh, between Defenders and Peep-o'-Day Boys. 20–30 Defenders killed.
September. Peep-o'-Day boys reorganize as the Orange Society. Orange attacks on Catholics in the North.
The new United Irishmen decide to co-ordinate with the Defenders.

1796

February. Wolfe Tone arrives in France to try to persuade French to mount expedition to Ireland.
March. Government introduces Insurrection Act to try to break Defenders.
16 December. French expedition of 14,000 men sails for Ireland. Storms at sea.
21 December. French arrive at Bantry Bay, down to 7, 000 men.
31 December. Galway militia, consisting of about 400 men, drawn up on beach to oppose French landing. (Which doesn't happen.)

1797

3 January. Last of French leave Bantry Bay.
United Irishmen and Defenders in Ulster increase drilling and raids for arms, parading openly, cutting down trees for pike handles.
Military respond with brutal searches for arms, burning down cottages, flogging people to get information.
March and May. Government makes proclamations in

Ulster demanding surrender of arms.
July. Dutch/French invasion planned (with the support of Wolfe Tone) but prevented by contrary winds.
8 December. Gen. John Moore lists the troops available to the government in Ireland as 76,791, of whom 11,193 are English or Scots. (The rest being Irish.)

1798

February. News arrives in Ireland that a third French invasion is planned.
12 March. Almost entire Leinster provincial committee of United Irishmen arrested.
March. Commander-in-Chief, Sir Ralph Abercromby, resigns at not being allowed to bring army under control.
April and May. Army, militia and yeomanry mount a campaign of torture to get information and find arms.
9 April. First meeting of National Grand Orange Lodge at Dublin.
19 May. Military leader of the United Irishmen, Lord Edward Fitzgerald, arrested. Dies of wounds in prison on 4 June.
21 May. United Irishmen John and Henry Sheares plan to capture military barracks at Loughlinstown and take Dublin. Plan discovered by militia officer. Sheares brothers arrested.
24 May. United Irishmen in Dublin issue orders for a rising.
About 1,000 rebels fight battle with troops at Naas, Co. Kildare.
Rebel attack on barracks and soldiers' billets at Prosperous, Co. Kildare. Many soldiers burnt, suffocated or impaled on pikes. Rebels routed.
25 May. Rebels begin to move on Carlow. Defeated. Hundreds killed. Brutal retributions.
Various unsuccessful risings in counties round Dublin. Unsuccessful.
A few days after the risings, 2,000 Catholic gentry make an address of loyalty to the King and regret that Catholic 'lower orders' took part.
26 May. Rising in Wexford and Wicklow starts with an incident at Boulavogue.
27 May. Father John Murphy's men win battle against North Cork militia. Many militiamen killed after battle by rebels.

5 June. Rebels take New Ross, then withdraw.
Wexford rebels massacre 200 Protestant prisoners at
Scullabogue.

June. Unsuccessful rising in Co. Antrim under Henry
Joy McCracken. Bloodily put down. McCracken
executed.

June. Unsuccessful rising in Co. Down under Henry
Monroe, also bloodily put down. Monroe executed.

Rebels lose Battle of Arklow against General Needham.

10 June. But Dublin Castle still in such a panic that
the Viceroy's wife, Lady Camden, and her family are
sent back to England.

11 June. The Viceroy says Ireland is lost unless more
troops are sent.

16 June. Five English regiments land at Waterford. By
the end of June, 12,000 English militia men are on the
way.

20 June. Massacre of prisoners by rebels on the bridge
at Wexford.

21 June. Successful attack by government forces under
General Lake on Wexford rebel forces at Vinegar Hill,
near Enniscorthy.

Rebels abandon town of Wexford as General John
Moore and his army approach. Town back in
government hands after 23 days of rebel occupation.

26 June. Further rebel defeat by government troops at
Kilcomney Hill, Kilkenny.

Father Murphy captured soon afterwards and hanged.

1 July. Rebel leaders hanged off Wexford Bridge.

July. General Sir John Moore, engaged in mopping up
operations in Co. Wicklow, comments on the
unpardonable acts of the yeomanry who shot people
after they had received certificates of pardon and
burned homes.

Commander-in-Chief Lord Cornwallis says the
yeomanry 'have saved the country but . . . now take the
lead in rapine and murder'.

8 July. Lord Cornwallis reports that Wexford rebels
now consist only of scattered bands.

After the rising, United Irishmen already in prison in
Dublin escape execution provided they give evidence
to the authorities about the origins of the United
Irishmen. They agree, but not naming names. Arthur
O'Connor, Thomas Emmet, W. J. MacNeven and

others are first imprisoned in Scotland, later allowed to go into exile in France or USA.

22 August. The French (flying British flags as a ruse) appear in Bay of Killala, Co. Mayo and take town of Killala with little opposition from local yeomanry. French General, Humbert, issues proclamation to the Irish to rise and join them. Local peasants join. Humbert moves south and defeats a much larger British force under General Lake at Castlebar.

8 September. Humbert is defeated by Lord Cornwallis at Ballinamuck. French prisoners sent home, Irish peasants slaughtered.

16 September. Not knowing about this defeat, another, much smaller, part of the French expeditionary force lands on Rutland Island off Donegal. Local peasants show no inclination to join in, so it goes away.

12 October. A third part of the French expeditionary force, with Wolfe Tone on board, is intercepted by Royal Navy off north coast of Donegal. Many prisoners taken, including Tone.

10 November. Tone tried and condemned to death in Dublin. Tries to commit suicide by cutting throat on morning he is to be hanged. Dies of wound a week later.

1798 and 1799	Various plots by Irish crews on British navy ships to rebel and hoist Green Flag discovered. Mutineers hanged and flogged.
1799	Still widespread fear of rebellion. Some rebel bands still out and roads impassible without military escort.
1803	23 July. Robert Emmet declares a provisional government and tries to seize Dublin Castle. Rising a failure.
	August. Robert Emmet caught, tried and hanged.
1815–1824	Some resumed activity by agrarian secret societies, spurred on by two potato famines.
1845	A government newspaper points out that the new system of railways being built in Ireland would make it easy to put down treason by bringing troops from Dublin to any point in Ireland within six hours. (To Daniel O'Connell's fury, one of his young and more hotheaded supporters publishes a piece on sabotaging railways.)

Potato famine. Agrarian secret societies more active again. Murders increase.

1846   Government responds with Coercion bill.

1847   January. Some of O'Connell's younger and more radical supporters and Smith O'Brien split and form Irish Confederation.
15 May. O'Connell dies.
Government passes Crime and Outrage Act.

1848   Year of revolutions in Europe.
March. Government prosecutes O'Brien, John Mitchel and Thomas Meagher for sedition.
May. O'Brien and Meagher released after jury fails to agree. Mitchel found guilty and deported.
July. Lord Lieutenant bans holding of arms in Dublin and some other counties. Habeas Corpus suspended.
23 July. O'Brien and friends unsuccessfully attempt armed rising in Co. Wexford then move on to Co. Tipperary.
26 July. O'Brien, with pistols in his coat and two supporters, marches into police station at Mullinahone, Co. Tipperary. Asks police to surrender. Police refuse. O'Brien leaves town.
29 July. O'Brien and supporters encounter police at Ballingarry, Co. Tipperary. Police open fire. Two people killed. Rebels go into hiding.
August. O'Brien arrested on station platform. Later tried for high treason and sentenced to death, but sentence reduced to transportation to Tasmania. Other plotters also transported. (O'Brien later pardoned, returns to Ireland.)

1849   Plan by Joseph Brennan to capture Queen Victoria on visit to Dublin comes to nothing.
September. Unsuccessful attack on police barracks at Cappoquin, Co. Waterford.

1854   Irish exile John Mitchel founds Irishmen's Civil and Military Republican Union in New York.

1855   The American Emmet Monument Association sends an emissary to Ireland to make contact with nationalists and offers to send 30,000 men. Nothing happens.

1856   James Stephens returns to Ireland from exile in Paris and tries to find signs of life in Irish nationalist movement. No success at first.

1857	The Emmet Monument Association sends another emissary. Stephens says that if the USA can send 500 men with Lee Enfields, plus money, Stephens will guarantee 10,000 men ready to rise in Ireland. Initial fund-raising in USA is disappointing.
1858	17 March. In Dublin, James Stephens and friends form a new secret society dedicated to the establishment of an independent democratic republic in Ireland. No name at first, but became Irish Republican Brotherhood. Funds arrive from America. May. Stephens's new organization joins forces with the Phoenix National and Literary Society of Skibbereen. Cover for a secret society under oath to fight 'at a moment's warning'. Some arrests for illegal oath-taking. October. Stephens goes to USA. Collects £600 in six months. 3 December. The Lord Lieutenant issues a proclamation offering £100 for information about oath-taking.
1859	Stephens and Irish exile O'Mahony set up an association in the USA which becomes the Fenian Brotherhood. In Dublin, RC Archbishop Cullen says anybody joining a secret society will be excommunicated.
1861	Young Ireland supporter, and 1848 rebel, Terence Bellew McManus, dies in California. Return of his body to Dublin for funeral, 10 November, gives recruiting boost to Stephens's organization.
1861 to 1865	American Civil War: Fenians including Meagher (see 1848) prominent on both sides.
1863	American Fenian convention in Chicago.
1864	Stephens goes to USA and tours Union armies, recruiting for his Brotherhood In Ireland, his assistant John Devoy tries to convert members of militias and British army to Fenianism. Some success.
1865	At American Fenian Brotherhood convention at Cincinnati, O'Mahony says: 'The Brotherhood is virtually at war with the oligarchy of Great Britain.' March. US Fenian representative T. J. Kelly visits Ireland and reports it ready for a rising.

As American Civil War ends, former officers make their way to Ireland.

September. A letter from Stephens saying it is the year for the rising is stolen and passed to authorities by informer.

Government arrests some leading Dublin Fenians. Stephens escapes, but is arrested in November. Escapes from prison, later goes to America again.

1866 February. Habeas Corpus suspended.

In Dublin, the first murder by Fenians of a suspected informer, George Clark.

April. Unsuccessful American Fenian attempt to invade Campo Bello, New Brunswick, by sea.

31 May. American Fenian invasion of Canada. First recorded use of name 'Irish Republican Army'. Fenians win an action against volunteers, then are cut off from reinforcements and have to retreat.

December. Stephens deposed as head of movement in Ireland by American Fenians, who are tired of waiting for action. They appoint T. J. Kelly instead.

1867 January. Kelly and other US Fenian leaders arrive in London and plan raid on Chester Castle and barracks for arms.

11 February. Fenians assemble in large numbers at Chester, but authorities have been warned of attempt and guard increased, so raid called off.

4 March. 'General' Massey, who was to command Fenian operations in Ireland, arrested at Limerick.

5 March. Fenian raid on Stepaside barracks, Dublin. Exchange of fire. Barracks surrender. So does police barracks at Glencullen. Exchange of fire between rebels and police at Tallaght, but momentum falters after arrest of Massey.

6–7 March. Various clashes. Drogheda, Co. Limerick. Police barracks at Ballyknockane, Co. Cork, captured. Police escorting prisoners to gaol in Waterford attacked by crowd.

8 March. *The Times* of London prints a proclamation from the 'Provisional Government of the Irish Republic'.

Military flying columns disperse rebels in the south and west of Ireland.

11 September. Fenian leader T. J. Kelly and Timothy

Deasy arrested in Manchester.
18 September. In Manchester about 30 Fenians raid prison van and rescue Kelly and Deasy. Police Sergeant Brett is mortally wounded. Killer escapes.
24 November. William Allen, Philip Larkin and Michael O'Brien hanged in Manchester for their part in raid.
13 December. 12 civilians killed when Fenians try unsuccessfully to rescue Richard O'Sullivan Burke from Clerkenwell Prison in London by blowing down wall. Fears of Fenians on the mainland are now widespread.
October. Central Protestant Defence Association founded to resist religious and social reforms. Ulster Defence Association also created: a front for the Orange Order.

1868   Protestant leader Thomas Ellis says his co-religionists 'will fight . . . with the Bible in one hand and the sword in the other'.

1871   IRB agrees to three-year trial of political, not military, route to Home Rule: Fenians adopt the ballot-box.

1879–1880   Land League campaign against eviction of farmers leads to widespread terrorism against land agents and others. Captain Boycott needs bodyguard of 7,000 soldiers.

1882   Phoenix Park murders: Lord Frederick Cavendish stabbed to death in Dublin by the Invincibles, an IRB group, hours after his arrival to promote new deal for Irish tenant farmers. Gladstone's political initiative damaged. New Coercion Act.

1883–1886   The Fenian Dynamite War hits civilian targets in England: US Senate gives dynamiters immunity from extradition.

1885   Metropolitan police scraps most of its cutlasses and rattles. Acquires 931 Webley revolvers.

1886   Orange Order recruits military volunteers to oppose Home Rule. Many British officers support them.

1912–1913   Tory leader Bonar Law threatens resistance to Home Rule 'outside constitution'. Unionists create Ulster Volunteer Force; smuggle rifles and machine-guns into Ireland. Republicans create Irish Volunteers and Connolly's Citizen Army.

1914	British army officers in 'Curragh Mutiny' as Unionists import more guns. Casement raises funds for Republican rifles, also imported into Ireland.
August 1914–November 1918	First World War: thousands of Irishmen of both communities serve with British army.
1915	Casement seeks Irish volunteers in Limburg p.o.w. camp; finds only ten.
1916	Easter. German guns and Casement land in Kerry. Promptly captured. Dissident wing of Irish Volunteers overrules Chief of Staff to launch a six-day revolution in Dublin: 220 civilians killed and 600 wounded as British use artillery. British turn military victory into political defeat a month later by executing rebel leaders, one by one in a six-day counter-revolution.
1919–1921	The Anglo-Irish War, the first modern terrorist and counter-insurgency conflict. British government forced to concede independence to 26-county Irish Free State.
1922	Irish Civil War results from armed opposition by Republican hardliners to terms of Anglo-Irish Treaty, recognizing six counties of Ulster as separate state of Northern Ireland under British jurisdiction. Ulster Protestants repudiate claims of a Catholic state that outlaws divorce and birth control.
1932–1938	Anglo-Irish economic war. This ends with Anglo-Irish Treaty. British cease boycott of Irish goods.
1935	Sectarian rioting in Belfast.
1939	IRA declares war on England. Bombs in England – notably Coventry post office – kill civilians. Second World War begins. Irish Free State remains neutral, though thousands of its citizens join UK forces.
1945	Second World War ends. Irish President de Valera expresses condolences to Nazi envoy on death of Hitler. Irish Free State becomes Irish Republic and leaves the Commonwealth.
1956–1962	IRA border campaign and raids on cadet armouries in England ends in acknowledged defeat when most Irish people withhold support.
1962–1969	IRA adopts new 'civil rights' strategy, combines with student activists of People's Democracy to provoke sectarian disorder.

| 1967 | Loyalist terrorists (members of Prince Albert Loyal Orange Lodge no. 1892) murder Catholic barman, Malvern Street, Belfast, in mistake for IRA veteran Leo Martin. |

1968 Violence results from NICRA marches at Dungannon and Armagh. Derry civil rights protest march organizers lose control; Young Socialists hit police with placards; RUC over-react, attack non-violent politicians with batons.

1969 Student anarchist march from Belfast to Derry provokes Loyalist mob attack as police watch. Cameron describes the tactic as 'calculated martyrdom'. RUC runs amok in Bogside. NICRA march at Newry led by People's Democracy agitators turns violent. Loyalist terrorist bomb Silent Valley water reservoir and other key points. This and other 'no-claim' attacks blamed on IRA, destabilizing O'Neill's reformist programme. Public order breaks down as RUC is beaten in Bogside. Armoured cars and machine-guns kill Catholic civilians in Belfast. London government does nothing: British soldiers permitted to intervene too late to avert sectarian war.

Split between two wings of IRA (traditionalists and socialists) formalized. Officials and Provisionals both oppose British army.

1970 Ballymurphy nationalists riot: army warns patrol, bombers might be shot. Both IRA factions start major terrorist campaigns apparently from a standing start: a unique event in the history of guerrilla warfare. Explosion at Derry IRA bomb factory: bomb-maker's daughters killed. Provisionals 'blooded' in first armed confrontation with Loyalists, East Belfast. Five Protestants shot dead, 26 wounded. One IRA man killed. Falls Road 36-hour military curfew, following arms search, disillusions many Catholics about role of British army. Five civilians killed and many others injured in gun battle between Officials and British soldiers. Army uses 'rubber bullet' to subdue rioters for first time. Two RUC men blown up by Crossmaglen car-bomb. Unapproved border roads spiked. Dublin arms trial: ministers accused of gun-running and financing IRA.

IRA man killed as he plants bomb at Belfast power transformer.

IRA receives Armalite rifles from USA.

1971
First British soldiers killed by Provisionals. Within 17 months, 100 soldiers have been killed by Republicans. Army starts shooting rioters. Unarmed RUC men shot dead by IRA in Belfast. Bomb attacks on police stations. Police, having been disarmed, are rearmed again. Unionist Minister John Taylor shot by IRA but survives. Three teenage Scottish soldiers, unarmed and off-duty, murdered in cold blood near Belfast, in a textbook use of violence to provoke a political backlash. Soldiers' girlfriends tarred and feathered by Republicans. Sgt Michael Willets, Parachute Regiment, throws himself on IRA bomb to save children at Belfast police station; awarded posthumous George Cross. Two Derry men shot dead by soldiers who claim they were armed. Riots follow and SDLP boycotts Stormont Parliament. Bombing campaign grows.

Internment of Catholics, many innocent, in Operation Demetrius, as army uses inaccurate Intelligence provided by RUC. This provokes massive reaction including intensive bombing campaign by both wings of IRA. Seventeen people killed in 36 hours. Loyalist terror group the UDA founded.

As bombing campaign accelerates, Catholic prelates ask, 'Who in their sane senses wants to bomb a million Protestants into a united Ireland?' Subsequently the Pope's pleas for peace will also be brushed aside by the IRA. IRA bombs a Protestant pub in Belfast, provoking creation of Ulster Defence Association. IRA bomb attacks begin in London, including Post Office Tower. In a shop on Protestant Shankill Road a baby boy aged seven months is murdered. Victims of assassination include Unionist Senator Jack Barnhill. Loyalists bomb McGurk's Bar, Belfast, killing 16 people: the heaviest single civilian body-count of the renewed Troubles.

1972
Bloody Sunday in Derry (14 unarmed civilians killed by Paras) followed by Bloody Friday in Belfast when 26 IRA bombs are detonated in Belfast, killing 11 people. IRA bombs the Abercorn Restaurant, Belfast,

where sisters shopping for a trousseau have their legs blown off; and Donegall Street shopping area. Official IRA bombs Aldershot; murders local boy serving in Irish Rangers, provokes outrage and calls ceasefire. Loyalist terrorists increase sectarian murders. Operation Motorman ends Republican no-go areas. IRA bombs Claudy as reprisal. First major gun battles between Protestants and army. Stormont wound up; direct rule from London imposed; major political victory for IRA. Sectarian gun-battles provoked by Republican and Loyalist terrorists. Out of 468 people killed in 1972, a total of 323 are civilians and 122 have been assassinated.

1973 Loyalist workers' strike, backed by guns, leads to violence: army kills two loyalists. IRA bombs in London follow border poll and preparations for new Assembly and herald mainland campaign. Bombs explode at Old Bailey and Great Scotland Yard. Irish government intercepts Libyan arms cargo intended for IRA. IRA seize helicopter to spring its leaders from Dublin prison yard.

1974 Nine soldiers, three civilians killed by IRA in M62 coach bomb. IRA team bombs, machine-guns London clubs and restaurants. Loyalist terrorists bomb Dublin: 22 dead. IRA bombs at two Birmingham pubs kill 21 people and injure 162, prompting Prevention of Terrorism Act. Ulster Workers' Council general strike, backed by paramilitary intimidation, brings down power-sharing administration. Security Forces powerless. First British soldier charged with murdering Catholic. More than 30 Republicans break out of the Maze. Provisionals declare ceasefire for talks to take place with UK government.

1975 Provisional IRA ceasefire lasts six months. Includes Provisional 'Incident Centres' to monitor events, sanctioned by London. IRA bombs breach ceasefire. Internment ends. Loyalist death squads (some UDR soldiers) kill Catholics including Miami Showband from Dublin. South Armagh Provos launch their own sectarian attacks on civilians before and after Miami Showband killings. Ten Republicans die in renewed feud between Provisional and Official IRA. In London, Balcombe Street siege ends with surrender of

IRA terror team. INLA (Irish National Liberation Army) emerges from split within Official IRA.

1975–1977   Shankill Butchers kill more than a dozen Catholics in Belfast, usually after prolonged torture in 'romper rooms'.

1976   Murder of ten Protestant workers by South Armagh Provos provokes commitment of SAS to the Province. IRA blows up British ambassador to Dublin, Christopher Ewart-Biggs, with culvert bomb later copied by Basque ETA terrorists. London government announces new strategy of 'police primacy' in running security operations in NI. The political effect is to hand over leadership of the war against terrorism to the Protestant-dominated RUC. Following deaths of two children – hit by terrorist car – 10,000 Catholics march for peace. The leaders ('peace women') attacked by Republican thugs. Sinn Fein Vice-President Maire Drumm murdered in Mater Hospital, Belfast.

1977   IRA bombing campaign in London. Captain Robert Nairac murdered by IRA after being detected while disguised as a civilian in Forkhill. His body never found: believed to have been dismembered and fed to pigs. RUC arrests of Loyalist terrorists are a body-blow to UVF. Leader of Shankill Butchers is one of many imprisoned. NI Secretary Roy Mason – hardline opponent of all terrorists – claims the tide has turned against them.

1978   IRA use 'air-fuel' weapon in horrific attack on La Mon House Hotel, NI, killing 12, injuring many more. SAS ambush kills IRA bomb team at Ballysillan post depot, Belfast. Army Intelligence assessment (the Glover Report) leaked: notes IRA reorganization into self-contained cells for greater security against penetration. It acknowledges that Republican activists are not mindless hooligans and sees no viable alternative to a continuing conflict. IRA blitz in NI and London. Two senior prison officers assassinated.

1979   INLA murders Airey Neave MP with car-bomb before Thatcher's election. USA blocks British attempt to extradite IRA bombers and halts export of revolvers to RUC. Lord Mountbatten blown up on holiday in Sligo; 18 Paras killed at Warrenpoint on same day;

IRA tells Pope, 'Force the only means of removing evil British'; IRA bomb blitz continues in NI.

1980   IRA hunger strikes begin in the Maze. Thatcher denies the prisoners political status. Hunger-strikes called off, temporarily.

1981   IRA prisoners resume hunger-strikes. Bobby Sands, first to die, has been elected MP. Thatcher claims hunger-strike 'may be IRA's last card'. IRA prisoners, who had killed SAS officer Captain Westmacott before surrendering by waving white sheet, use smuggled guns to break out of prison. Hunger-strikes end after ten Republican deaths. London gives way to prisoners' rejection of prison uniform. Foundation laid for later prison 'republics' within NI. Sinn Fein publicly adopts 'Armalite/ballot box' twin-track strategy. USA declares Ian Paisley *persona non grata*. IRA continues bombing: 16 killed at Droppin' Well disco.

1982   IRA bombs ceremonial cavalry and bandstand in London parks, killing 11 servicemen; INLA kills two children with bomb in Belfast; unarmed IRA men killed in RUC ambush, first of 'shoot-to-kill' controversies; INLA murders 17 in bomb attack on NI discotheque; RUC shoot and kill two INLA leaders. INLA kills 17 people with Ballykelly pub bomb.

1983   38 IRA men escape from the Maze; prison staff scapegoated by government; INLA fires into Protestant chapel indiscriminately, killing three worshippers; IRA bombs Harrods store, London, crowded with Christmas shoppers. Six killed; 90 injured. Edgar Graham, Unionist politician, shot dead by IRA.

1984   Gerry Adams wounded by Ulster Freedom Fighters assassination team; European Parliament calls on British to ban plastic bullets in riot control, since the weapon is lethal. London ignores this. Trawler *Marita Ann* stopped near Kerry carrying cargo of IRA guns from the USA; Grand Hotel, Brighton, bombed by IRA during Conservative conference, murdering five people, almost killing Premier Thatcher.

1985   Nine RUC officers killed by IRA mortar attack on Newry police barracks; IRA starts killing civilians rebuilding Security Force establishments.

1986
Loyalist rioters protest against Anglo-Irish Agreement and intimidate RUC families; nationalists murdered by Loyalist assassination teams. Acquittals in Christopher Black appeal signal end of 'supergrass' (informer) trials.

1987
Feud between INLA and splinter group IPLO provokes 13 killings; IRA bomb attacks on British military bases in Germany including the open, undefended camp at Rheindalen; UVF kills IRA man who planned the Maze prison escape; Lord Justice Gibson blown up; SAS kills eight IRA men at Loughgall; French authorities intercept trawler *Eksund*, loaded with Libyan arms for IRA; worshippers at Enniskillen cenotaph, attending Remembrance Day service, bombed by IRA, causing 11 deaths. Civil rights veteran Nell McCafferty declares this led her to repudiate IRA claim to political legitimacy.

1988
RUC seizes major UDA armoury; Irish police uncover IRA arms depot on Donegal beach; SAS kills three unarmed IRA bombers at Gibraltar; using grenades, Loyalist terrorist Michael Stone kills three mourners at Belfast funeral of Gibraltar Three; funeral procession of one of the mourner-victims halts car with two British soldiers in civilian dress, who are lynched, butchered and stripped; IRA attacks against British on Continent; IRA bombs van carrying soldiers who had participated in charity run, kills six; army helicopter crash-lands after IRA machine-gun attack; SAS kills three IRA men as they open fire on police barracks; London government imposes part-censorship on broadcasters, forbidding use of Republican voices, but broadcasters use actors instead to utter the same words.

1989
Provisional IRA disbands its undisciplined West Fermanagh team; Loyalist arms procurement team arrested in Paris in company of South African arms team, provoking row between London and Pretoria; British Intelligence files on Republicans leaked to Loyalist assassins; IRA campaign continues in 'war of three theatres' – NI, Britain and Germany. Bomb targets in England include Ten Hill barracks, Shropshire; Mill Hill, London; and Royal Marine band musicians at Deal, Kent, where eight bandsmen are killed.

1990

Soldiers dressed as civilians kill robbers armed with replica weapons in apparent 'shoot-to-kill' episode; army undercover agent Brian Nelson arrested following inquiry into leak of Intelligence to Loyalist assassins; Dublin refuses British request for extradition of two Maze prison escapees; inquiry into British Intelligence leaks finds collusion between Loyalist assassins and soldiers; IRA kills tourists in Holland in mistake for British soldiers; bombs Carlton Club; Stock Exchange; murders Ian Gow MP, inflicting terminal political damage on Premier Thatcher. Paras, including Lee Clegg, kill joy riders, a public relations and legal 'own goal'; IRA employs 'human bombs' using blackmail and coercion to sacrifice bomb carriers as well as soldiers; Loyalist assassins murder Republicans and their relatives in attrition campaign of counter-terror.

1991

IRA arson attacks in Belfast and Manchester; mortar bomb attack on Downing Street; IRA begins 'big bomb' campaign including attack on Protestant housing estates; responds to loyalist assassinations with lethal witch-hunt for informers, usually killing the wrong people; bomb attacks on Musgrave Park Hospital, Belfast, and Victoria station, London. 'Birmingham Six', wrongly convicted of Birmingham pub bombings, released after 16 years; NI slides towards overt sectarian war expressed as 'tit-for-tat' murders.

1992

IRA kills eight Protestant workers with culvert bomb as they drive home from work on Security Forces base; Loyalist assassins shoot dead five Catholics at Belfast bookmaker's shop; IRA bombs Christmas shoppers in London's Oxford Street; SAS kills Kevin O'Donnell and other IRA men as they attack RUC with heavy machine-gun (O'Donnell, in UK court, had sworn he was 'a devout Catholic' not an IRA supporter); IRA scores bull's-eye when it bombs Baltic Exchange, distorting British insurance market; IRA arms bunkers found in Irish Republic; MI5 takes over from Special Branch as lead agency against Irish terror in Britain; Paras open fire on Catholic crowd outside pub in Tyrone; UDA banned; IRA bombs Belfast forensic laboratories by creating mock motor-accident, through which a damaged vehicle is used as a Trojan Horse which passes laboratory defences; IRA bomb attacks on civilians in NI and Britain intensify: civilian body-count is 76, highest for 16 years. IRA murders alleged informers Gregory Burns, Sean Burns and Aiden Star of Portadown for links with security forces and 'King Rat' (Billy Wright). Wright assassinated in the Maze prison December 1997.

1993 IRA bombs Warrington gas works; IRA sniper using American .5 Barrett rifle kills fourth British soldier in South Armagh; Father (later Mr) Denis Bradley, Derry priest, key member of 'The Link' – the back-channel for secret talks between the Provisional IRA and UK government – drafts message to the British: 'The war is over. We need your help to end it.' The IRA denies that the note represented its real policy. Martin McGuinness says the story is a lie. Two children murdered by IRA bomb at Warrington shopping centre; Loyalist assassins continue sectarian murders; massive peace rally in Dublin; IRA bombs NatWest Tower in City of London; St Ethelburga's Church in Bishopsgate; six no-warning bombs in north London, and civilian targets in NI including Magherafelt (town centre demolished).

1994 IRA bombers attack fishmonger's shop on Protestant Shankill Road, Belfast, killing nine civilians and one bomber, Thomas Begley, whose coffin-bearers include Gerry Adams. IRA subsequently (31 August) declares 'complete cessation of military operations'. Gerry Adams meets President Clinton at White House as IRA continues to plan operations.

1996 Canary Wharf, London, bomb marks end of 17-month IRA ceasefire. Other bombs follow at Charing Cross Road, Aldwych, Old Brompton Road, Hammersmith Bridge (in London); Bognor Regis and Brighton (bike bombs); Manchester.

1997 IRA adopts 'chaos strategy' to paralyse airports and motorways with bombs and false alarms. Targets include 150th Grand National steeplechase, won (after postponement) by Ulster-born jockey Tony Dobbin who says, 'It is shameful; makes you ashamed to say you are from there.' Double-bomb attack penetrates outer defences of army HQ at Lisburn, NI. IRA

sniper with Barrett Light .5 heavy rifle kills
Lance-Bombardier Stephen Restorick at checkpoint.
SAS team ordered to hunt those responsible. IRA
assassins try to gun down Unionist politician as he
visits sick son in Belfast children's hospital. In July,
two months after the election of Tony Blair's New
Labour government, the IRA renews its 'complete'
ceasefire. In December, the Republican splinter group
INLA murders Loyalist assassination maestro Billy
Wright inside the Maze prison, possibly with IRA
complicity. Loyalist sectarian killings begin anew.
'Peace process' endangered. IRA high command has
already warned Sinn Fein that it must achieve
substantial political progress by March 1998 or it will
go back to war. Body-count since 1969 now
approaches 4,000 out of population of 1·5 million. The
cost of damage to property expertly estimated at £25
billion.

1998   January–March: Republican bomb and mortar attacks
at Enniskillin, Moira, Portadown and Armagh: splinter
groups blamed.

10 April: Good Friday Peace Agreement forms basis
for new political alignments in Ireland including
guarantees of peaceful politics instead of violence and
Dublin's promise – subject to referendum – to
abandon claims to Northern Ireland until majority
there agrees to reunification. Sinn Fein does not
formally sign the agreement but acts as if it will,
subject to its own conference approval. Gerry Adams's
caveat: 'This is a phase in our struggle.' Orange Order
opposes the deal.

22–23 May: Referenda in both parts of Ireland. In the
North, 71.12 per cent vote to accept the deal; 28.88
per cent oppose it. In the Republic, 94 per cent are in
favour.

28 May: RUC Chief Ronnie Flanagan says terror
groups still armed and in training.

30 May: Junior Orange march attacked with explosives.

31 May: Suspected drugs dealer shot dead in
Dungannon. IRA blamed.

25 June: New Assembly elections: Pro-peace Unionists
take most seats; pro-peace deal Social Democratic and
Labour Party takes most votes: a turning point in
Ulster politics.

July: Orange Order defies Parades Commission; claims right to march through nationalist neighbourhood at Drumcree, Armagh, and threatens to 'paralyse Ulster' if the march is blocked. Stand-off begins as security forces bar the way. Loyalist terrorists shoot at RUC officers and Catholic civilians; torch Catholic homes and ten churches; kill three children of mixed marriage with nocturnal firebomb. Moderate Unionists withdraw support from Orange extremists.

Republican terrorists compromised by informer. An attempt to plant fire bombs in London is nipped in the bud.

Leo McKinstry, a Belfast Protestant, reminds his people (in a *Daily Mail* article): 'This tiny statelet of just 1.5 million people swallows more than £8.3 billion of British Government money every year.' Others note that the latest Drumcree stalemate has caused £100-million of damage. The cost of policing the stand-off is estimated to be £2 million per day.

September: Sinn Fein peace offensive linked to President Clinton's visit to NI; Gerry Adams declares violence 'must be for all of us now a thing of the past – over, done with and gone.' Martin McGuinness, chief negotiator for Sinn Fein, appointed as party representative on arms decommissioning team. Following Omagh bomb, Blair government makes new anti-terrorist law to 'mop up' breakaway terrorist groups.

RUC announces closure of six military OPs and VCPs. More than 160 local RIR soldiers voluntarily return guns kept for personal protection.

October: Gerry Adams says it is 'not within the gift of Sinn Fein' to persuade the IRA to disarm. He adds: 'Don't kick a dog to see if it is asleep.'

November: Martin McGuinness, when asked why no IRA arms had yet been handed over, replied: 'I'll give you a good reason. The IRA won't do it. That's the reason.'

Mowlam tells RUSI: 'Decommissioning of paramilitary arms is an essential part of the Good Friday Agreement and must move forward with all the other parts.' And 'We have a decommissioning body meeting with all the parties linked to paramilitary groups.'

Catholic West Belfast football team, Donegal Celtic, obeys an order from Sinn Fein not to play a fixture against an RUC team.

Irish leader Bertie Ahern says: 'Ireland will be united in my lifetime.'

December: Trimble/Hume deal to rule NI together in power-sharing executive of twelve, running ten government departments. Sinn Fein excluded in continuing row over IRA arsenal. LVF destroys first weapons. Portadown Protestants clash with RUC.

1999

January: Blair, challenged by Hague as paramilitary beatings and murders continue, says ceasefire still holds. Labour MPs propose end to early release of terrorists. Mowlam visits the Maze prison to reassure Loyalist prisoners after LVF leader Billy Wright is murdered inside the prison by INLA inmates. Lord Tebbit, a survivor of the 1984 Brighton Hotel bomb attack, alleges that Mowlam's secret agenda is to keep IRA 'fully operational.' IRA murders its critic and former intelligence officer, Eamon Collins.

February: IRA claims radical breakaway groups have stolen weapons. McGuinness tells interviewer: 'I cannot get the IRA to surrender.' Opposing factions face off in NI Assembly. Uproar as McGuinness objects to opponents describing his party as 'Sinn Fein/IRA.' Ahern, Irish leader, says Sinn Fein should be kept out of NI government unless IRA decommissions weapons and also points out that Sinn Fein has benefited from release of terrorist prisoners. In England, MI5 accused of losing track of a Republican bombing team sent by the Continuity IRA to renew the terrorist campaign. Reports suggest a Loyalist terror group, the Red Hand Defenders, have acquired a fresh cache of weapons. In some form, the war is set to resume.

15 March: Civil rights lawyer Rosemary Nelson murdered by Loyalist terrorists. RUC under attack for alleged refusal to provide her with protection following her claims to have been threatened by some officers. Mrs Nelson's evidence, meanwhile, was sent to the Director of Public Prosecutions following a report from the Independent Commission for Police Complaints.

17 March: Frankie Curry, leading Loyalist terrorist linked to Red Hand Defenders, shot dead in Belfast by masked men believed to be other Loyalists in gang turf war.

17–19 March: Washington summit, hosted by President Clinton and attended by Prime Ministers Blair and Ahern, Unionist leader David Trimble and Sinn Fein's Gerry Adams ends without clear commitment to arms decommissioning. Adams says he cannot deliver IRA decommissioning. Blair, Ahern and Clinton accept that IRA's failure to disarm will not keep Sinn Fein out of a new power-sharing executive in Northern Ireland. Everyone knows that to

admit Sinn Fein without decommissioning will provoke a
Unionist rejection of the peace process.

19 March: IRA sniper Bernard McGinn convicted of murdering Lance Bombardier Restorick. With other South
Armagh IRA men Michael Caraher, Seamus McArdle and
Martin Mines, arrested by SAS in 1997, McGinn is sentenced to a total of 640 years and three life terms linked to
the murders of nine soldiers. In practice, all four convicts
will be released after sixteen months, in July 2000, under the
terms of the Good Friday Agreement. Caraher, the team
leader, had been represented by Rosemary Nelson.

21 March: Report on telephone tapping and electronic surveillance, including bugging, by Lord Nolan reveals that
security and intelligence services in Britain are bugging
more people and intercepting more letters than at any time
since World War II. A *Sunday Times* report says: 'The trend
is the opposite of what was expected. Surveillance has always
been closely linked to the violence in North Ireland, which
has subsided.' The Orwellian Machine, as predicted in the
history, now seeks fresh employment at home.

Chronology of the Peace Process, 1999/2000

Throughout 1999 the peace process limped like some battlefield casualty towards a political field hospital at
Stormont. The 'casualty' needed the tenacious support of an
American – the retired Senator George Mitchell – if it was
not to collapse on the way. Enemies of the process, as it
turned out, were not only terrorist extremists, but also the
British military intelligence officers. Officers who secretly
converted Gerry Adams's car into a mobile recording studio,
complete with electronic tracing gear, as part of their own,
apparently private, war on the IRA, regardless of political
sensitivities.

These were the clearest steps on a zig-zag path towards an
end (for the time being) of the Irish War:

1999

10 March: Deadline set for devolving powers to NI set by
UK Prime Minister Tony Blair passes without result.
Although Blair asserts on 2 June that the IRA has made a
'seismic shift' in its position – implying a readiness to end
the armed struggle – there is continued political stalemate as
the IRA retains its arsenal and refuses to accept that it is
bound by the Good Friday Belfast Agreement of 1998. Sinn
Fein claims that its electoral support entitles it to places in
the reformed, devolved government of NI. Unionists insist
on linking paramilitary disarmament to Sinn Fein's place in
government.

Retired Senator George Mitchell summoned back from the United States to break the deadlock and revive an expiring peace process as chairman of all-party talks. By October he admits that the process is in trouble.

London's Minister for NI, Dr Mo Mowlam, declares that the IRA ceasefire is intact, despite Republican gun-running operations from Florida and IRA murders of alleged informers. She resigns and is replaced by Peter Mandelson, a controversial ex-television producer valued by Prime Minister Blair for his ability to influence editors, a practice known as 'spin doctoring.'

Loyalist terrorists continue to make sectarian pipe-bomb attacks on Catholics. All paramilitaries are free to conduct punishment beatings, shootings and enforced exile upon their own communities.

In the autumn, as the British continue to release imprisoned terrorists, an official British team headed by ex-Hong Kong governor Christ Patten recommends 175 reforms for the RUC including a manpower cut from 13,500 to 7,500. In October, the Chief Constable Sir Ronnie Flanagan threatens to resign if police strength is cut before the terrorist threat is reduced.

27 November: In a major political breakthrough the Unionists abandon their 'No Guns/No Government' ultimatum as the Ulster Unionist Council votes to transfer power from London to a Northern Ireland executive, with two out of ten seats going to Sinn Fein. The IRA – not a party to the Belfast Good Friday Agreement – retains its weapons for the time being but agrees to discuss decommissioning with a supervisory team led by Canadian General John de Chastelain. Unionist leader David Trimble puts his own time-bomb under the deal: he will quit if the IRA does not disarm by February 2000.

2 December: UK and Irish governments sign joint treaty creating new cross-border institutions. Dublin waives its claim to the Six Counties. London passes control of Northern Ireland to a local power-sharing executive including ex-IRA chieftain Martin McGuinness and Sinn Fein leader Gerry Adams. Direct rule from London ends. The IRA appoints its intermediary – believed to be Padraic Wilson, a Maze prisoner – to talk to General John de Chastelain. His arms decommissioning body now seeks an audit of the IRA arsenal.

12 December: The IRA informally reveals that it plans to begin decommissioning on 16 January 2000, following a first

meeting with de Chastelain. London's new Northern Ireland Secretary, Peter Mandelson, prepares to announce major British troop withdrawals from Ulster 'in the mid to long term.' Suddenly, peace appears to be an emerging reality, rather than a feeble aspiration. For now, an exhausted IRA has had to abandon its core aim – reunification of Ireland by force – and Dublin has dropped its provocative claim to the territory of a separate state of Northern Ireland. Victims of the war, including IRA survivors, ask themselves and their neighbours what the sacrifices were for. But everyone is pleased that peace has returned to Ireland.

2000   8 January: DPP decides not to prosecute RUC officers alleged to have threatened Rosemary Nelson.

GLOSSARY

Aintree: A steeplechase course near Liverpool, UK; a spiritual home for many Irish jockeys and horses, targeted for disruption by the IRA as part of a 'chaos strategy.'

AMD: IRA shorthand for 'anti-metal detector.'

ANFO: An IRA home-made explosive combining ammonium nitrate with fuel oil.

'Annie': An IRA home-made explosive combining nitrobenzine and ammonium nitrate; used as the explosive charge with some IRA mortars.

Apprentice Boys of Derry: A 'Loyal Order,' similar to the Orange Order (see below), commemorating the action of thirteen apprentice boys who slammed shut the gates of Derry in the face of King James II's soldiers, 1689. The Apprentice Boys celebrate the event with a march on 12 August each year around the elevated walls that overlook Catholic Bogside.

ASU: Active Service Unit. An IRA cell engaged in violence.

'B' Squadron: One of four company-sized elements of the Special Air Service Regiment, with an especially controversial record in the war against Republican terrorists.

Bayeux Tapestry: A famous work of art, depicting French/Norman conquest of England, 1066.

Beaver: A light fixed-wing aircraft used by the Army's aviators, the Army Air Corps.

Black-and-Tans: A temporary militia licensed to kill in the war of Irish Independence, 1919–21.

Black Watch: British/Scottish infantry regiment usually composed of Protestants.

Bogside: A Catholic and Republican-dominated sector of Derry; flaunted its rejection of Northern Ireland through its famous mural proclaiming 'Free Derry' in the sixties; scene of the Bloody Sunday massacre, 30 January 1972.

Bombard: British designation for a simple IRA anti-armour missile and launcher.

Bombardier: A corporal in the British Royal Regiment of Artillery.

By-election: An election in a single British constituency to replace a dead or retired parliamentary representative.

Cabinet, the: Inner circle of senior government ministers.

Glossary

CAC: Continuity Army Council. Fundamentalist Republican armed group opposed to any solution of the Irish problem other than the enforced withdrawal of Britain from the Six Counties of Northern Ireland.

Calmucks (also Kalmucks): Mongolian migrants to Russia and China.

Carlingford Lough: A long inlet on the northeast coast of Northern Ireland, where sovereignty is shared between the Province and the Republic; a haunt of smugglers and British marines engaged in maritime stop-and-search operations.

Cashier (verb): Military punishment imposed upon disgraced officers, requiring dismissal and exclusion from further public service.

CID: Criminal Investigation Department. The professional detective service in every British police force.

Citizens' Defence Committees: Local vigilante groups operating in sectarian ghettoes, usually controlled by paramilitaries.

Clann na Gael: US Irish Republican movement; the American wing of the original Fenian Brotherhood, founded in 1858. In 1926 it formally pledged to give 'undivided support, physically, morally and financially to Oglaigh na hEireann (Irish Volunteers) to secure by force of arms the absolute independence of Ireland.'

Coldstream Guards: Heavy infantry regiment of British army.

Continent, the: Mainland Europe, as distinct from the British Isles.

Co-op Mix: An IRA home-made explosive combining sodium chlorate and nitrobenzine.

COPs: Close Observation Platoons. Raised in 1977 as an element of uniformed battalions in Northern Ireland to conduct static, prolonged surveillance of terrorist suspects.

Coroner: Legal officer appointed to enquire into sudden deaths; powers of investigation into reasons beyond autopsy evidence stringently limited in Northern Ireland.

Cossacks: Cavalry soldiers from southeast Russia.

Counter-Gangs: Security force 'SWAT' teams disguised as pseudo-terrorists. Used by the British in Palestine, 1946–48, and Kenya, 1954.

CRA (or NICRA): Northern Ireland Civil Rights Association. A broad-based political campaign seeking equal rights in the context of Northern Ireland as part of the UK,with equal rights for Catholics; used as a stalking horse by the IRA as part of its campaign to reunify Ireland under its control.

CRIS: Crime Report Information System. A police computer programme on which the London Metropolitan police spent £20 million.

Cromwell, Oliver: The first and only English 'President'; a Puritan general who decapitated a king and declared himself Lord Protector. Massacred Irish garrisons in 1649. His name is a synonym for British overkill in Ireland.

CS: Corson and Stoughton. Name of a riot control agent, technically a form of 'smoke,' named for the scientists who first synthesised it in 1928; often described as 'CS Gas.'

Cumann na mBan: Women's IRA; used as fire-bombers, bomb-makers, intelligence officers and couriers.

Curragh Mutiny, the: A threat by senior British officers in 1914 to disobey the London government rather than deter a Protestant uprising.

CWIED: Command Wire Improvised Explosive Device.

DAAG: Direct Action Against Drugs. An IRA front organisation, suppressing selected areas of drug dealing by assassination. Within limits it is effective in achieving this aim, confirming that a solution can be worse than the problem it seeks to address. Possibly used to 'blood' IRA Volunteers when the IRA was publicly on ceasefire.

Dail, the: The Dublin parliament governing the 26-county Republic of Ireland.

Defenders: Irish Roman Catholic society formed at the end of the 18th century in opposition to the Peep-o'-Day Boys and the Orange Order.

Derry (aka Londonderry or 'Stroke City'): An ancient port near Donegal, scene of a successful resistance operation by Protestants when besieged by the Army of King James II in 1689. The name 'Derry' derives from the original Gaelic name and is favoured by Catholics. The official name is 'Londonderry.'

Derry Fusiliers (aka Derry Young Hooligans or DYH): Youths and girls operating as apparently spontaneous street protesters to bombard security forces with rocks and petrol bombs; sometimes an orchestrated, Republican 'rent-a-mob.'

'Dets' (Detachments): see 14 Intelligence Company.

Devon & Dorset Regiment: An English county infantry regiment of the British army.

Dhofar: A mountainous province of Oman, Britain's client state in the Gulf; scene of a colonial war from 1970–76.

DNA: Deoxyribonucleic acid. Complex molecules embodying coded instructions for hereditary characteristics; genetic 'fingerprints.'

Downing Street: Street off Whitehall, London; site of Prime Minister's office; political symbol similar to White House.

E4A: Undercover surveillance unit of the RUC; the police equivalent of the Army's 14 Intelligence Company.

Escort: A small, cheap automobile.

Fabianism: Political attrition; a moderate Socialist philosophy believing in 'the inevitability of gradualness.'

FAIT: Families Against Intimidation & Terror. A non-sectarian grassroots movement opposing the violence of paramilitary groups upon people of the same religious persuasion.

Falls Road: Catholic heartland of Belfast and a Republican stronghold. Subjected to British military curfew, 3–5 July 1970.

FCA: Forsa Consanta Aitiuil. Irish National Guard.

Fenian: Originally a member of the secret society, the Fenian Brotherhood, a revolutionary movement raised in the 19th century to fight British occupation of Ireland; latterly a term of abuse directed at Catholics by Loyalists.

Fianna: Mythical warriors led by Finn MacCumhail; collective name for some Republican groups, such as the Fianna na hEireann, the IRA youth wing.

4 Field Survey Troop: Now-defunct cover name for Special Forces surveillance/hit team in Northern Ireland. Others included MRF and NITAT.

FRU, the: Force Research Unit or Field Reconnaissance Unit. An agent-handling team of the British army drawn from the Intelligence Corps, running its own network of informers inside terrorist groups, often in competition with the RUC Special Branch. Allegedly it collaborated with Loyalist murder gangs.

G-2 (properly, GSO-2): British General Staff Officer Grade II. Often – as G-2 (Int) – a military intelligence officer with the rank of major.

'G' Squadron: A company-sized element of the Special Air Service Regiment, largely recruited from volunteers serving in the heavy infantry Guards regiments.

Gaeltacht: An area of Ireland dedicated to native Irish culture including the language; a centre for Irish studies.

Garda: A member of Garda Siochana.

Garda Siochana (plural, Gardai): National police force of the Irish Republic.

GCHQ: General Communications Headquarters. The British equivalent of the National Security Agency, with which it works closely.

GOC: General Officer Commanding. Senior military rank, usually a three-star officer.

Gordon Highlanders: A British/Scottish infantry regiment.

GPS: Global Positioning (Satellite) System. A modern navigational aid, adapted experimentally by the IRA as a guidance system for unmanned vehicle bombs.

[Royal] Green Jackets: British infantry regiment, originally raised to fight against Americans during the War of Independence. So called because its men preferred to wear green, blending with the foliage, rather than traditional redcoats. First British troops to be armed with rifles.

Guardian, the: Left of centre UK broadsheet newspaper.

Harrow: A small town near London; a private school for privileged, rich children.

HEAT: High Energy Anti-Tank. A missile warhead. The IRA's own version was based on drawings in technical, military manuals and developed by trial and error.

HME: Home-Made Explosives. The Irish have a range of HME recipes, some-times boosted by commercial or military plastic high explosives such as Semtex.

HOLMES: Home Office Large Major Enquiry System. A Home Office com-puter programme to co-ordinate data on organised crime.

Home Counties: Rural/suburban local authorities nearest to London.

Home Secretary/Home Office: Minister/Ministry of the Interior.

IED: Improvised Explosive Device. British term for all home-made bombs.

INLA: Irish National Liberation Army. Military wing of the Irish Republican Socialist Party, active since 1975, specialising in political assassinations and pub bombings.

14 Intelligence Company (aka '14 Company,' the 'Detachments' or the 'Dets'): A special intelligence-gathering team, armed but dressed in civilian clothes, recruited from men and women already serving in more orthodox UK military units for close reconnaissance missions. One of many special, temporary teams created by the British for the Irish War. All its members are volunteers.

Intelligence Corps (aka the 'Green Slime' from their green berets): Military intelligence specialists of the British regular army.

IPG: IRA Improvised Projected Grenade.

IRA: Irish Republican Army. A guerrilla movement claiming to inherit the man-tle of legitimate government over the whole of Ireland from the revolutionary Proclamation of 1916.

IRB: Irish Republican Brotherhood. Predecessor to IRA, founded in 1858.

Irish Special Branch: Detective force, part of national police service of the Irish Republic, the Garda Siochana, countering political crime.

Islander: A light, twin-engine aircraft used for many purposes including police surveillance.

Jacobins: French revolutionaries of the 18th-century Terror.

Kenya/Mau Mau Campaign: A colonial war, 1954, in which novel methods of counter-insurgency were tested by the British soldier Frank Kitson and later recycled in Northern Ireland. These included security force teams disguised as terrorists and known as 'pseudo-gangs.'

King's Own Scottish Borderers: British light infantry regiment drawn from the Scottish Lowlands, notably the city of Glasgow; traditionally wears 'trews' (tartan trousers) rather than the Highlanders' kilt.

Law Lords: Upper House of Parliament sitting as a Supreme Court.

Lilywhites: Terrorists with no criminal record.

Long Range Desert Group: British reconnaissance team set up during the Western Desert campaigns of World War II, to work behind enemy lines.

Lord Chancellor: Senior British legal officer, similar to head of the Supreme Court.

Loyalists: Believers in a mystical union with the British monarchy; ready to shoot to defend their notion of loyalism. Loyalist extremists shade into Protestant death squads that assassinate Republicans.

Luton: Industrial centre north of London with large expatriate Irish population.

Maginot Line: An elaborate fixed, fortified defence line built by France in the 1930s; synonym for the futility of static defence.

Marseillaise: French national anthem; revolutionary song of the First Republic.

Maze Prison: A prison at Long Kesh, near Lisburn for political detainees and convicted terrorists.

MBE: Member of the Order of the British Empire. A decoration for merit awarded to worthy sherpas of British society.

Mess (Officers' or Senior NCOs'): The living quarters of military personnel above the basic rank of enlisted men.

MI5: Military Intelligence, Department 5 (aka 'Box 500,' after its postbox address in London). UK counter-intelligence agency whose officers do not have police powers but often act as if they do.

MI6: see SIS.

MLA: Martial Law Area. So designated by the British during the Irish War of Independence, 1919–21.

MP: Member of Parliament. In practice an elected member of the Lower House in the UK.

MRF: Mobile Reconnaissance Force. An undercover British counter-insurgency team, recruited largely from the Paras, run during the early 1970s. It ran its own agents and engaged in a private war against Republicans. Disbanded after its assassination attempts became known.

National grid: The electricity supply system linking power stations with consumers; a strategic target among IRA terrorists in England and by NATO in Serb-occupied Kosovo.

NCIS: National Criminal Intelligence Service. Police intelligence-collation team.

NCO: Non-commissioned officer (e.g., Sergeant).

Nimrod: A maritime reconnaissance spy plane similar to the P3 Orion, used by the RAF to track illegal Irish arms cargoes.

NITAT: Northern Ireland Training Team. A unit training soldiers in England and Germany to prepare them for service in NI; also used as a cover name by Special Forces working in the Province.

Northern Ireland Secretary: London's Ruler in Northern Ireland after Stormont was abolished in favour of direct rule in 1972.

OBE: Officer of the Order of the British Empire. A decoration for merit awarded to the upper classes of British society.

Oglaigh na hEireann (singular, Oglach): IRA Volunteers.

OP: Observation Post (military).

Orange Order (aka Loyal Orange Institution): A Protestant cult, embodying closed rituals and public parades; the largest Protestant organisation in Northern Ireland with around 100,000 active members; founded in 1795, it still wields great political influence behind the scenes.

Parachute Regiment (aka the 'Red Devils' or 'Paras'): Airborne infantry, similar to 82nd Airborne.

Patten Enquiry: Commission appointed by UK government to recommend reforms of the RUC, chaired by Chris Patten, former Governor of Hong Kong.

PD: People's Democracy. Now extinct political grouping of various left-wing factions; worked with IRA in 1969 to destabilise Northern Ireland.

Pearse, Patrick (1879–1916): Commander of the 1916 Dublin Uprising; president of the Provisional government; executed by the British and thus made a martyr in Irish eyes. A zealot who believed in the purifying power of blood sacrifice.

Petroleuses: Female fire bombers. The term refers to the alleged arsonists of the Paris Commune in 1871.

PFLP: Popular Front for the Liberation of Palestine. A left-wing Palestinian guerrilla/terrorist group.

PIRA: Provisional IRA. A faction of the IRA believing in the physical force tradition as the prime means to reunify Ireland under its control; the main mechanism for armed resistance to the British and Scots/Irish presence in Northern Ireland. Main player in the renewed Irish War.

Positive Vetting: A stringent process of security checks imposed on individuals given access to classified material.

PRIG: Projected Recoilless Improvised Grenade. The IRA's version of the RPG-7 rocket propelled grenade.

Province, the: A synonym for the state of Northern Ireland.

PTA: Prevention of Terrorism (Temporary Provisions) Act. A law enabling the British authorities to hold a suspect for up to seven days without reference to habeas corpus.

PVCP: Permanent Vehicle Check Point. A British Army control point.

Q & A Brief: Question and Answer Brief. A guidance document issued to military public affairs officers.

'Q' Cars: Military vehicles, fitted with special equipment, camouflaged as normal civilian automobiles.

QC: Queen's Counsel. A senior barrister-at-law.

RAF: Royal Air Force. UK equivalent of USAF.

RC: Radio Controlled bomb.

Red Hand: Traditional Ulster symbol sometimes misused by Loyalist terrorists as a nom-de-guerre, e.g., 'Red Hand Defenders,' the group that claimed responsibility for the murder of the civil rights lawyer Rosemary Nelson on 15 March 1999.

Rhodesia: Former British colony in southern Africa; now Zimbabwe: a resort of many British special forces personnel after service in Northern Ireland.

RIC: Royal Irish Constabulary. One of two civilian police services in Ireland before Partition, 1921.

Royal Irish Rangers: British army infantry regiment recruiting from both religious factions in Ireland.

Royal Scots: British infantry regiment composed of Scots.

RPG-7: Rocket Propelled Grenade Mark VII. Soviet-designed missile launcher, widely exported.

RUC: Royal Ulster Constabulary. A largely Protestant police service created in Northern Ireland in 1922 as part of the Partition process. Its equipment included armoured cars and .3 caliber machine-guns. Since 1976, the controlling counter-terrorist agency in Northern Ireland. UK government favours its replacement by a new Northern Ireland Police service.

RUC Special Branch: A detective force, the best-informed counter-intelligence team in Northern Ireland. Distrust between UK Army intelligence agencies and RUC Special Branch is sometimes mutual.

RUSI: Royal United Services Institute for Defence Studies. A learned institute in London.

Sandhurst: Home of the Royal Military Academy, near London; the military college where British officer cadets are trained.

SAS: Special Air Service Regiment. An arm of UK special forces, whose operations are often clandestine and sometimes deniable. Some SAS soldiers act as the executive arm of British Intelligence agencies, notably the Secret Intelligence Service, aka MI6 (see above).

Semtex: Czech-manufactured, odourless plastic high explosive.

SF: Ambiguous initials signifying either Security Forces or Sinn Fein, depending upon the context.

Sherwood Foresters: A British county regiment drawing volunteers from the county of Nottinghamshire.

Shropshire: A rural county in England.

Shropshire Light Infantry: A British regiment drawing volunteers from that county.

Sinn Fein ('Ourselves Alone'): The oldest Irish Republican party, founded in 1906.

Sinn Fein Conjuror's Outfit: Bomb-making equipment.

SIS: Secret Intelligence Service (aka MI6 – Military Intelligence 6; 'Box 850' after its post office box address in London; 'Six'; 'the Friends'): Britain's overseas espionage service, whose members are given Foreign Office cover; often recruited from British armed services including Special Forces.

Six Counties, the: A synonym for the state of Northern Ireland, aka the Province, but not for historic Ulster, which comprises nine counties.

Slotted: UK Special Forces jargon for 'killed.'

SMIU: Special Military Intelligence Unit, Northern Ireland. Temporary, ad hoc formations run by the Intelligence Corps to work in liaison with the Royal Ulster Constabulary.

Socialist Worker: A newspaper published among Trotskyite Socialists in Britain. Its worker-control gospel appealed to some Republicans.

SOE: Special Operations Executive. A British guerrilla force running indigenous resistance operations in occupied Europe and Asia during World War II.

Special Branch, the (founded 1883 as the Irish Special Branch): An arm of the London Metropolitan Police, countering espionage, subversion and terrorism in conjunction with MI5. Not the same as the RUC Special Branch or the contemporary Irish Special Branch.

Special Powers Act: Civil Authorities (Special Powers) Act (Northern Ireland), 1922. This act permitted indefinite internment without trial and the suspension of basic liberties from habeas corpus to press freedom; a cornerstone of Unionist rule.

Sticky (or Stickie): Official IRA, the Marxist-led IRA that sought a grassroots political route to Irish reunification, using provocation and destabilisation ('agitprop' tactics) successfully, only to lose out to the traditionalist Provisional IRA after the street battles of 1969. Known as 'Stickies' because of their custom of sticking Easter lilies on their coats during the annual commemoration of the 1916 Dublin Rising.

Stormont: Originally the Protestant-dominated parliament building (and Unionist Government headquarters) outside Belfast, from which Northern Ireland was ruled from 1922 until 1972 when London imposed direct rule through a single Minister. Still the seat of government locally.

Sultan's Special Force: An elite unit of the army of Oman, invariably commanded by a British SAS officer and run with the assistance of other British officers.

Supergrass: An informer for the authorities against paramilitaries. As used in Northern Ireland, part of a process of virtual justice, abandoned when convictions failed on appeal.

Taig: A term of abuse used by Loyalists to describe Catholics. Derived from 'teague,' or a Gaelic proper name, Tadhg (Thady).

Tam-o'-Shanter: Distinctive Scottish tartan bonnet; in some contexts, a Protestant symbol.

Territorials: UK National Guard.

Thatcher, Lady (formerly Margaret, Mrs, aka 'the Iron Lady'): British Prime Minister, 1979–90, whose uncompromising attitude to security in Northern Ireland inflamed the conflict, notably during the IRA hunger strikes.

Tommy: British equivalent of a GI.

Tory Party (aka Conservative Party): The right-wing political party, roughly equivalent to the Republican Party, traditionally an ally of the Unionist Party.

TPU: Timer/power units. Delay mechanisms attached to detonators on terrorist bombs.

UDA: Ulster Defence Association. Largest Protestant paramilitary organisation, started in 1971 to co-ordinate Loyalist vigilante groups.

UDR: Ulster Defence Regiment. A part-time, voluntary reserve, similar to National Guard, set up in 1970 to replace the Ulster Special Constabulary (see below). This in turn was penetrated by Loyalist extremists, some of whom waged their private war against Republicans using uniforms, guns and intelligence obtained from their links with the rest of the British army. The UDR was merged with a regular line regiment, the Royal Irish Rangers, in 1991.

UFF: Ulster Freedom Fighters. Illegal Loyalist terror group, responsible for many political and sectarian assassinations.

Ulster Special Constabulary (aka 'B Specials'): A part-time, voluntary, armed police militia dominated by Loyalist extremists and disbanded in 1970. Many ex-members joined the Ulster Defence Regiment.

Unionist Party: With its fellow-Protestant parties, the traditional ruling party in the Stormont government of Northern Ireland; latterly split into several factions.

UVF: Ulster Volunteer Force. Loyalist terror group sometimes described as the 'secret Protestant Army.'

Western Approaches: The Atlantic approaches to the Irish coast, long regarded as of great strategic value.

Whitehall: A street in central London; also the administrative centre of UK government.

Yellow Card: Official instructions to British soldiers about when it is in order to shoot; a document of dubious legal value.

Yomping: British military slang for a fast, forced march across rough country.

ZANU: Zimbabwe African National Union. A nationalist movement opposed to white rule in the former Rhodesia; some leaders targeted for assassination by British veterans of Northern Ireland.

BIBLIOGRAPHY

Sources consulted and quoted from include the following:

PART I: THE GREAT DECEPTION

BOOKS

Bell, J. Bowyer, *The Irish Troubles – A Generation of Violence, 1967–1992* (Dublin: Gill and Macmillan, 1993).

Boyd, Andrew, *Holy War in Belfast* (Tralee, Co. Kerry: Anvil Books, 1970).

Devlin, Bernadette, *The Price of My Soul* (Deutsch, Pan, 1969).

Foot, Paul, *Who Framed Colin Wallace?* (London: Pan Books, 1990).

Geldard, Ian and Keith Craig, *IRA, INLA: Foreign Support and International Connections* (London: Institute for the Study of Terrorism, 1988).

Insight (*Sunday Times*), *Ulster* (London: Times Newspapers, 1972).

Kee, Robert, *The Green Flag: A History of Irish Nationalism* (London: Weidenfeld and Nicolson, 1972).

McCana, Proinsias, *Celtic Mythology* (London: Hamlyn, 1970).

Styles, Lieut-Col. George, GC, *Bombs Have No Pity: My War Against Terrorism* (London: William Luscombe, 1975).

OFFICIAL REPORTS

Cameron, the Hon. Lord, DSC, Prof. John Biggart, CBE and James Joseph Campbell, *Disturbances in Northern Ireland: Report of the Commission appointed by the Governor of Northern Ireland*, Cmd 532 (Belfast: HMSO, September 1969).

Compton, Sir Edmund, GCB, KBE, Edgar S. Fay, QC and Dr Ronald Gibson, CBE, *Report of the Enquiry into Allegations Against the Security Forces of Physical Brutality in Northern Ireland Arising out of Events on the 9th August, 1971*, Cmd 4823 (London: HMSO, 1971).

Widgery, The Rt Hon. Lord, OBE, TD, *Report of the Tribunal Appointed to Enquire into the Events of Sunday, 30 January 1972, which Led to Loss of Life in Connection with the Procession in Londonderry on that Day* (London: HMSO, 1972).

Wilson, Harold, *House of Commons Official Report, 13 May 1972* (London: HMSO, 1972).

ARTICLES

Goulding, Cathal, 'The New Strategy of the IRA' (interview with Jack Dowling in *This Week* and reprinted in), *New Left Review*, November–December 1970.

Greig, Ian, 'Arms and Arms Running', *Intersec Magazine*, June 1994.

Halliday, Fred, '7 *Days* Talks to Cathal Goulding – Official IRA Chief of Staff', 7 *Days*, 1 March 1972.

Hamden, Toby, 'Republican Grandfather takes on the Big Man', the *Daily Telegraph*, 24 June 1998.

Holland, Mary, 'IRA Man Joe Cahill Fights his First Election at 78. Against Ian Paisley. A bit cheeky?' the *Observer*, 21 June 1998.

Kennedy-Pipe, Caroline and Colin McInness, 'The British Army in Northern Ireland 1969–1972: From Policing to Counter-terror', *Journal of Strategic Studies*, Vol. 20, no. 2, June 1997.

McCann, Eamonn, 'After 5 October 1968', *International Socialism*, April–June 1972.

Myers, Kevin, 'I Admit I was Wrong', the *Sunday Telegraph*, 12 April 1998.

O'Doherty, Malachi, 'Revealed: Priest who was Ulster Peace Link Man', the *Observer*, 28 June 1998.

—— 'Who Stopped the Killing? The Father of the Peace', the *Observer*, 28 June 1998.

Rosselli, Mark, 'Ulster Foes Exposed on Secret Path to Peace', the *Observer*, 5 December 1993.

Trench, Richard, 'Talking to the Provisional Leaders', 7 *Days*, 12 January 1972.

—— 'Belfast': The NICRA Conference', 7 *Days*, 16 February 1972.

Trench, Richard, et al., 'Report from Ireland', 7 *Days*, 12 January 1972.

OTHER SOURCES

Dillon, Martin, *The Long War: The Last Colony*, Channel 4 documentary, 4 July 1994.

PART II: THE BRITISH SOFT-WAR MACHINE

BOOKS

Bell, J. Bowyer, *The Irish Troubles – A Generation of Violence, 1967–1992* (Dublin: Gill and Macmillan, 1993).

Fitzgerald, Garret, *All in a Life: an Autobiography* (London: Macmillan, 1991).

Flackes, W. D., *Northern Ireland: a Political Directory 1968–1983* (London: Ariel Books, BBC, 1983).

Geraghty, Tony, *The Bullet-Catchers: Bodyguards and the World of Close Protection* (London: Grafton, 1988).

────── *Who Dares Wins: The Special Air Service, 1950 to the Gulf War* (London: Warner Books, 1993).

Insight (*Sunday Times*), *Ulster* (London: Times Newspapers, 1972).

Kelley, Kevin, *The Longest War: Northern Ireland and the IRA* (Dingle, Co. Kerry: Brandon, 1982).

Mullan, Don and Others, *Eyewitness Bloody Sunday: The Truth* (Dublin: Wolfhound Press, 1997).

Murray, Raymond, *The SAS in Ireland* (Cork: Mercier Press, 1990).

Reed, Edwin Harold, *A Short Guide to the Present Campaign in Northern Ireland*, unpublished MS (1972).

Rennie, James, *The Operators: On the Streets with 14 Company* (London: Century, 1996).

Urban, Mark, *Big Boys' Rules: The SAS and the Secret Struggle against the IRA* (London: Faber and Faber, 1992).

OFFICIAL REPORTS

Gardiner, Lord, *Report of the Committee of Privy Counsellors appointed to consider authorised procedures for the interrogation of persons suspected of terrorism: Minority report*, Cmd 4901 (London: HMSO, March 1972).

Keith of Kinkel, Lord, Lord Browne-Wilkinson, Lord Slynn of Hadley, Lord Lloyd of Berwick and Lord Nicholls of Birkenhead, *R. v Clegg (1995)* (1 All ER 34).

ARTICLES

Anon., 'Protect Catholics Call by Dublin', *The Times*, 28 July 1970.

Anon., 'Journalist Cleared of Belfast Charge', *The Times*, 28 July 1970.

Anon., 'GOC "Had Power to Impose Curfew in Belfast"', *The Times*, 9 September 1970.

Anon., 'Stalker Affair Inquests Abandoned', *Independent*, 9 September 1994.

────── 'IRA Intercepts British Intelligence Documents: British Spies Operating in 26 Counties, *Republican News/Daily Telegraph*, January 1998.

Cohen, Nick, 'Former Police Chief Blasts "Macho" Force', *Independent on Sunday*, 21 April 1996.

Davies, Caroline, 'IRA's Final Insult to Grieving Family', *Daily Telegraph*, 29 February 1996.

Halliday, Fred, 'Oman: British Lies Hide Colonial War', *7 Days*, 12 January 1972.

Kelsey, Tim, 'MI5 Says 80% of Terror Plots Foiled', *Independent*, 13 June 1994.

Kirby, Terry, 'Terrorists Jailed for Bomb Campaign Plot – MI5 agent in hiding after infiltrating, then testifying against Republican Group', *Independent*, 17 December 1993.

Mackinnon, Ian, 'IRA Bomb Plot Leader is Jailed for 25 Years', *Independent*, 9 November 1994.

McKittrick, David, 'British Spies in Ireland', *Irish Times*, 22 April 1980.
——— 'Prison Warder Given Life for Role in IRA Murder', *Independent*, 22 June 1990.
——— 'Priest Puts Faith in Justice to Overcome Ulster's Troubles', *Independent*, 8 August 1991.
——— 'Military Agent Who was "Out in the Cold"', *Independent*, 30 January 1992.
——— 'The Nelson Case Exposed a Legal Nonsense at the Heart of the Informer System: thin dividing line in secret world of Army agents, *Independent*, 4 February 1992.
——— 'Army "Let Ulster Loyalists Kill 5"', *Independent*, 9 June 1992.
——— 'Inquiry Call over Killing of Solicitor', *Independent*, 19 February 1993.
——— 'Marines Verdict Attacked by MPs and Rights Groups', *Independent*, 24 December 1993.
——— 'Legal Hurdles Reduce Chances of Conviction', *Independent*, 24 December 1993.
——— '25 Years on, Ghosts Return to Challenge the Official Truths about Bloody Sunday', *Independent*, 18 January 1997.
——— 'Bloody Sunday Pledge from Mowlam', *Independent*, 20 March 1997.
Macleod, Scott and Others, 'From Here to Eternity', *Time Magazine*, 5 September 1988.
Magee, Patrick, 'Do They Mean Us? Patrick Magee, aka the Brighton Bomber, knows a thing or two about the Troubles. So he can hardly believe what he sees in the films and books that reach him in the Maze prison', *Guardian*, 3 September 1997.
Murdoch, Alan, 'Para Tells of Bloody Sunday "Kills"', *Independent*, 17 March 1997.
——— 'Blair Handed New Bloody Sunday File', *Independent*, 25 June 1997.
Newsinger, John, 'From Counter Insurgency to Internal Security – Northern Ireland 1969–1992', *Small Wars & Insurgencies*, Spring 1995 (London: Frank Cass).
O'Brien, Conor Cruise, 'Can the Army Ever Leave?', *The Times*, 10 August 1989.
Randall, Colin, 'Bullet Tests "Show Clegg was Wrongly Convicted"', *Daily Telegraph*, 18 November 1997.
Rose, David and Eamonn Mallie, 'Computer Chaos Hampers War on IRA', *Observer*, 6 December 1992.
Savill, Richard, 'Ulster Shoot-to-kill Inquests Closed as Subpoena Fails', *Daily Telegraph*, 9 September 1994.
Scott-Barrett, Lieutenant-General Sir David, 'Time to Free the Two Scots Guards', *Daily Telegraph*, 25 February 1997, and *Sunday Telegraph*, 2 March 1997.
Toolis, Kevin, 'IRA Kidnap Foiled by Mother's Super-bleep', *Mail on Sunday*, 25 June 1989.

Ward, Stephen, ' "Proud" IRA Bombers Jailed for 30 Years', *Independent*, 14 May 1994.

Ware, John, David McKittrick and Geoffrey Seed, 'Fear "Junkie" Who Marked Men for Death', *Independent*, 9 June 1992.

Winchester, Simon, 'How the SAS Moved in on the Terrorists', *Guardian*, 1976.

OTHER SOURCES

Alderson, John, Correspondence with the author, 9 September 1997.

Carver, Field Marshal Lord, GCB, CBE, DSO, MC, Letter to the author, 1 August 1996.

Hailsham, Lord, KG, CH, FRS, Letter to the author, 5 March 1998.

Mates, Colonel Michael, MP, Interview with the author, 4 December 1996.

O'Callaghan, Sean, *Address to the Crime Writers' Association*, London, 1997.

Taylor, Peter, *Provos*, BBC 1 documentary, 7 October 1997.

PART III: THE IRISH HARD-WAR MACHINE

BOOKS

Archer, Dennis R. R. et al., *Jane's Infantry Weapons, 1978* (London: Macdonald and Jane's, 1978).

Bell, J. Bowyer, *The Irish Troubles – A Generation of Violence, 1967–1992* (Dublin: Gill and Macmillan, 1993).

Boyd, Andrew, *Holy War in Belfast* (Tralee, Co. Kerry: Anvil Books, 1970).

Coogan, Tim Pat, *The Troubles – Ireland's Ordeal, 1966–95 and the Search for Peace* (London: Hutchinson, 1995).

Geldard, Ian and Keith Craig, *IRA, INLA: Foreign Support and International Connections* (London: Institute for the Study of Terrorism, 1988).

Greig, Ian, *Op. Cit.*

Kelley, Kevin, *The Longest War: Northern Ireland and the IRA* (Dingle, Co. Kerry: Brandon, 1982).

McCana, Proinsias, *Celtic Mythology* (London: Hamlyn, 1970).

MacIntyre, Tom, *Through the Bridewell Gate: A Diary of the Dublin Arms Trial* (London: Faber and Faber, 1971).

Meiring, Johan, *Major André Dennison MLM BCR, 24 July 1935–3 June 1979*, in J. R. T. Wood, *The War Diaries of André Dennison* (Gibraltar: Ashanti, 1989).

Reed, Edwin Harold, *A Short Guide to the Present Campaign in Northern Ireland*, unpublished MS (1972).

Salmon, Trevor, *Unneutral Ireland: An Ambivalent and Unique Security Policy* (Oxford: Clarendon Press, 1989), by permission of Oxford University Press.

Bibliography

OFFICIAL REPORTS

Anon., *Statement on Defence Estimates, 1989* (London: HMSO, 1989).

ARTICLES

Anon., 'Loyalists Try to Justify Killing', *Sunday Telegraph*, 26 May 1991.
—— 'Sinn Fein "Will Never Surrender"', *Observer*, 23 February 1992.
—— 'Intern IRA Godfathers', leading article, *Daily Express*, 26 April 1993.
—— 'Belfast Wedding Terror', *Observer*, 3 July 1994.
—— 'The War Process', *Sunday Telegraph*, 11 February 1996.
—— 'A Reward for the Bombers', *Independent on Sunday*, 3 March 1996.
Bevins, Anthony, '"IRA Has an Ethical Dimension"', *Observer*, 28 November 1993.
Bevins, Anthony and Dennis Staunton, 'MI5 "Foiled IRA Plot to Kill Adams"', *Observer*, 9 April 1995.
Bew, Paul, 'Will Loyalists Hold Their Fire?', *Independent*, 20 February 1996.
Boggan, Steve, David Connett, David McKittrick and Richard Brennan, 'IRA Attack Signals New Campaign', *Independent*, 11 March 1994.
Boyne, Sean, 'Uncovering the Irish Republican Army', *Jane's Intelligence Review*, August 1996.
Brown, Colin and Phil Reeves, 'Security Leak Puts Credibility of RUC and Army at Risk', *Independent*, 31 August 1989.
Brown, Colin, David McKittrick, David Connett, and Martin Whitefield, 'More "Spectaculars" to Follow Heathrow', report of Gerry Adams's remarks after Heathrow mortar attack, *Independent*, 11 March 1994.
Cicutti, Nick, 'Premiums to Rise after IRA Bomb Costs £400m', *Independent*, 13 July 1996.
Coone, Tim, 'Regrouping by Loyalists May Heighten Violence: the shadowy connections of the paramilitaries', *Financial Times*, 9 February 1992.
Coughlin, Con and Others, 'Murder of Innocents' issue, *Daily Mail*, 28 March 1993.
Cox, Michael, 'Bringing in the "International": the IRA ceasefire and the end of the Cold War', *International Affairs*, Vol. 73, no. 4, October 1997.
Daily Mail Reporters, 'London Blitzed' issue, *Daily Mail*, 26 April 1993.
Elliott, Valerie and David Wastell, 'Special Insurance Plan for Companies Facing IRA Blitz', *Sunday Telegraph*, 22 November 1992.
Esler, Gavin, 'Explosive Developments: the IRA's Bomb Technology' *The Listener*, 19 June 1986.
Farrell, Nicholas and Valerie Elliott, 'Terrorist Sleepers on Mainland Caught Security Chiefs Off Guard', *Sunday Telegraph*, 11 February 1996.
Hardy, James, 'Adams Says "Sorry" for Massacre at Enniskillen', *Sunday Telegraph*, 9 November 1997.

Henry, Ian, 'Speedboat Patrol to Combat IRA Threat', *Sunday Telegraph*, 12 May 1996.

Hornblower, Margot and Edward Curran, 'Tragic "Mistakes" by the IRA: A bungled bombing raises questions about the terrorists' tactics', *Time*, 8 August 1989.

Kelsey, Tim and Peter Koenig, 'Libya Will Not Arm IRA Again, Gaddafi Aide Says', *Independent*, 20 July 1994.

McDonald, Henry, 'Smuggled US Guns for IRA Truce Rebels: Seventies weapons supply line reopens as dissidents defy Adams and McGuinness', *Observer*, 16 November 1997.

McKinnon, Ian, '40 Injured as IRA Mortar Bombs Hit Shopping Area', *Independent*, 30 July 1994.

McKittrick, David, 'Dublin Admits Garda Leak to IRA', *Independent*, 18 April 1991.

—— 'Murder of Ulster Couple Fuels Fears over Future Targets', *Independent*, 8 September 1992.

—— 'Ulster Bill Dwarfed by £750m City Blast', *Independent*, 9 December 1992.

—— 'IRA Faces Blame for Beating Councillor', *Independent*, 26 March 1994.

Miles, Tim, 'No. 10 Bomber Tells IRA to End the Killing,' *Daily Express*, 21 June 1996.

Murdoch, Alan, 'The Game's Up, Charlie: for decades the Irish have been puzzled by the lifestyle of Charles Haughey, and now they're starting to learn the whole truth', *Independent on Sunday*, 13 July 1997.

—— 'Fresh Inquiry into Haughley's Finances', *Independent*, 29 August 1997.

Myers, Kevin, 'The Prime Minister and the Tycoon: how Haughey was finally disgraced', *Sunday Telegraph*, 13 July 1997.

—— 'On Tuesday Sinn Fein Abandoned the Bullet. On Thursday the IRA said it never would. Kevin Myers is not fooled by their supposed split – it is all part of their strategy', *Sunday Telegraph*, 14 September 1997.

Ogden, Christopher, 'Deadly Games: Britain's army and the IRA play tit for tat', *Time*, 8 August 1989.

O'Brien, Conor Cruise, 'Quit Now We're Ahead? No way', *Independent*, 7 January 1994.

Pithers, Malcolm, 'Tim Parry, Victim of IRA Bomb Blast, Dies after Ventilator is Switched off', *Independent*, 26 March 1993.

Reeves, Phil, 'Former MP Supports Maze Escaper', *Independent*, 6 October 1993.

Rose, Peter and Tony Halpin, 'Mortar Terror at Terminal 4', *Daily Mail*, 14 March 1994.

Seamark, Michael, 'Helicopter Hero Foils IRA Attack', *Daily Mail*, 21 March 1994.

Taylor, Peter, 'War and Peace' (interviews with Shane Paul O'Doherty and others), *The Listener*, 9 August 1989.

Wolmar, Christian and Stephen Ward, 'IRA Bombs Stock Exchange', *Independent*, 21 July 1990.

OTHER SOURCES

Taylor Peter, *Provos: The IRA and Sinn Fein*, BBC 1 documentary, 23 September 1997.

PART IV: A NATION ONCE AGAIN?

Seventeenth and Eighteenth Centuries

BOOKS

Collins, M.E., *Ireland, 1478–1610* (Dublin Educational Co. of Ireland, 1980).

Cullen, L.M., *The Emergence of Modern Ireland, 1600 to 1900* (London: Batsford, 1981).

Daugherty, William E. and Morris Janowitz, *A Psychological Warfare Casebook* (Baltimore, MD: Johns Hopkins Press, 1958).

Elliott, Marianne, *Wolfe Tone, Prophet of Irish Independence* (New Haven and London: Yale University Press, 1989).

Fitzpatrick, Brendan, *Seventeenth Century Ireland – The War of Religion*, New Gill History of Ireland (Dublin: Gill and Macmillan, 1988).

Hay, Edward, *History of the Insurrection of the County of Wexford AD 1798* (Dublin: John Stockdale, 1803).

Kee, Robert, *The Green Flag* (London: Weidenfeld and Nicolson, 1972).

Lecky, William Edward Hartpole, *History of Ireland in the XVIII Century* (London: Longmans, Green and Co., 1902).

Macaulay, Lord, *History of England* (London: Heron, 1967).

Musgrave, Sir Richard, *Memoirs of the Different Rebellions in Ireland* (Dublin: Milliken, and London: Stockdale, 1801).

Oman, Carola, *Sir John Moore* (London: Hodder and Stoughton, 1953).

Tillyard, Stella, *Citizen Lord: Edward Fitzgerald 1763–1798* (London: Chatto and Windus, 1997).

ARTICLES

Adamson, John, 'The High Society Terrorist', *Observer*, review of *Citizen Lord*, 1997.

Bartlett, Thomas, 'The Catholic Question in the Eighteenth Century', *History Ireland*, Spring 1993.

Canavan, Tony, 'Making a Hole in the Moon: the rescue of Princess Clementina', *History Ireland*, Winter 1993.

Gahan, Professor Daniel, 'The Military Strategy of the Wexford United Irishmen in 1798', *History Ireland*, Winter 1993.

Nineteenth Century

BOOKS

Allason, Rupert, *The Branch – A History of the Metropolitan Police Special Branch 1883–1983* (London: Secker and Warburg, 1983).

Bourke, Marcus, *John O'Leary: A Study in Irish Separatism* (Tralee, Co. Kerry: Anvil Books, 1967).

Cobban, Alfred, *A History of Modern France, Vol 2, 1799–1871* (London: Pelican, 1965).

Comerford, M., *A New History of Ireland – Ireland in the Union, II: 1870–1921*, edited by W. E. Vaughan (Oxford: Clarendon Press, 1996), by permission of Oxford University Press.

Gould, Robert W. and Michael J. Waldren, *London's Armed Police* (London: Arms and Armour Press, 1986).

Kee, Robert, *The Laurel and the Ivy (Charles Parnell)* (London: Penguin, 1994).

Keneally, Thomas, *The Great Shame – A Story of the Irish in the Old World and the New* (London: Chatto and Windus, 1998).

Lampson, Locker G., *A Consideration of the State of Ireland in the Nineteenth Century* (London: Constable, 1907).

Longford, Elizabeth, *Queen Victoria, Born to Succeed* (New York: Harper Row, 1964).

McCarter, Private William, *My Life in the Irish Brigade: The Civil War Memoirs of Private William McCarter, 116th Pennsylvania Infantry*, ed., Kevin E. O'Brien (Campbell, CA: Savas, 1997).

O'Brien, Conor Cruise, *Ancestral Voices: Religion and Nationalism in Ireland* (Dublin: Poolbeg, 1994).

O'Leary, John, *Recollections of Fenians and Fenianism* (London: Downey and Co., 1896).

Perkins, Dexter, Van Deusen and G. Glyndon, *The United States of America, A History Since 1865* (New York: Macmillan, and London: Collier-Macmillan, 1968).

Quinlivan, Patrick and Paul Rose, *The Fenians in England, 1865–1872* (London: John Calder, 1982).

Rafferty, Oliver P., *Catholicism in Ulster, 1603–1983: An Interpretive History* (C. Hurst, 1994).

Rutherford, John, *The Secret History of the Fenian Conspiracy* (London: Kegan Paul, 1877).

Ryan, Desmond, *The Phoenix Flame – A Study of Fenianism and John Devoy* (London: Arthur Barker, 1937).

Willis, Grania, *The World of the Irish Horse* (London: Weidenfeld and Nicolson, 1992).

ARTICLES

Clarke, Dennis, 'Portraying Irish America: Trans-Atlantic Revisions, *History Ireland*, Winter 1994.

Davis, Professor Norman, 'West Best, East Beast ?', *Oxford Today* (the University Magazine), Hilary Issue 1997.

Donnelly, James S. Jnr, 'The Terry Alt Movement, 1829–1831', *History Ireland*, Winter 1994.

Gray, Dr Peter, 'The Triumph of Dogma: Ideology and Famine Relief', *History Ireland*, Summer 1995.

O'Grada, Professor Cormac, 'Devastating Years When the Luck of the Irish Ran Out', *European*, 24 June 1994.

Twentieth Century

BOOKS

Bennett, Daphne, *Margot: A Life of the Countess of Oxford and Asquith* (London: Gollancz, 1984).

Bennett, Richard, *The Black & Tans* (London: Edward Hulton, 1959).

Butler, Ewan, *Barry's Flying Column* (London: Leo Cooper, 1971).

Clarke, Thomas J., *Glimpses of an Irish Felon's Prison Life* (Cork: National Publications Committee, 1970).

Collins, Eamon with Mick McGovern, *Killing Rage* (London: Granta Books, 1997).

Connolly, James, *Labour, Nationality and Religion* (Dublin: New Books Publications, 1910; reprinted 1954, 1962).

—— *Labour in Irish History* (Dublin: New Books Publications, 1971).

—— *Revolutionary Warfare* (Dublin: New Books Publications, 1968; originally published in 1915 under the title, *Insurrectionary Warfare*).

Coogan, Tim Pat, *The IRA* (London: Fontana 1987).

Cosgrave, W. T. *Arthur Griffith* in *Dictionary of National Biography*, 1922–30 (1937).

Dillon, Martin, *The Enemy Within: The IRA's War Against the British* (Doubleday, 1994).

Grigg, John, *Lloyd George from Peace to War 1912–1945* (Oxford: Clarendon Press, 1965).

Hayes-McCoy, G. A., ed., *The Irish at War: the Thomas Davis Lectures* (Cork: Mercier Press, Cork and RTE, 1964).

Insight (*Sunday Times*), *Ulster* (London: Times Newspapers, 1972).

Knightley, Phillip, *The First Casualty: the War Correspondent as Hero, Propagandist and Myth Maker* (London: Quartet Books, 1975).

Mac Thomais, Eamonn, *Down Dublin Streets 1916* (Irish Book Bureau, Joseph Clarke).

Mercer, Derrik et al., *Chronicle of the World* (London: Longman, 1989).

Quinn, Colonel Patrick, *The Irish Air Corps* in *The Air Forces of the World* (London: Salamander).

Rolleston, T. W., *Celtic Myths and Legends* (London: Studio Editions, 1994).

Smith, Michael, *New Cloak, Old Dagger* (London: Gollancz, 1996).

Taylor, A. J. P., *English History 1914–1945* (Oxford: Clarendon Press, 1965), by permission of Oxford University Press.

Taylor, Rex, *Assassination: the Death of Sir Henry Wilson and the Tragedy of Ireland* (London: Hutchinson, 1961).

Townsend, Charles, *The British Campaign in Ireland 1919–1921: The Development of Political and Military Policies* (Oxford: Oxford University Press, 1975), by permission of Oxford University Press.

Travers, The Very Rev. Charles J., *Sean MacDiarmada (1883–1916)* (Cavan: Cumann Seanchais Bhriefne, 1966).

Vaughan, W. E. (ed.), *A New History of Ireland VI – Ireland Under the Union, II, 1870–1921* (including essays by R. V. Comerford and F. S. L. Lyons) (Oxford: Clarendon Press, 1966).

ARTICLES

Cooney, Patrick and John Gaskell, 'I Know Who Shot Michael Collins says Irish Priest', *Sunday Telegraph*, 10 November 1996.

De Cogan, Donard, 'Ireland, Telecommunications and International Politics 1866–1922', *History Ireland*, Summer 1993.

Keegan, John, 'When Britain Turned Terrorist', *Sunday Telegraph*, 9 February 1993.

Murphy, Brian, 'Review of "Revolutionary Government in Ireland: Dail Eireann 1919–22"' (by Arthur Mitchell, Gill and Macmillan), *History Ireland*, Autumn 1995.

Phoenix, Eamon, 'New Light Shed on Stormont's "X" Files', *History Ireland*, Winter 1996.

Roberts, Andrew, 'Iron Fist Behind Irish Talks', *Sunday Telegraph*, 10 January 1993.

Selth, Andrew, 'Ireland and Insurgency: The Lessons of History', *Small Wars and Insurgencies*, August 1991 (London: Frank Cass).

Addenda to the 2000 Edition

ARTICLES

Anon., 'Adams: I Can't Deliver Guns', *Belfast Telegraph*, 17 March 1999.

——— 'Peace Process Facing Real Threat: Mitchell', *Belfast Telegraph*, 5 October 1999.

——— 'IRA/Sinn Fein "Insult"', *Guardian*, 16 February 1999.

——— 'Don't Create Any Martyrs, SAS Squad Was Ordered', *Daily Telegraph*, 20 March 1999.

Bamber, David, Alan Murray and Jenny McCartney, 'Mowlam Authorised Bugging of Gerry Adams's Car', *Sunday Telegraph*, 12 December 1999.

Binyon, Michael, 'The Mitrokhin KGB Archive', *The Times*, 13 September 1999.

Cracknell, David, 'We Used to Say: First Guns, Then Government. Now It's Government, Then Guns', *Sunday Telegraph*, 21 November 1999.
—— 'IRA "Will Start Disarming on January 16" ', *Sunday Telegraph*, 12 December 1999.
Fletcher, Martin, 'Sinn Fein Demands Backing for Assembly', *The Times*, 20 April 1998.
—— 'Peace Will Not Come', *The Times*, 5 March 1999.
—— 'Sinn Fein Votes to Abandon Force', *The Times*, 11 May 1998.
Fletcher, Martin et al., 'US Links with Britain "Worst since 1773" ', *The Times*, 16 August 1996.
Gurdon, Hugo and Toby Harnden, 'Clinton Plea to Ulster Leaders As Terrorist Is Shot Dead', *Daily Telegraph*, 18 March 1999.
Harnden, Toby, 'RUC Calls in Kent Police and FBI', *Daily Telegraph*, 17 March 1999.
—— 'RUC Faces a Crisis of Confidence', Op. Cit.
—— 'Sinn Fein Leaders Call for a Tactical "Yes" Vote', *Daily Telegraph*, 11 May 1998.
—— 'Unionists in First Sinn Fein Talks', *Daily Telegraph*, 18 February 1999.
Jones, George, Hugh Davies and Toby Harnden, 'Blair Gives Ground on IRA Arms Handover', *Daily Telegraph*, 19 March 1999.
McCann, Eamonn, 'Bloody Sunday Truth "Was Known 25 Years Ago"', *Observer*, 19 September 1999.
McDonald, Henry, 'Former IRA Terrorist Tells Provos to Disarm', *Observer*, 10 October 1999.
McKittrick, David, 'Adams: We Will Never Give Up the Fight', *Independent on Sunday*, 7 December 1997.
—— 'Ulster Lawyers "Threatened by RUC" ', *Independent on Sunday*, 21 March 1999.
MacKinnon, Ian, 'Early Release Plan for 100 Terrorists "Is No Amnesty" ', *Independent*, 14 July 1995.
Mullin, John, 'IRA Admits Killing Widow Who "Disappeared" 26 Years Ago', *Guardian*, 5 December 1998.
—— 'Mowlam Damned', *Guardian*, 27 April 1999.
—— 'IRA Gives Peace a Chance', *Guardian*, 18 November 1999.
Mullin, John and Nicholas Watt, 'Ulster Takes the Leap of Faith', *Guardian*, 30 November 1999.
Oliver, Ted, 'Freed Women Take Total to 200', *Daily Telegraph*, 11 November 1998.
Randall, Colin, 'Tears As Clegg Is Cleared of Murder', *Daily Telegraph*, 12 March 1999.
Shrimsley, Robert, 'Arms Deadlock after Adams's No. 10 Meeting', *Daily Telegraph*, 10 January 1999.
Sheehan, Maeve, 'Secret Phone Tapping Soars', *Sunday Times*, 21 March 1999.

Sengupta, Kim, 'Demons Haunt the Scarred Children of Omagh', *Independent On Sunday*, 3 January 1999.
Walker, Christopher, 'Sister's Anguish', *The Times*, 15 September 1999.
Williams, David and Nick Craven, 'Murdered Lawyer "Was Refused Protection" ', *Daily Mail*, 17 March 1999.

OFFICIAL REPORTS
USIS Washington File, American Embassy, London, 10-03-99: 'Senator George Mitchell to Be Awarded the Medal of Freedom'.

OTHER SOURCES
Taylor, Peter, *Loyalists*, BBC 2 Television, March 1999.

INDEX

Hopkins, Adam 181, 182
Hughes, Francis 99
Hughes, Oliver and Anthony 126–7
Humbert, General 360
Hume, John 207
hunger-strikers 76, 97–8, 99–101, 183,
    341, 370
Hunt, District Inspector 335
Hurson, Martin 99
Hussein, Saddam 76
Hutton, Lord Chief Justice 103
Hyland, Bernadette 239

identity, Irish 350–1
Improvised Explosive Devices (IEDs)
    204
Improvised Projected Grenade (IPG)
    195–6
informers 339
    British Intelligence 111, 131, 133,
        137, 151–4
    and Fenian Brotherhood 302–5
    RUC 157–8
INLA (Irish National Liberation Army)
    151–2, 153–4, 212, 369, 370, 371
Innocent XI, Pope 251
Institute for the Study of Terrorism 174
Intelligence 130–1, 133–64
    aliases 147
    Artificial 160–1
    bugging and listening devices 135
    and Close Observation Platoons
        140–1, 142
    and computers 158–61
    and decoy holiday 135, 146
    failure to notice arms traffic from
        Libya 183
    and '14 Int Company' 139–40, 155
    and FRU 151, 155–6, 236
    growth of computerized in Britain
        163
    information management 158–9, 160
    and informers 111, 131, 133, 137,
        151–4
    leaks on Republicans to Loyalists
        from 229–30, 371, 372
    and Mobile Reconnaissance Force
        137–8
    and RUC 136, 142, 143, 157 *see also*
        RUC special Branch

and SAS 130–1, 134, 139
system and organization of 135
training of officers 141–2
see also M15; M16; surveillance
Intelligence Corps 130–1, 141, 155
Intelligence and Security Group 130,
    139, 155
internment 97, 244
    (1956–58) 3–4, 43
    (1971–72) 43–51, 136, 367
    consideration of by Stormont 45–6
    effect of 41–2
    eruption of violence after 50–1
    and European Commission on
        Human Rights 94
    failure 52
    implementation and round-up of
        suspects in Operation
        Demetrius 46, 48
    information obtained from
        interrogation 51–2, 53
    interrogation and treatment of
        prisoners 46–7, 48–52, 83, 94
    release of prisoners 68, 69
Invincibles 310, 312–13, 331, 364
IPG (Improvised Projected Grenade)
    196–7
IPLO 371
IRA (Irish Republican Army) 3–12,
    333–4, 348, 353–4
    advise on avoiding forensic trap
        82–90, 103
    agitation campaign approach 6–9, 10
    and Anglo-Irish Treaty 242–3
    assassinations in 1919, 335, 336
    assets 68
    and 'back of envelope treaty' with
        British xviii-xix, 23–4, 27, 93
    and Bloody Friday 70, 71–2
    and Bloody Sunday 58, 60–1, 62, 64
    bombing campaign in Britain *see*
        Britain
    and Catholics 7, 9, 10, 23, 27, 39, 112
    and ceasefires *see* ceasefires
    and civil rights movement 7, 11–12,
        13–14, 135, 352, 365
    co-ordination of operations 167–8
    communication problems 154–5
    contingency plan against sectarian
        attacks on Catholic areas 352–4